JEWS IN THE HUNGARIAN ECONOMY
1760-1945

The Andrew and Pearl Rosenfeld Research Project on the History of the Jews of Hungary and the Habsburg Empire (founded in 1985) is part of the Ben-Zion Dinur Institute for Research in Jewish History (Institute of Jewish Studies) of the Hebrew University of Jerusalem. Together with the Joseph and Margaret Fettman Chair on the History of the Jews in Central Europe (founded in 1977), the Rosenfeld Project aims at furthering research in the field of Hungarian and Habsburg Jewish History.

THE HEBREW UNIVERSITY OF JERUSALEM

The Joseph and Margaret Fettman
Chair on the History
of the Jews in Central Europe

The Andrew and Pearl Rosenfeld
Research Project on the History of the
Jews of Hungary and the Habsburg Empire

JEWS IN THE HUNGARIAN ECONOMY 1760-1945

Studies Dedicated to Moshe Carmilly-Weinberger on his Eightieth Birthday

EDITED BY MICHAEL K. SILBER

THE MAGNES PRESS, THE HEBREW UNIVERSITY
JERUSALEM 1992

Distributed by the Magnes Press
POB 7695 Jerusalem 91076

ISBN 965-223-783-3

Printed in Israel

Contents

Preface

Although the field of economic history has been recognized as an important desideratum of Jewish history ever since the inception of modern Jewish scholarship some one hundred and seventy years ago, the number of serious academic studies devoted to the topic has been disappointingly few. In the last two decades, however, as part of the remarkable expansion of Jewish studies in general, several important books and articles began to fill the lacuna. One of these was William O. McCagg's *Jewish Nobles and Geniuses in Modern Hungary* published in 1972. McCagg's book was not only one of the first in the recent crop of studies in Jewish economic history, but also one of the first monographs on Hungarian Jewry to appear since World War II. While a handful of scholars pursued the study of Hungarian Jewry in Israel and the United States, until that time Hungarian historians under the Communist regime shied away from writing Jewish history. (The important exception was the research sponsored by the Rabbinical Seminary in Budapest under supervision the late Alexander Scheiber.) On the other hand, the field of economic history received special impetus in communist Hungary for obvious reasons and made considerable strides. And even if these numerous articles and books did not always explicitly mention Jews as such, the prominent role played by Jews in Hungary's economy made it inevitable that these studies would enrich our historical knowledge of Hungarian Jewry.

As liberalization proceeded apace in Hungary, occasional pieces on Hungarian Jewish history began to appear in respected academic journals. Finally, in 1984, the first academic conference on the subject took place in Budapest on the fortieth anniversary of the Hungarian Holocaust, organized by the late György Ránki, the Director of the Institute of Historical Studies of the Hungarian Academy. The following year, a number of scholars gathered in Paris at the invitation of Victor Karády and Yehuda Don to discuss the social and economic history of Central European Jewry, with heavy emphasis on Hungary.

When the newly founded Rosenfeld Project at the Hebrew University considered the idea of sponsoring a conference on Hungarian Jewry, it seemed only natural to concentrate on economic history in light of the extensive work already done in the field. The conference would provide the opportunity to explore in an explicit manner the economic activities of the Jews in Hungary, always a sensitive subject. A large contingent of Hungarian historians led by Iván T. Berend, the President of the Hungarian Academy and György Ránki, met in Jerusalem in January 1988 with colleagues from the United States, Canada, France and Israel. The papers in this volume, largely revised and expanded, were first presented at that forum.

The conference was an opportunity for the Hebrew University to honor Professor Moshe Carmilly-Weinberger on his eightieth birthday. Professor Carmilly, formerly chief rabbi of Cluj and a historian in his own right who taught for many years at Yeshiva University in New York, was instrumental in the establishment of the Andrew and Pearl Rosenfeld Research Project and the Joseph and Margaret Fettman Chair at the Hebrew University, both devoted to furthering the study of Hungarian Jewry. These studies are dedicated to him in honor of his scholarship and lifetime activity on behalf of Hungarian and Transylvanian Jewry, as well as in grateful recognition of his services to the Hebrew University.

Many debts were incurred in the process of organizing the conference and editing this volume. Over the years, Andrew and Pearl Rosenfeld have been a constant source of encouragement, it is their support which made the conference and this volume possible. A similar debt is owed to the Strauss family, the sponsors of the Fettman Chair. Avraham Harman has always taken a keen interest in advancing the study of Hungarian Jewry at Hebrew University during his tenure both as president and chancellor. My mentor, Professor Jacob Katz who serves as the chairman of the Rosenfeld Project, was closely involved in the planning of this conference. I also benefited from the sound advice of past and present members of the board of the project, in particular Israel Ephal. The late Professor Ránki, an outstanding historian whose lecture marked his last public appearance before his untimely death, aided in the conception of the conference. The organizational burden, conducted often at long-distance was considerably lightened by the help I received from Daniella Ashur of the Dinur Center, and especially from Anat Peri. Thanks are due to Lenn Schramm for his skillful editing; William Templer for translating Péter Hanák's paper from the German; Erzsébet Somogyvári, Susan Smadja and Mimi Gess for typing several difficult texts; Janet Bar-Shalev for careful copyediting; Dr. György Haraszti and Rama Friedlander for the index; Techiya Rosenthal for the jacket design and Dan Benovitch and his staff at the Magnes Press for their patient cooperation. The Diaspora Museum made available a copy of the jacket illustration; my thanks to Chana Gilad and especially Natalia Berger. During the years I worked on the manuscript, I received funding from several sources: the American Council for Learned Societies-Social Science Research Council, the Soros Foundation and the Rosenfeld Foundation. I gratefully acknowledge their support.

And finally, a word of gratitude to members of my family for their forbearance.

Michael K. Silber

Moshe Carmilly-Weinberger

Moshe Carmilly-Weinberger
An Appreciation

It is in every way appropriate that the proceedings of the first conference to be held on the History of Hungarian Jewry at the Hebrew University should be dedicated to Professor Moshe Carmilly. The conference was held on the occasion of his eightieth birthday and was a tribute to his notable services to the Hungarian Jewish community, his participation in organizing the rescue of Transylvanian Jews during and after World War II by facilitating their migration to Israel and his determination to preserve for posterity the significant contribution of Hungarian Jewry to the Jewish people as a whole.

Professor Carmilly is a unique combination of scholar, educator and organizer. The Hebrew University is deeply indebted to him for his initiative in the creation at the University of the Joseph and Margaret Fettman Chair on the History of the Jews in Central Europe and the Andrew and Pearl Rosenfeld Research Project on the History of the Jews of Hungary and the Habsburg Empire. The first public activity of the Rosenfeld Project was the organization of the conference and this volume of the conference's proceedings is the first major publication in English of the Project.

The transformed political situation in Hungary has resulted in the development of many contacts between Hebrew University scholars and their colleagues in Hungary, as well as with the Jewish community of Hungary. In the School for Overseas Students at the Hebrew University there is now a substantial number of students from Hungary. It can, therefore, be confidently expected that in the course of time the activities of the Fettman Chair and the Rosenfeld Project will increase.

It is good to know that Professor Carmilly continues with vigor and dedication his efforts to develop the work of the Fettman Chair and the Rosenfeld Project and to encourage the growing contacts between the Hebrew University, Hungarian Jewry and the Hungarian academic community.

Avraham Harman

This volume of the proceedings of the conference on the Economic History of Hungarian Jewry held in January, 1988 is dedicated to Professor Moshe Carmilly-Weinberger in honor of his eightieth birthday. This is a well deserved act of recognition for without his moral and material support of Hungarian Jewish history at Hebrew University, the conference would never have taken place. This is an occasion to pay him tribute for having persistently prodded scholars of Hungarian background like myself to dedicate at least part of our time and energy to a field of research closed to most historians because of the linguistic barrier. He himself, although interested in many other branches of knowledge (as the bibliography of his publications reveal), never wavered in seeing this assignment as his first obligation.

Jacob Katz

On Three Continents

Eliyahu Yeshurun

Childhood and Education

Dr. Moshe Carmilly (Moses Weinberger) was born in Budapest on 7 April 1908. He was the eldest son of Solomon Weinberger and Rosa Spitzer, who both perished in Auschwitz in June 1944. Solomon Weinberger was a student of Rabbi Yitzhak Bunim Sopher (the *Shevet Sopher*, 1842-1906), head of the famous yeshiva in Pressburg (now Bratislava, Czechoslovakia); and of Rabbi Moshe Shmuel Glasner (1877-1923), the rabbi of Cluj (Kolozsvár, Klausenburg), a great rabbinical authority and one of the courageous Zionist leaders among the Orthodox rabbis. His wife, Rosa Spitzer, was the daughter of Rabbi Shmuel Arye Spitzer of Szilágykraszna, Transylvania. (Szilágykraszna was called "the little Eretz Israel", *das klein Eretz Israel*). It was a deeply religious, ultra-orthodox Jewish community, led by Rabbi Baruch Bendet Lichtenstein (1883-1944). The Weinberger children (Moshe, Ernest and Rudolph) were raised and educated in a very religious home, but were also given a secular education.

Young Moshe was six years old when the archduke Franz Ferdinand, nephew and heir of the emperor Franz Joseph I (1848-1916), was assassinated, the deed that unleashed World War I. The emperor's death at the height of the war put an end to the "golden age" that the Jews had enjoyed during the 68-year reign of the *Judenkaiser* (as the antisemites were wont to call him).

When he completed elementary school in a small Romanian village (Vaskoh-Vascău, Bihar county, Transylvania), his parents sent him to the Jewish junior high school in the neighboring city of Nagyvárad (now Oradea, Transylvania) where there was a dynamic Jewish community. The junior high school, which had been founded by the local Orthodox congregation in 1888, was the only Jewish junior high school in Transylvania before World War I. In addition to the required public-school curriculum, students were educated in Bible, Talmud, and *Shulchan Aruch*. It was a rigorous program, with eight hours of daily classes.

In 1921, he followed his parents to Szatmárnémeti (now Satu Mare, Romania), where his father was employed by the Status quo ante congregation, and enrolled in the local public junior high school.[1] After graduating from that school he studied for three years in the local yeshiva, under the directorship of Rabbi Eliezer David Grinwald, author of the commentary *Keren le-David* and an ardent anti-Zionist who in his later years was inclined toward Hasidism. Moshe's only study was now the Talmud, its commentaries and *musar* (ethical) literature. In 1924 Moshe was sent to the Rabbinical Seminary of Budapest, one of the great rabbinical seminaries of Europe.[2] Among the luminaries of Jewish scholarship who taught there between 1877 and 1942 were Mózes Bloch, Vilmos (Binyamin Zev) Bacher, Ignaz Goldziher, David Kaufman, Lajos (Yehudah Arye) Blau and Michael Guttman.

Weinberger completed the 10-year course of study at the Seminary in only 9 years (1924/25-1933/34). During the fall semester of 1930/31, he studied at the *Jüdisch-Theologisches Seminar* in Breslau, under the rectorship of Professor Michael Guttman, where his teachers included Yitzhak Heinemann, a prominent scholar in Jewish-Hellenistic literature, Israel Rabin (Bible), Albert Lewkowitz (Philosophy) and H. J. Zimmels (Jewish history).[3]

At that time, the rector of the Budapest Rabbinical Seminary was Lajos Blau, a prolific scholar and the author of many works in biblical and Talmudic scholarship and Jewish history. Blau championed studying the past of the Jewish people in the light of modern scholarship. He also maintained that Talmud study was not only for the sake of finding the logical result of the hairsplitting debates conducted by the sages, but also a method of learning about the way of life of the Jewish people in Palestine and Babylonia. For Blau the Talmud was a treasure trove of the cultural, social, and economic life of the Jewish people. It was, therefore, logical that Blau should suggest the theme of Weinberger's dissertation—*The Social Conditions of the Jews in the Talmud*.[4]

On Blau's retirement in 1933, Michael Guttman returned from Breslau to his *alma mater* and became its rector. Guttman was well-versed in mathematics and

1 *Salaj-Szilágy megye és zsidóságának Emlékkönyve*, ed. David Giladi (Tel-Aviv, 1989), pp. 269-272 and Hebrew section pp. 305-306. The Jewish communities in Hungary after the Congress held in Budapest in 1869 were divided into three autonomous religious organizations: Neolog (conservative), Orthodox and Status quo ante.

2 See *The Rabbinical Seminary of Budapest Centennial Volume, 1877-1977*, ed. by Moshe Carmilly-Weinberger, (New York, 1986).

3 *Das Breslauer Seminar. Jüdisch-Theolologisches Seminar (Fraenckelscher Stiftung) in Breslau 1854-1938. Gedächtnisschrift*, ed. Guido Kisch, (Tübingen, 1963), p. 438; *Bericht des Jüdisch-Theologischen Seminars—Hochschule für Jüdische Theologie für das Jahr 1931*, p. 9.

4 *A zsidóság szociális helyzete a Talmudban* [The Social Conditions of the Jews in Light of the Talmud] (Ph.D. diss., Budapest, 1934). 24 p.

astronomy and a master of modern Hebrew. Like Blau, he avoided *pilpul* in teaching the Talmud and used modern teaching methods.

The rectors, Blau and Guttman, and teachers like Bernát Heller (renowned in biblical scholarship), Simon Hevesi, Chief Rabbi of Budapest, a great orator and Professor of Philosophy and Homiletics, and Abraham Hoffer, Professor of Codes, all had great influence on their students. These were the teachers who shaped and educated the small student body. The heavy double program in Jewish and secular subjects was very demanding. A rigorous discipline prevailed in the institute. The majority of students sustained themselves by tutoring. It was a hard life, but a rewarding one.

The Rabbi

In June 1934, Weinberger received his Ph.D. *summa cum laude* from the University of Budapest. In those years it was dangerous for a Jew to enter the university buildings. Antisemitic atrocities were daily affairs. Jewish students were attacked and frequently evicted from classrooms. The non-Jewish professors, among them many antisemites, were unwilling to defend the rights of those Jewish students who were admitted by the *numerus clausus* law of 1921 which limited Jewish enrollment in the general student body to six percent. That same year, upon completion of his studies at the Rabbinical Seminary of Budapest, Moshe Weinberger was called to the pulpit of the Neolog (conservative) congregation in Cluj-Kolozsvár, the capital of Transylvania, a university city with a dynamic Jewish community. In 1935 Weinberger married Sara Güns, a descendant of Rabbi Akiba Eger-Güns. She was a great source of encouragement and an indefatigable helper in Weinberger's multifaceted and sometimes life-endangering activities. She died on October 13, 1972, in New York, after a long illness. In 1975, Carmilly-Weinberger married Rhoda Trotzky of New York, an educator and communal leader.

The Jews of Transylvania

A Jewish Renaissance had taken place in Transylvania and Banat with its focal point at Cluj-Kolozsvár where a large Orthodox, a fairly strong Neolog, and a small Hasidic community had developed.

At first the Neolog congregation, established in 1881, shared rabbis with the neighboring Neolog congregation of Nagyvárad (Oradea Mare). Among them were Rabbi Isaac Kunstadt and the world-renowned Dr. Alexander Kohut, editor of the encyclopedic work *Aruch Hashalem*.[5] In 1891, the Kolozsvár congregation was able to engage its own rabbi, Dr. Mátyás Eisler, a graduate of the Budapest Rabbinical Seminary and a teacher at the Jewish Teacher's Institute in Budapest. Rabbi Eisler served the Neolog congregation for 40 years, until his death in 1930. Eisler was a great spiritual leader, a Zionist, president of the Organization of Neolog and Status quo ante communities in Transylvania and Banat, and a lecturer in Oriental studies at the University of Kolozsvár; he was also the first Jewish historian of Transylvanian Jewry.[6]

In 1918, at the end of World War I, Transylvania, with a Jewish population of 200,000, was awarded to Romania. Transylvanian Jewry had a positive world outlook. On November 20, 1918, a Zionist organization was established in Cluj-Kolozsvár with the tacit consent of the Romanian government. The Romanian authorities hoped that the Zionist movement, with its Hebrew cultural and educational program, would weaken Hungarian influence in the region. The rise of Nazism in the 1930s confronted rabbis and communal leaders in Central and Eastern Europe with enormous social, economic, and immigration problems.

Antisemitism had existed in Romania for centuries, but now it was reinforced by Nazism. Already in 1920, university students from all over Romania held their first congress in Cluj and decided to exclude Jewish students from their organization, demanding the application of the *numerus clausus* in Romanian universities. In 1927 the Iron Guard conducted a pogrom in Transylvania, vandalizing synagogues and desecrating Torah scrolls in Oradea Mare, Huedin, Cluj and other cities. In the 1930s, the Jews were thrown from railway cars. Newspapers followed the *Stürmer* style and agitated against the Jews. Antisemitic laws and orders were passed by the Goga-Cuza government (December 1937-February 1938) and by the dictatorial regime of King Carol II (February 1938-September 1940). Under the slogan "Romania for the Romanians", harsh measures were taken to eliminate Jews from economic life. Non-Jewish workers had to constitute 80 percent of the work force in every

5 Julius Fischer, "Dr. Alexander Kohut: Ein Lebensbild," *Jubilee Volume on the Fiftieth Anniversary of the Franz Joseph Rabbinical Seminary* (Budapest, 1927), pp. 152-199; Dr. József Schweitzer, "Dr Kohut Sándor (1842-1894)," *Memorial Volume for the Jews of Cluj-Kolozsvár* (New York, 1970), pp. 71-73, 89-94; M. Carmilly-Weinberger, "Sophrim ivriyim memotza hungari beartzot habrit" [Hungarian Hebrew Writers in America] *Migvan: Studies in Hebrew Literature in Honor of Jacob Kabakoff*, ed. Stanley Nash (Lod, 1988), pp. 229-241.

6 *Memorial Volume for the Jews of Cluj-Kolozsvár*, pp. 56-58; 79-86; M. Weinberger, "Eisler Mátyás irodalmi müködése" [The Bibliography of Dr. Matthias Eisler], *Hitközségi Értesitő* 1, 4 (Cluj, August, 1936), pp. 3-5; 1, 5-6 (September, 1936), pp. 4-6; 1, 7-8 (October-November, 1936).

factory. Jewish businesses were liquidated by taxation, Jewish lawyers were excluded from the bar, the licences of physicians and pharmacists were reviewed in order to limit their practice. Jews who did not hold Romanian citizenship were deported.

Rabbi of Cluj-Kolozsvár

It was in these circumstances that Moshe Weinberger assumed the position of Chief Rabbi of Cluj-Kolozsvár in September 1934, and continued in the post until May 1944. His first activity was the reorganization of Jewish education, especially at the secondary-school level. He learned Romanian in order to teach Judaism to high school students in the official language of the state, as required by law. Regular youth services were introduced on the Sabbath. Special care was taken to teach Hebrew to facilitate the emigration of youth and adults to Palestine. In cooperation with the Zionist organizations, courses were conducted for adults in Bible, Jewish history, Jewish education, and art. Weinberger succeeded in laying the foundations for a much-needed Jewish cultural center. He was instrumental in establishing the Esther Order, an institute for Jewish nurses (the only one of its kind in Romania).

In the social domain, besides taking part in the work of the local charitable organizations, he focused his attention on general economic and social problems. In 1939 he helped establish the Central Office for the Solution of Social Problems together with other Jewish congregations in Transylvania, both Orthodox and Neolog. One of the organization's urgent tasks was aiding the refugees who had escaped from the Nazis and arrived in Cluj-Kolozsvár. The refugee-aid committee established in Cluj in 1936 was unable to deal with the increasing numbers of refugees. Hence in 1939, at Weinberger's initiative, a Regional Organization of the Transylvanian and Banat Jewish Congregations was organized, with headquarters in Cluj-Kolozsvár, to care for the hundreds of refugees from Eastern and Central Europe.[7]

In the course of his refugee-aid work Weinberger was once detained at the local police station and interrogated for many hours. It seems that two German spies had infiltrated the mass of Jewish refugees and had received financial aid from his organization. After being warned against a recurrence of this situation he was released.

On August 30, 1940, in the wake of an agreement between Germany and Italy, North Transylvania, with its capital Cluj-Kolozsvár, was handed over to

7 See the *Memorial Volume for the Jews of Cluj-Kolozsvár*, pp. 227-235, 300-304 and pp. 144-149 in the Hebrew section.

Hungary. Refugee aid became a clandestine operation. A special committee was formed to deal with the refugee problem, whose magnitude grew daily. With the help of liberal-minded Romanians, an escape route was established near Cluj-Kolozsvár, over which hundreds of Jews found their way into Romania and from there to Palestine. This rescue operation, in which Weinberger played a major role, was commemorated on April 7, 1987, when Dr. Raoul Sorban, Professor of Art at the University of Bucharest, was recognized as a "Righteous Gentile" by the Yad Vashem Institute in Jerusalem.[8]

8 Adrian Riza, *Románia Pámint al Sperantei. Fascism si Anti-Fascism pe Meleaguri Transilvane. Reteaua Omeniei* [Romania the Land of Hope: Fascism and Anti-Fascism in the Transylvanian Region. The Network of Humanity] (Bucharest: Almanah Luceafarul, 1986), pp. 63-92; "Un Pom pentru Raoul Sorban" [A Tree in Honor of Raoul Sorban], *Minimum* I, 1 (Tel Aviv, April, 1987), pp. 7-8; "Raoul Sorban la Yad Vashem" [Raoul Sorban at Yad Vashem], *Ibid.* I, 2 (May 1987), pp. 8-10; Adrian Riza, "The Network of Humanity," *Romania* V (390) (Bucharest: Romanian News Agency, 1987), pp. 26-28 (in English, French, German and Spanish); "Professzor Raoul Sorban bukaresti egyetemi tanár kitüntetése" [Raoul Sorban University Professor in Bucharest was Awarded the Title of "Righteous Gentile"], *Menóra-Egyenlőség* XXVI (Toronto, 21 August 1987), no. 1181; Naphtali Krausz, "Prof. Raoul Sorban: ani omer sheani yehudi lamrot sheze lo nachon," *Maariv* (Tel Aviv: 5 April 1987); Adrian Riza, "After 44 Years," *Romanian News* (Bucharest, July 9, 1988); *Din Istoria Multimilenara a Daciei. Transilvania si Banat. Documente si Marturii,* ed. J.C. Dragan [From the Thousand Years of Dacia. Documents and Witnesses] (Roma: Revista Fundatiei Dragan, 1987), no. 3-4, pp. 281-310; "Autograf Prof. Moshe Carmilly-Weinberger U.S.A.," *Tribuna Romaniei* (Bucharest, 1 August 1988); Moshe Carmilly-Weinberger, "Gyermek reményim s bánatim tanyája," *Uj Kelet* (Tel Aviv, 29 July 1988); *Menóra Egyenlőség* (Toronto, 19 August 1988); *Magyar Hirek* 42, 2 (Budapest, 22 January 1989), pp. 18-19; Mircea Vajda, "Am Venit sa Multumesc Poporului Roman Prietenilor Mei" [Köszönetemet jöttem kifejezni a román népnek, köztük barátaimnak] *Tribuna* (Cluj-Napoca, 9 June 1988); Moshe Carmilly-Weinberger, "Ajutorul Romaniei in Actiunea de Salvare a Evreilor din Timpul Nazismului" [The Help of Romania in the Rescue Operation of Jews in the Time of Nazism] a lecture delivered at the Nicolai Iorga Institute of History, Bucharest on 27 May 1988, printed in *Almanah Luceafarul* (Bucharest, 1988), pp. 47-56; *Europa si Neamul Romanesc* (Milan, 17 October 1988), no. 196, pp. 9-16; *Curentul* 60 (Munich, November-December, 1988), pp. 1-2; Mircea Musat-Ion Ardeleanu, "Romania Dupa Marea Unire" [Romania After the Union], *Editura Stiintifica si Enciclopedica* (Bucharest, 1988), vol. 2, pp. 1309-1311; Constantin Mustata, "Convorbire cu Moshe Carmilly-Weinberger fost Sef Rabin al Clujului. Din Viltoarea unor Ani Dramatici" [Interview with M. Carmilly-Weinberger formerly Chief Rabbi of Cluj, From the Storm of Dramatic-Years], *Almanah Flacara* (Bucharest, 1989), pp. 140-148; M. Carmilly-Weinberger, "1940-1944. In Acele Vremuri Grele, Poporul Roman si-a pastrat demnitatea si omenia" [1940-1944. In Those Difficult Times Romania has Saved her Dignity and Humanity], *Magazin Historic* XIII, 10 (Bucharest, October 1989), pp. 40-42; Adrian Riza, *Romania Pamint al Sperantei. Istoria Fara Pete Albe. Salvarea Evreilor din Teritorul de Nord-West al Romaniei 1940-1944. Pagini Antifasciste. II. Arhivele Incep Sa Vorbeasca* [Romania the Land of Hope. History without White Spots. Rescuing Jews from the Nord-West Part of Romania 1940-1944. Antifascist Pages. II. The Archives Start to Speak], (Bucharest: Almanah Luceafarul, 1989), pp. 113-162.

On May 2, 1944, the *Judenrat* sent Moshe Weinberger into Romania in order to increase the number of crossing points on the Hungarian-Romanian border. After escaping over the border, like hundreds of Jewish refugees before him, he reached Turda (Romania) and proceeded to Bucharest. There he mobilized the local Jewish leadership: Chief Rabbi Dr. Alexander Safran, Dr. W. Filderman, head of the Jewish Congregation in Bucharest and chairman of the council of the Union of Jewish Communities in Romania, and A. L. Zissu, the renowned Romanian Zionist leader. The Jewish leadership in Bucharest wasted no time and embarked on activities on behalf of the Jews of Hungary and the refugees who had escaped into Romania. Alexander Safran called on the papal nuncio, Monsignor Cassulo. Filderman appealed to the ambassadors of the United States, Soviet Union, and Great Britain in Istanbul and escorted Moshe Weinberger to the office of the International Red Cross in Bucharest. Meanwhile Zissu obtained from the Romanian authorities some legal assurances for the refugees already in Romania. With the help of Professor Raoul Sorban, Weinberger was received by Juliu Maniu (1873-1953), head of the National Peasant Party, and twice premier of Romania (1928 and 1932-1933). Juliu Maniu gave them 1,200 blank identification cards of the National Peasant Party for distribution to Jewish refugees or Jews in Cluj-Kolozsvár trying to cross the border. Professor Sorban returned to Kolozsvár with the 1,200 identification cards, but by that time no Jews were left in the city. He returned to Bucharest with the devastating news—all the Jews had been deported and the synagogue of the Neolog congregation bombed. All efforts in Bucharest were in vain because of the rapid deportation of the Jews of Cluj-Kolozsvár and other cities of North Transylvania. In six weeks, more than 140,000 Jews were sent from that region to the extermination camps of Auschwitz and Maidanek.[9]

In order to strengthen the spiritual life of his congregation, in May 1936 Weinberger began to publish a monthly bulletin, *Hitközségi Értesitő*, which, because of censorship by the Romanian and later the Hungarian authorities, appeared under different titles *(Raport Lunar, Havi Jelentés)* until its closure by the Hungarian authorities in 1943.[10] In addition to the usual congregational

9 This tragic chapter in the history of the North-Transylvanian Jews was later described by Weinberger in articles published in the Yad Vashem bulletins, in the *Memorial Volume for the Jews of Cluj-Kolozsvár*, in his lectures in Jerusalem, later transmitted by *Kol Yisrael* and at the Nicolae Iorga Institute of History, Bucharest. See in particular his "Irgun lehatzalat yehudim be-Transylvania bimei hashoah" [Organization Rescuing Jews in Transylvania in the Time of the Holocaust], *Proceedings of the Ninth World Congress of Jewish Studies* (Jerusalem: World Union of Jewish Studies, 1986), Vol. II, pp. 211-216 and Alexander Safran, *Resisting the Storm, Romania 1940-1947, Memoirs* (Jerusalem: Yad Vashem, 1987), pp. 114, 208.

10 Microfilm copies of *Hitközségi Értesitő* are in the New York Public Library (Jewish Section) and at the Yad Vashem Library, Jerusalem.

news, the bulletins contained sermons delivered by Weinberger in the synagogue, historical essays, and book reviews. It informed the Jewish communities of Transylvania and Banat of the struggle of the Jewish people in Germany under the Nazi regime and of the daily restrictions imposed on them. The news from Nazi Germany published in the bulletins was a harbinger of the future. *Hitközségi Értesitő* became so successful that many other congregations in Transylvania started to publish their own bulletins (Brassó, 1939; Arad, 1939; Nagyvárad, 1940; Marosvásárhely, 1940; the Orthodox congregation in Cluj-Kolozsvár).[11]

On December 25, 1939, when King Carol II visited Cluj, Weinberger delivered a welcoming address in Romanian on behalf of the Jewish communities. The king was favorably impressed and told the governor of Transylvania, Dr. Coriolanu Tâtar, that he would like to have Weinberger as the Chief Rabbi of Romania.[12]

In September 1940, following the Hungarian annexation of North Transylvania, the antisemitic laws and regulations that had been in effect in Hungary since 1938 were applied there as well. The refugee problem and the anti-Jewish laws, which restricted Jewish participation in social and economic life, imposed a heavy burden on the Jewish communities.[13] The immediate limitation on the number of Jewish students in public high schools posed a sudden and serious problem.

During the visit to the city of Bálint Homan, the Hungarian minister of education and a well-known antisemite, a delegation headed by Weinberger

11 Jewish scientific and religious life was revitalized after the election of Weinberger according to György Gaal, "Magyar nyelvü zsidó irodalom Romániában" [Jewish Literature in Romania written in Hungarian], *Évkönyv* 1983/84, ed. Scheiber Sándor (Budapest: A Magyar Izraeliták Országos Képviselete, 1984), pp. 135, 140.

12 On November 1939, Dr. I. Niemerower, the chief rabbi of Romania, who served in that capacity from 1921 until 1939 and was the representative of Romanian Jewry in the Senate, died and with his demise the position became vacant. Weinberger was the only rabbi from Transylvania who participated in the election with seven other candidates. Dr. Alexander Safran was elected by a majority vote. He fulfilled his task with dignity and showed heroism in the years of persecution. In December 1947, Safran was forced by the Romanian authorities to leave the country. He left for Switzerland where he became chief rabbi of Geneva. See Adrian Riza, "The Network of Humanity," *Romania* V (390) (Bucharest: Agerpres, 1987), pp. 26-27; *Hitközségi Értesitő Havi Jelentés* V, 1 (Cluj: January, 1940), pp. 1-2; Jacob Geller, *The Rise and Decline of a Community: The Ashkenazim and Sephardim in Romania, 1919-1941* (Hebrew) (Tel Aviv: Moreshet, 1985), pp. 124-125; Theodor Lavi, *Roumanian Jewry in World War II. Fight for Survival* (Hebrew) (Jerusalem: Yad Vashem and Hitachdut Olei Romania, 1965), pp. 107-112 and Alexander Safran, *Resisiting the Storm*, pp. 277, 287, 296-301.

13 Nathaniel Katzburg, *Hungary and the Jews 1920-1943*. (Ramat Gan: Bar Ilan University, 1981), pp. 60-212.

called upon him and requested permission to establish two high schools for Jewish students. The minister agreed to the request. Within six weeks, thanks to the help of a renowned educator, Márk Antal, formerly head of the *Tarbuth* high schools in Cluj, two high schools were established, one for boys and one for girls. The new schools opened their doors on November 3, 1940, with an enrollment of more than 600 students.[14]

Weinberger was the school superintendent, and also taught Bible and Jewish history to the upper classes. He organized Sabbath youth services in the main synagogue, with the full participation of the student body. These services became one of the focal points for hundreds of boys and girls who received a positive Zionist education. These Jewish high schools, under the leadership of Márk Antal and later of Dr. Endre Bach, quickly became two of the best educational institutions in North Transylvania.

When the Jews were deported from Kolozsvár, in May and June of 1944, the schools ceased operation. Hundreds of students perished with their teachers in the gas chambers of Auschwitz and Maidanek. In New York, in 1968, at the initiative of Weinberger, their former teacher and rabbi, those few who survived founded the Alumni Association of the Jewish High Schools in Kolozsvár.[15] In October, 1990, a fiftieth anniversary reunion was held by the one hundred and fifty survivors and their families in Israel.

The Zionist

In his youth, Moshe Weinberger was influenced by the Zionist daily *Uj Kelet* (New East), first published in Cluj in December of 1918. During the 22 years it was published in Transylvania it informed Hungarian-speaking Jewry about the dangers of the Diaspora and educated and guided them towards Zionism. In part as a response to the rampant antisemitism he encountered during his student years in Budapest and later in Breslau, Weinberger became a Zionist. The writings of Martin Buber and the articles published in the *Jüdische Rundschau* (Berlin) also played their part. After his election as Chief Rabbi of the Jewish congregation in Cluj-Kolozsvár he found himself at the center of the Zionist political and cultural movement in Transylvania. While in Cluj-Kolozsvár, he did not affiliate with any Zionist political party, but participated in the cultural

14 *A Kolozsvári Zsidó Gimnáziumok Évkönyve az 1940-41, 1941-42, 1942-43 tanévröl* [Annuals of the Jewish High Schools in Kolozsvár] (Kolozsvár: Az iskola igazgatósága), p. 15; *Antal Márk Emlékkönyv* (Márk Antal Memorial Volume), ed. by Mózes Weinberger (Kolozsvár, 1943), pp. 9-38 (Hungarian and Hebrew).

15 *Memorial Volume for the Jews of Cluj-Kolozsvár*, pp. 114-129.

activities of the Central Organization for Cultural Affairs of the Zionist Movement in Transylvania and Banat. Many of the sermons he delivered, in both Hungarian and Romanian, dealt with the future of the Jewish people and urged *aliya*. In April 1942, in a speech to the Jewish students of Budapest, he called on them to emigrate to Palestine.[16]

In response to the Hungarian annexation of North Transylvania, Chief Rabbi Weinberger declared, in an article that appeared in the last issue of *Uj Kelet* (September 14, 1940): "We were and we remain Jews!" It implied that under the Romanian government the Jews had declared themselves to be a Jewish minority and it was their intention to continue living as such under their new Hungarian rulers. As Hungarian citizens they would fulfill their obligations, but in essence they would remain Jews. This situation indeed became a reality in light of the anti-Jewish legislation of the Hungarian government. When he arrived in Palestine on July 12, 1944, Moshe Weinberger realized his Zionist dream, but under such tragic circumstances that he could not have imagined them even in his darkest nightmares.

In Eretz Israel

While in Bucharest, Weinberger received the devastating news from North Transylvania that no Jews were left in Kolozsvár. It was decided that Dr. Ernő Marton, editor in chief of *Uj Kelet* and a former member of the Romanian parliament, who had escaped to Romania would remain in Bucharest, while Moshe Weinberger would leave for Istanbul, where the Office of Rescue Operation was headed by Chaim Barlas. Jewish refugees could escape Nazi Europe through the ports of Romania (Constanza, Sulina) thanks to the efforts of Zissu, the Romanian Zionist leader. On June 19, 1944, despite pressure from Nazi Germany and Great Britain, the deputy prime minister, Mikhail Antonescu (no relation to the antisemitic dictator Ion Antonescu), agreed to the establishment of an emigration office in Bucharest, headed by Zissu. Four ships, the *Kazbek, Bulbul, Mefkure, Morina,* belonging to ORAT (Romanian Tourist Organization), a shipping firm owned by Romanian citizens, were permitted to sail from Constanza by virtue of an agreement concerning "orphans from Transnistria, political refugees from other countries who could not remain in Romania, and Jews who wanted to emigrate."[17] The *Kazbek*, built as a freighter, left Constanza on July 7, 1944, with 712 refugees including

16 *Képes Családi Lapok. Zsidó Lap* [Illustrated Family Journal: A Jewish Journal], ed. by Jenő Lévai LXIII, 16 (Budapest: 26 April 1942], p. 10.

17 Theodor Lavi, *Roumanian Jewry in World War II*, pp. 97-101.

Weinberger and his wife. Later he described in articles the *Kazbek*'s journey to Turkey, flying the flag of the International Red Cross. Three weeks after the *Kazbek* sailed, the *Mefkure* left Constanza with 379 people. It sank after being torpedoed in the Black Sea by a German U-boat on August 5, 1944; only four passengers and the ship's captain survived.[18] When the Kazbek arrived in the Bosporus, Weinberger was met by Chaim Barlas who came out in a motorboat accompanied by two Turkish officers. The Turks refused to issue transit visas to those who did not possess an immigration certificate for Palestine issued by the British government. These refugees could not disembark on Turkish territory and continued their journey by rail through Turkey, Syria and Lebanon. On July 12, 1944, Weinberger reached Haifa, where, along with the other refugees, he was held in the detention camp at Atlit. While in Atlit he met Yitzhak Gruenbaum, then the head of the Jerusalem headquarters of the *Vaad Hahatzala* (rescue committee) in Jerusalem. After his release from Atlit he appeared before the *Vaad Hahatzala* committee and provided them with firsthand information about the situation of Hungarian Jewry. In meetings, public appearances and newspaper articles, Weinberger tried to alert the leadership and the public in Palestine to the tragic situation in Hungary.[19]

After two months in Palestine, Weinberger settled down and dedicated himself to Jewish education. His first job was as principal of the elementary school (*Mizrachi*) in Afula; next he became assistant principal of the Bilu school in Tel Aviv. In 1948, after the establishment of the State of Israel, he took a leave of absence from his teaching post and was assigned to the Ministry of Foreign Affairs. There he headed the divisions of Hungary, Romania and Finland in the East European Department. After a few months at the Foreign Ministry he was appointed Immigration Officer and Cultural Attaché at the Israeli Legation in Budapest. To satisfy the Foreign Ministry requirement that Israeli representatives abroad adopt Hebrew names, he chose the name "Carmilly." After two years with the Foreign Ministry, Carmilly returned to education. He served as deputy director of the Department of Education and Culture of the city of Netanya, where he strengthened the educational system by establishing new schools and introducing varied cultural and artistic programs. During that period the Wingate Institute for Physical Education, near Netanya, was established. After two years he took over the principalship of the Tchernichowsky high school in Netanya. In 1957 Carmilly was invited to teach at Yeshiva University in New York, where he taught Bible, Hebrew language and literature, and

18 Chaim Barlas, *Hatzala bimei hashoa* (Tel Aviv: Hakibutz Hameuhad, 1975), pp. 182-196; *Memorial Volume for the Jews of Cluj-Kolozsvár*, pp. 233-234, 304.

19 *Ibid.*, pp. 234-235, 304; *Davar*, 31 July 1944; *Hazman*, 30 July 1944; *Hamashkif*, 27 July 1944.

Jewish history for 19 years. In 1966, the student body of the Teacher's Institute at Yeshiva University chose him Teacher of the Year. In 1976, he retired as Professor Emeritus of Jewish Studies and as an "Outstanding Educator of America".

Scholarship

Reviewing Moshe Carmilly's scholarly work over the last 50 years we see that his main interest was in three major disciplines: (1) Jewish history, (2) Hebrew literature, and (3) art. He did pioneering work in all three fields.

Jewish History

In Jewish cultural history Moshe Carmilly opened a new chapter by researching the attitude of the Jewish people to freedom of speech and expression. Many books and articles had been written about censorship in general or about the restrictions that the non-Jewish world placed on Hebrew works. But no work had been published concerning the attitude of the Jewish people towards its own work.

The first comprehensive volume, beside his many articles on that subject, was *Sefer ve-Sayif* [Book and Sword: Freedom of Expression and Thought among the Jewish People] published in 1966.[20] This work covers the subject from the biblical period until the twentieth century. Carmilly discusses, in chronological order, more than 200 Hebrew books that were criticized, attacked, censored, banned, or destroyed. His interest in freedom of speech resulted in his second work, *Censorship and Freedom of Expression in Jewish History* published in 1977 where the subject was treated by topics (e.g., Censorship and the Talmud; the Kabbalah; the Enlightenment; the Battle against Hasidism; Halachic, Apologetic, Economic, and Political Considerations; Erotic Literature).[21] In his introduction to the second edition of William Popper's *The*

20 New York: Sura-Yeshiva University. See Zvi Erényi, "Bibliography of Dr. Moshe Carmilly-Weinberger," in this volume no. 104 as well as nos. 107, 121, 156, 157, 158-166. [From hereon references to this bibliography will cite only the item number.]

21 New York: Sepher-Hermon. See no. 166. A recent review praised its pioneering merit: "The work of M. Carmilly-Weinberger is as far as I know the first book in the English language which treats in an almost exclusive manner internal censorship....Each chapter that the author consecrates to censorship could be developed and become the subject of a book, but its merit is truly due to the fact that its theme is just as big as it is unknown.... This work opens to the interested public passionate, ambiguous, unknown problems of censorship exerted in Jewish circles on specific Jewish texts." *Révue des Études Juives* 145 (1986), 460-461.

Censorship of Hebrew Books (1969), he brought that work up-to-date by incorporating the censorship exercised by the Church and secular authorities in the nineteenth and twentieth centuries. He also contributed articles to the *Encyclopaedia Judaica* on various aspects of censorship.[22]

Hebrew Literature

His pioneering work *Yalkut ha-meshorerim ha-ivriyim mi-Hungaria* published in 1977[23] is the first systematic treatment of an unknown chapter of Hebrew literature. In it he discussed the development of Hebrew poetry in the last two centuries and unearthed more than one hundred anthologies of Hebrew poetry written by Jews in Hungary. The volume includes the bio-bibliographies and selected poems of twenty-six poets. (He also published a companion bibliography of 110 works.)[24] In his introduction Carmilly analyzed the themes chosen by these poets (e.g., the love of the Hebrew language and of *Eretz Israel*, antisemitism, Romanticism) and emphasized the intellectual affinity with other Hebrew cultural centers (Vienna, Prague, Jerusalem, Cracow). These poets kept alive the spark of Hebrew literature in Hungary and were the forerunners of modern Israeli poets of Hungarian origin such as Avigdor Hameiri, Mordechai Avi-Shaul and Itamar Yaoz-Keszt.[25] Carmilly has also written many articles in Hebrew, English, and Hungarian about the history of Hebrew poetry in Hungary.[26]

The Holocaust

Carmilly dealt with the Holocaust, especially with the tragedy of the North-Transylvanian Jewish communities, in his *Memorial Volume for the Jews of Cluj-Kolozsvár* (1970, 2nd ed.: 1988).[27] This work covers not only the history of the Jewish community in Cluj-Kolozsvár, but also that of Transylvanian Jewry from the seventeenth century on, presenting its cultural, educational, religious, and economic development. The Holocaust is the subject of many articles by Carmilly in Hebrew, English, Romanian and Hungarian, published in

22 Nos. 121, 156-158.

23 *Yalkut hameshorerim ha-ivriyim mi-Hungaria, min hameah 18 vead yameinu: Im mavo bio-bibliographiyah* [Hebrew Poets of Hungary from the Eighteenth to the Twentieth Century, with Introduction and Bio-Bibliography] (Tel Aviv: Eked).

24 "Hitpatchut hashirah haivrit be-Ungaria" [The Development of Hebrew Poetry in Hungary], *Areshet* 4 (1966), 368-417; 5 (1972), 254-265.

25 *Yalkut hameshorerim ha-ivriyim mi-Hungaria*, pp. 134-144; 145-151; 197-204.

26 Nos. 109, 131, 137, 165, 208.

27 See no. 213 for the full reference.

the *Yad Vashem* bulletins, memorial volumes, and periodicals. *The Rabbinical Seminary of Budapest, 1877-1977: A Centennial Volume* (1986), edited by Carmilly-Weinberger, is a memorial to an august institution which lost hundreds of students and faculty members in the destruction of Hungarian Jewry. The *Centennial Volume* dedicated to the seminary was published with the collaboration of many contributors, most of whom were educated at the seminary. The volume, which includes scholarly articles about various Jewish disciplines (Bible, Talmud, Jewish history, philosophy, Oriental studies, Hebrew language and literature, folklore) reveals the greatness of that institution. Many of his book reviews dealt with works connected with the Holocaust. [28]

He was instrumental in the publication of the religious melodies sung by the Hasidic population of North Transylvania (Maramures region). These melodies, collected by the late Professor Max Eisikovits, a renowned composer and director of the Academy of Music and of the Opera in Cluj-Kolozsvár, were published as *Songs of the Martyrs: Hassidic Melodies of Maramures* (1980). Eisikovits saved these melodies in the last hours before the Jews of North Transylvania were deported in April and June 1944. In the introduction Carmilly-Weinberger analyzed the development of the Hasidic *niggunim* (melodies) in Eastern Europe and their influence on the songs of the Hasidim in Maramures.[29]

Art

Recently, Carmilly-Weinberger's interest has turned to general art. He studied the question of freedom of expression in artistic creation. Does the artist, painter, or sculptor have the freedom to express artistic ideas without any restrictions? Does he encounter the same severe censorship as writers do? Carmilly-Weinberger presented his findings in *Fear of Art: Censorship and Freedom of Expression in Art* (1986). It is a pioneering work, an inquiry into the attitude of religious and secular authorities, kings, and political leaders towards art through the ages. How was modern art accepted in different parts of the world under different regimes? He also considers the reaction to eroticism in art and the fate of art under totalitarian dictatorship.

In an article "The Jew in Courbet's and Goya's Art," he deals with antisemitism in painting and the paradoxical attitude of painters towards the Jew.

28 One book review dealt with Jewish education in Nazi Germany, another with the concentration camp near Lvov, and yet another, with the negative attitude of the Western world. See nos. 108, 115, 202.

29 No. 180.

Courbet, the socialist, head of the Commission des Beaux Arts in Paris, depicted the Jew as a "parasite" in his *L'atelièr du peintre* [The painter's studio, 1855]. Goya, braving the Inquisition in Christian Spain, depicted in many of his drawings the suffering Jew, whose only sin was "being a Jew".[30]

Many of his articles in Hebrew, Hungarian, Romanian and English deal with topics related to Jewish history (Solomon Loewisohn as historian; the problem of assimilation; ransoming Jews in the seventeenth century; the settlement of Sephardic Jews in Transylvania), Jewish booklore (the love of the book in *Sepher Hasidim* as compared with that in *The Philobiblon* of Richard de Bury, Bishop of Durham), and folklore (the Magic Bird).

In addition to the memorial volume on the Budapest Rabbinical Seminary, Carmilly edited two jubilee volumes in Romania dedicated to Dr. Pinchas Löwy, Dr. Menachem Lenke, rabbi of Lugoj and Dr. Jacob Singer, rabbi of Timisoara (1939) and to Márk Antal (1943). He was also co-editor of the *Samuel Belkin Memorial Volume* (1981).[31]

Sermons

Many of the sermons and lectures delivered by Carmilly during the last 50 years have been published. They mirror a conscientious and responsible spiritual leader who used the pulpit to teach and guide his congregants. Many of his speeches appeared in *Hitközségi Értesitő* or were printed separately. One of his most famous speeches, *Sirt az Isten* [God Wept] was delivered in New York on May 25, 1969, at the Memorial Service on the twenty-fifth anniversary of the destruction of Hungarian Jewry. The speech still echoes among the Hungarian-speaking Jews and has been reprinted and quoted many times.[32]

Carmilly has been invited to lecture at numerous universities (Hebrew University, Jerusalem; Bar-Ilan University, Ramat Gan; University of Sydney, Australia; Fordham University, New York; Lehman College, New York; at the inauguration of the Jewish Studies Program at Budapest University; at the Institute of Art and History in Bucharest), Zionist organizations, and congregations. He has appeared on television and radio in the United States, Romania, Australia, and Israel. He has been a regular lecturer at the World Congress of Jewish Studies at Jerusalem.

30 No. 205, 216.
31 Nos. 42, 82, 183.
32 For the full bibliography of his sermons see nos. 2, 22, 43, 57, 74, 79, 85, 120, 214. For the impact of of his sermons in Transylvania, see the remarks of Lajos Marton in *Uj Kelet* (Cluj-Kolozsvár, April 1939).

In the last few years he has dedicated himself to preserving the heritage and rich cultural past of Hungarian-speaking Jews. He was instrumental in the establishment of a chair and a research project at the Hebrew University: in 1977, the Joseph and Margaret Fettman Chair on the History of the Jews in Central Europe; in 1985, the Andrew and Pearl Rosenfeld Research Project on the History of the Jews of Hungary and the Habsburg Empire. His firm belief is that such institutions will preserve the history of that once glorious Jewry.

His organizational talent was put to use in the founding of the Jewish high schools in Kolozsvár in 1940, in the establishment of the *Immanuel Loew B'nai Brith Lodge* in Netanya (1955), and in the organization of the alumni associations of the Rabbinical Seminary of Budapest and of the Jewish High Schools of Kolozsvár in New York.

In 1986 his half-century of scholarly and scientific work was recognized by an honorary degree (Golden Diploma) conferred by the Lóránd Eötvös University (formerly Péter Pázmány University) in Budapest. In 1990, an Institute of Judaic Studies carrying his name was established by the Babes-Bólyai (formerly Franz Joseph) University in Cluj-Kolozsvár, the capital of Transylvania. He received the Károly Roboz Literary Award for his *Censorship and Freedom of Expression in Jewish History* (New York, 1977) and *Fear of Art* (New York-London, 1986).

Bibliography of Moshe Carmilly-Weinberger

Zvi Erényi

1933

1. "A szegénység fogalma a Talmudban" [The Definition of Poverty in the Talmud]. *A Blau Lajos Talmudtudományi Társulat Évkönyve*. Vol. 1, pp. 29-37.

1934

2. *Istenért-emberért: beszéd, 5695-1934 Rosh HaShanah első napján* [For God and Man: Sermon on the First Day of Rosh HaShanah 5695-1934]. Cluj-Kolozsvár: A kolozsvári izr. hitközség. 15 p.
3. *A zsidóság szociális helyzete a Talmudban* [The Social Conditions of the Jews in the Talmud]. Ph.D. diss., Pázmány Péter University, Budapest. 24p.

1935

4. "A jámborok könyvéről" [Sepher Hassidim]. *Zsidó Naptár az 1934-1935 Polgári Évre*. Cluj. Vol. 1, pp. 1-5.

1936

5. "Bucsúzó Dr. Kecskeméti Lipót nagyváradi főrabbitól" [Eulogy of Dr. Leopold Kecskeméti, Chief Rabbi of Nagyvárad-Oradea]. In *Emlékkönyv Dr. Kecskeméti Lipót temetéséről, életrajz adataival*. Nagyvárad-Oradea, June 9, pp. 29-30.
6. "Dr. Blau Lajos." *Uj Kelet*. Cluj, March 8.
7. "A cluji hitközség" [The Jewish Community in Cluj]. *Zsidó Naptár 5696-1935/36*. Cluj-Oradea. Vol. 2, pp. 48-55.
8. "Dr. Eisler Mátyás főrabbi irodalmi működése" [The Bibliography of Chief Rabbi Dr. Matthias Eisler]. *Monitorul Comunitatii Izraelite - Hitközségi Értesítő*. Cluj. Vol. 1, no. 4 (August), pp. 3-5; nos. 5-6 (September), pp. 4-6; nos. 7-8 (October-November).
9. "A húsvéti fáklya" [The Torch of Easter]. *Múlt és Jövő*. Budapest. Vol. 26, pp. 140-143 (translation from the Romanian of "O Fáclie de Pasti," by I. L. Caragiale).
10. *Monitorul Comunitatii Izraelite-Hitközségi Értesítő* [Bulletin of the Jewish Community of Cluj]. Cluj. Vol. 1. Ed. by Mózes Weinberger.
11. "Ötvenéves a templomunk" [The Fiftieth Anniversary of Our Synagogue]. *Monitorul Comunitatii Izraelite - Hitközségi Értesítő*. Cluj. Vol. 1, nos. 5-6, pp. 2-3.
12. "Valamit a halotthamvasztásról" [Cremation]. *Zsidó Naptár 5696-1935/36*. Cluj-Oradea.

Vol. 2, pp. 128-132.

13. Review of *Almanahul Evreesc-Jüdisches Jahrbuch - Zsidó Évkönyv és Naptár, 1936-37/ 5697. Monitorul Comunitatii Izraelite - Hitközségi Értesítő.* Cluj. Vol. 1, nos. 5-6, p. 7.
14. Review of *Gerechtigkeit*, ed. by Irene Harand. *Monitorul Comunitatii Izraelite - Hitközségi Értesítő.* Cluj. Vol. 1, p.11.
15. Review of *Hebrew Union College Annual*, vol. 10 (1936). *Monitorul Comunitatii Izraelite - Hitközségi Értesítő.* Cluj. Vol. 1, nos. 5-6, p. 6.
16. Review of *Moses Mendelssohn: ein jüdisches Schicksal in Deutschland*, by Otto Zarek. *Monitorul Comunitatii Izraelite - Hitközségi Értesítő.* Cluj. Vol. 1, nos. 2-3, p. 11.
17. Review of *Palesztina* by Lajos Lazar. *Monitorul Comunitatii Izraelite - Hitközségi Értesítő.* Cluj. Vol. 1, no. 4, p. 9.
18. Review of *T. G. Masaryk* by Aladár Váradi. *Monitorul Comunitatii Izraelite - Hitközségi Értesítő.* Cluj. Vol. 1, no. 4, pp. 6-7.
19. Review of *Weise von Zion* by Otto Friedrich. *Monitorul Comunitatii Izraelite - Hitközségi Értesítő.* Cluj. Vol. 1, nos. 2-3, p. 11.
20. Review of *A zsidóság története: az ókortól napjainkig* [The History of the Jews from Ancient Times to the Present] by Simon Dubnov with an appendix by the translator, Bence Szabolcsi, "A zsidóság története Magyarországon" [The History of Jews in Hungary]. *Monitorul Comunitatii Izraelite - Hitközségi Értesítő.* Cluj. Vol. 1, no. 4, p. 9.

1937

21. *A cluji Izraelita Hitközség Havi Jelentése* [Bulletin of the Jewish Community of Cluj]. Vol. 2. Ed. by Mózes Weinberger.
22. *A templomos lelkek: A cluji congr. izraelita hitközség templomának félévszázados jubileumán, 1936 december 13-án* [The Souls of the Synagogue: a Sermon Delivered on the Synagogue's Fiftieth Anniversary, Dec. 13, 1936]. Cluj. 8 p. [Also in *Cluji Izraelita Hitközség Havi Jelentése* (Bulletin of the Jewish Community of Cluj), vol. 2, no. 1, pp. 1-5.]
23. "Az aranyhíd: Rosh HaShanah, 5698" [The Golden Bridge: Rosh HaShanah, 5698]. *Cluji Izraelita Hitközség Havi Jelentése* vol. 2, nos. 7-8, pp. 1-3.
24. "A cluji izraelita hitközség rabbijai" [The Rabbis of the Jewish Community of Cluj-Kolozsvár]. *Zsidó Naptár* vol. 3, pp. 105-112.
25. "Hitközségünk multjából" [From Our Community's Past]. *Cluji Izraelita Hitközség Havi Jelentése* vol. 2, nos. 3-4, pp. 9-11; nos. 5-6, pp. 13-15.
26. "Maimonides mint codificátor" [Maimonides as Codifier]. *B'nai B'rith Bulletin* (Cluj).
27. "A megtérésről" [On Repentance]. *Cluji Izraelita Hitközség Havi Jelentése* vol. 2, nos. 7-8, pp. 5-7.
28. "T. G. Masaryk" [in Romanian]. *Cluji Izraelita Hitközség Havi Jelentése* vol. 2, nos. 9-10, pp. 7-10.
29. "Telket vásároltunk" [We Bought Land]. *Cluji Izraelita Hitközség Havi Jelentése* vol. 2, nos. 11-12, pp. 1-2.

1938

30. *Raport Lunar* [Bulletin of the Jewish Community of Cluj]. Vol. 3. Ed. by Mózes Weinberger.
31. "Bűn és megtérés" [Sin and Atonement]. *Raport Lunar* vol. 3, nos. 9-10, pp. 83-84.
32. "Dr. Adorján Armin." *Raport Lunar* vol. 3, nos. 1-2, p. 12.
33. "Egy vizcsepp az olajban" [A Drop of Water in Oil]. *Raport Lunar* vol. 3, nos. 3-4, pp.

28-29.

34. "Fényjel az éjszakában: Rosh HaShanah, 5699" [Light in the Night: Rosh Ha-Shanah, 5699]. *Raport Lunar* vol. 3, nos. 9-10, pp. 73-74.
35. "A hitéleti statisztika fontosságáról" [On the Importance of Statistics in the Evaluation of Religious Life]. *Raport Lunar* vol. 3, no. 11, pp. 97-99; no. 12, pp. 113-115.
36. "Hitközségek és azoknak szervezete Németországban" [The Jewish Communities of Germany and their Organization]. *Raport Lunar* vol. 3, nos. 9-10, pp. 86-89.
37. "A németországi zsidó menekültekért" [Assisting the Jewish Refugees from Germany]. *Raport Lunar* vol. 3, nos. 9-10, p. 76.
38. "Pace" [Peace]. *Raport Lunar* vol. 3, nos. 1-2, pp. 2-5. [Sermon in Rumanian on the occasion of the promulgation of the new constitution, 13 March 1938].
39. Review of *A circumcisió: vallási és orvosi tanulmány* [Circumcision: a Religious and Medical Study], by Ferenc Tóbiás Strohli, Dr. Ernő Grünwald and Dr. Gyula Lasz. *Raport Lunar* vol. 3, nos. 3-4, verso of title-page.
40. Review of *Ifjainkkal és öregeinkkel: zsidó imakönyv, magyarra korszerűen átültette és magyar alkalmi imákkal bővítette Dr. Fényes Mór* [With Our Young and Elders: a Prayerbook with Hungarian Translation]. *Zsidó Naptár* vol. 4, pp. 121-127.
41. Review of Kurt Wilhelm, *Von Jüdischer Gemeinde und Gemeinschaft (Aus Gemeindebüchern, Satzungen und Verordnungen ausgewählt und deutsch herausgegeben)*. *Raport Lunar* vol. 3, no. 11, p. 112.

1939

42. ספר היובל לכבוד הרבנים ד״ר פנחס לוי (טארגו־מורש), ראש אגודת הרבנים שבטרנסילווניה, ד״ר מנחם לנקה (לוגוז׳), וד״ר יעקב סינגר (טימישוארא) ליום מלאת להם שבעים שנה לחייהם. יצא לאור ע״י ד״ר משה מרדכי ווינברגר. קלוז׳, תרצ״ט.
Emlékkönyv [Jubilee Volume in Honor of Dr. Pinehas Löwy (Tårgu Mures), Head of the Rabbinical Organization of Transylvania, Dr. Menahem Lenke (Lugoj), and Dr. Jacob Singer (Timisoara) on their Seventieth Birthdays] (Hungarian, Hebrew and Romanian). Edited by Moshe Mordechai Weinberger (= Erdély-Bánáti Rabbiegyesület Kiadványa: Közlemények, no. 2) Cluj: Erdély-Bánáti Rabbiegyesület. 107+23 p.
43. *Erő és szellem* [Physical and Spiritual Power: Sermon Delivered on Shavuot, 5699]. Cluj. 8 p. (First published in *Raport Lunar* vol. 4, no. 6 [1939], pp. 49-53.)
44. *Raport Lunar* [Bulletin of the Jewish Community of Cluj]. Vol. 4. Edited by Mózes Weinberger.
45. "II. Carol királyt üdvözlő beszéd" [Address Welcoming King Carol II on His Visit to Cluj]. *Universul* December 26. (Also published on the same date in *Viitorul* and *Curierul Israelit Bucuresti*.)
46. "Discursul tinut la receptie in sale prefecturii (27.II. 1939)" [Discourse Delivered at the Reception at the Cluj Prefectural Hall, 27 February 1939]. *Raport Lunar* vol. 4, nos. 3-4, p. 19.
47. "Dr. Marton Aron püspök beiktatása" [Greetings Offered at Dr. Aron Marton's Installation as Bishop of Transylvania]. *Raport Lunar* vol. 4, nos. 1-2, p. 10.
48. "A hitéleti statisztika fontosságáról" [On the Importance of Statistics in the Evaluation of Religious Life]. *Raport Lunar* vol. 4, nos. 1-2, pp. 4-6; nos. 3-4, pp. 20-24.
49. "Isten a hegyek felett" [God Above the Mountains: Shavuoth, 5699]. *Raport Lunar* vol. 4, no. 5, pp. 33-35.
50. "Kulturális élet hitközségünkben" [Cultural Life in Our Congregation]. *Raport Lunar* vol. 4, no. 9-10, pp. 105-106.
51. "Menekültek segélyezése" [Assistance for the Refugees]. *Raport Lunar* vol. 4, nos. 9-10, p. 111.
52. "A menekültekért" [Help the Refugees!] *Uj Kelet* (Cluj), September.

53. "Mit csinál a hitközség?" [The Activities of the Congregation]. *Raport Lunar* vol. 4, nos. 7-8, pp. 89-91.
54. "Porszemek futása" [The Swift Flight of Sand]. *Raport Lunar* vol. 4, nos. 7-8, pp. 81-82.
55. "Predica ocazionalâ tinutâ la aniversarea constitutiunei noui, 27.II.1939" [Sermon on the Anniversary of the New Constitution]. *Raport Lunar* vol. 4, nos. 3-4, pp. 17-18.
56. "A sírfeliratok szövegéről" [On the Text of Epitaphs]. In *Dr. Lőwy Pinchas Emlékkönyv*, Cluj, pp. 31-39.

1940

57. *Az Istenkereső ember* [Man in Search of God]. Eulogy of Dr. Lipót Kecskeméti, Chief Rabbi of Nagyvárad, in the *Zion* Synagogue, 30 May 1937, Oradea Mare-Nagyvárad. (First published in *Erdélyi Zsidó Évkönyv 5701 - 1940/41* [Kolozsvár] vol. 6, pp. 40-44; also as an off-print.)
58. *Jelentés az 1940. szeptember-december hónapokról* [Report for September-December, 1940]. Kolozsvár. 21 p.
59. *Raport Lunar* [Bulletin of the Jewish Community of Cluj]. Vol. 5. Edited by Mózes Weinberger.
60. "Beteljesült a prófétai látomás" [The Fulfillment of the Prophetic Vision (of Ezekiel)]. *Jelentés az 1940. szeptember-december hónapokról* (Kolozsvár), pp. 1-3. (Reprinted in *A kolozsvári zsidó gimnáziumok Évkönyve az 1940-1941 iskolai évről*. Kolozsvár, 1941, pp. 5-6 [Also in *Uj Kelet*, 14 September 1940].
61. "Dr. Lenke Manó főrabbi" [Eulogy of Rabbi Dr. Manó Lenke, Chief Rabbi]. *Raport Lunar* vol. 5, nos. 6-7, p. 95.
62. "Az Erdély-Bánát területén kötött vegyesházasságok a számok tükrében" [Statistics of Mixed Marriages in Transylvania and Banat]. *Erdélyi Zsidó Évkönyv 5701-1940/41* [Kolozsvár] vol. 6, pp. 92-98 [Also as an off-print].
63. "Győzelmek az éjszakában" [Victories in Dark Times]. *Raport Lunar* vol. 5, no. 4, pp. 41-43.
64. "Historia Sef-Rabinatului" [The History of the Chief-Rabbinate]. *Curierul Israelit* (Bucharest), February.
65. "Mit csinál a hitközség?" [The Activities of the Congregation]. *Raport Lunar* vol. 5, no. 5, p. 75; nos. 6-7: 96-97.
66. "Mózes" [Moses]. *Raport Lunar* 5, no. 5, pp. 61-62.
67. "Öfelsége látogatása városunkban" [The Visit of King Carol II to Cluj, 25 December 1939]. *Raport Lunar* vol. 5, no. 1, pp. 1-2.
68. "Olvassuk a Megillát" [Reading Megillat Esther]. *Raport Lunar* vol. 5, nos. 2-3, pp. 17-18.

1941

69. *Értesítés és tudnivalók az őszi ünepekkel kapcsolatban a hitközség tagjai számára* [Information and Instruction for Congregation Members Concerning the High Holidays]. Kolozsvár. 7 p.
70. *A kolozsvári kongresszusi izraelita hitközség jelentése az 1941. május-junius hónapokról* [Report of the Jewish-Neolog Congregation for the Months May-June, 1941]. Edited by M[ózes].W[einberger]. Kolozsvár. 20 p.
71. *Peszáchi jelentés* [A Passover Bulletin]. Kolozsvár. 20 p.
72. "Grof Teleki Pál miniszterelnök" [Eulogy of Prime Minister Count Paul Teleki]. In *Peszáchi jelentés*. Kolozsvár, p. 10.
73. "A györelmi dal" [The Song of Triumph (Passover, 5701)]. In *Peszáchi jelentés*. Kolozsvár, pp. 1-2.

74. "A halálszekér" [The Death Carriage: Eulogy at the Funeral of Dr. Béla Konrád, President of the Jewish Community of Nagyvárad, 10 January 1941]. *Hitközségi Értesítő* (Nagyvárad, Shevat 5701-February 1941), pp. 11-12.
75. "Imádkozzunk!" [Let's Pray!]. In *Értesités és tudnivalók az őszi ünepekkel kapcsolatban a hitközség tagjai számára*. Kolozsvár, pp. 1-2.
76. "A zsidó gimnáziumokért!" [Support the Jewish High Schools]. In *A kolozsvári kongresszusi hitközség jelentése az 1941. május-junius hónapokról*. Kolozsvár, pp. 1-3.

1942

77. *Peszáchi jelentés* [A Passover Bulletin]. Edited by M[ózes].W[einberger]. Kolozsvár. 32 p.
78. "Antal Márk". In *Izraelita Tanügyi Értesítő* (Budapest), December, 1942.
79. "Jirmijáhu világnézete" [The World Outlook of Jeremiah]. In *A kolozsvári izraelita koedukációs gimnázium Évkönyve az iskola fennállásának 22.-ik évében*. Kolozsvár, pp. 3-5.
80. "A zsidó ifjuság kivándorlásáról" [On the Emigration of the Jewish Youth]. *Képes Családi Lapok* (Budapest) vol. 63, no. 16 (26 April), p. 10.
81. Review of *Héber nyelvkönyv magántanulók, tanfolyamok és középiskolák részére* [Modern Hebrew Textbook for Self-Study and for Junior and Senior High Schools], by Mór Mannheim. *Múlt és Jővö* (Budapest), vol. 32 (July, 1942), p. 11.

1943

82. *Antal Márk Emlékkönyv* [Márk Antal Memorial Volume]. Edited by Mózes Weinberger. Kolozsvár. 5-287-XIII p. (in Hungarian and Hebrew).
83. *A kolozsvári kongresszusi izraelita hitközség jelentése az 1943. május-augusztusi hónapokról* [Report of the Neolog Congregation for the Months of May-August, 1943]. Edited by M[ózes].W[einberger]. Kolozsvár. 10 p.
84. "Chananja, Misael és Azarja" [Chananya, Mishael and Azarya]. In *A kongresszusi izraelita hitközség jelentése az 1943. május-augusztusi hónapokról*. Kolozsvár, pp. 3-4.
85. "Fejével emelkedett ki" [The Man of High Intellect]. In *Antal Márk Emlékkönyv*, pp. 41-44.
86. "Indexre tett héber könyvek" [Prohibited Hebrew Books]. In *Antal Márk Emlékkönyv*, pp. 166-188.
87. "Fel-lábon álló zsidóság" [Jewry that Stands upon One Foot]. In *Zsidó Diáknaptár*, edited by Dezső Fried and Béla Gábor. Kolozsvár.

1946

88. "Adatok az erdélyi zsidóság történetéhez" [Archival Material for the History of the Jews in Transylvania]. In *Jewish Studies in Memory of Michael Guttmann*, edited by Samuel Löwinger. Budapest, pp. 283-296.

1947

89. ביל״ו: גליון להורים ולתלמידים, שנה א. תל אביב: יוצא לאור ע״י ועד ההורים וחבר המורים של בית הספר ביל״ו, ניסן תש״ז (משה וינברגר, חבר מערכת).
90. הגורמים בחינוך. ביל״ו א, חוברת אייר-סיון תש״ז, עמ׳ 3-4.
91. החינוך בדברי חז״ל. ביל״ו א, חוברת אייר-סיון תש״ז, עמ׳ 10.
92. יצחק ארי־גור, אדם בישראל במשפט ובתולדה. הצופה, י״ז שבט תש״ז (ביקורת). (נתפרסם גם בתוך: חינוך. תל־אביב, תש״ז.)

1948

93. החינוך בדברי חז״ל. ביל״ו ב, חוברת טבת-שבט תש״ח, עמ׳ 4.

94. מטרתינו. ביל״ו ב, חוברת אדר-ניסן תש״ח, עמ׳ 26.

95. תפקידנו. ביל״ו ב, חוברת טבת-שבט תש״ח, עמ׳ 5.

96. "A középiskolai nevelés Izraelben [High School Education in Israel]. *Az Idő* (Tel Aviv), 25 February, pp. 1-6.

1962

97. גשרים. גיליונות: בטאון בית הספר התיכון ע״ש שאול טשרניחובסקי. נתניה, תשכ״ב. שנה יא, מס׳ 2-3, עמ׳ 12.

98. מלחמת קיום. ניר: בטאון תלמידי בית המדרש למורים. ניו־יורק: ישיבה אוניברסיטה, תשכ״א. עמ׳ 14-16.

1964

99. אהבת הספר בספר חסידים ובפילוביבלון. סיני נו, עמ׳ קנט-קעה (גם כתדפיס).

100. צפון טראנסילווניה בימי השואה ונסיונות הצלה. ידיעות יד ושם 32, עמ׳ 8-19 (גם כתדפיס).

101. "The Tragedy of Transylvanian Jewry." *Yad Vashem Bulletin* 15, pp. 12-27 (translation of no. 100; also as an offprint).

1965

102. הוראה מה היא? ניר: בטאון תלמידי בית המדרש למורים. ניו יורק: ישיבה אוניברסיטה, תשכ״ד-תשכ״ה. עמ׳ 69.

103. משוררים עבריים בטראנסילווניה. סיני נז, עמ׳ קמ-קנט (גם כתדפיס).

1966

104. ספר וסייף: חופש הביטוי והמחשבה אצל עם ישראל. ירושלים-ניו־יורק: מכון סורא ע״י ישיבה אוניברסיטה, תשכ״ז. 290 עמ׳.

105. אהבת ציון ושפתה בשירה העברית בהונגריה. בצרון כז, עמ׳ 119-128 (גם כתדפיס).

106. התפתחות השירה העברית בהונגריה. ארשת ד, עמ׳ 368-417 (גם כתדפיס).

107. ספרים מוחרמים במשך הדורות. פרקים ד, עמ׳ 223-241 (גם כתדפיס).

108. S. Colodner, *Jewish Education in Germany under the Nazis* בתוך: בצרון נד, עמ׳ 44-45 (ביקורת).

109. "Hebrew Poetry in Hungary." In *Hungarian Jewish Studies*, vol. I, ed. Randolph L. Braham. New York: World Federation of Hungarian Jews, 1966, pp. 295-342.

1967

110. חלקה נשכחת: על ספרות וסופרים עבריים בהונגריה. הדאר מו, עמ׳ 293-294.

111. חנוך יהודי בטראנסילבניה בימי השואה. ידיעות יד ושם 38, עמ׳ 16-22. (נדפס מחדש בתוך: ספר הזכרון ליהדות קלוז׳-קולוז׳וואר. ראה מס׳ 127. גם כתדפיס.)

112. ספר ספר וגורלו: ספרים שהושמדו בידי מחבריהם. הדאר מז, עמ׳ 49-51.

113. "Jewish Education in Transylvania in the Days of the Holocaust." *Yad Vashem Bulletin* 21, pp. 21-27. (Reprinted in *Memorial Volume for the Jews of Cluj-Kolozsvár*.)

114. "Sephardic Jews in the Development of Transylvania." *The American Sephardi* 1, no. 2. pp. 39-44.

115. Review of *The Janowska Road* by Leon Welicker-Wells. *Jewish Social Studies* 29, no.

2, pp. 135-136.

1968

116. הטרגדיה של יהודי טראנסילבניה. בתוך: לזכר קהלת קולוז'וואר-קלוז'. תל־אביב: חוג יוצאי קולוז'בר בישראל, תשכ"ה. עמ' 72-79.

1969

117. גורמי התבוללות בדורינו. הדאר מח, עמ' 245-246 (יצא לאור גם בתוך המשקיף: בטאון תלמידי המכללה ע"ש אלישבע מיכאל שע"י ישיבה אוניברסיטה, ב, גליון ב, ערב פסח תשכ"ט, עמ' 2-4.
118. הגדה מעוטרת מבורגנלנד. הדאר מח, עמ' 342-343 (גם כתדפיס).
119. הפילאנטרוף והפילוביבלון היהודי: דברים שנאמרו לזכרו של ד"ר יצחק ריבקינד ז"ל. הדאר מ (ג' אדר תשכ"ט), עמ' 264-265.
120. *Sirt az Isten: Emlékbeszéd a magyarországi zsidóság tragédiájának huszonötéves fordulóján, 1969 május 25-én megtartott emlék-istentiszteleten, Park East Synagogue, New York* [God Wept: Memorial Speech Delivered on the Twenty-Fifth Anniversary of Hungarian Jewry's Tragedy at the Memorial Service Held on May 25th, 1969 at the Park East Synagogue]. New York: World Federation of Hungarian Jews, 1969, pp. 3-7. (Reprinted in *Memorial Volume for the Jews of Cluj-Kolozsvár*. See no. 138. Also in *Uj Kelet*. [Tel-Aviv: 4 May 1978], p. 4; *Menóra-Egyenlőség*. [Toronto: 10-17 April 1987].)
121. "Censorship and Jewish Writers." Introduction to William Popper, *The Censorship of Hebrew Books*. New York: Ktav, pp. I-XXXI.
122. "The Life of Spanish Jews in the Balkans: In Light of Documents." *The American Sephardi* 3, no. 1-2, pp. 113-115.

1970

123. *A kolozsvári zsidóság emlékkönyve - Memorial Volume for the Jews of Cluj-Kolozsvár.* ספר הזכרון ליהדות קלוז'-קולוז'וואר. בעריכת משה כרמילי-וינברגר. ניו־יורק, 1970. 313 עמ'. (עברית, הונגרית ואנגלית).
124. ארגוני תרבות וספורט. בתוך: ספר זכרון ליהדות קלוז'-קולוז'וואר. עמ' עו-פ.
125. הארגונים הארציים של הקהילות (בקולוז'וואר). בתוך: ספר הזכרון ליהדות קלוז'-קולוז'וואר. עמ' פד-פז.
126. בתי כנסת ובתי מדרש, מוסדות צדקה, הלשכה הסוציאלית. בתוך: ספר הזכרון קלוז'-קלוז'וואר .עמ' סא-עה.
127. חנוך יהודי בטרנסילוניה. בתוך: ספר הזכרון ליהדות קלוז'-קולוז'וואר. עמ' קכט (ראה לעיל מס' 111).
128. יהודי טרנסילוניה בתרבות ההונגרית. בתוך: ספר הזכרון ליהדות קלוז'-קולוז'וואר. עמ' קכט (ראה להלן מס' 154).
129. כתבי ד"ר משה כרמלי-וינברגר: ביבליוגרפיה (1934-1970). בתוך: ספר הזכרון ליהדות קלוז'-קולוז'וואר. עמ' מ-מו (גם כתדפיס נפרד).
130. מרוץ עם המות. בתוך: ספר הזכרון ליהדות קלוז'-קולוז'וואר. עמ' קמד-קמט (ראה להלן מס' 152).
131. משוררים עבריים בטרנסילבניה. בתוך: ספר הזכרון ליהדות קלוז'-קולוז'וואר. עמ' קיב-קכח (ראה לעיל מס' 103).
132. הנביא ישעיהו והמחשב האלקטרוני (קומפיוטר). ניר: בטאון תלמידי המכללה ע"ש אלישבע מיכאל ע"י ישיבה אוניברסיטה. עמ' 33.
133. הקהילה האורתודוכסית והקונגרסאית (בקולוז'וואר). בתוך: ספר הזכרון ליהדות קלוז'-קולוז'וואר. עמ' כו-לט.
134. ראשית הישוב היהודי בקולוז'וואר. בתוך: ספר הזכרון ליהדות קלוז'-קולוז'וואר. עמ' טז-כה.
135. שאלת הפליטים בטרנסילוניה. בתוך: ספר הזכרון ליהדות קלוז'-קולוז'וואר. עמ' פא-פג.
136. שואת יהודי צפון טרנסילוניה. בתוך: ספר הזכרון ליהדות קלוז'-קולוז'וואר. עמ' קל-קמג (ראה לעיל מס'

100, 116 ולהלן מס׳ 151).

137. שירת יהדות הונגריה ב״חבצלת״ (ירושלים). בתוך: תלפיות ט, חוב׳ ג-ד (ניו־יורק), עמ׳ 853-886 (גם כתדפיס נפרד).

138. שמים בכו. בתוך: ספר הזכרון ליהדות קלוז׳-קולוז׳וואר. עמ׳ יג-טו (ראה לעיל מס׳ 120).

139. תכנית הלימודים החדשה. בתוך: המשקיף ג, מס׳ ו (ג׳ כסלו תש״ל), עמ׳ ג.

140. התנועה הציונית בטרנסילוניה. בתוך: ספר הזכרון ליהדות קלוז׳-קולוז׳וואר. עמ׳ פח-פט.

141. כתבי־יד עבריים בכריכת ספרים לועזיים. בתוך: הדואר מט, עמ׳ 170. ביקורת על:
Sándor Scheiber, *Héber Kódex maradványok magyarországi kötéstáblákban: A középkori magyar zsidóság könyvkultúrája. (Hebräische Kodexüberreste in ungarischen Einbandstafeln: die Bücherkultur der ungarischen Juden im Mittelalter).*

142. "Az Erdély-Bánát területén kötött zsidó vegyes házasságok a számok tükrében" [Statistics on Intermarriages in Transylvania and Banat]. In *Memorial Volume for the Jews of Cluj-Kolozsvár,* pp. 168-172 (reprint of no. 62).

143. "Five Protocols." In *Memorial Volume for the Jews of Cluj-Kolozsvár,* pp. 305-313.

144. "A Héber kultúra Erdélyben" [Hebrew Culture in Transylvania]. In *Memorial Volume for the Jews of Cluj-Kolozsvár,* pp. 172-185.

145. "Hitközségek: az orthodox hitközség és Chevra Kadisa; a kongresszusi hitközség" [Jewish Congregations: The Orthodox Congregation and Chevra Kadisha; the Congressional (Neolog) Congregation]. In *Memorial Volume for the Jews of Cluj-Kolozsvár,* pp. 31-78.

146. "Jewish Education in Transylvania in the Days of the Holocaust." In *Memorial Volume for the Jews of Cluj-Kolozsvár,* pp. 269-276.

147. "A kolozsvári zsidó gimnáziumok története" [The History of the Jewish High Schools in Kolozsvár]. In *Memorial Volume for the Jews of Cluj-Kolozsvár,* pp. 114-129.

148. "A kolozsvármegyei zsidóság és az 1848-49-es szabadságharc" [The Jews of Kolozsvár County and the 1848-49 War of Independence]. In *Memorial Volume for the Jews of Cluj-Kolozsvár,* pp. 13-28 (reprint of no. 88).

149. "Sephardic Jews in the Development of Transylvania." In *Memorial Volume for the Jews of Cluj-Kolozsvár,* pp. 263-268 (reprint of no. 114).

150. "Statisztikai adatok Kolozsvár zsidóságáról az 1919-1936-os években" [Statistical Data Concerning the Jews of Cluj-Kolozsvár during the Years 1919-1936]. In *Memorial Volume for the Jews of Cluj-Kolozsvár,* pp. 105-113.

151. "The Tragedy of Transylvanian Jewry." In *Memorial Volume for the Jews of Cluj-Kolozsvár,* pp. 286-304 (translation and reprint of nos. 100-101, 116).

152. "Versenyfutás a halállal" [Race with Death]. In *Memorial Volume for the Jews of Cluj-Kolozsvár,* pp. 213-235 (translation of no. 130).

153. "Zsidó ejtőernyősök" [Jewish Parachutists]. In *Memorial Volume for the Jews of Cluj-Kolozsvár,* pp. 248-249.

154. "Zsidók Erdély magyar kulturájában" [The Participation of Jews in the Hungarian Culture of Transylvania]. In *Memorial Volume for the Jews of Cluj-Kolozsvár,* pp. 202-210 (translation of no. 128).

155. "Zsidók Erdélyben" [Jews in Transylvania]. In *Memorial Volume for the Jews of Cluj-Kolozsvár,* pp. 7-12.

1971

156. "Censorship: Church Censorship, Government Censorship, Jewish Censorship." *Encyclopaedia Judaica*. Jerusalem: Keter. Vol. 5, pp. 276-281. [Reprinted (author's name omitted)] in Raphael Posner and Israel Ta-Shema, ed., *The Hebrew Book: an Historical Survey*. Jerusalem: Keter, 1975, pp. 184-187.]

157. "External and Internal Censorship of Hebrew Books." *Jewish Book Annual* 28, pp. 9-16. [Reprinted in *Essays on Jewish Booklore*. New York: Ktav, Jewish Book Council of

America, n.d., pp. 398-405.

158. "Haskamah (Askamah)." *Encyclopaedia Judaica*. Jerusalem: Keter. Vol. 7, pp 1452-1454.

1972

159. התפתחות השירה העברית באונגריה. ארשת ה, עמ׳ 254-265 (גם כתדפיס נפרד).

1974

160. יצחק יהודה גולדציהר, דרשת הבר־מצוה. בתוך: ספר היובל לכבוד ד״ר יהושע פינקל. עורכים שמחה בנימין הוניג ואריה ליב סטיצקין. ניו־יורק: ישיבה אוניברסיטה. עמ׳ 185-199.

161. סופרים יהודים ומוסד הצנזורה במערב אירופה. הגות עברית באמריקה. תל־אביב: ברית עברית עולמית. עמ׳ 120-130 (גם כתדפיס נפרד).

1975

162. שלמה לויזון כהיסטוריון. בצרון סז (תשרי-חשון תשל״ו), עמ׳ 20-27.

1977

163. ילקוט המשוררים העבריים מהונגריה מן המאה ה-18 ועד ימינו. עם מבוא וביו-ביבליוגרפיה. תל־אביב: עקד. 207 עמ׳.

[English title-page: *Hebrew Poets of Hungary (18th-20th Century), with an Introduction and Bio-Bibliography*.]

164. בית המדרש לרבנים בבודפסט בן מאה שנה. הדאר נו, (כ״א אדר תשל״ז), עמ׳ 295-296.

165. רומנטיזם בשירה העברית בהונגריה. בתוך: דברי הקונגרס העולמי השישי למדעי היהדות. ירושלים: האיגוד העולמי למדעי היהדות. כרך ג, עמ׳ 229-240 (גם כתדפיס נפרד).

166. *Censorship and Freedom of Expression in Jewish History*. New York: Sepher-Hermon Press, Yeshiva University. 295 p. (also in paperbound edition).

167. "Százéves a budapesti Rabbi-Szeminárium" [The One Hundredth Anniversary of the Rabbinical Seminary in Budapest]. *Uj Kelet* (12 September).

168. "Történelem nem hal meg" [History does not Cease to Flow]. *Uj Kelet* (16 December).

1978

169. על מטבע אחת של בר־כוכבא שנתגלתה בהונגריה. הדאר נז (ט״ו אדר ב׳ תשל״ח), עמ׳ 318-319 (נוסח עברי של מס׳ 171).

170. יומנו של יצחק גולדציהר. הדאר נז (ער״ה תשל״ט), עמ׳ 659-662 (ראה מס׳ 174). ביקורת על: Ignac Goldziher, *Tagebuch*, edited by Alexander Scheiber.

171. "Egy Magyarországra elvetődött Bar-Kochba érem" [A Bar-Kochba Coin Found in Hungary]. *Uj Kelet* (6 January). [Originally a lecture delivered at the Hebrew University on Dec. 21, 1977 at the inauguration of the Joseph and Margaret Fettman Chair for the History of the Jews in Hungary. Also published in *Menóra-Egyenlőség* (Toronto), 28 January 1978.]

172. "A Nilushal és az aszimiláció" [The Nile-Catfish and the Problem of Assimilation]. *Uj Kelet* (22 December).

173. "Sirt az Isten" [God Wept]. *Uj Kelet* (4 May) (see no. 120).

1979

174. "Nincs kihez fordulnom csupán naplómhoz" [My Diary Is My Only Consolation].

Review of Ignac Goldziher, *Tagebuch*, ed. Alexander Scheiber. *Uj Kelet* (16 and 23 March).

175. "Százéves a *Hatikva*" [The Centennial of *Hatikva*]. *Uj Kelet* (3 August).

1980

176. טיול בסין. הדאר נט (י״א ניסן תש״ם), עמ׳ 321-320; (ט׳ אייר), עמ׳ 367-366; (ט״ז אייר), עמ׳ 379-378; (א׳ סיון), עמ׳ 395-394.
177. יובלו המאה של בית המדרש לרבנים שבבודאפשט. הדאר נט (ה׳ אדר תש״ם), עמ׳ 238 (חתום: משה בן שלמה).
178. "Prayer of a Jew." *New York Times* (30 September), p. A26 (letter to the editor).
179. "Sírkövek, ha megszólalhatnának" [If Tombstones Were Able to Speak]. *Uj Kelet* (26 December).
180. "The Songs of the Martyrs." Introduction to *Songs of the Martyrs: Hassidic Melodies of Maramures* by Max Eisikovits. New York: Sepher-Hermon Press.
181. "Tűzbe vetem szótáram kéziratát, ha nem segítenek: Ben Jehudah könyörgő sorai prof. Bacherhez" [If I Do Not Receive Assistance, I Will Throw the Manuscript of My Dictionary into the Fire: Ben Yehudah's Plea to Prof. Bacher]. *Uj Kelet* (29 February), p. 9.
182. "Utiélmények a Kinai Népköztársaságban" [Travel Impressions of China]. *Uj Kelet* (18 March; 18 April; 9 May; 16 May).

1981

183. ספר זכרון לשמואל בלקין. עורכים משה כרמלי וחיים ליף. ניו־יורק: המכללה ע״ש אלישבע (אירנה) מיכאל, ישיבה אוניברסיטה. 280 עמ׳.
184. כוחו של ״פדיון שבויים״. הדאר ס (ט׳ מרחשון תשמ״ב), עמ׳ 11; (ט״ז מרחשון תשמ״ב), עמ׳ 23 (גם כתדפיס נפרד).
185. פרוש תהלים מצונזר של ר׳ שלמה בן עטיה. בתוך: ספר זכרון לשמואל בלקין. ניו־יורק: המכללה ע״ש אלישבע (אירנה) מיכאל, ישיבה אוניברסיטה. עמ׳ 62-55 (גם כתדפיס נפרד).
186. אוטוביוגרפיה של הרב אליהו יונג. הדאר נט (כ״ה שבט תשמ״א), עמ׳ 187-186. ביקורת על: *The Path of a Pioneer: The Autobiography of Leo Jung.*
187. "Aki megelőzte Wallenberget" [A Precursor of Wallenberg]. *Uj Kelet* (30 October).
188. "Nehéz történelmet írni" [It is Difficult to Write History]. *Uj Kelet* (8 May).

1982

189. פדיון שבויים יהודיים במאה הי״ז בהונגריה. בתוך: דברי הקונגרס העולמי השמיני למדעי היהדות, חטיבה ב: תולדות עם ישראל. ירושלים: האיגוד העולמי למדעי היהדות. עמ׳ 83-77 (גם כתדפיס נפרד).
190. "A Fettman kathedra teljesiti feladatát" [The Fettman Chair Fulfills Its Task]. *Uj Kelet* (June), p. 11.
191. "Ne csinálj magadnak faragot képet" [Thou Shalt Not Make for Thyself a Graven Image], *A Hid* [Literary Supplement to *Uj Kelet*] (9 March), p. 7.

1983

192. "Lax A. Salvator" (Necrology). *Uj Kelet* (22 April), p. 4.
193. "The Magic Bird." In *Fields of Offerings: Studies in Honor of Raphael Patai*, ed. by Victor D. Sanua. London and Toronto: Associated University Presses, pp. 129-141 (also as an off-print).

1984

194. קברה הראשון של חנה סנש ז״ל. הדאר סב (כ״ב סיון תשמ״ג), עמ׳ 423.
195. תרבות אשכנזית או תרבות ספרדית איזו היא העילית ביותר. הדאר סג (ט״ו סיון תשמ״ד), עמ׳ 460-461.
196. ישעיה תשבי כמשורר. ביקורת על ישעיה תשבי ‹אליהו קידר›, שביבי אלטה. הדאר סג (י״ג כסלו תשמ״ה), עמ׳ 92-93.
197. המצבות מספרות. הדאר סג (כ״ד אלול תשמ״ד), עמ׳ 603. ביקורת על: Alexander Scheiber, *Jewish Inscriptions in Hungary.*
198. "The Pronunciation of the Letter 'H'." *New York Times* (1 December 1984), p. 22.

1985

199. ארגון להצלת יהודים בימי השואה. הדאר סד (כ״ה סיון תשמ״ה), עמ׳ 460-461; 474-475; 492-493.
200. פרופ׳ אלכסנדר שייבר ז״ל (1913-1985). הדאר סד (ו׳ ניסן תשמ״ה), עמ׳ 311.
201. ה׳ אימבר כסופר אנגלי. הדאר סד (ער״ה תשמ״ו), עמ׳ 607-608. ביקורת על: *Master of Hope*: *Selected Writings of N. H. Imber*, by Jacob Kabakoff .
202. "A magárahagyott zsidóság" [The Abandoned Jews]. Review of *The Abandonment of the Jews: America and the Holocaust, 1941-1945* by David S. Wyman. *Uj Kelet* (4 October), p. 6.

1986

203. ארגון להצלת יהודים בטרנסילוניה בימי השואה. בתוך: דברי הקונגרס העולמי התשיעי למדעי היהדות, חטיבה ב, כרך ב. ירושלים: האיגוד העולמי למדעי היהדות. עמ׳ 211-216 (גם כתדפיס).
204. *The Rabbinical Seminary of Budapest Centennial Volume, 1877-1977.* Edited by Moshe Carmilly-Weinberger. New York: Sepher-Hermon Press, Alumni Association of the Rabbinical Seminary of Budapest. IX-XIII+334 p. (English) + 4-54 p. (Hebrew).
205. *Fear of Art: Censorship and Freedom of Expression in Art.* New York, London: R.R. Bowker. VIII+249 p.
206. בית המדרש לרבנים בבודפשט והישיגיו. בתוך: *The Rabbinical Seminary of Budapest Centennial Volume, 1877-1977,* pp. 7-18 (Hebrew section).
207. "Censorship Foreign to the Jewish Spirit." *B'nai B'rith International Jewish Monthly* 100, no. 5 (January), pp. 19, 32.
208. "Hebrew Language and Literature." In *The Rabbinical Seminary of Budapest Centennial Volume. 1877-1977,* pp. 205-214.
209. "Jewish Historiography of Transylvania, Banat and Croatia." In *The Rabbinical Seminary of Budapest*, pp. 238-241.
210. "One Hundred Years of the Seminary in Retrospect." In *The Rabbinical Seminary of Budapest*, pp. 3-47.
211. "The Students." In *The Rabbinical Seminary of Budapest*, pp.143-148.
212. סופרים עברים ממוצא הונגרי בארה״ב. בתוך: מגוון: מחקרים בספרות העברית ובגילוייה האמריקניים מוגשים ליעקב קבקוב במלאות לו ארבעים שנה. התקין וערך שלמה נש. לוד: מכון הברמן למחקרי ספרות. עמ׳ 229-241 (גם כתדפיס).

1988

213. *Memorial Volume for the Jews of Cluj-Kolozsvár*. Second edition. New York: Sepher Hermon Press (Reprint of no. 123).
214. "Az utolsó főpap" [The Last High-Priest]. *Menóra - Egyenlőség* (Toronto) 19 February,

p. 4 (Eulogy of Prof. Alexander Scheiber held on 6 January 1988 in Jerusalem).

215. "Egy burgenlandi, illusztrált Haggadah" [An Illustrated Haggadah from Burgenland]. *Uj Kelet* 8 May, p. 6.

216. "The Jew in Courbet and Goya's Art." In *Occident and Orient: A Tribute to the Memory of Alexander Scheiber*. Edited by Róbert Dán. Budapest: Akadémia Kiadó - Leiden: E.J. Brill, pp. 39-52 (also as an off-print).

217. "Gyermek reményim és bánatim tanyája" [The Village of My Hopes and Sorrows]. *Uj Kelet* 29 July and *Menóra - Egyenlőség* 19 August.

218. "Ajutorul Romaniei in Actiunea de Salvare a Evreilor in Timpul Nazismului" [The Help of Romania in Rescuing Jews during the Time of Nazism]. *Europa si Neamul Romanesc*. Milan, October 1988. Vol. XVII, no. 196, pp. 9-16 (Lecture delivered at the Nicolae Iorga Institute of History, Bucharest on 27 May 1988). Also in *Curentul* (Münich), November-December, pp. 2-3; *Almanah Luceafarul* (Bucharest), pp. 47-56.

1989

219. "Szülőhelyem és bánataim földjén" [My Journey to Transylvania]. *Magyar Hírek* 42, 2, pp. 18-19.

220. "1940-1944. In acele vremuri grele. Poporul Roman si-a pastrat demnitatea si omenia" [1940-1944. In those difficult times Romania saved her dignity and humanity]. *Magazin Historic* 13, 10 (October), pp. 40-42.

221. "Salvarea evreilor din teritorul de Nord-West al Romaniei, 1940-1944" [The Rescue Operation from the North-West Territory of Romania, 1940-1944: A Roundtable]. In *Almanah Luceafarul*. Bucharest, pp. 114-162.

1990

222. "A North-Transylvanian Tale: Days when Proselytes shared Martyrdom of Jews." *Martyrdom and Resistance*. New York. 4 p.

223. "Az utolsó főpap" [The Last High-Priest]. *Uj Élet* (15 April and 1 May). (Eulogy of Prof. Alexander Scheiber, rector of the Rabbinical Seminary of Budapest, see no. 214.)

224. "Rendhagyó tiszteletadás" [Unprecedented Respect]. *Uj Kelet* (28 September), p. 5 (On the Tenth Anniversary of the Demise of Marton Aron, Bishop of Transylvania).

I

Jews and Entrepreneurship

A Jewish Minority in a Backward Economy: an Introduction

Michael K. Silber

"As far as I am acquainted with the various European states, I know of no country where the Israelite population exercises as much weight in its numbers, spiritual talent, activities and wealth, on the one hand, and is as significant in the economy with its peculiar social conditions, on the other hand, as in Hungary."[1] When Ágoston Trefort, the Hungarian Minister of Education and Religion, made this declaration on the floor of the Hungarian Parliament in 1874, he was not too far off the mark. Although it could be argued that Jews played an even greater economic role in the Pale of Settlement in Russia or in neighboring Galicia, these were both regions in larger political and economic units within which the relative importance of the Jews dropped considerably. To be sure, in Germany, too, Jews left their imprint on the economy, but in no other European country (perhaps the Kingdom of Poland excepted) did the Jews play such a dominant role both in the upper reaches and the lower levels of economic life, in the diversity of their impact on almost every sector—agriculture, industry, commerce and the free professions—as in the Kingdom of Hungary.[2]

Before it was drastically reduced in size in the wake of the First World War, Hungary was composed of areas which were to become large parts of the new states of Czechoslovakia, Romania, Yugoslavia and Austria. In 1910, the Jewish population of this greater Hungary was fast approaching the million mark, and it was Europe's largest Jewry outside the Russian Empire. Budapest had over 200,000 Jews who constituted almost a quarter of the capital's population; it was the largest Jewish community on the continent after Warsaw.

1 Árpád Zeller, *A magyar egyházpolitika, 1847-1894* [Hungarian Church Politics, 1847-1894], 2 vols. (Budapest, 1894), vol. II, p. 281.

2 Jewish "domination" of the economy was, and is, of course, a much harped upon theme in antisemitic literature. This does not, however, mean that the phrase is meaningless and cannot be treated in a neutral fashion. Yehuda Don's *relative domination index* or László Katus's *index of participation* (see their papers below)—both defined as the share of Jews in any one sector or occupation divided by their proportion in the total population—provide objective, quantitative measures which prove highly useful in comparing the economic role of Jews in various countries. Such indices indicate that in the commercial sector, for example, the Jews of Hungary scored the highest in Europe. See pp. 258-260 below.

The proportion of Jews in the entire country was around five percent, placing Hungary in an intermediate position between Poland (close to ten percent) and Germany (somewhat under one percent).

The more sensational statistics on the disproportionate economic role of Hungarian Jews are generally well-known and were often cited both by apologetic-minded well-wishers who were concerned to place "Jewish contributions" on the record,[3] as well as by antisemites who sought proof that nothing less than a conspiracy was afoot to achieve domination over Christian Hungary.[4] And there is no denying that the figures were impressive indeed. The 1910 census revealed the high proportion of Jews among Hungary's professionals—they constituted 49% of the doctors, 45% of the lawyers and 42% of the journalists—while the percentage of Jews among those engaged in commerce was 47%.[5]

The disproportionate share of Jews in commerce and later in the professions, their prominence among the economic elite, not only in Hungary, but elsewhere as well, has often occasioned speculation about how being Jewish has affected their distinctive economic patterns. Did the Jews share some specific group characteristics, some cultural orientations which gave them an edge, particularly in the modern capitalist market? Of course there was no lack of antisemites who sought to trace the Jewish propensity to commercial activity to "innate" racial characteristics. Jewish culture and religion, they argued, were fashioned by these inherent dispositions and were nothing but the reflections of an inborn business mentality. Others, rejecting this crude racism, reversed the equation, asking instead what specific features of Jewish culture—whether Judaism or more sophisticatedly, the ethic of Judaism—may have helped mold economic orientations suited to modern capitalism. The Holocaust has clearly discredited among respectable scholars the notion of primordial attributes, and to a certain extent it has made even the Weberian concept of a particular ethic uncomfortable. While recognizing the importance of culture in shaping economic behavior, the tendency in recent scholarship has been to play down the role of Jewish cultural orientations[6] and to emphasize instead the social dimension, the fact of being a

3 See for example M. Gelléri, "Zsidók a magyar közgazdasági életben" [Jews in Economic Life], in Count Hermán Zichy and Gy. M. Derestye, eds., *Magyar zsidók a milleniumon* [Jews at the Hungary's Millennium] (Budapest, 1896), pp. 44-51.

4 Alajos Kovács, *A zsidóság térfoglalása Magyarországon* [The Jewish Conquest of Hungary] (Budapest, 1922) and *A csonkamagyarországi zsidóság a statisztika tükrében* [The Jewry of Mutilated Hungary in the Mirror of Statistics] (Budapest, 1938).

5 For these statistics, see László Katus's study below.

6 Mordechai Levin, "Economic Attitudes and Behavior in Jewish Tradition: An Examination of Sombart's Thesis in Light of *Musar* Literature and Memoirs" (Hebrew) *Zion* XLIII (1978), 235-263. See however the chapter entitled "Commerce and Currency: Cultural Sources of Entrepreneurialism," in Hillel Levine, *Economic Origins of Antisemitism: Poland and its Jews in the Early Modern Period* (New Haven and London, 1991), pp. 75-135 and Jacob Katz, "Thoughts on the Relationship between Religion and Economy" (Hebrew), *Tarbitz* LX (1991), 99-111, esp. 111.

minority. The peculiar contours of the Jewish occupational structure, it is argued, can be best understood as part of a general theory on the economic activities of minorities.[7]

Ethnic and religious minorities tend to find niches in the economy which the indigenous populations for reasons having to do with high risk or low social prestige have traditionally shunned. And although ethnic groups often suffer various degrees of legal and social discrimination, they also enjoy certain advantages by virtue of being minority. They are psychologically more highly motivated to succeed in economic life to compensate for their exclusion from the social and political spheres; they arrive with practical experience and cultural traditions of economic behavior which give them an edge over the native population still shackled by religious and cultural constrains; they benefit from the solidarity and trust which a tight-knit minority enjoys; and they have access to connections and resources which result from being part of a far-flung diaspora.[8]

But clearly being a minority is no prescription for economic success. There may be levels of discrimination so high or competition so intense that minorities can end up being restricted to very narrow economic roles with little opportunity for advancement. This was the experience of Chinese immigrants in the United States in the late nineteenth century who came to occupy a very marginal niche in the overall economy. On the other hand, minorities need not necessarily be relegated to peripheral roles as the success of those Chinese who landed on the more hospitable shores of Latin America demonstrates.[9] In regions like Southeast Asia and East Africa, middleman diasporas such as the Chinese and Indians constituted the middle-class of their host countries. Therefore in considering the economic fate of minorities, we must note not only their specific cultural orientations and social characteristics, but also the environment in which they function. First and foremost this means the specific economy, the way it is structured, the degree, pace and direction of its development, and the like. But inevitably, noneconomic factors must also come into play. If this is true of the economy in general, then certainly it holds in the case of minorities and of Jews in particular. "In the economics of Jews," Simon Kuznets has observed, "the noneconomic elements are important almost to the point of dominance."[10] The

7 See for instance the introduction to Nachum Gross, ed., *Jews in Economic Life: Collected Essays in Memory of Arcadius Kahan* (Hebrew) (Jerusalem, 1985), p. 11; Avraham Barkai, *Jüdische Minderheit und Industrialisierung* (Tübingen, 1988), pp. 44-47. W.E. Mosse, *Jews in the German Economy: The German-Jewish Economic Élite, 1820-1935* (Oxford, 1987), pp. 12-20 has a brief, excellent overview of the various theories of Jewish economic behavior.

8 A recent survey can be found in Howard E. Aldrich and Roger Waldinger, "Ethnicity and Entrepreneurship," *Annual Review of Sociology* XVI (1990), 111-135.

9 B. Wong, "A Comparative Study of the Assimilation of the Chinese in New York City and Lima, Peru," *Comparative Studies in Society and History* XX (1978), 335-358.

10 Simon Kuznets, "Economic Structure and Life of the Jews," in Louis Finkelstein, ed., *The Jews*, 3rd ed. (New York, 1960), vol. II, p. 1658.

role of the specific society and state must be taken into account in assessing the economic development of the Jews.

The studies in this volume examine the economic role of Jews in the specific environment of Hungary. (Two of the studies stray to neighboring Vienna, but this is understandable considering its large Hungarian enclave.) Their theme is to trace Jewish economic patterns as they were shaped by the complex interaction of social and cultural group characteristics with the opportunities afforded by the particular environment. These factors were not static, and it is their dynamic which provides the history of Jewish economic activity in Hungary.

Of overriding importance was Hungary's economic backwardness.[11] By whatever indices one chooses, Hungary on the eve of the 1848 Revolution lagged considerably behind not only such pioneers of industrialization as England or Belgium, but latecomers like Germany.[12] It shared the typical features of the region sandwiched between Russia to the east and Germany to the west: a large population of enserfed peasants; a politically powerful and numerous nobility (some five percent of Hungary's population); and a weak urban class of largely foreign extraction. Yet, as contemporaries often noted, it was almost a rule of thumb that the more backward the economy, the more opportunities it offered for Jews. "This is why more Jews live in villages and small towns than in a cultivated and well-populated city. This is why more Jews live in coarse Turkey and Russia-Poland-Hungary than in the more cultivated western countries."[13]

There were, of course, also disadvantages to this backwardness. Jewish emancipation, for instance, was granted relatively late in 1867, and legal discrimination certainly hampered economic activity. Nevertheless, as we shall see, well before their full political emancipation, Hungarian Jews attained a considerable measure of "economic emancipation".

In the eighteenth century, numerous legal restrictions on residence and occupations obtained. Many of the royal towns exercised their right "not to tolerate Jews", as did an assortment of "privileged" areas. Besides these legal restrictions, settlement was dependent upon receiving permission of the local landlord. While this was usually forthcoming, there were also exceptions.

11 See the review in Daniel Chirot, "Causes and Consequences of Backwardness," in Daniel Chirot, ed., *The Origins of Backwardness in Eastern Europe: Economics and Politics from the Middle Ages until the Early Twentieth Century* (Berkeley-Los Angeles-London, 1989), pp. 1-13. On Hungary, Andrew C. Janos, *The Politics of Backwardness in Hungary, 1825-1945* (Princeton, 1982).

12 László Katus, "Economic Growth in Hungary during the Age of Dualism (1867-1913)," in E. Pámlényi, ed., *Social-Economical Researches on the History of East-Central Europe*, Studia Historica LXII (Budapest, 1970) and Iván T. Berend and György Ránki, *The European Periphery and Industrialization, 1780- 1914* (Cambridge, 1982), pp. 13-18.

13 János Édes, "A zsidók polgárositása ügyében" [On the Matter of Jewish Embourgeoisement], *Jelenkor*, 26 May 1841, p. 165.

The occupational restrictions were just as onerous. Jews could not own land (not even the rustical land of the serfs) and were excluded from the merchant and craft guilds. Although Jews could become doctors, they were prohibited from studying and practicing law, entering the civil service or occupying any position of authority over Christians (including that of teacher or professor).

While Jews managed to circumvent some of the residential and occupational limitations, these discriminatory measures had an undeniable effect on the occupational structure of Hungarian Jewry. Péter Hanák and László Katus's studies in this volume highlight the largely rural nature of Jewish economic activity in the eighteenth century. Both refer to a 1768 census which revealed that about two-thirds of the Jewish population was engaged as either village *arendars* who leased such noble monopolies as distilleries, inns and mills, or itinerant traders who plyed their wares in the countryside.

The gradual alleviation of legal restrictions began with the Edict of Toleration issued by Joseph II for Hungarian Jewry in 1783. Joseph's policy toward Jewish economic activities was influenced by a contradictory mix of mercantilistic and physiocratic ideas. He viewed their heavy involvement in petty trade and innkeeping as economically harmful and morally corrupting. Jews, in his opinion, not only brought ruin on the peasant population by engaging in usury and encouraging alcoholism, but their occupations were also "unproductive" in light of the physiocratic theories of the day. (The term carried moral, as well as economic connotations.) It was the task of the state to intervene, educate and channel Jews away from their existing endeavors into such "productive" pursuits as agriculture and industry. By creating new economic opportunities (and insisting upon educational reforms), Joseph hoped to speed up the integration of the Jews into the general body of useful citizens. The Edict and subsequent legislation lifted the restrictions on settling in the cities, permitted Jews to join the guilds, and encouraged them to practice crafts and till the land. On the other hand, measures were proposed against peddling and leaseholding, and prohibiting, in general, Jewish settlement in the countryside for those not engaged directly in agriculture.[14]

Aside from breaching the walls of some of the royal cities, Joseph's economic policies had little practical results—in any case widespread opposition caused him to repeal most of his controversial legislation on his deathbed. Nevertheless, already during his reign there were officials in his Chancellery who demonstrated a greater appreciation of Jewish commercial activities. Arguing against the proposal to exclude Jews from leasing in the countryside, Vice-Chancellor Count Karl Pálffy and Court Councilor Count Franz Eszterházy raised several points in their favor. True, leasing invariably involved some abuses, but there was nothing to indicate that Christians behaved any differently.

14 "Sistematica Gentis Judaicae Regulatio," *Magyar Zsidó Szemle* [from hereon *MZsSz*] XIII (1896), 367-374, esp. 374 and Henrik Marczali, "A magyarországi zsidók II. József korában" [Hungarian Jewry in the Era of Joseph II], *MZsSz* I (1884), 353-363.

"It is a fact," they added, "that no Christian lessee can accomplish on the manor what a Jewish lessee can accomplish. The reason for this is the much more modest and inferior living standard of the Jews." Moreover, barring Jews from the *arenda* would have grave negative consequences for the little credit and commerce there was in Hungary. The Jew also proved of benefit to the peasant by buying up his raw produce and putting it to use.[15]

These themes—the moral corruption and economic harm of Jewish occupations on the one hand, the great utility of Jews in a backward environment, on the other—were to be echoed over and over again in the years to come. The balance between the two swung in favor of the Jews somewhere around the 1830s and the timing, which coincided with the beginnings of nationalism and political reform, as well as the agricultural "take-off" in Hungary, was clearly not fortuitous. Even before this time, the Jews had found important patrons among Hungary's magnates (such as Pálffy and Eszterházy of the Chancellery) and middle nobility. With their considerable resources, these noblemen helped Jews evade the residential disabilities and the guild restrictions which continued to be in force, at least on paper.[16] The more liberal nobles also began the campaign to remove the discriminatory legislation. Hont county, located in the mining region where Jews were not permitted to settle, instructed its delegates to the 1825-27 Diet to urge the assembly to revoke the law, because "it finds their presence and residence useful. Since they further commerce and increase the flow of trade, they bring no small benefit to the tax-paying people, and even more to the landlords by easing the sale of their crops. Through the agency of the Jews, there is greater circulation of money in the entire region."[17]

With the rise of nationalism, the reform-oriented political elites became even more sensitive to the need to modernize the economy. In order to create a strong nation-state, the economy had to be thoroughly transformed: serfdom had to be abolished and replaced by more efficient wage labor; transportation and communications had to be improved by creating new roads, canals, bridges and railways; credit had to be made available through savings and commercial banks. A start was made in this direction already in the 1830s. By the next decade, various patriotic societies for the promotion of industry, trade and agriculture had sprung up. Many leading nobles themselves became involved in some sort of entrepreneurial activity by establishing factories on their estates, sponsoring

15 Henrik Marczali, "Egy emlékirat II. József korából" [A Memorandum from the Era of Joseph II], *MZsSz* II (1885), 406-410.

16 See especially the studies of Géza Eperjessy: *Mezővárosi és falusi céhek az Alföldön és a Dunántúlon (1686-1848)* [Market-Town and Village Guilds on the Great Plains and Transdanubia, 1686-1848] (Budapest, 1967), pp. 122-139; "A zsidó iparűzők a reformkori szabad királyi városokban" [Jewish Craftsmen in Royal Free Cities in the Era of Reform], *Századok* CXVII (1983), 711-740; and *A szabad királyi városok kézművesipara a reformkori Magyarországon* [Craftsmen in Royal Free Cities in Reform Era Hungary] (Budapest, 1988), pp. 150-173.

17 Hont county delegates at the 208th session of the 1825-1827 Diet, *Diary 1825/27*, vol. V, pp. 214-216.

various banks, rail and steamship companies, as well as appearing on the boards of these associations.[18] But clearly a much broader sector of the population was needed to implement this transformation.

The problem was that Hungary lacked an autochthonous middle-class. Neither the broad stratum of the Magyar lower nobility nor the peasantry were prepared or willing to engage in commercial pursuits. Such activity was regarded as something essentially immoral and degrading, not suited to the Magyar spirit.[19] This had not always been so. The price revolution of the sixteenth century had brought increased involvement in trade and commerce on the part of the Hungarian nobility. However, with the decline of the agricultural boom in the middle of the next century, the nobility began to withdraw from commercial pursuits, developing an increasingly negative attitude toward trade. By the eighteenth century, instead of marketing their own produce they came increasingly to rely on foreign grain merchants to carry out this function. Commercial activity came to be regarded as alien activity. "The nobleman ignorant of and uninterested in market relations became the characteristic figure of the majority of the ruling class."[20]

Granted that economic entrepreneurship became the exclusive province of ethnic minorities in Hungary, but why were the Jews singled out for success in the nineteenth century among Hungary's numerous nationalities and religions? In the previous century, the towns had been dominated by burghers of German origin and much of the trade in the countryside was plied by Armenians and "Greeks"—meaning Serbs, Macedonians Greeks and others of Balkan origin.[21] These last had much in common with Jews. "Shrewd like the Jew/Greek," went a popular saying.[22] Many of the discriminatory measures restricting residence and limiting competition with the German or Magyar townsfolk were aimed not only at Jews, but also against these groups. As a cohesive minorities, they enjoyed strong family and commercial connections with the Ottoman Empire

18 An English-language introduction to the period and one of its key figures is George Barany, *Stephen Széchenyi and the Awakening of Hungarian Nationalism, 1791-1841* (Princeton, NJ, 1968).

19 Deploring the low status of trade, one publicist complained that even an honest, noble-minded Christian merchant risked being dubbed "Jew". He estimated the number of Jews among Hungary's "commercial estate" as 60,000 out of a total of 77,709. János Erdélyi, *Nemzeti iparunk* [Our National Industry], edited and annotated by Elek Fényes (Pest, 1843), pp. 85, 317-318.

20 Pál Zsigmond Pach, "Business Mentality and Hungarian National Character," *Études historiques hongroises 1985* (Budapest, 1985), vol. II, pp. 131-160.

21 On the towns see Dénes Oszetzky, *A hazai polgárság társadalmi problémái a rendiség felbomlásákor* [Problems of the Hungarian Burgher Society in the Era of Feudal Dissolution] (Budapest, 1935); on the "Greeks" see Traian Stoianovich, "The Conquering Balkan Orthodox Merchant " *Journal of Economic History* XX (1960). A recent study is Zoltán Ács, "Marchand grecs en Hongrie aux XVIIe-XVIIIe siècles," in Ferenc Glatz, *Ethnicity and Society in Hungary: Études historiques hongroises 1990,* vol. 2 (Budapest, 1990), pp. 41-58 which has a good bibliography on the subject.

22 This saying, "Ravasz, mint a zsidó-görög", was already cited one of the earliest proverb collections by András Dugonics, *Magyar példa beszédek és jeles mondások* (Szeged, 1820).

which gave them a decided edge in the grain and livestock trade. But by the 1830s and 1840s, Jews had displaced these once ubiquitous "Greeks". "For the last twenty-five years," noted a publicist in 1847, "the Serb Orthodox communities in Transdanubia and west of the Tisza have been dwindling steadily, because many Serbs are migrating to Serbia." Serbian shopkeepers in the villages "had vanished completely and now one hardly finds any shopkeepers except Jews."[23]

These Balkan merchants, as Péter Hanák suggests in this volume, illustrate what can happen to the entrepreneurial spirit of a minority once it is allowed unrestricted access to the entire range of occupations. By the beginning of the nineteenth century, much of the discrimination aimed at Balkan merchants in the previous centuries had been abolished. On the other hand, Maria Theresa's legislation in 1774 had in effect forced them to choose between returning to the Balkans or renouncing their connections with Turkey. Once they lost the advantages of the Levant trade, the "Greeks" abandoned the commercial sector, choosing instead to invest in urban and rural real estate. The German burghers often adopted similar strategies though several generations later. Like the Greeks, they opted out of trade, and preferred to buy real estate, get ennobled, join the army or enter the civil service. This was to prove a crucial difference between them and the Jews who continued to be barred from these careers.

Although occupational restrictions did persist, Jews were not denied ready access to the new opportunities presented by the expansion of the agricultural market. Hanák points out that the vertical network stretching from the wealthy wholesalers in Pest and Vienna down to the lowly peddlers in the villages, proved strategically advantageous when the demand for Hungarian agricultural products rose. It was also fortunate that precisely in these decades immigration of Jews from the neighboring lands reached its peak tripling the number of Hungarian Jewry from about 80,000 in the 1780s to about a quarter of a million by 1825. The willingness to take risks, to dodge guild regulations, to lead a frugal life-style, to be on the lookout for the smallest profit, all these set the Jews apart from the majority of Hungary's population.

Nevertheless, in her study of entrepreneurship among the wholesale merchants in *Vormärz* Pest, Vera Bácskai cautions against exaggerating the specificity of Jewish economic behavior. Generalizations about the particular character of Jews can best be gauged only when the economic activities of Jews *and* non-Jews in the same sector or occupation is compared. She dismisses, for instance, the notion that Jewish entrepreneurship can be explained in terms of competition between Christian native sons and Jewish newcomers. On the contrary, more Jewish wholesalers were local born than Christian (mostly of German origin). Her findings demonstrate that both the preponderance of Jews

23 Bárándy, *Über Ungarns Zustände* (Pressburg, 1847), p. 8 as quoted by C.A. Macartney, *The Habsburg Empire*, 1790-1918 (New York, 1969), p. 225. For the actual share of Jews in commerce in different categories of towns in 1828, see Vera Bácskai, *Towns and Urban Society in Early Nineteenth-Century Hungary* (Budapest, 1989), pp. 83-85.

at the uppermost reaches of the commercial elite, and their entrepreneurial spirit have been overestimated. Dividing the first fifty years of the nineteenth century into three almost equal periods, she notes that the Jewish share in the grain trade fluctuated and apparently was not as great as once thought. She also points out that Jews did not have a monopoly on enterprise, nor were they all necessarily innovators. Many in fact, were quite conventional businessmen. Nevertheless, she agrees with Hanák that ultimately what differentiated between the two groups was the greater range of career opportunities open to non-Jews. The choice to opt out of commerce was available to sons of Christian wholesalers and by mid-nineteenth century this option was increasingly exercised.[24]

Bácskai's article reminds us of the importance of timing and periodization when assessing Jewish entrepreneurship. Take for example their role in the beginnings of industrialization in Hungary in the pre-1848 period. Aside from a notable exceptions such as Goldberger and Spitzer families who set up cotton-printing plants and an occasional oil refinery, most Jewish merchants were quite cautious about investing their capital in risky industrial ventures. The machine building industry, for instance, was entirely initiated by non-Jewish foreigners. As we shall see, only later when many of the early industrial enterprises were transformed into joint-stock companies in the 1860s did Jewish merchant capital come to play an important role in the industrialization of Hungary.[25]

By mid-nineteenth century, the legal status of the Jews had improved substantially, opening new economic opportunities. While a proposal to emancipate the Jews by the Lower House in 1840 was frustrated by both the Upper House and the king, a compromise piece of legislation emerged which came close to granting "economic emancipation". Most important was the permission to settle in the cities (although Jews continued to be excluded from the mining towns until 1860) and to buy urban real estate. This had a great impact on the Jews whose share in the urban population rose from 4.6% in 1827 to close to 12% in 1869. Although most Jews continued to live in villages and small market towns, a substantial portion chose to move to the cities. In his study on urbanization in this period, Peter Hidas notes that whereas the non-Jewish urban population remained pretty much stagnant, there was a remarkable rush by Jews to the cities. Moreover, the nature of the Jewish urban population was different from the non-Jewish. Employing several quantitative methods, Hidas was able correlate the presence of Jews with commercial occupations, a

24 See Vera Bácskai, *A vállakozók előfutárai: Nagykereskedők a reformkori Pesten* [Precursors of Entrepreneurs: Wholesale Merchants in Reform Era Pest] (Budapest, 1989).

25 See the following: Gyula Mérei, *Magyar iparfejlődés, 1790-1848* [Industrial Development in Hungary, 1790-1848] (Budapest, 1951); Emma Lederer, *Az ipari kapitalizmus kezdetei Magyarországon* [The Beginnings of Industrial Capitalism in Hungary] (Budapest, 1952) and Sándor Gyömrei, "A kereskedelmi tőke kialakulása és szerepe Pest-Budán 1849-ig" [Commercial Capital Formation and its Role in Pest-Buda until 1849], *Tanulmányok Budapest múltjából* XII (1957), 197-278.

correlation which was highest toward the end of the period. (According to his calculations, 92% of the presence of merchants in 1869 could be explained by the presence of Jews.)

It was in this post-1848 generation that the basis for the new urban professions was laid. In these decades the neo-absolutist government intervened forcefully in Jewish affairs, ordering the creation of a network of Jewish elementary schools. The number of such schools grew by leaps and bounds. Similarly, it is from 1850 that a steady acceleration began in the proportion of Jews in secondary schools and institutions of higher learning, a process which peaked sometime around the mid-eighties. Graduates of these institutions were to form the growing cadres of free professionals and white-collar commercial employees of the cities, further diversifying the Jewish occupational structure.

In 1849, full emancipation was granted first by the imperial government in March and by the rebels at the end of July. Until Franz Joseph revoked this legislation in 1853, Jews enjoyed full equality. Jewish emancipation coincided with serf emancipation. Jews could now legally own rural real estate, and it became readily available under the new conditions as the bothersome restrictions on the sale of noble estates were abolished, land was parcelled out among the peasants, and wage labor came to replace serf labor. Many no doubt anticipated that with removal of occupational restrictions, Jews would expand their activities beyond petty commerce to all spheres of economic activity, especially to agriculture. In any case, even before emancipation some Jews had been personally engaged in agriculture. "It is not at all rare," wrote a correspondent from Ungvár in 1841, "to see a Jew work a leased land or a vineyard with his bare hands." An 1846 report recorded 429 Jews in Bereg county who earned their livelihood exclusively by tilling the soil, and listed an additional 41 innkeepers and *arendars* who also worked small plots of land.[26] Emancipation created a minor land rush as new opportunities to buy land presented themselves. Mortgaged noble property which in *Vormärz* could not have been legally transferred to Jewish ownership, now became available. "Ever since the new legislation," reported the commissioner of the Kassa district in 1850, "Jews acquire daily more and more plots of land which they work splendidly because

26 *Pressburger Zeitung* LXXVIII (1841), 416 and Henrik Pollák, "Adatok a magyar izraeliták statisztikájához" [Statistical Data on Hungarian Jewry], *Első magyar zsidó naptár és évkönyv 1848-ik szökőévre* [The First Magyar Jewish Calendar and Yearbook for 1848] (Pest, 1848), p. 120. The papers of the Weissburg family from Erdőbénye in Zemplén county reveal that they had purchased the first of several vineyards in the Hegyalja region as early as 1787, although it may well be that legally Jews had much greater leeway in acquiring vineyards than rustical land. Even so, one occasionally encounters the term "serf" [*jobbágy*] in the Jewish censuses and apparently in the northeast region of Hungary the phenomenon was not unheard of. See Roger W. Weiss, *The Weissburgs: A Social History* (Chicago: The Kimbark Press, 1975), document 1, p. 65 and Ignác Acsády, "A magyar zsidók 1735-38-ban" [Hungarian Jewry in 1735-38] *IMIT Évkönyv* 1897, p. 182 and Bernát Mandl, "Magyarországi zsidók földmivelési törekvései a XVIII. században" [The Agricultural Ambitions of Hungarian Jewry in the Eighteenth Century], *IMIT Évkönyv* 1907, pp. 280-298.

they are endowed with capital and intelligence. Within a decade they will probably own most of the estates." The shortage of available labor had caused the price of leases to drop, and Jews had little competition. "The Jews have no problem getting workers anywhere because they pay, whereas this is more difficult for the noble landlords. They are not trusted; it is feared that they plan to reinstate the obligatory performance of labor."[27]

In the coming years, with a brief hiatus between 1853 and 1860 when Jews were again forbidden to own land, smaller and larger estates were purchased by Jews throughout Hungary. "In few countries, and most probably none in Europe," explained a Jew in 1857, "is the ability to own land of such importance from a national-economic, as well as fiscal point of view, as in Hungary."[28] As the commercialization of Hungarian agriculture proceeded in the years to come, not only owning, but also leasing land came to play an important role in Jewish economic activity. It signalled an important shift in Jewish leasing patterns in eastern Europe where from the middle of the seventeenth century Jews had largely withdrawn from leasing entire estates, and turning instead to more modest *arendas* such as inns and mills. In the first half of the nineteenth century, just under a third of Hungarian Jewry were *arendars*, while in the northeast region, well over half. The fate of these *arendars* once the noble monopolies were abolished in 1848 still remains to be explored, but certainly a sizeable number shifted to land ownership or leasing.

In her study, Julianna Puskás traces the shifting patterns of Jewish landleasing over a period of eighty years. Short-term leasing had been common before 1870; in the subsequent period long-term investment became the rule. Some one-fifth of the total land was leased, but of the large estates (over 1000 *hold*; 1 *hold* being equal to 1.42 acres), more than half. While in the northeast regions Jews owned and leased small properties, Jewish presence was especially noticeable among the lessees (70 to 75%) and owners (20%) of the large estates. These lessees were often in the forefront of rationalizing and modernizing Hungarian agriculture. Puskás sees the rising importance of rented agricultural land as an indication of the transition to a capitalist economy; in those regions where modernization was more advanced, landleasing played a less important role. She concludes with a note of caution: modern studies of Jewish economic activity tend to concentrate on their innovative role, evading the touchy issues posed by the interethnic relations between owners and lessees and lessees and peasants. Jewish enterprise must not be studied in a vacuum,

27 Heinrich Swieceny to Carl Geringer, Kaschau 7 May 1850, "Bericht des Caschauer k.k. Ministerial Kommissärs über die Bereisung des Zempliner Comitats," in MOL D55 Geringer. Általános iratok. 1850:8802. The document was first summarized in Oszkár Sashegyi, ed., *Munkások és parasztok mozgalmai Magyarországon, 1849-1867* [Movements of Workers and Peasants in Hungary, 1849-1867] (Budapest, 1959), pp. 24-25.

28 Sándor Knopfler, "Érdekes folyamodvány a sátoraljaújhelyi mintafőiskola ügyében" [An Interesting Petition in the Matter of the Sátoraljaújhely Model High School], *MZsSz* XXVII (1910), 364-367.

but within the context of the particular, traditional character of Hungarian social and economic structures. Only the interaction between the two can "explain the remarkably fast integration and mobility of the Jews in Hungary."

Jewish involvement in agriculture, whether as owners or lessees, was always a sensitive matter in Hungary where the specter of a Jewish "conquest" of Christian-Magyar land had loomed large ever since the 1848 Revolution. The statistical evidence was an antisemite's nightmare. Just before the First World War, around seven percent of Hungarian Jewry was engaged in agriculture, but their share in the total population of this sector was less than a half of one percent, about a tenth of what their proportion in the population called for. Therefore, it seemed quite scandalous to the statistician Alajos Kovács, that close to one-seventh of the middle and large estates, those which he claimed had been previously in the hands of the nobility, had come to be owned by Jews, all in the space of only sixty years.[29]

For Kovács, land was a good indicator of wealth in Hungary,[30] but assessing the wealth and the role of Jews in Vienna proves much more difficult. William McCagg tries to do just this by using a variety of sources to reconstruct the wealth of the Viennese Jewish elite during three stages, from the days of the Court Jews at the end of the seventeenth century through the *Vormärz* period and finally from the *Gründerzeit* up until the dissolution of the Empire in 1918. The nature and sources of Jewish wealth in Vienna shifted in time as did the relative importance of Jews in the capital's economy. From the glorious days of Samuel Oppenheimer and Samson Wertheimer, when Jews not only supplied the imperial armies, but performed other vital administrative functions as well, Jewish wealth and importance declined toward the second half of the end of the eighteenth century. It was the quarter of a century of the French Wars that saw a new stratum of bankers and wholesale merchants elevated to wealth. Many of the wholesalers had come from Hungary and carried on trade in Hungarian agricultural products, so that "all told, the turn-of-the-century boom in Hungary's agricultural trade was a major source of early nineteenth century Viennese Jewry's wealth." The Napoleonic Wars brought another source of wealth: a banking revolution, marked by the appearance of the Rothschilds who were to transform and internationalize Viennese banking. As in commerce, so too in banking, the share of Jews steadily grew in the *Vormärz* period. The early pattern of wealth, the landlessness, persisted in this era because Viennese Jews, like their counterparts in Pest, were still barred from owning real estate. Nevertheless, McCagg points to Prague where precisely during these years Jews built dozens of textile factories on what must have been their own landed property. The last period again marked a turn in the nature of Jewish wealth. The old family-oriented private banks and firms increasingly gave way to the

29 Kovács, *A zsidóság térfoglalása Magyarországon*, pp. 45-49.

30 Indeed more than 55% of the highest tax-payers among Hungarian Jews in the 1880s were lessees and landowners. See Censor [Gusztáv Beksics], *Társadalmunk és nemzeti hivatásunk* [Our Society and our National Vocation] (Budapest, 1884), ch. 8.

impersonalized joint-stock companies. Wealth now had to be gauged by other means, no longer direct ownership, but rather in terms of economic power and control. Jews came to occupy important posts in key financial and commercial institutions, but because of the growing sensitivity to the Jewish presence in these bodies, the number of Jews in visible positions of power was often masked by padding the board with Gentile notables. The role of the banks was dominant; they held control of most of the industrial joint-stock companies.

But Jewish wealth should not blind us to the other side of the story. John Komlos warns against glowing generalizations which tend to exaggerate Jewish economic success. True, there were Jews who enjoyed spectacular affluence, and yes, the occupational structure of the Jews differed from that of non-Jews. Neither, however, necessarily implied that the masses of Jews were better off than their Christian counterparts. He reminds us of the wretched conditions in which many Jews lived at the turn of the century and turns to anthropometric evidence as a proxy for income to gauge their standard of living. As recent studies have shown, the nutritional status of a population is a good indicator of economic well-being, and this in turn is reflected in human stature.[31] Since social status has been strongly correlated with stature, a comparison of the heights of Viennese Jews with the rest of the population should establish if indeed Jews enjoyed a higher standard of living. The best and most extensive source for such information is the height of soldiers, and the evidence Komlos marshals for the 1860-1920 period points consistently to a shorter Jewish population among Viennese-born men. Similar evidence gleaned from a smaller sample of young women suggests that Jewish teenagers reached menarche later than Christians. Both call into question the accepted stereotype of Jewish prosperity. Komlos's conclusions are borne out by contemporary statistics on the comparative stature of Jewish and non-Jewish soldiers in the Hungarian army at the turn of the century. The average height of almost 78,000 recruits was found to be 164.6 cm, but of the Jews only 163.3 cm. Indeed, throughout Eastern Europe, despite considerable variations in stature, Jews were consistently about one centimeter shorter than the majority populations.[32] One is reminded of an objection raised by Johann David Michaelis in 1782 to granting Jews equality. He maintained that they should be denied such rights, because they would be incapable of fulfilling their military obligations. "It is held that the

31 John Komlos, *Nutrition and Economic Development in the Eighteenth-Century Habsburg Monarchy: An Anthropometric History* (Princeton, 1989).

32 Maurice Fishberg, "Probleme der Antropologie der Juden: II. Die Körpergrösse," *ZDSJ* III (1907), 101-104, 120-129, esp. p. 126 and 128. One can learn about nutritional intake, specifically meat consumption, from the varied evidence available on the kosher meat tax. One factor which perhaps should not be overlooked is that kosher meat is always more expensive. An interesting report on the kosher meat tax dating from 1830 noted that because of the depression, meat consumption had declined in Galicia to less than 40% of what it had been in 1815. Viktor Hofmann von Wellenhof, "Die Sonderbesteuerung der jüdischen Bevölkerung in Galizien und der Bukowina bis zum Jahre 1848," *Vierteljahrschrift für Sozial- und Wirtschaftsgeschichte* XII, pp. 432.

conduct of modern warfare requires a specific minimum height for soldiers...If this claim be true, very few Jews of the necessary height will be found who will be eligible for the army."[33] Considering the Spartan existence many Jews led, this should not come as a surprise. Adolf Munk (1830-1907), the father of the famous ethnographer Bernard Munkácsi, described a childhood of wretched misery in the Slovak highlands. His father, a peddler who was on the road for most of the week, carried "a one hundred and twenty [!] pound pack of goods on his shoulder as he went from village to village...The bread which he put in his satchel was good enough to last a whole week and he did not eat cooked food until he returned on Fridays." As for his children, meat was a rare treat and there was never even a piece of fat in their soup. "While we experienced great hunger, we had enough bread to fill our stomachs although we did lack warm food...From Sabbath to Sabbath we never saw boiled or rich foods, the kind that is pleasurable to the palate...We wearied of eating dry bread every morning and night." His diet consisted of peas, lentils and the ever-present potatoes.[34]

Such abject poverty was often noted in censuses before 1850. One tax conscription dating from 1817 listed as much as one-third of Hungarian Jewry in the category of the "impoverished".[35] By the second half of the nineteenth century, however, such misery seems to have disappeared at least in the western part of the country. Peddlers who had once constituted the bulk of Jews engaged in commerce, seem to have acquired wagons, set up general goods stores, or moved to the cities and become clerks and salesmen. László Katus's data on the occupational structure of Hungarian Jews in 1768 and again between 1900 and 1930, points in part to this shift. He analyses the structure of occupations and of social groups among Hungarian Jews, and then goes on to compare Jews and non-Jews. What emerges is two strikingly different structures, which are actually "complementary and interdependent substructures within the same national economy and the same national society." Despite the changes in the nineteenth century, Katus observes that the sectors in which Jews traditionally were concentrated in pre-modern times—trade, crafts and innkeeping—kept their pride of place "although, of course, in forms adapted to the developing and

33 *The Jew in the Modern World: A Documentary History,* edited by Paul R. Mendes-Flohr and Jehuda Reinharz (Oxford, 1980), p. 38.

34 The Munk family lived in a small one-room house. "Our doors and windows were open because of broken latches and locks and the snow brought in the cold...The furnishing consisted of a bed, a chair, a table and a lamp...Wash basin, combs and brushes were unknown in our house...There were not many plates and most of the time only one person could eat at a time. There were only two or three chairs and most of the children had to eat standing because there was no place to sit...At night two or three of the children slept in the parents' bed...We did not have any pillows or comforters and my blanket was an old piece of clothes." Adolf Munk, *Autobiography (1830-1907)* (Typewritten MS, the English translation by Steven Nadasy of the Hungarian translation by several hands of the original Hebrew, now lost), pp. 6-10. I wish to thank William McCagg for drawing my attention to Munk's memoirs and sending me a copy.

35 Raphael Mahler, *History of the Jewish People in Modern Times* (Hebrew) (Tel Aviv, 1976), vol. II, 2, p. 301.

industrializing modern economy." Nevertheless, new fields did open up. As a result of emancipation Jews appeared in agriculture and the free professions, while the rapid economic development and industrialization of Hungary in the Dualist Era created new opportunities for entrepreneurs "in large-scale industry, in railway construction, in trading companies, in joint stock banking."

Although the economic structure of Hungarian Jewry underwent extensive transformation in the nineteenth century, change was not uniform, and there was considerable regional variation. Victor Karady analyses these variations in light of the 1910 census and finds consistent correlation between the religious divisions among Orthodox and Neolog (moderate Reform) Jews (perhaps the sharpest in Europe at the time), and various indices of modernization such as socio-professional stratification, urbanization, educational attainments and demographic data. While the Neolog strongholds were located in the urban centers, the Orthodox were based in the villages and small towns of the largely underdeveloped regions of the north and northeast. We can also note that it was probably not by chance that the introduction of Jewish religious reform in Hungary coincided with the beginnings of economic modernization in the late 1820s, or that Reform achieved a dominant position in Hungarian Jewry in the 1840-1870 period, during the first decades of intensive urbanization.

Economy made its impact not only on religion, but on politics as well. The relationship between economy and politics is multifaceted and raises a host of interesting problems. One that we can briefly touch on here is the sensitive issue of Jewish power. Did Jews translate their considerable economic attainments into political power?

Antisemites, of course, did not hesitate to answer in the affirmative, asserting that Jews dominated Hungarian society. But the question of political power is by no means an easy one to gauge. It is undeniable that by virtue of their wealth and education, Hungarian Jews did constitute a sizeable part of the middle and upper classes, while conversely, only a minority belonged to the urban and rural proletariat. During most of the pre-emancipation era (at least until 1860), even wealthy, ennobled Jews were often denied the elementary political rights of non-Jewish commoners. But in the post-1867 period, this changed. In Dualist Hungary where a *liberal*, but not *democratic* system of limited suffrage obtained, only six percent of the total population enjoyed the political franchise. However, a considerably larger percent of Jews enjoyed the vote, since voting rights were based mainly on education and property qualifications.[36] The electoral system further favored Jews in that half the seats at county assemblies or municipal councils was automatically reserved for the so-called virilists, the highest tax payers. By the 1880s, according to one source, Jews constituted at least a fifth of the virilist throughout forty-odd

36 R. W. Seton-Watson, *Corruption and Reform in Hungary: A Study of Electoral Practice* (London, 1911), pp. 101, 168-169.

counties.[37] The electoral advantage which Jews (especially wealthy ones) enjoyed was a factor, no doubt, in checking the advance of antisemitic parties, especially in cities with sizeable Jewish populations.[38]

And yet, while Jews enjoyed considerable electoral strength as voters, their actual political power was in fact quite modest. In such non-Magyar ethnic areas as Slovakia and Transylvania where Jews formed a sizeable proportion of eligible voters, elections were almost completely rigged by the powerful, political machine of the ruling party. Jewish votes may have made a difference in municipal elections; their impact on state and county politics was negligible. Their proportion among members of Parliament or among state civil servants never surpassed five or six percent, the exact ratio of Jews in the general population. Although not entirely barred from political power, they did not play the role their economic prominence warranted. They were excluded from the upper echelons of government which continued to be dominated by the nobility, and only in 1917, on the eve of the dissolution of the monarchy was an (unconverted) Jew first named to a cabinet post (Vilmos Vázsonyi).

Interestingly, forty years earlier Jewish prospects did not seem so dim. During the first decade of the Dualist Era, two Jews came very close to being appointed as ministers with economic portfolios (surely no coincidence). The journalist Ede Horn (Ignatz Einhorn, 1825-1875) had distinguished himself as a financial analyst of the first rank. (As a young man, he had served as the preacher of the radical reform society in Pest and as a chaplain in the rebel forces of 1849.) In 1870, he was elected to Parliament, and five years later, was named secretary of state in the Ministry of Agriculture, Industry and Commerce. Horn became the first Jew to hold such a high ranking post in the civil service, second only to the minister. (The next Jewish secretary of state was appointed only in 1913.) The press reported that just before his premature death in 1875, Horn was slated to succeed his minister. That same year, when Kálmán Ghiczy resigned as Minister of Finance, Moritz Wahrmann (1832-1892) was seriously considered for this much more important post (one which served as a steppingstone to the office of Prime Minister for several of its incumbents), and only a serious eye ailment prevented his appointment. Wahrmann, the subject of

37 My estimates based upon the detailed lists in Censor, *Társadalmunk és nemzeti hivatásunk*, ch. 8. See also Gyula Szekfű, *Három nemzedék és ami utána következik* [Three Generations and What has Happened Since Then] (Third ed.: Budapest, 1935), p. 312 and Janos, *Political Backwardness in Hungary,* pp. 113-114. I have been unable to locate a similar work of Censor's dating to 1887 which János makes reference to.

38 The contrast around fin-de-siècle between liberal Budapest, where half the voters were Jewish (they constituted somewhat less than a quarter of the city's inhabitants), and Vienna, where Karl Lueger's antisemitic Christian-Social party rose to power thanks to a newly enfranchised, Gentile lower middle class, is instructive. Compare Janos, *Political Backwardness in Hungary,* p. 117 and John Boyer, *Political Radicalism in Late Imperial Vienna: Origins of the Christian Social Movement, 1848-1897* (Chicago, 1981), pp. 85-86. Of course, other factors also played a role to make Budapest different, which is why we find prominent Jewish industrialists leading the campaign for universal suffrage at the beginning of the century. See George Deak's paper below, pp. 219-223.

Károly Vörös's biographical sketch, filled several important positions in Jewish communal life, serving in the 1880s as president of the Budapest community. He was the first Jew to be elected to Parliament where over the years he exercised considerable influence as chairman of the Finance Committee.

The fiercely nationalistic economic policies advocated by Wahrmann, geared toward strengthening the independence of Hungarian financial and industrial institutions, was moderated by a realistic appreciation of the need to foster close economic ties with the Austrian half of the Monarchy and to attract foreign investors and markets. This, in a nutshell, summarized the economic orientation of most of the Jewish elite, and until the end of the nineteenth century, it coincided with the general policies of the various governments. The political ruling class dominated by the nobility sought to create a modern state and economy in concert with the mostly Jewish middle class. It ensured a liberal legislative climate favorable to the modernization of agriculture and to industrialization based at this stage mainly on agricultural products. Government cooperated closely with commercial, financial and industrial interests by creating the necessary infrastructure, by extending state subsidies and by raising protective tariffs. Yet it would be unfair to brand the Jewish economic elite as no more than a subservient tool in the hand of a corrupt ruling class, nor must we exaggerate the identity of their interests. George Deak points out in his study of the politics of *GyOSz*, an industrial lobby with a large Jewish membership, that by the turn of the century, as the government increasingly espoused economic policies favoring powerful agrarian interests at the expense of industry, the comfortable arrangement between state and Jewish capital was becoming undone. The history of the *GyOSz* reveals the limited political power exercised by Jewish capitalists, but also their willingness to challenge the government, not only over economic policy, but social and political issues, as well as.

The Hungarian-Jewish economic elite did much to transform the Hungarian economy from the second half of the nineteenth century until the end of the First World War.[39] The first generation of these men were usually grain merchants who moved into industry and finance in the *Gründerzeit* of the 1860s. Typical of agrarian Hungary, it was the foodstuffs industry (not textiles as in western and central Europe) which inaugurated the industrialization of the country as early as 1839. Although as noted, Jews played only a modest role in the initial stages of industrialization, by the 1860s they began to invest heavily, first in flour milling (by the 1880s Budapest had become the second largest milling center in the world after Minneapolis), and later, in sugar beet refining. Wahrmann was an outstanding representative of these early merchant bankers, investing heavily in

39 Three indispensible studies on the Jewish economic elite are William O. McCagg, *Jewish Nobles and Geniuses in Modern Hungary* (New York, 1972); Károly Vörös, *Budapest legnagyobb adófizetői, 1873-1917* [The Highest Tax-Payers of Budapest] (Budapest, 1979); and László Varga, "The Great Generation of the Hungarian Bourgeoisie," *Acta Historica* XXX (1984), 353-379.

the burgeoning milling industry in the 1860s.[40] In banking, a converted Jew, Moritz Ulmann, had pioneered the first commercial bank in Hungary in 1841, but not until the 1867 Compromise did a modern banking system "take-off". Banks, small and large, mushroomed from only 36 credit institutions in 1848 to 107 in 1867, 637 in 1873, and 5993 by 1913. Jews played a leading role as private bankers, bank directors, managers and clerks. Foreign money powers, the most important of which was the Viennese Rothschild's *Creditanstalt*, helped in the capitalization of these banks and invested heavily in the expansion of Hungary's railways in the years immediately following the Compromise.[41]

But the truly great entrepreneurial breakthrough in industry and finance came in the next generation when a handful of extraordinarily talented Jews guided Hungary to a large measure of economic independence and modernization. László Varga's study of Manfréd Weiss, who he terms "the greatest personality" among the economic elite at the turn of the century, shows how Weiss transformed and diversified the family milling industry into one of the world's largest armaments industries. It was his generation which expanded Hungarian industry beyond its traditional agricultural base. As a model entrepreneur, Weiss espoused a "crisis strategy" which not only took advantage of economic opportunities, but helped shape and create them. His contemporaries in the financial sector, transformed not only the banking system, but also industry by heavy bank investment in key industrial firms such as the Ganz Works and the Rimamurányi-Salgótarján Iron Works.

The fact of their being Jewish certainly affected the lives of these men. It played a role in their international connections with the largely Jewish-run firms in Austria and Germany; in their choice of marriage partners, social circles and business associates; in their at times overeager nationalism tempered by a dose of cosmopolitan common sense.[42] And on occasion their Jewishness could even spur them on to suggest economic sanctions against antisemitic regimes such as Romania and Russia.[43]

40 See Vilmos Sándor, "A Budapest nagymalomipar kialakulása 1839-1880" [The Formation of Budapest's Milling Industry], *Tanulmányok Budapest múltjából* XIII (1959), 315-422; McCagg, *Jewish Nobles and Geniuses, passim* and György Kövér, *Iparosodás agrárországban: Magyarország gazdaságtörténete, 1848-1914* [Industrialization in an Agrarian Country: The Economic History of Hungary] (Budapest, 1982).

41 For the role of the Rothschilds in Hungary see József Radnóti, *Kornfeld Zsigmond* (Budapest, n.d.). See also the studies of György Kövér: *Iparosodás agrárországban*, pp. 38-68; "Egy kereskedő-bankár kapcsolatrendszere (Kohn I.I. 1869-es csődperének tanulságai)" [A Merchant-Banker's Connections (The Evidence of I.I. Kohn's Bankruptcy Proceedings)], in *Rendi Társadalom-Polgári Társadalom* I (Salgótarján, 1986), pp. 321-329; and *1873. Egy krach anatómiája* [1873: The Anatomy of a Crash] (Budapest, 1986).

42 As chairman of the Budapest Stock Exchange, the banker Zsigmond Kornfeld insisted that brokers bid exclusively in Magyar on the floor. Radnóti, *Kornfeld*, p. 85. For his social circles and cultural life, *ibid.*, pp. 32-33, 52, 145-146.

43 In 1875, both Ferenc Chorin and Wahrmann urged Parliament that the trade agreement then being negotiated with Romania be linked to the improvement of Jewish legal status. Wahrmann dramatically opened his speech, "As the honorable House knows, I too am a

Antisemitism was also a factor closer to home. The prominence of Jews in the economy fueled antisemitic claims that Jewish capital was taking over Hungary. Sensitive to such accusations, many institutions sought to play down the presence of Jews on their board of directors. When the question arose of promoting Zsigmond Kornfeld to the chairmanship of the Credit Bank, he was opposed by a liberal member of the board on the grounds that no Jew should occupy a post best reserved for a member of the aristocracy.[44] The exclusion of unconverted Jews from the upper echelons of the administration not only limited their impact on formulating economic policy, but also deprived them of one of the important avenues of horizontal career advancement, the move from business to civil service and politics, and vice versa.

It is a historiographical commonplace to speak of an unspoken contract, a sort of an ethnic division of labor between the two leading elements of the Hungarian middle class, the Jews and the gentry. The former would restrict their activities to the private economic and professional sectors, whereas the latter would monopolize the public political and administrative sphere, thus avoiding any conflict of interest and minimizing competition. This arrangement, in itself a symptom of the backwardness of Hungarian society, began to come apart toward the beginning of the century. Jews increasingly became involved in politics, their numbers in the civil service and Parliament grew, and a few converted Jews even entered the cabinet. Non-Jews, on the other hand, increasingly turned to business careers, while the pace of growth of Gentiles in the professions began to overtake that of the Jews.

The terms of this unspoken contract were further violated with the collapse of the Dual Monarchy, when Jews became highly visible in positions of political power in the brief-lived Károlyi and Kun governments. On the other hand, with the dismemberment of Hungary, the size of the state apparatus was greatly reduced, accelerating the trend of non-Jews to enter into business and the professions. Hungary became the first country in the interwar period to institute a *numerus clausus* law limiting the proportion of Jews entering the universities and the professions. The growing intervention of the state in the economy became the hallmark of the interwar era. Mária Kovács, who has previously explored antisemitism within the legal and medical professions, tackles here the engineers, the profession most linked to the modern economy and traditionally the least tied to the Magyar gentry. They came to espouse a curious blend of anti-capitalist, reactionary modernism, implementing the *numerus clausus* law

Jew," to loud acclaims from the audience. For the text of the speech, see Ignatz Reich, "Wahrmann Mór," in his *Beth-El: Ehrentempel verdienter ungarisches Israeliten,* 3 vols. (Pest, 1878), vol. III, pp. 23-27. For Kornfeld's rather ineffectual gesture in protest against the Russian loan during the Russo-Japanese War, see Radnóti, *Kornfeld*, p. 37.

44 Kornfeld did get the appointment with the help of Count Pallavicini, a former managing director, who remarked, "Although I am a conservative and an antisemite, I oppose Mr. Lukács the liberal, and support Kornfeld!" Radnóti, *Kornfeld*, pp. 39-41, 52.

with particularly stringency. Consequently, Jewish engineers were driven out of the growing public sector and industry; the proportion of Jews in the profession plummeting from a high of 40% in the prewar era to less than 16% by 1937. Nevertheless, Kovács points out that the engineers came to view the anti-Jewish legislation of the late 1930s with dissatisfaction since it failed to truly transform the economy and realize their *étatist*-technocratic utopia.

The growing competition in the professions and business between Jews and Gentiles signalled a new phase in the economic history of Hungary. If the conditions of backwardness had positioned the Jews in a favored starting position at the initial phase of modernization, with economic development the importance of Jews in the economy began decline. And antisemitism was not the only factor. In his analysis of Hungary's economic elite in the interwar period, György Lengyel notes that as managerial professionalization, Jewish business leaders were placed at a disadvantage. While Jews in general were better educated than the average and disproportionately represented among the more technically oriented fields in the secondary and higher institutions of learning, the educational level of the Jewish business elite was actually lower than of their Gentile counterparts. The Jewish elite, once distinguished for its flexibility and innovative edge, now, because its criteria of recruitment remained largely traditional, was actually slower to adapt to the professionalization process.

Many of the features of Jewish economic behavior that we have sketched for Hungary were to be found in other countries in eastern and central Europe. Although throughout the region Jewish occupational structure was considerably transformed in the course of the modern era, it retained its specificity down to the Second World War. Scholars agree that this specificity can be explained by a combination of cultural orientations and social characteristics on the one hand, and the environment on the other; they differ, however, in the weight they assign to the variables. The closing papers by Yehuda Don and György Ránki debate the relative importance of inner propensities versus external circumstances. Drawing on the Jewish experience in east-central Europe during the interwar period, they reexamine many of the points advanced by Simon Kuznets in his seminal article on Jewish economic behavior. While Don tends to emphasize the importance of peculiar Jewish characteristics and suggests that one can speak of a common economic history of the Jews, Ránki argues for the decisive importance of the specific environment in shaping the particular features of Jewish economic behavior.

This volume does not pretend to be an exhaustive history of Jews in the Hungarian economy, although it does provide solid building blocks toward such a study. Hopefully the papers raise important questions and suggest fruitful lines of inquiry for further research not only in Hungarian Jewish history, but for Jewish history and the economic histories of minorities, in general.

Jews and the Modernization of Commerce in Hungary, 1760-1848

Péter Hanák

The nineteenth century was a decisive period, indeed a kind of "golden age" in the rapid modernization of Hungary, the rise of the Jewish middle class and its assimilation to Hungarian culture and society. As obvious as the close interlinkage between these three processes may appear today in historical retrospect, those developments were most certainly surprising, even alarming, for contemporaries at the time.

At the end of the eighteenth century, Hungary was a backward agrarian country, characterized by a still operative system of serfdom and other feudal institutions. 4.5 percent of the population belonged to the stratum of privileged nobility, and only a fifth of that circle, some 30,000 families, were estate owners with true power.[1]

The bulk of the Jewish population that had immigrated during the course of the century lived in dire circumstances, in appalling poverty, eking out a living as itinerant tradesmen, pedlars or leaseholders. The Jews lived isolated from the Christian population. They had been welcomed particularly by the enlightened members of the estate-owning aristocracy, who accepted them in the villages and on the manorial estates under their jurisdiction.[2] The free royal towns and numerous market centers, in contrast, denied Jews permission to settle there.

At this time, not even the most optimistic Hungarian patriots thought that it would be realistically possible to modernize the country at a rapid pace in the near future, and fewer still could have imagined that the Jews would come to play a key role in this process. At the beginning of the nineteenth century in Hungary, the Jewish inhabitants there were unfamiliar with Hungarian customs, and had far closer links with German culture and the German language. Yet the logic of history seldom conforms to the logic of abstract reason. Rather, history

1 *Magyarország története 1790-1848* [History of Hungary, 1790-1848], ed. Gyula Mérei and Károly Vörös (Budapest, 1980), pp. 486-488.

2 *Ibid.*, pp. 579-580.

in its evolvement follows the undulating paths of organic development, the tectonic motion of strata having an effect over a longer term.

A still unresolved question in the economic and social development of Hungary in the eighteenth century is why no ethnic Hungarian entrepreneurial bourgeoisie was able to develop from the midst of traditional agrarian society. It is well-known that at the time the country was partitioned, it was the German "bourgeois merchants" (*mercatores civiles*) who acquired key positions in commerce and achieved a monopoly in important branches of trade. Rich Vienna-based firms and their domestic agents gradually obtained control even over the once prosperous Hungarian cattle trade.[3] The blossoming commercial houses that had been granted municipal rights and autonomy, as well as special licenses, soon found themselves faced, at the end of the seventeenth and during the eighteenth century, with dynamic competitors in the person of Balkan merchants who had relocated from the Turkish empire. These merchants, frequently called *Turci* or "Greeks" (and whose ranks in fact included Greek, Serbian and Macedonian elements), along with the Armenians who had settled in Transylvania, developed a thriving trade with the Levant.[4]

Initially, they traded mainly in foodstuffs, coffee and spices, but soon also managed to penetrate Hungarian domestic trade. For a long period, many of them were unsuccessful in obtaining the municipal rights as citizens confirming their final settlement in a locality; rather, they remained itinerant tradesmen and cattle dealers doing business at open markets. They bought up the abundant produce and products from the market centers and villages directly, and then sold and redistributed this merchandise. In so doing, they not only tapped a new field in internal commerce, but also constituted what was a new type of tradesman in the evolving Hungarian economy: *wholesale buyers*.

The eminent Hungarian historian, Mihály Horváth, has written that the Greeks, starting at the end of the seventeenth century, slowly displaced the Saxons from the southern area of the country, the territory beyond the Tisza; however, their original home area, the Zips (Szepes), was also conquered. It was there they bought up the local linen and made great fortunes from the work

3 Martin Schwartner, *Statistik des Königreichs Ungarn* (Ofen, 1809^2), vol. 1, pp. 138-139; S. Mihály Horváth, *Az ipar és kereskedés története Magyarországon a három utolsó század alatt*[History of Industry and Commerce in Hungary during the Last Three Centuries] (Buda, 1840), p. 173; Ferenc Eckhart, *A bécsi udvar gazdasági politikája Magyarországon Mária Terézia korában* [The Economic Policy of the Viennese Court in Hungary at the Time of Maria Theresa] (Budapest, 1922), pp. 213-216.

4 Schwartner, *Statistik*, pp. 137-139; Eckhart, *A bécsi udvar gazdasági politikája*, pp. 244-251; Schäfer László, *A görögök vezetőszerepe Magyarországon a korai kapitalizmus kialakulásában* [The Leading Role of the Greeks in the Genesis of Early Capitalism in Hungary] (Budapest, 1930), esp. pp. 10-11, 29-38.

of the highly industrious inhabitants in Zips.[5] The Greeks played a decisive role in the establishment and strengthening of early Hungarian capitalism: they founded trading firms, created a smoothly functioning commercial network, organized shipping on the Danube all the way to Vienna, and were thc first modern bankers, who introduced mortgage and security ("Lombard") loans, bonds and exchange.[6]

However, starting at the close of the eighteenth century, the dynamism and leading role of the Greeks declined. Many of them settled, bought estates and vineyards, were granted municipal rights, and in some cases were even integrated into the ranks of nobility. In the 1820s, after their Greek homeland had gained independence, many returned to Greece. The place they—and the rapidly assimilating Armenians—had occupied was now taken over by a numerous and tenacious group of industrious merchants, the Jews.

Alongside the Germans, Greeks and Armenians, often in tough competition with them, the Jews proceeded to develop modern commerce in Hungary, and they were the most successful in accumulating capital and building thriving enterprises. The Greeks, Serbs and Armenians were pushed into the commercial background, and even the Germans now played only a secondary role in the economic modernization of the country.

Why was it the Jews who were able to supplant other groups and assume a leading role? At this juncture, I do not wish to enter into that now hoary discussion about the presumed "economic talents" and intellectual virtues of the Jewish people. That discussion, ranging from the bitterly antisemitic invective of Rohling and the racist perspective of Sombart, the negative views of Weber to the positive assessment by Thorstein Veblen, continues unabated.[7] Here, I would like to delve into the reasons behind the outstanding success enjoyed by Hungarian Jewry in the economic life of the country. Two major topics should be stressed: the dimension of social structure and the specific historical situation in which the Jews found themselves—and in which they advanced during the course of the nineteenth century.

5 Horváth, *Az ipar és kereskedés története*, p. 308.

6 Schäfer, *Görögök vezetőszerepe*, pp. 38-46; Mihály Pásztor, *A százötven éves Lipótváros* [150 Years Lipótváros] (Budapest, 1940), pp. 59-63.

7 See, for example, Werner Sombart, *Die Juden und das Wirtschaftsleben* (München, 1920), esp. pp. 242-258, 340-355; Max Weber, *Die protestantische Ethik* (München/Hamburg, 1968), vol. I, pp. 174, 261 and *Wirtschaft und Gesellschaft* (Tübingen, 1980^5), pp. 367-370, 353; Thorstein Veblen, "The Intellectual Preeminence of Jews in Modern Europe," in: *The Portable Veblen*, ed. Max Lerner (New York, 1948), pp. 467-479; Peter Pulzer, *The Rise of Political Antisemitism in Germany and Austria* (New York, 1964), pp. 3-15.

What was the principal structural and situational difference?

The Christian merchants—Hungarians, Germans, Greeks, merchants with rights as municipal citizens, wholesale buyers—constituted a major component of the feudal society at the time. They had recognized rights and organizations, and occupied specific rungs in the hierarchy of prestige on the basis of their ranking and wealth. As a result of their favorable position, they were guided in economic life primarily by caution and prudence, and by conservative principles of conduct and living. One of their characteristic commercial tenets was: "Better to own dead capital than to take risks in uncertain ventures".[8]

A merchant who had become wealthy did not branch out into large-scale enterprises, but rather generally aspired to acquiring a title of nobility. He was made a nobleman either in recognition of his meritorious service or for his contributions for "noble" (agrarian) purposes. He would also provide one or another of his sons with a good education so that he might become an esteemed intellectual and respected figure in the community.[9]

In contrast, the Jews, insofar as they did not undergo baptism, were excluded from feudal society. This marginalized Jewish community, living outside the city walls or in villages, oppressed and despised by the populace, enjoyed the specific advantage of exclusion, and were thus able with relative ease to become the pioneers of capitalist economy—those elements acting to stimulate modernization, especially in modern central and east-central Europe.

The historical situation in this region toward the end of the eighteenth century was also favorable for their advancement and rise. Enlightened absolutism had accepted the idea that Jews settle and engage in economic activity, and during the era of Joseph II, it had expressly supported this idea. At that time, the Habsburg monarchy had already entered a period of rapid economic growth and expansion, but was sorely lacking a national market and trading network. "On Hungarian soil, we find only retail tradesmen—a trading class does not exist."[10] Even the situation fifty years later was characterized by

8 Franz Schams, *Vollständige Beschreibung der königlichen Freystadt Pest in Ungarn* (Pest, 1821), p. 465.

9 Many examples can be found in the works of Béla Kempelen: *Magyar nemes családok* [Hungarian Noble Families], 11 vols. (Budapest, 1911-1932) and *Családkönyv* [Family Album] (Budapest, 1940). On the Wurm family, see *Magyar nemesi családok*, vol. I, (Budapest, 1911), pp. 80-81; on the Heinrich family, *ibid.*, vol. V (Budapest, 1913), pp. 16-17. On those same families cf. also Károly Vörös, *Budapest legnagyobb adófizetöi 1873-1917* [Budapest's Largest Taxpayers, 1873-1917] (Budapest, 1979), pp. 19, 51-54.

10 György Komoróczy, *A magyar kereskedelem története* [The History of Hungarian Commerce] (Budapest, 1942), p. 57. It is noteworthy that this view extends all the way back to the 18th century. For example, the statistician M. Schwartner remarked: "The ordinary Hungarian from the middle and lower classes is not very responsive to the whistles and cries of the heteroglots surrounding him...and encourages purchases as little

that same historian as follows: "Within the depths of the world of feeling and thought of Hungarian society, there was a mood inimical to commerce...." Recognition of the necessity for modernization "did not fundamentally change the old feudal attitudes of society, which regarded involvement in commerce as incompatible with the only 'elegant' occupation in the economy."[11]

Hungarian commerce declined notably in the third quarter of the eighteenth century. The factors responsible for this decline were not merely the poor transportation conditions, that virtually paralyzed trade in natural produce, and the partitioning of Poland, which was a hard blow especially for trade in wine—rather, a key causal element was the economic and tariff policy of the imperial court in Vienna. That policy fostered the industrialization of the western areas of the Habsburg Empire at the expense of Hungary.[12]

However, those unfavorable circumstances underwent a stormy change at the end of the century under the impact of the Turkish wars, and then for another 25 years during the French wars. The long period of conflict created a stable and certain market, while the Napoleonic continental system gave artificial assurance to market stability. Thus, this was indeed a highly favorable moment in economic history when the Jews *in large numbers* began to enter economic life throughout the monarchy as wholesale buyers, army contractors, privileged wholesalers and their commission agents.

In acquiring predominance in trade, the Jews benefitted from two main advantages. First of all, their numbers had increased dramatically during the eighteenth and early nineteenth centuries, and they soon outnumbered all rivals. Secondly, since most free imperial cities and many market centers had denied them citizen rights, they had been forced to settle in villages around the great estates. There are no reliable figures on their number up to 1787. The figure of 12,000 listed for the 1735 conscription or that of some 20,000 for 1768 can hardly be regarded as accurate. These numbers were heavily underestimated in preparations for fixing of the "tolerance tax" for the Jewish community. In reality, the census under Joseph II was more accurate; its figure of 83,000 Jews climbed in the span of 20 years to 127,000, and soared by the 1840s to a quarter of a million.[13]

as the Herrenhuthers. His main proclivity leads him to engage in farming and animal husbandry....He hardly belongs in any sort of stylish clothing shop...." Schwartner, *Statistik*, vol. I, p. 203.

11 *Ibid.*, p. 57.

12 Eckhart, *A bécsi udvar gazdasági politikája*, pp. 49-54, 77-78.

13 Alajos Kovács, *A zsidóság térforglalása Magyarországon* [The Expansion of Jewry in Hungary] (Budapest, 1922), pp. 9-11. Ernő Marton, *A magyar zsidóság családfája* [The Genealogical Family Tree of Hungarian Jewry] (Klausenburg [Kolozsvár], 1941), pp. 48-58.

Yet such predominance demographically cannot, despite its magnitude, have been decisive for gaining economic superiority. That complex phenomenon in economic history can only be interpreted in connection with the entire complex and web of interactions operative in Hungarian and Jewish social structure. The structure of Jewish society at the time was similar to that of German Jewry, as David Landes has pointed out.[14] The overwhelming majority of Jewish immigrants were impoverished, consisting of pedlars, unskilled laborers, employees, distillers and beggars. Numerous conscriptions between 1740 and 1848 demonstrate that a third of the Jews were beggars and workers without any property or assets; the majority of the rest were leaseholders and itinerant tradesmen.[15]

Thus, the rich Jewish entrepreneurs, who had been prohibited from hiring Christian workers, were able to employ their own impecunious co-religionists: consequently, enough manpower was readily available. This circumstance helps explain why one can find a striking number of relatives and assisting family members in the tally of Jewish households. The key factor here is that the vertical structuring of Jewish society corresponded to the pattern of stratification based on the capitalistic division of labor.

The lower stratum of Jewish society was composed of the most impoverished pedlars, the rag-collectors. They were constantly on the road, pipe in mouth and bundle on their back (which explains the origin of their name in Latin: *dorsarius*). These rag-and-bone men sold the village inhabitants such items as needles, thread, and ribbon, and collected rags, the hides of dead animals, honey, feathers, etc. On the order of rich merchants, they sold or picked wormwood, so valuable for the tanners. In 1811, the government introduced regulations to control the sphere of peddling activity and the articles

14 David S. Landes, "The Jewish Merchant," *Leo Baeck Institute Yearbook* 19 (1974), 12-15.

15 Authentic proof of this can be found in the conscription of 1767-1768. Of the 5,440 family heads listed, 1,686 are marked "no profession" or "profession unknown". The great majority of those without any vocation were extremely poor. However, fully three-quarters of those with a trade or profession were pedlars (57.8 percent) or artisans (17.5 percent). See *Magyar-Zsidó Oklevéltár* [Monumenta Hungariae Judaica], 18 vols. ed. Sándor Scheiber, (Budapest, 1974), vol. XVI, pp. 13-18. A conscription of the year 1780 indicated that 282 persons (47 percent of those employed in Somogy) were in arrears with the payment of the "tolerance tax" ("causalitates insufficientiae ad solvendam Taxam Tolerantialem Judeorum"). Among them were 99 impoverished beggars, who were unable to pay even a single *forint* in taxes. Cf. *Somogy megyei levéltár* [SML], Conscriptio Iudeorum et taxa-tolerantialis, 1744-1844, 286. The conscription of Somogy county from 1815 lists 609 Jewish heads of households. Of these, 111 (18.4 percent) were totally impoverished, 212 (35 percent) were pedlars, and 141 (23 percent) were poor artisans. The table was published by Ferenc Szili, *Somogy megye kereskedelme a kései feudalizmus korában* [The Trade of Somogy County in the Age of Late Feudalism] (Kaposvár, 1988), p. 123. See also notes 24, 25 below.

which might be sold, and placed a strict prohibition on itinerant trade by cart. That prohibition was not revoked until 1836, after these restrictions had been rendered obsolete by the new needs of society.[16]

The itinerant tradesmen equipped with a cart (*quaestores ambulantes*) were at a higher rung in the hierarchy. They bought and sold goods regularly, and in large quantities, and also even shipped such merchandise. If they received approval from the estate owner or the municipality, they were able to buy a house or inn and maintain or rent a place for storing stock. Merchants with an open shop who were authorized to buy and sell various commodities stood even higher in the pecking order. The Jewish merchants and itinerants in the province were often the commission agents of wholesale firms in Pressburg, Vienna and Pest, until they themselves had amassed sufficient wealth to go independent.

Let us look at one illustrative example of this structure. Located in the southwestern corner of the country, in the county of Zala, was the market town Nagykanizsa of the count Batthyány, an important commercial center. At the top of local society, the rich merchants, including several privileged wholesalers, enjoyed a special position. They hired itinerant traders, agents, popularly termed "Croatian travellers". Using large two-horse carts, they travelled across Croatia and Slovenia all the way to the Adriatic, and northward as far as Fünfkirchen and Lake Balaton. They would purchase grain, raw hides, slivovitz, honey and other commodities. They transported the raw products to Nagykanizsa, where they were worked, cleaned and purified by the wholesale firm and then brought to market in Graz, Trieste or Vienna.[17]

These large carts did not, of course, return empty from Vienna and Trieste, but rather were laden down with iron and textile goods, spices, coffee and foodstuffs. It should also be noted that the itinerant tradesmen placed orders with local innkeepers and pedlars to assemble the desired items or put them aside in advance so that the "Croatian travellers" would not need to waste valuable time in a given locality.

Peddling was everywhere a transitional form of trade that, as Sombart stated, "was suited to revolutionizing the traditionalistic-static economic outlook of pre-capitalist man". The pedlar had to think about the needs of his clientele and the selling of commodities, and thus "develop economic rationalism in his

16 Although Joseph II had given permission in December 1787 for Hungarian Jews to engage in itinerant trade, the governor and the Austrian authorities prohibited it once again in 1811. See SML Közgyülési jegyzőkönyvek [Acta Congregationis—Protocols of the Assembly] 1811, No. 699, 722. But the counties did not take the prohibition all that seriously, cf. Szili, *Somogy megye kereskedelme*.

17 Barbarits Lagos, *Nagykanizsa* (Budapest, 1929), p. 291. A report from Somogy County indicates that Jews there were generally poor agents of the rich Nagykanizsa wholesalers. See SML Acta Congr. 1818, No. 1661; Szili, *Somogy megye kereskedelme*, p. 122.

mind". Peddling as a trade everywhere was "engaged in most extensively by Jews...frequently, only as such were they able to penetrate into the structure of European economic life."[18]

This was also true of the East European Jewish pedlars. Although they cannot accurately be classified as entrepreneurs, they did constitute a preliminary stage on the way to full entrepreneurship. As mentioned earlier, if a successful pedlar obtained a permit from his estate owner or the responsible authority, he was able to buy or rent a house or storage stockroom in the city, while other Jews were granted permission to maintain a small open shop for buying and selling various commodities. Thus, there was an *organic path* leading from peddling to wholesale entrepreneurship, even though but few were able to traverse it successfully.

However, there was another organic path, just as important, open to enterprising and reliable Jewish pedlars and small merchants—namely that of leaseholder on a large estate. Lease (*arenda*) did not originally mean a lease on land, but rather the leasing of the *jura regalia minora*—that of a taverner's license, along with mill and butcher shop. The arrendator was authorized to maintain a village inn with license as taverner, along with a distillery; he was also permitted to trade in wines from the respective estate, and sometimes in other alcoholic products. Thus, for many Jewish families, a village pub and a brandy distillery as a home business constituted the veritable royal road for social advancement.

The tavern was not only a place where various agricultural products, ranging from wool and hides to feathers and leather, could be stored; it also served as the point of departure for the most varied and diverse careers for the *arrendator*: customary was advancement to a small shopkeeper, a dealer in grain or cattle; many moved ahead to become liquor manufacturers or land leaseholders. Later in the nineteenth century, an opportunity finally arose to become landowners.

A relatively good picture of the occupational distribution of the Jewish community in the middle of the eighteenth century can be gathered from the 1767-1768 conscription.[19] The conscription covers only 40 counties in Hungary proper, listing 5,440 families, some 20,000 persons. Occupation is noted in the case of 3,754 heads of household.

18 Werner Sombart, *Der moderne Kapitalismus*, Vol. II/1 (München-Leipzig, 1929^7), pp. 449-450.

19 The conscription is not complete. Missing were Croatia-Slovenia, Transylvania, the Landmark and numerous counties. Cf. Jenő Házi, "Az 1767/8. évi országos zsidóösszeirás," *Magyar-Zsidó Oklevéltár*, vol. XVI, pp. 15-20.

Table 1: Occupational Distribution of Hungarian Jews, 1767-1768

Category	Number	Percentage
Merchants	1821	48.5
Leaseholders, innkeepers	639	17.0
Distillers	639	17.0
Artisans, tradesmen	655	17.4
Total	3754	99.9

If we break down the category of merchants, we can note the following:

Table 2: The Distribution of Jewish Merchants, 1767-1768

Subcategory	Number	Percentage
1. *Mercatores*	308	17.0
2. *Quaestores specificati*	467	25.6
3. *Quaestores non-specificati*	393	21.6
4. *Quaestores cum minutioribus mercibus*	348	19.1
5. *Quaestores ambulantes*	305	16.7
Total	1821	100.0
Total itinerant traders (3, 4, 5)	1046	57.4

These figures indicate that 17 percent of Jewish merchants in 1768 belonged to the property owning *mercatores* of higher standing; a quarter was composed of *quaestores*, specialized in a specific branch, while just over 57 percent, the preponderant majority, were poor itinerants and pedlars. We have as yet no similarly evaluated conscription from a later period. A comparison of local material from the county administrations indicates that there was an evolving tendency over the course of the next half century for an increase in the number of *mercatores* and specialized *quaestores*, and that university professions also appear in the employment classification data for Hungarian Jewry.

The other problem associated with the rise of the Jewish middle class—its position and actual situation in the recipient society—is closely bound up with the internal stratification in the Jewish community. As mentioned, the majority of Jews were living on manorial estates or villages under estate jurisdiction due to the prohibition on settling within cities. That discrimination, though socially humiliating, ultimately proved very useful in facilitating Jewish economic activity and the rise of the Jews to the role of capitalist entrepreneurs. Jewish merchants lived in villages, in the very heart of agricultural areas: thus, right from the beginning, they were situated in close proximity to the actual and potential market. They were always well-informed about the quantity of products, prices and consumer needs, as well as the more general situation of the consumer.

The Jews were not a group that was separated and cut off from the village farming community. On the contrary, they played a role as middlemen between the estates, the villages, the market centers and the large trading firms. Correspondingly, they provided both the small farmers and large landowners with indispensable services. The traditional urban-based merchants were unable to compete with this diverse set of functions as middlemen, buyers and money-lenders. This is the reason why "bourgeois" merchants in the towns, conservative noblemen and notables often launched bitterly vehement attacks against the Jewish businessman, the so-called "usurer". The first genuinely professional statistician, for example, Martin Schwartner, baldly termed the Jews a "plague" harmful both for the country and the people.[20] Even the liberal patriot, Ferenc Kölcsey, voiced his condemnation of Jewish economic activity, especially the distilling of spirits.[21] István Széchenyi, the first great reformer, who was not especially enthusiastic about Jews, posed the more realistic question: "Would not all products be spoiled for many a person if the Jew did not search for them... Many view all this trading activity... with contempt, they believe they are born of more noble blood...."[22]

In the period when the commodities market was undergoing dynamic expansion, prices for agricultural products continued to rise at a slow rate, and Jewish merchants, leaseholders and credit-lenders proved to be highly useful and practical. This is what established the enduring *community of interests* between Hungarian liberal nobility and the Jewish commercial middle class, a bond lasting for almost a century. It contributed both to the modernization of the country and the assimilation and Magyarization of Jews in Hungary.

20 Schwartner, *Statistik,* vol. I, pp. 142-149. The term "plague" (*Landplage*) was used to refer to both Jews and Gypsies. See p. 149.

21 Ferenc Kölcsey, *A szatmári adózó nép állapotáról* [On the Situation of the Taxpaying Populace of Szatmár County] (1829).

22 István Széchenyi, *Hitel* [Credit], ed. Béla Iványi-Grünwald, (Budapest, 1930), p. 381.

It can be easily noted that the vertical structuring of Jewish mercantile society was largely in keeping with the extended horizontal—one might say geographical—distribution of the commercial functions and posts. The commercial network formed a nationwide chain extending from the poor Jewish pedlar, his bundle in hand, on to the rich and respected wholesaler and capitalist entrepreneur. On the one hand, that network functioned as a cohesive organization of small business units; on the other, it served as a progressively evolving, infrastructured national market.

It is here that one can grasp what is an essential feature of western capitalist development and related developments in Hungary. In the West, as underscored especially by Weber, capitalism realized a rational organization of labor in trade and new industries; in Hungary, however, early capitalism founded an organization of labor in *commerce*, in the commercial network of the country. That organization, to a certain extent, fulfilled the same function as plant organization in industry, and helped correspondingly to facilitate the transition to industrial capitalism during the course of modernization.

This organized commercial network was the solid foundation for maintenance and advancement of the Jewish middle class, and its younger generation. This network provided that class with security, an economic bastion in the struggle against urban "bourgeois" guild tradesmen, the authorities—and particularly in the struggle to combat superstitious beliefs and prejudices.

Our sources indicate that the main figure in village trade was the leaseholder, as a key link in the trade network, along with the itinerant trader. He rented the manorial inn, the butcher shop, the mill—and increasingly, leased small and larger-size tracts of land. Cases are also known in which the Jewish leaseholder acquired the exclusive right to purchase the honey production, raw hides and other goods of individual large estate owners.[23] This is understandable, since the preponderant majority of estate owners had no circulating capital, personnel or business contacts, and thus had to sign a contract with the leaseholder. In general, the owners demanded payment of rent in advance; in return, they guaranteed a monopoly on sales of all kinds of commodities, wine, alcohol, including the right to operate a liquor distillery.

A surprisingly large segment of immigrants gained a living by rental of an inn, some other lease or a liquor distillery. The 1769 conscription in Szatmár

23 SML. Protocolli Contractuum Dominii Mernye, 1827-1834. These files contain numerous contracts between the estate administration and the buyers. The protocols of Somogy County contain an interesting agreement between the estate administration of Széchenyi and a Jewish trader regarding the "privilege" to sell all rags to him exclusively. Cf. Szili, *Somogy megye kereskedelme*, pp. 95-101, 130.

County registered 177 Jewish families; 74 of them were leaseholders (42 percent), 20 were tradesmen, 35 distillers (including employees, this amounted to 48 persons, i.e., 27 percent); in addition, 15 were listed as beggars.[24] In two districts of the neighboring county of Szabolcs, of 134 families, there were 50 leaseholders, 30 tradesmen (some of these also rented an inn), 43 involved with distilling (32 percent), and 8 persons were classified as beggars without possessions of any kind.[25] In the most eastern county, Máramaros, 136 of 182 families (ca. 75 percent) lived from distilling hard liquor.[26] However, that was mainly characteristic of the eastern and northeastern sections of the country.

In the western counties, the number of distilleries was low. In 1781 in Somogy County, nearly half of all those employed were itinerant traders; a third made a living as craft artisans or by rental of an inn, and the authorities registered only 7 percent beggars there (in Sopron 5 percent, in Moson 2 percent).[27] One can also note that leasing of land spread principally in the more agriculturally developed western regions. Such leasing was a veiled form of land ownership in the first half of the nineteenth century, since Jews until 1849 were prohibited from owning an estate.

Let us explore two connected problems in greater detail at this juncture: (1) the damage caused by Jewish distillers and (2) the usury that formed the basis for many Jewish fortunes. We might dispose of these questions swiftly by the brief assertion that trade in liquor and usury were natural phenomena of capitalist development, especially during the period of "original accumulation". Yet beyond the limits of this general thesis, it is useful to point out that alcoholism and distillation of spirits were not something introduced into Hungary by the Jews. The conscription figures on the Greeks and the general conscription of 1770 on operating inns (*Conscriptio Educillatorum*) clearly show that all groups in the population—German and Greek merchants, noblemen, even the most powerful magnates and the poorest of vintners—were involved in the production of wine and brandy.[28]

The sole difference was that the large estate owners shifted the burden of work to their servants and the business of selling to the Jewish leaseholders, who were obliged to pay extra taxes for the distillery and for sales. In the Kisvárda district in Szabolcs County, 48 out of 70 distilleries were operated by

24 *Szabolcs megye Levéltára* [SzML], IV, A. 1, fasc. 35. Conscriptio Judeorum 1769.

25 *Ibid.*, fasc. 35, N. 22-23.

26 See notes 15, 19.

27 SML. Conscriptio Judeorum 1744-1844, 286.

28 SML. Conscriptio Educillatorum, fasc. 35, N. 17. We have a valuable collection from the communities of Baranya County, compiled by István Taba in *Baranya megyei Levéltár* [BML]. *Községtörténeti Lexikongyüjtemény*. It is clear from the data for the various communities that all groups in the population were involved with distilling.

Jews, and 25 were in the hands of entrepreneurs from the minor nobility.[29] In the market town Siklós, liquor was distilled and sold exclusively by German and Greek merchants.[30] We know with some certainty that the number and proportion of Jewish distillers increased at a very rapid rate from the end of the eighteenth to the middle of the nineteenth century, and then declined in the second half of the last century, when the liquor factories gradually squeezed the small individual producers out of business.

Naturally, one can strongly condemn distilling and trade in brandy from the medical and moral standpoint. Yet such condemnation has never led to a halt in drinking as a popular need, no matter how strictly the sale and consumption of hard liquor was prohibited. Seen from the perspective of economic history, distilling was a general and effective way of achieving a high profit with minimal investment. The raw materials were cheap—indeed, windfall fruit cost nothing—and the primitive distillation apparatus, the small vat where self-made brandy was made, were all inexpensive and home-made. Usury can also be viewed as a similar means of capital accumulation that had been branded for centuries by the church and Christian ethics, but never effectively eliminated. It is a fact that usury in the period of original accumulation was an especially heavy burden for farmers, and for agricultural producers in general.

Our sources indicate that the interest rates in rural areas were high during this period. An extended form of usury was the security ("Lombard") loan. In the spring, the creditor offered a loan for the grain then in leaf, the wool of the young lamb, the wine harvest. He received that money plus a substantial interest after the harvest. A rate of 100 percent was no rarity.[31] As mentioned, the security loan was introduced by Greek businessmen, but ecclesiastical and secular institutions as well as Jewish innkeepers and merchants also played a key role in spreading different forms of usury. After the economy was badly paralyzed as a result of the lack of sufficient credit, usury was not supplanted until the development of the modern system of credit and the consolidation of interest rates.

It was specifically the lack of credit at the beginning of the nineteenth century that led to a substantial rise in the volume of credit transactions. The list of mortgage loans in Somogy County for the period 1813-1819 enumerates some 600 cases with a total value of 4.7 million forint. Jewish creditors were involved in 20 percent of the cases, and accounted for 10 percent of the total value of

29 SML. Conscriptio Judeorum, 1770. Fasc. 35, N. 22.

30 BML. Taba collection.

31 György Szabad, "A hitelviszonyok" [Credit Conditions], in: *A parasztság Magyarországon a kapitalizmus korában, 1848-1914* [The Farming Class in Hungary in the Era of Capitalism], ed. István Szabó (Budapest, 1965), vol. II, pp. 187-189.

loans. The interest rate was around 8 percent, and was identical with the interest rate of noblemen, churches and other financial sources interested in the credit business.[32] If we look at the protocols on bankruptcy proceedings for the same county (1839-1847), we find nearly similar percentages.[33]

Surveying Jewish economic activity in the modernization of the country from the last third of the eighteenth century to the middle of the nineteenth century, it is not possible to discover any sort of special or secret method in accumulation. The prime objective difference was not in the means or methods of accumulation, of making money, but rather in respect to the circulation of the accumulated capital—or, in modern parlance, the *investment strategy*. For Christians, the possibility existed for hierarchical advancement and integration into the nobility by becoming wealthy and purchasing an estate, or earning or otherwise acquiring a title of nobility.

In contrast, Jews were not emancipated until the middle of the century, and not fully so until 1868. Down to the 1840s, they were prohibited from owning real estate in the cities, obtaining municipal citizenship, practicing an academic profession (aside from a few exceptions, medicine being the most frequent) or being given a post in the civil service. In the period under consideration, they were legally blocked from any opportunity to invest in property. At best, they could only rent land—yet during this period, that was not as yet completely safe and profitable.

Thus, the Jewish entrepreneurs were forced, so to speak, to reinvest their accumulated capital in business, and to expand their entrepreneurial activity to new areas, since few other avenues were open to them at the time. The Jewish merchant was able to climb only from step to step of the network in vertical fashionyet to do so, he had to be a highly capable, true entrepreneur. One might formulate the dynamics of the process as follows: in this sphere and during this period, there was a tendency for a kind of "natural selection" to operate.

A few examples can help to illustrate this. The Weidman family from Moravia became wealthy wool merchants in this way. After they had changed their name to Wodianer, they moved to Pest and established a business specializing in the sorting and washing of wool. In the 1840s, the baptized Wodianer family was ennobled, received landed property, and participated in founding several banks and in the construction of the railway. Female members of the third generation made good matches, marrying wealthy business magnates and noblemen.[34]

32 SML. Protocollum debitorum intabulatorum 1813-1820.

33 *Ibid.*, Index intabulat., 1 Feb. 1839 - 1 May 1847.

34 Béla Kempelen, *Magyarországi zsidó és zsidó eredetü családok*, 3 vols. (Budapest, 1937-1939), vol. I, pp. 42-46; idem, *Magyar nemes családok*, vol. XI, pp. 132-133; Gyula

In a similar manner, the Koppely family was integrated into Hungarian nobility under the new name of Harkányi, and the Ullmann family under the Magyar name of Szitányi. The latter came from Moravia to Pressburg (Bratislava), and became famous as contractors for the army. Initially they were the agents of a large tobacco factory, and then set themselves up as independent tobacco merchants. Mór Ullmann was the founder of the first Hungarian bank, the Commerce Bank in Pest, and was a supporter and follower of Louis Kossuth.[35] Mózes Lackenbach, son of a poor itinerant tradesman, settled in Nagykanizsa and amassed a fortune there. Under Joseph II, he was granted the title "royal and imperial privileged wholesaler". The head of the respected firm played a leading role in the local community of the faithful and in cultural life in Nagykanizsa.[36]

As we noted, many wealthy Jewish families followed the example of their Christian occupational colleagues at the beginning of the nineteenth century: they rose into the nobility, conforming to the ruling classes and adapting to their form of life; in most instances, this entailed giving up or scaling down their capitalist enterprise. How is it possible nonetheless that in the second half of the nineteenth century, more and more Jewish entrepreneurs advanced to the top of the pyramid?[37]

One reason may have been that the price exacted for being ennobled and integrated into nobility initially was conversion to Christianity—and many pious, believing Jews were unprepared for that step. They preferred to refuse title, rank and a noble marriage, and to remain with their business. The economic factor was that the Jewish commercial middle class, after gaining in strength and numbers, was able to compensate for the richest Jewish entrepreneurs receding from the picture by tapping the ranks of the clever businessmen, endowed with great talents. In this connection, one can mention the members of the families Sándor Deutsch, Manfréd Weiss, Fellner, Brüll, Kohner, Herzog, Chorin and Kornfeld.

The rising Jewish entrepreneurs and intellectuals compensated for legal discrimination, the ban on their entering the "finer" professions—i.e., the

Mérei, *Magyar iparfejlödés* [Hungarian Industrial Development] (Budapest, 1951), pp. 170-171; Emma Lederer, *Az ipari kapitalizmus kezdetei Magyarországon* [Beginnings of Industrial Capitalism in Hungary] (Budapest, 1952), pp. 73-75; William O. McCagg Jr., *Jewish Nobles and Geniuses in Modern Hungary* (Boulder, 1972), pp. 55-56; *Zsidó Lexikon* (Budapest, 1929), p. 965.

35 Mérei, *Magyar iparfejlödés*, pp. 40, 170; McCagg, *Jewish Nobles and Geniuses*, pp. 59-63; Kempelen, *Magyar nemes családok*, vol. 10, pp. 450-451; *Zsidó Lexikon*, p. 924.

36 Barbarits, *Nagykanizsa*, pp. 253-254, 290.

37 This question was posed by György Ránki at a joint conference in Jerusalem, 4 January 1988. See his paper in this volume.

positional inferiority of the Jewish middle class—by utilization of situational advantages. The deeply articulated Jewish social structure and the abundant reserves possessed by the upper and middle classes offered excelled possibilities for this.

In conclusion, I would like to venture an answer to the question broached at the very beginning: why the Jews? Why were they the most successful businessmen—why was it they who formed the backbone of the newly evolving entrepreneurial stratum in Hungary?

1. Jews surpassed their rivals not only in numbers, but also in respect to the social embourgeoisement: that structure extended from the wealthy capitalist entrepreneurial stratum to the poor employees and workers. Nonetheless, there was basically no stratum of Jewish farmers. Within this complex, the broad commercial middle class, structured both vertically and horizontally (geographically), had a decisive role. *That class functioned as a socially cohesive network—and simultaneously as the territorially coherent infrastructure of domestic trade and commerce.*

2. The Hungarian Jews entered into economic life at a very favorable point in time, when the French wars and then the rapid development of the industrial revolution in the West (including the western provinces of the Habsburg monarchy) had assured the presence of a dynamically expanding market, and had generated a growing demand for Hungarian agricultural products. Austrian and Bohemian textile factories competed for Hungarian wool. Mihály Horváth noted that most Hungarian domestic traders made their wealth based on this product.[38] "The entire world wants to engage in trade…the country is crawling with tradesmen, especially those trading in grain," wrote Pál Magda in describing the decade beginning in 1810.[39] The period from 1815 to the March 1848 revolution was certainly a shining era for the region as a whole and for Hungary: *the evolving modernization, which held out such great promise, coincided with the victory of liberalism and the emancipation of the Jews.*

3. The Hungarian land-owning nobility played a key role in stimulating modernization and emancipation and in promoting the binding ideals of liberalism. That nobility was apparently spurred on by its vital interests, the pressure to introduce contemporary economic methods and land improvement in order to manage its economy profitably. Yet the nobility's interests were in harmony with its European education and outlook and its liberal nationalism—a

38 Schwartner, *Statistik des Königreichs Ungarn* (Ofen, 1809²), vol. 1, pp. 363, 369; Horváth, *Az ipar és kereskedés története*, p. 308.

39 Pál Magda, *Neueste statistisch-geographische Beschreıbung des Königreichs Ungarn, Croatien-Slavonien* (Leipzig, 1834²).

liberalism that had, among other things, advanced the notion of Jewish emancipation and integration. Thus, Hungarian nobility was more tolerant and more prepared for various types of cooperation than was the administration in Vienna or the domestic urban German bourgeoisie.

4. The existing social, political and legal situation compelled the Jewish entrepreneurs to seek their main field of endeavor and realization within economic life, since other avenues were blocked. That is the reason why they developed their specific investment strategy, endowed with a historically refined sense of business a strategy that was absolutely in keeping with the spirit of capitalism. Instead of accumulating and amassing dead capital, the now wealthy tradesmen and bankers constantly reinvested their capital in further ventures. First, they took part in the construction of the railroads, and then in the development of shipping on the Danube and the mill industry. During the second half of the century, they turned with growing interest and capital reserves toward the young and developing branches of Hungarian large-scale industry and the evolving credit system.

Translated by Bill Templer, Tel Aviv University

Jewish Wholesale Merchants in Pest in the First Half of the Nineteenth Century

Vera Bácskai

A comparative analysis of the careers of both Jewish and Christian wholesale merchants in Pest in the first part of the nineteenth century can uncover many phenomena that might remain hidden in a study focusing exclusively on Jewish merchants.[1] The main sources for this study were the minutes and membership rolls of the commercial corporations of Pest, drawn from the papers submitted to the council of Pest between 1800 and 1848, the Jewish censuses, the applications for tolerance and wholesale licences, and inventories of the assets of persons under investigation. I also used the contemporary directories of firms; but because such data were less reliable, the research was limited to those merchants who, as members of the Civil Commercial Corporation, or possessors of licences from the City Council, verifiably carried on wholesale activity. There were 230 such merchants in the first part of the century; I have managed to collect more or less substantial data about 88 corporation members and 142 Jewish wholesale merchants.

These data confirm the recurrent statements found in the historical literature that the overwhelming majority of wholesale merchants were Jewish. In fact, Jews constituted two-thirds of the wholesale merchants of Pest, although this proportion gradually decreased throughout the half century.

In terms of economic cycles, the first half of the nineteenth century can be divided into three periods of roughly the same duration. The first period covered the two decades from the mid-1790s to the final defeat of Napoleon. The years of French wars and the continental blockade were a time of economic prosperity. War-related contracts, the flourishing commercial life, increased demand, and,

1 This paper is based upon the results of my book-length monograph: Vera Bácskai, *A vállalkozók előfutárai: Nagykereskedők a reformkori Pesten* [Pioneer Entrepreneurs: Wholesale Merchants in Pest in the Age of Reforms] (Budapest, 1989). Full documentation is provided there.

not least, the profits of smuggling multiplied the formerly small capital of the merchants of Pest and promoted the development of wholesale activity.

The agricultural and bank crisis following the French wars paralyzed business activity and led to many bankruptcies. In addition, the customs policy of the empire, favoring the economic development of the Austrian provinces and blocking that of the merchants of Pest, exacerbated the situation. It is true that the role of Pest in domestic and foreign trade became more and more important during the period from 1815 to 1830. Still, these years were not characterized by the vivid commercial life of the previous decade; both spectacular new-found wealth enrichment and spectacular bankruptcies were rare in the 1820s; the wholesale firms established then had more solid economic bases, their management was more reliable—and hence they had greater survival power. In the main this period saw the emergence in Pest of the sectoral wholesale and retail trade.

Thanks to this moderate development, a progressive merchant group, with relatively large capital assets, could build on the economic prosperity that began in the 1830s and continued, except for several years of bad harvests, until 1847.

The first period of prosperity was practically synonymous with the emergence of the wholesale trade in Pest: between 1800 and 1815, 58 individuals received permission to enter wholesale trade—and 70% of them were Jewish. Despite the unfavorable conditions that prevailed during the fifteen years of recession, 55 wholesale firms were founded—but only 62% of them were Jewish-owned. Finally, in the 1830s and the 1840s the proportion of Jewish merchants among the founders of the 117 new firms was only 57%.

The data demonstrate that, contrary to common belief, Jewish merchants did not play an overwhelmingly dominant role in the produce trade and credit operations at the end of the 1830s. From the outset only one-third of the wholesale firms established during this half-century were engaged in produce trade, transport, and credit operations, while the majority specialized in crafts and textiles. These fields of wholesale trade underwent a great development during the first decade of the century, attracting Jewish merchants too: whereas in 1800 only one-third of the Jewish wholesale firms dealt exclusively or partly in handmade and manufactured products, more than two-thirds of those established after 1830 did so. When the boom ended, many Jewish produce merchants changed their field of activity, either getting out of the produce trade or handing over the management to a family-member. In its place, they started a new form of wholesale activity based on handicrafts. Nevertheless, most of these enterprises failed.

By the middle of the century the proportion of Jewish produce merchants had decreased: before 1830, more than one-third of Jewish merchants were in the produce trade; during the next two decades hardly more than one-fourth of them engaged in it exclusively. At the same time, the proportion of such firms owned by (Gentile) members of the commercial corporation increased from 10% at the beginning of the century to 30%. The produce trade and credit operations became increasingly important in the business life of Christian merchants; not only were more and more new firms established in these areas, one-third of former handicrafts and textile merchants turned to this type of commercial activity. Hence almost two-thirds of the Christian merchants were engaged in this field in the 1840s, compared to only one-third of the Jewish merchants.

Before 1815 three-quarters of the wholesale firms dealing with the produce trade were directed by Jews; after 1830, however, nearly half of the credit operations and transport businesses belonged to members of the corporation. In the absence of data on capital and turnover, we cannot prove that the Jewish merchants dominated the produce trade and credit operations, despite the decisive share of Jewish merchants at the beginning of the nineteenth century and their dominant role in the second half of the century. It should be noted that in the first half of the nineteenth century Jewish merchants deliberately entered wholesale textiles, which had previously been considered a privilege of corporation members.

Two-thirds of all wholesale merchants were born in Hungary and almost one-third of them were born or grew up in Pest. No more than 20% had come from abroad. (The origin of the others is unknown.) When this is broken down by religious affiliation, the native-born accounted for 71% of the Jewish merchants and 59% of the corporation members. The greatest difference between the two groups in this regard was at the beginning of the century: 57% of corporation members and 76% of Jewish merchants who began their commercial careers in the years 1800-1815 were Hungarian born. The figures increased to 69% and 86% among those who established firms in 1830-1847. The ratio of native-born between the two groups was closest to one during the recession, when they accounted for three-quarters of both groups, taking into account those who had already been living in Hungary before settling in Pest.

The proportion of locally born merchants showed a different picture in the two groups: among the Gentiles at the beginning of the century, they accounted for only 10%, whereas by the 1830s one-third of the Christian wholesalers came from families living in Pest and Buda. Among the Jewish merchants, by contrast, the proportion of the locally born decreased from 39% to 31%, partly as a result of the emigration of the sons of successful wholesale merchants and mainly due to the gradual drying up of the sources of immigration of Old Buda.

The majority of the Jewish merchants who poured into the city had previously lived in market towns in the upper western parts of Hungary and Transdanubia. Most of the merchants coming from abroad had arrived from the territory of the Austrian empire: the Christian ones mainly from the Austrian provinces, the Jewish ones from Bohemia and Moravia.

A considerable number of the firms established in the first half of the century were unable to contribute to greater concentration of capital because of their short lives: slightly more than half of the firms existed for less than 20 years—in many cases even less than 10 years; only one-fifth of the wholesale firms survived until 1870. Despite this fact, exactly half of the 86 registered wholesale firms listed in the directory of 1871/72 had been established before 1848.

The ratio of Jewish firms that lasted for more than 20 years exceeded that among the Christian firms (59% versus 45%).

The native merchants were slightly more successful in business than were the immigrants. Whereas 57% of native merchants operated for more than two decades and one-fifth of them were still active as wholesale firms or banks at the beginning of the 1870s, the corresponding figure for immigrants' firms was 17%. This advantage enjoyed by the natives characterized the Jewish merchants only during the first decade of the century.

The operating life of a firm depended not only on economic conditions but also on, for instance, demographic factors, as well as the personal abilities of the owners. It is supposed that many closures during the 1830s and the 1840s were due to the inability of the owners to adjust to the requirements of the developing bourgeois conditions.

Insolvency was a frequent occurrence during the recession, but it did not always lead to liquidation. Practically every firm suffered from the effects of the crisis; only the credit-worthy commercial houses, with sound fiscal bases and appropriate sources of capital, could eventually retrieve their losses. In boom times, however, the number of firms with weak bases increased. It is not by chance that 47% of the firms established between 1800 and 1815 and 57% of those opened in the post-1830 boom closed down in less than 20 years. Those established between 1816 and 1830 survived longer.

To survive the recession Jewish merchants applied a special strategy. Many of them turned from the produce trade to handicrafts and textiles formerly considered to be the privilege of the corporation members. The advantage of this type of trade derived from the fact that they purchased the products directly from the producers—the factories of Vienna—and could therefore compete successfully by offering lower prices than the corporation members who purchased their goods from the wholesale merchants who visited the Pest markets.

Changing the range of products could frequently only delay bankruptcy. Those who were facing failure could return to the produce trade, which they may have never given up. This can be proved by the fact that their sons and sons-in-law persisted in this trade. In many cases, returning to the produce trade did not mean giving up handicrafts activity; instead, such activity was contracted out to merchants who had come to Pest from Pressburg, Transdanubia, and Moravia, but lacked tolerance or permission to reside there, in return for a percentage of the profit. Around 15% of the Jewish merchants who began their careers in the years of prosperity ultimately entered this sort of arrangement. In 1820 ten, in 1831 thirty-one Jewish merchants were charged with "unlawful trade activity"; in most cases it was proved that were fronting for others. Consequently, taking the advice of both the Civil and Jewish Commercial Corporation, they closed their firms.

The switch to or parallel operation of produce and handicraft trade did assure a certain flexibility and more advantageous conditions, which helped Jewish merchants weather the critical periods of recession better than their Christian competitors, who had to fulfill the rules of the corporation, which prescribed compulsory activities.

It may also have been prestige that stimulated the establishment of new handicraft wholesale firms. Owning a shop that was open year-round and obtaining tolerance procured higher status in the social hierarchy of the town and among the merchants themselves. Among the 1,356 Jewish heads of family registered in 1833, 12% had the permission of tolerance and 11% had the permission of residence. The corresponding ratios were 57% and 35% among wholesale merchants, 10% and 12% among other merchants, 7.6% and 7.4% among other persons.

The possibility cannot be excluded that those who turned to the textile trade during the recession may have intended transferring their licenses to others from the outset, and that the necessary financial transfusion might have come from those who later continued to operate the firm in their names. In other words, the new textile wholesalers associated with other merchants in order to maintain their commercial activity, which was against the law; the outside merchant supplied the capital and the goods, while they provided the premises and the permits for the establishment of the new firm.

A longer commercial lifespan did not automatically guarantee considerable accumulation of capital nor mean an entrepreneurial contribution to the economic development of the country via investment in industry or bank credit. It could only facilitate the creation of the preconditions of entrepreneurial business by a continual and relatively large accumulation of profits and by meeting the requirements of flexible management and adaptability during the recession.

Of the 113 firms that existed for more than 20 years, 57 retained their traditional management methods. They did not change their original scope of activity, showed little interest in the economic and political events of the time, and took little part in the undertakings of the reform era. Neither these businessmen nor their descendants were at the head of industrial firms or banks in the second half of the century.

The other 56 merchants changed their business according to requirements; they located new markets and became active participants and initiators in the reform era. These businessmen and their descendants played leading roles in stock companies during the second half of the century.

The majority of these merchants went into business between 1815 and 1830. Two-thirds (62%) of the wholesale firms established in this period existed for more than 20 years. More than one-quarter of the owners were entrepreneurs. On a confessional breakdown, the ratio was one-third among the Christian merchants and slightly less than one quarter among the Jewish businessmen. This disparity diminished during the years of prosperity, when 23% of corporation members and 19% of Jewish merchants were entrepreneurs. The Christian wholesale merchants developed their modern management approach during the recession; more precisely, it was during this period that the wholesale trade in a broad sense emerged. The Jewish merchants, by contrast, did not venture beyond short-term adjustments. It should be taken into consideration that those Jews with the most daring entrepreneurial spirit moved the center of their business to Vienna.

One-fifth of the merchants who began their careers after 1830 were entrepreneurs in some sense; thc Jewish merchants played a dominant role among them. Obviously, the removal in the 1840s of the barriers to residence helped the wealthiest and more mobile Jewish merchants to move to the capital from the countryside. Moreover, it is likely that the modernization of wholesale activity that took place among the corporation members during the recession was also effected among Jewish merchants after 1830.

There was a higher proportion of the native-born among the entrepreneurial than among the traditional merchants, especially among the Christians. Only at the beginning of the century did natives of Pest have a dominant share among the Jewish merchants. The explanation for this is, on the one hand, the removal by the elite to Vienna, and, on the other hand, the failure during the recession of firms that had prospered during the boom. Their replacements were provincial merchants with broader knowledge and more modest management strategies.

The establishment of firms by the vast majority (84%) of the entrepreneurial merchants was preceded by relatively protracted commercial activity in Pest, where they, or their fathers, had engaged in wholesale or retail activity. In many cases they were the heirs of an established firm. Their new firms were supported by larger capital sources, more professional practices, and more solid business relationships than those of the traditional merchants, half of whom started commercial activity as wholesale merchants on their till capital.

Merchants of the entrepreneurial type were more closely involved in public affairs. Some 70% of the Christian entrepreneurs participated in the government of the city, compared to only one ennobled individual from among the traditional merchants. The public activity of the Jewish wholesale merchants was limited to their religious community, and here many of the entrepreneurs played a leading role.

Many entrepreneurial firms of Christian wholesale merchants survived for only one generation. The still-active founders of advanced age did not expect their firms to continue; they wanted their sons to be bureaucrats or military officers and married their daughters to members of these social strata or the intelligentsia. They did not intend to increase their profits and continue the business, but to advance and promote their heirs in the social hierarchy. It is interesting that in this period it was the traditional merchants whose principal motives were to accumulate capital and develop the firm. Most of the owners of firms founded after 1830, especially those carrying on parallel commercial and industrial activity, did find and train an appropriate successor.

Before 1848, ennoblement or acquisition of country estates was rare: only 10 wholesale merchants—three Catholics, four Greek Orthodox, and three Jews—were ennobled. The majority continued in business after being ennobled. In some cases the next generation gave up the business. In any event, they did not invest their capital in country estates; instead they bought up urban property that produced rental income. It was not an unknown phenomenon, among both the Catholic and Greek Orthodox merchants, that neither the ennobled generation nor their heirs ceased commercial activity. Among the Jews (Ullmann, Wodianer) ennoblement even intensified their entrepreneurial activity.

Property holding and business success, however, could not give even the illusion of social promotion or assimilation for the Jewish merchants in Pest; even in the 1840s, by which time they could become full members of the Wholesale Corporation, conversion was the only way to gain social status and public functions (cf. the career of Ferenc Bernát Weiss). Nevertheless, few Jews were baptized before the middle of the century.

Thus the ultimate goal of Jewish wholesale merchants was to become bankers and wholesale merchants among the Viennese bourgeoisie. Only some of them were able to attain this level; even fewer advanced higher in the economic-financial hierarchy. This sort of career required large-scale commercial activity and large sources of capital—an extraordinary economic accomplishment. Nevertheless, a Viennese career remained a dream for most; the attainable reality was a firm in Pest, in the center of the country, despite all the confining regulations—especially for the only son or the sons-in-law of a tolerated head of family. Since no son wanted to renounce the possibility of an advantageous position, they followed a special strategy: the elder sons endeavored to obtain the tolerance on their own right, so that the younger ones could inherit the father's privilege. They relied on the support of the higher governmental authorities against the leadership of the city, who sought to limit the number of Jewish inhabitants. All the same, outstanding results, large-scale governmental contracts, and broad business relationships were required to succeed in this.

In contrast with earlier generations of corporate wholesale merchants, the Jewish ones trained their sons to a business career so as to guarantee the future direction of the firm. They also merged the firms of several family members. This strategy was characteristic of the first decades of the century, and its success was proved by the presence of owners and heirs of Jewish firms established before 1848 in the wholesale trading and stock-company enterprises of the 1870s.

It is well-known that only a portion of commercial capital was invested in industrial undertakings (much of it outside Hungary). The barriers to national industrial development made such investments risky and of small profit for the merchants who wanted to embark on industrial undertakings. They could expect greater results by extending their commercial activity and engaging in financial affairs. It hardly needs to be emphasized that the entry and circulation of commercial capital into industry was not so straight and simple as the theoretical model would have it. For instance, the sons of dyer families (Boscovitz, Kanitz) in Old Buda became wholesale merchants and bankers. Their industrial enterprises had a short life, and their industrial capital soon flowed to trade and financial affairs. The Goldberger factory was the only exception among the industrial undertakings established at the beginning of the century. The Christian Valero, owner of a silk factory, also paid more and more attention to his financial business.

The experience derived from the conditions of the first part of the century may have influenced the wholesale merchants of Pest who started their careers before 1848 to prefer commercial and credit businesses to establishing or financing industrial undertakings, at least up to the end of the 1890s, which is as far as we can follow their careers. Consequently, it was those wholesale merchants who came to Pest and entered business after 1848 who played the principal role in the establishment of factories during the second half of the century.

A certain sort of *citoyen* consciousness can be observed in the behavior of the wholesale merchants of Pest, starting from the end of the eighteenth century: the mentality of the citizen who makes a considerable contribution to the economic development of the country, increases government revenues through relatively high taxes and customs receipts, and promotes the public institutions to solve social problems. This certainly characterizes the Jewish merchants, who requested trade and residence permits in return for their services for the country, and not as a special boon. They referred to their success in making trade flourish, developing the national industry, and promoting the social welfare—in other words, to their patriotic activity. It is the consciousness of a tax-payer citizen that can be felt in the protest of Moses Grünhut over the unfavorable transfer of his market stall in 1821: he thinks he deserves better attention, as a tax-payer of the town for 20 years, than an immigrant shoemaker who had been frequenting the market for only a short time.

The category of productive citizen occupied an important place in the bourgeois value system, as reflected by the text of wills. Enoch Kern, in his will (dated 1823) urged his sons to be loyal to their country and to make sure that their activity served the national purpose. David Herzfelder and Mark Pollak encouraged their heirs to be faithful and good citizens, religious, humanistic, and generous persons, by preserving the property and making the firm prosper.

Economy, diligence, religious observance, charity—and, starting in the 1850s, loyalty to superiors and the preservation of public reputation—constituted the key elements of the bourgeois value system as reflected in the wills of these merchants: a value system parallel to that of the bourgeoisie in the most developed country of the time. Reading these wills, we can recognize the obvious pride the testators had in their accomplishments. Charity, originally held to be a religious-moral duty, acquired an ever-more important role, alongside the results achieved by good business management, as a way to gain social status. Making charitable benefactions to non-Jewish recipients was a signal that such philanthropy was no longer a matter of observing moral and religious commandments, but rather a contribution to the public weal reflecting a certain consciousness of civic responsibility. This is confirmed by the fact that charity received more and more publicity; there can be no doubt that one of its functions was to promote the donor's reputation.

The sources on which I relied were especially rich in information about matrimonial connections, seldom developed among the Jewish merchant families in Pest, but which, after the 1830s, typified the Viennese merchant families. Marriage between first and second cousins was not an extraordinary event. Similarly, endogamy was much less frequent among Christian wholesale merchants.

These documents give us an intimate view of many families: they report conflicts between in-laws (e.g., Móric Ullmann and Rudolf Wodianer), cases of prodigal sons (among the Jewish families, Móric Rosenfeld), reasons for frequent divorces, or the conversion and marriage of the 16-year-old daughter of

Adam Mauthner. Housing conditions, furnishings, even wardrobes can be reconstructed from the inventories of estates. These documents can inform us about the merchants' property and commercial capital, although exact data about the latter are seldom available.

The documents studied, however, cannot give satisfactory information about the most important factors—methods of business management and modes of commercial activity. Hence these must be evaluated indirectly. A more detailed analysis of commercial life would require other types of sources—for example, records of bankruptcy proceedings, mortgage deeds, and, not least, materials from the archives in Vienna.

II

Wealth and Occupations

Jewish Wealth in Vienna, 1670-1918

William O. McCagg

During that crucial era when central Europe leapt into the industrial age, the century from Joseph II's accession until the 1870s, the region's political center, Vienna, was known as a pleasant place for Jews to live and became a principal seat of Jewish wealth.[1] After 1873, as high industrialism began, the rise of modern antisemitism altered the Austrian political landscape and made the city a rather less desirable place for them to live. Now Budapest, the other great Danubian political and economic center, attracted numerous Jewish settlers, acquiring a larger number of Jews than Vienna. Nonetheless, the really rich Jews remained in the Austrian capital. Then as now it was a matter of curiosity who these wealthy Jews were.

At the time, especially to antisemites, the answers seemed easy. Who were the rich Jews? Why, "they" were the bankers! "They" were the stock exchange kings! However, when it came to giving the specifics about the wealth of Viennese Jews, in other words, when the economists and historians got busy, the task of identification seemed suddenly more difficult. It remains so for us today, and this for three main reasons.[2] First, the Austrian state didn't collect or keep full information. The authorities, of course, did draw up lists of rich people: the highest tax payers had to be identified, because they had special voting rights. But these lists were based on real property and did not cover the intangible dividends off which, after 1870, many rich people lived. Further, the original lists are now lost and the published ones, at least in Vienna, contained no economic information and were so long that they are of little help in

I am obliged to several conference participants, but especially to John Komlos for careful criticisms of the draft of this paper.

1 Standard accounts of the history of Vienna Jewry are Ludwig Bato, *Die Juden Wiens* (Vienna, 1928); Hans Tietze, *Die Juden Wiens* (Vienna, 1933); for the older period, Alfred Francis Pribram, *Urkunden und Akten zur Geschichte der Juden in Wien*, 2 vols. (Wien, 1918); and for the later period, Marsha Rozenblit, *The Jews of Vienna, 1867-1914* (Albany, 1983) and Robert Wistrich, *The Jews of Vienna in the Age of Franz Joseph* (Oxford, 1989). Since I deal extensively with Vienna Jewry in my *A History of Habsburg Jews, 1670-1918* (Bloomington, 1989), only the most necessary material will be cited in the following notes.

2 In the following, I am especially indebted to talks with Dr. Franz Baltzarek of Vienna University.

identifying a narrow elite. In addition, the state was "liberal" in its attitudes. As a result, though its statisticians generalized about wealth, they shied away from correlations with religion[3] and used profession, not income, as their primary economic category. Their figures tell a great deal about the correlation of religion and occupation, but practically nothing about who within the occupational groups, much less the religious groups, was rich, who poor.[4]

The second reason it was difficult to identify Jewish wealth in pre-1918 Vienna had to do with the Vienna Jewish religious community or *Kultusgemeinde*. That organization certainly knew better than the Austrian state exactly who among the confessional Jews had great wealth. The community taxed this wealth regularly, and published lists of the higher tax payers. But never would the community let an outsider near the actual records from which it might be possible to specify who was really rich, and how rich. Then thirdly, the wealthy Viennese Jews themselves did their very best to hide, fearing the muck-raking vigor of antisemite statisticians. Some converted, with the result that they dropped off even the *Kultusgemeinde* lists of wealthy Jews. Others—and this group included Rothschild himself—tended to let "straw men," often Christian lawyers, represent them in business affairs. As early as the 1880s it was perceptible that Jewish controlled firms were systematically watering down the number of Jews in their directorships—Rothschild's *Nordbahn* was a good example of a "Jewish" firm that made itself look Christian.[5]

Today, the calculation of Jewish wealth is even more difficult. The eye-witnesses—the bankers who knew the secrets—are all dead. There has been vast destruction—for example, in 1927 most of the city's registered wills, along with many business books, burned in the *Justizpalast* fire; then in 1938 the Nazis destroyed many Jewish business firm archives, including the greatest of them,

3 The census office introduced correlations according to confession for the first time in 1895. See *Dr. Bloch's Österreichische Wochenschrift* XVI (1899), 66-67.

4 A few attempts have been made to assess Jewish poverty in old Austria, for example, Leo Goldhammer, *Die Juden Wiens: Eine statistische Studie* (Leipzig, 1927); Jakob Thon, *Die Juden Österreich* (Berlin, 1908); and Alfred Nossig, ed., *Jüdische Statistik* (Berlin, 1903). But about Jewish wealth we are singularly ill informed. There is no equivalent for Austria to the work of the antisemitic Hungarian statistician, Alajos Kovács, who tried between the wars to assess the specifically Jewish sector of Hungary's wealth: *A zsidóság térfoglalása Magyarországon* (Budapest, 1922). One reason for this lack of parity between the Austrian and Hungarian statistical literature may be that Austrian Jewry had most of its estates in the Bohemian Crownlands. Alajos Kovács's main index of wealth was landownership, and as an official at the Budapest Royal Statistical Office after 1918, he had access to census materials from which to make correlations between landholding and religion. Comparable access was not available to interwar Cisleithian antisemites, because the material was in liberal Czechoslovakia.

5 Cf. *Dr. Bloch's Österreichische Wochenschrift* XII (1895), 42-43.

the Rothschild archive; next, the war took its toll of the administrative records at the Vienna *Rathaus* and Lower Austrian Land archives; and finally, the tax records of the *Kultusgemeinde* archive suffered a great deal of damage before their transportation in the 1960s to Jerusalem.[6] In all, though it is often still possible to find material about the wealth of Jewish individuals and families of old Vienna, such research is extremely painstaking, and any sort of generalization tends to be impossible.

Hence the present essay which is an effort to obviate the need for precise information about the wealth of the Vienna Jews by describing its parameters. We will deliberately adopt a broad perspective so as to perceive in successive major periods what were the peculiarities of Jewish wealth—what were the kinds of property involved, generally speaking where did it come from, and how over time did it change. We will develop control groups of various sorts so as to suggest what proportions of Vienna's private wealth was in Jewish hands. At the end, we will suggest through individual examples what the fate of Jewish wealth may have been.[7]

II

Let us start with an aphorism: In modern Vienna, Jewish wealth preceded the advent of the Jews themselves. This is so, because the Habsburgs expelled the city's Jewish population in 1670, and then for a century allowed a very small number of extremely wealthy Jews to live in their *Residenzstadt* while maintaining a rigid bar on any sort of larger Jewish community there.

Foremost in this tiny elite were the greatest of the German Jewish *Hoffaktoren*, or court Jews, Samuel Oppenheimer, who financed Leopold I's liberation of Hungary from the Turks,[8] and Samson Wertheimer, who underwrote both Prince Eugen's campaigns eastward and the Habsburg resistance to Louis XIV in the War of Spanish Succession.[9] When these two died in 1703 and 1724 respectively, the Throne allowed their children, and a few

6 There is a considerable card file in the archive, but it refers primarily to people who were still paying taxes in the 1930s.

7 My methodological model is in *Jewish Nobles and Geniuses in Modern Hungary* (Boulder, Colo. and New York, 1972, reissued with revised preface, 1986), ch. 2.

8 See Max Grunwald, Samuel Oppenheimer und sein Kreis (Wien, 1913); Jean Bérenger, *Finances et absolutisme autrichien* (Paris, 1975); and Ferenc Szakály, "Oppenheimer Sámuel működése különös tekintettel Magyarországi kihatásaira," in *Magyar Zsidó Oklevéltár*, 18 vols. (Budapest, 1971), Vol. XIV, pp. 31-78.

9 See David Kaufmann, *Samson Wertheimer, der Oberhoffaktor* (Wien, 1888); as well as relevant sections in Grunwald, *Oppenheimer* and Heinrich Schnee, *Die Hoffinanz und der moderne Staat*, 6 vols. (Berlin, 1953-67).

in-laws, notably the Sinzheimers and Arnsteiners, to stay on;[10] and then one by one it invited other wealthy Jews to settle at Vienna. In the 1730s, for example, Karl VI summoned a Spanish Jew, Don Diego d'Aguilar, to advise him on economic matters, not only allowing him free residence in the capital, but also, astoundingly, letting him organize a religious community for Sephardic Jews from the Ottoman Empire who visited the city.[11] Later on, Maria Theresa granted comparably free access to Vienna to a number of wealthy Bohemian Jews who in her name collected taxes on tobacco, on salt and on Jews—people like Israel Hönig of Kuttenplan, Salomon Dobruschka of Brünn, and Joachim Popper of Prague.[12] She also tolerated the presence of one or two new German military provisioners, for example Abraham Wetzlar, who figured towards the end of the reign as the richest individual in Vienna, and who after his conversion in 1777 won nobility as Wetzlar von Plankenstern.[13] Yet all this time these same rulers maintained the bar on native Ashkenazic Jews so strictly that in 1740 only 12 Jewish families in all had permission to live in the capital. When Maria Theresa died in 1780 the number of Jews was on the increase: there were now about 50 families with perhaps 570 family members and servants present. However, only 25 of the families were actually "tolerated" on a more or less long term basis. None of them were allowed the right to pursue their religion in public, nor were they permitted any legal corporative existence.[14]

The *Hofbefreiten*, as many of these people were known, have been studied extensively, so we may deal with them perfunctorily here. They are vitally important for our subject, however, not only because they were the original accumulators of Jewish wealth in the city, but also because they set a style for the city's latter-day rich Jews. They were models which subsequent generations of Jewish rich men might imitate, or, more importantly, avoid.

The first important quality of their wealth was its derivation from a very narrow professional base—above all from money lending, from money exchange and from dealing in jewels. This concentration, which as it happens

10 These people may best be traced through Bernard Wachstein's extraordinary *Die Inschriften des alten Judenfriedhofes in Wien,* 2 vols. and supplement (Wien, 1930, 1936); and Israel Taglicht, *Nachlasse der Wiener Juden im 17. und 18. Jahrhundert* (Wien, 1917).

11 See Rudolf Till, "Geschichte der Spanischen Juden in Wien," in *Jahrbuch der Verein für die Geschichte der Stadt Wien* V-VI (1946-47), 110 ff.

12 Samuel Krauss, *Joachim Edler von Popper* (Wien, 1925).

13 See Klaus Edel, *Karl Abraham Wetzlar Freiherr von Plankenstern* (Wien, 1975).

14 For lists of the eighteenth century Vienna Jews, and for the size of the community, see Pribram, *Urkunden und Akten*, vol. I, pp. liv, lvii, lxvi, and 374 ff., 608-10; vol. II, pp. 120-132. The lists attribute a profession to each name which may be matched with Wachstein's *Inschriften*. The following remarks are based substantially on a collection of cards bearing information about these people derived from Pribram, Wachstein and other sources.

Jews shared with many Christian businessmen in Vienna, stemmed from medieval restrictions on trade that existed in the capital. Manufacturers were rigidly cut off by law from the business of buying and selling wares. Bankers, likewise, whether Christian or Jewish, were barred from the buying and selling of goods; and importing and exporting were also rigidly regulated. Jews were not subject to such specialization in the German states outside of Vienna. The great German *Hoffaktoren* were usually by definition not only purveyors of money and jewels to the court, but army suppliers, dealers in every sort of ware from grain to horses, from weapons to uniforms and boots. Certainly Oppenheimer and Wertheimer and the people who after them held the specific title of *Hoffaktor*, were prominent in the trade in wares. In the early group of tolerated Vienna Jews, however, these were the minority by far. Typically, on a 1763 list of 57 prominent Viennese Jewish individuals, seven were jewelers or coin dealers, and 33 were, so far as one can determine, lenders and changers of money.[15] Of the remaining 17 (30%), two were visiting rabbis, one was a tutor in the Wertheimer house, one was a hospital attendant, and the rest were of unknown profession. Only two, who were *Hoffaktoren*, clearly dealt in wares.

The second and outstanding aspect of Jewish wealth at Vienna in the eighteenth century was, of course, its absolutely mobile character. From Oppenheimer down, the *Hofbefreiten*, despite their towering reputations for wealth, owned no real property, not even the houses they lived in. Elsewhere in the old German *Reich*, in cities where Jews could live legally, for example in Prague, rich Jews could own houses in specified districts. In Vienna they had to rent, sometimes from converted Jews like the von Sonnenfels brothers, more often from local aristocrats or burghers. And of course, outside Vienna they were barred absolutely from land-ownership, not just as Jews, but as non-nobles. The rich eighteenth century Vienna Jews certainly possessed tangible property, above all jewels, coins and costly objects; but they contrasted dramatically in their landlessness with the Christian rich people of their time and place, who tended to measure wealth exclusively in terms of land.

Their sensitivity to being thus different was in no way better attested than through the behavior of those who left the Jewish faith. Wetzlar von Plankenstern, for example, the convert about whom we are best informed, started in the very year of his conversion to buy estates and houses. When he died in 1799, he was no longer the richest banker in Vienna, but had become one of the most considerable house-owners. Though he could no longer endow his children with much cash, he gave them real estate enough to have lasted them a

15 For the list, see Bernard Wachstein, "Die Gründung der Wiener Chevra Kadischa im Jahre 1763," in *Mitteilungen zur Jüdischen Volkskunde* XIII (1910), 9-12. The professional identifications are derived from Wachstein's *Inschriften*, passim.

century had they not drunk it away.[16] All told, there was an elastic-band quality built into the pattern of Jewish wealth here. Because landlessness was enforced upon these people, they had a special craving for it.

The third important quality of Viennese Jewish wealth in the eighteenth century was what we may call its "administrative" derivation. The *Hoffaktoren* generically, and the Jewish ones in particular may be said to have derived their wealth from administration, because all of them built up their positions through credit relationships through extensive personalized contacts both with small-town money-lenders all over the Germanies, and with estate owners who alone in the feudal system could cough up the fruits of the land that the armies and courts needed. A *Hoffaktor* succeeded only if he could procure supplies cheaply, and to procure effectively, every one of them had to possess this sort of network.

At Vienna, there was also something else that made an administrative network of sorts an integral part of the property of every *Hoffaktor*. Nowhere else in Europe were specifically administrative skills in such high demand among the court money-men as at this capital, for the scale of business here was enormous. No other German potentate possessed such vast dominions as Vienna's masters, nor did any other undertake such titanic tasks as the Habsburgs at Vienna. Further, one may recall that until Napoleonic times, the emperors did not possess a united treasury, but derived their income from *regalia* and estates in various lands with whose nobilities they negotiated individually. Since prior to Maria Theresa's reforms in the 1750s the war office was administratively primitive, this diversity of income meant that the Army supplier himself had to put the whole vast financial packet together. The well-known story of Samuel Oppenheimer is ample testimony to the special administrative character of Viennese Jewish wealth. Who but an eerily independent administrative power could have organized the defense of Vienna in 1683, and the subsequent liberation of Buda, on only a month or two notice?[17]

One may not pretend that all the wealthy Jews of Vienna in the eighteenth century were of Oppenheimer's administrative breed. By mid-century the governmental bureaucracy had assumed more modern form and had acquired administrative skills after the French and Prussian models. Bankers no longer had to possess the administrative skills of their predecessors. Nonetheless, it seems notable that the aforementioned d'Aguilar came to Austria not as an army

16 See Edel, *Wetzlar*, pp. 197 ff, 242 ff. For the comparable tendency of other wealthy converts in this era, see Hanns Jäger-Sunstenau, "Die geadelten Judenfamilien im vormärzlichen Wien," (Ph.D. dissertation, Wien, 1950), pp. 93-98.

17 This point is made especially by Szakály, "Oppenheimer Sámuel," p. 66 and by Bérenger, *Finances et absolutisme*, pp. 203-205, 269, 459.

provisioner, as even Oppenheimer had, but as a tax advisor: he came from Iberia to advise the emperor how best to set up a state tobacco monopoly. In subsequent decades, the rising class of Jews in Vienna's hinterland, the Bohemian lands, consisted of people who prospered in the administration of taxes. They picked up d'Aguilar's tobacco legacy in particular. Even while he was in Vienna, the government had found it impossible to set up a viable tobacco monopoly for the lack of sufficient bureaucratic personnel. After he left, the tax on tobacco was farmed out; and time and again (to the manifest disgust of Maria Theresa) the wealthy Bohemian Jews outbid their Christian competitors in the government auctions. An Austrian Tobacco Monopoly was finally established in the 1780s by a Jew, Israel Hönig, on the basis of his family's private credit network.[18] To this extent the wealth of the rich Jews under consideration was built on what today we would call "bureaucracy."

In concluding this opening part of our essay, it is well to stress that Jewish wealth was only intermittently significant at Vienna in the eighteenth century. In 1700, of course, Oppenheimer and Wertheimer were the dominant figures in the state's finances. When Oppenheimer died, the state attempted to deny its debt to him, and as a result was suddenly faced with bankruptcy on the eve of a war. By reneging on its debts to Oppenheimer, it cut off entirely its credit elsewhere. But precisely because of this terrifying spectacle, the Habsburgs for decades thereafter seem to have favored Swiss Protestants, Greeks, Englishmen, and Italians—anybody but Jews—as their bankers in Vienna.[19] Jewish wealth at Vienna in this century was only a shadow of what it had been before, and what it would be again.

III

The turn of the century brought substantial changes and this first of all through an increase in the Jewish community's size. The handful of bankers and jewelers that had constituted Vienna Jewry in the mid-eighteenth century expanded by 1800 to about 1200 souls, and by 1840 to somewhere between 2000 and 7000. In relation to the third of a million people who crowded into bustling Vienna by

18 See the classic works on the tobacco industry, Joseph von Retzer, *Tabakpachtung in der österreichischen Ländern von 1670-1783* (Wien, 1784); and Jerome E. Brooks, *Tobacco: Its History Illustrated by Books, Manuscripts and Engravings in the Library of George Arents Jr.*, 5 vols. (New York, 1937-1943), vol. III as indexed. Cf. Leopold Kompert, "Israel Hönig" in *Jahrbuch für Israeliten* (1847-1848), pp. 120-144.

19 See Hans von Mikoletsky, "Schweizer Händler und Bankiers in Österreich" in *Österreich und Europa. Festgabe für Hugo Hantsch* (Graz, 1965), pp. 169 ff.; and Helen Kuraic, "Die Wiener Niederleger im 18. Jahrhundert," (PhD dissertation, Wien, 1946).

the 1840s, the dimensions of the city's Jewry seem small. And they are small relative to the hundreds of thousands of Jews who lived at the time in the most "Jewish" of the Habsburg lands, Galicia, and who were now overflowing rapidly into northern Hungary. But from our point of view, the change was significant: in our search for the richest Jews, we no longer have to do with a tiny handful of "millionaires," living apart. We must somehow identify a wealthy elite within a growing population.[20] Such an elite is identifiable because Leopold II (1790-92) stabilized a system according to which any Jew could get permission to live and do business in Vienna if he or she possessed a certain wealth.[21] Under this system the number of "tolerated" Jewish family heads rose from the 25 of 1780 to about 125 from 1800 to 1835, and then to 197 by 1847. The lists of the tolerated became more or less equivalent to lists of the truly wealthy, as opposed to the thousand-odd hangers-on and servants. There were exceptions: some wealthy Jews (for example the Gomperzes, who were tolerated at Brno, and the Figdors, who had special dispensation) managed to live in Vienna without "toleration," and the Rothschilds, who lived there as "foreigners". And there were invariably some "temporary tolerees" on the lists—people of modest wealth who were allowed to remain in the capital because they carried out Jewish ritual functions, or rendered special services for the government. Still, the toleree lists give us for the entire period up to 1848, a reasonably precise measure of who among the Jews was truly rich, who not. Table 1 is a summary of who these *Tolerierten* were by profession.

20 The best estimates of Vienna's nineteenth century Jewish population are gathered in Siegmund Husserl, "Die israelitische Kultusgemeinde Wien," *Ost und West* (1910), 519-520.

21 Under Maria Theresa, the income from Jewish taxes was the following: 7500 fl. annually from the 23 tolerated families who paid the state for their "tolerated" residential rights, and 5600 fl. annually from the *Leibmaut*, or body tax, which each "untolerated" Jew had to pay upon entering Vienna. By the end of Joseph II's reign, however, 73 families were paying in all only 6292 fl., and even this seemed a violation of Joseph's abolition of the *Leibmaut*. Meanwhile, the government, alarmed by an influx of Jews, was looking for a new tax system. In an on-going debate, it was decided to offer long-term "toleration" in the city to individuals who could prove they possessed a wealth of 10,000 fl. and pay a small annual fee. *Hoffaktoren* and ennobled Jews might likewise have indefinite residence, barring bankruptcy. Persons of lesser wealth could receive "tolerance" on a short term (usually three-year) basis. In so far as possible, the poor were to be excluded. See Pribram, *Urkunden und Akten*, vol. I, pp. lxxiv, lxxxvii, xci-xcii; and vol. II, p. 46. With time, the requirements rose—by 1817 the rich had to demonstrate a wealth of 50,000 fl. Furthermore, there were intensive efforts to restrict immigration—for a time even the rich were only admitted if they became wholesale merchants, *Grosshändler*, and then only on short-term! Then after 1830, the rules were gradually relaxed. See Pribram, *Urkunden und Akten*, vol. II, pp. 78, 104-105, 272.

Table 1: The Tolerated Jews of Vienna, 1787-1847

A. Development by Profession

	1787	1790	1804	1807	1812	1823	1827	1834	1847
I. Money									
a. Exchange	15	16	12	13	14	9	11	9	15
b. Jewels	13	13	13	13	10	11	9	9	11
Total	28	29	25	26	24	20	20	18	26
% of total	46%	31%	21%	20%	18%	15%	16%	15%	13%
II. Wholesale									
a. Deliveries	3	5	4	3	1	2	2	2	1
b. *Grosshändler*	2	4	14	14	15	36	33	36	35
c. *Commis*	2	2	3	4	4	2			
Total	7	11	21	21	20	40	35	38	36
% of total	12%	12%	17%	16%	15%	30%	28%	31%	19%
III. Produce									
a. Leather	1	1	1	1	1	2	4	4	6
b. Oil, Potash		1		1	1	2	2	2	7
c. Distilling		1			1				2
d. Raw produce	1	2	10	10	10	4	4	5	12
e. *Gal. Sensal*			3	3	8	8	7	8	6
f. Agricultural *Sensal*						1	1	1	11
g. Horses		6	3	5	5	4	2	2	2
Total	2	11	17	20	26	21	20	22	46
% of total	30%	20%	14%	15%	20%	16%	16%	18%	23%
IV. Textile									
a. Silk	2	5	10	10	11	8	8	6	5
b. Wool	4	7	10	10	0	8	4	3	6
c. Cotton	1	1	1	1	1	1	2	4	8
d. General	1	1	4	4	5	3	8	9	15
Total	7	13	25	25	26	20	24	22	34
% of total	12%	14%	21%	19%	20%	15%	19%	20%	17%
V. Manufactured goods	0	4	4	5	2	2	2	2	
% of total	0%	0%	3%	3%	4%	1%	1%	1%	1%
VI. Functional									
a. Ritual	11	13	19	20	16	12	10	8	7
b. Medicine	2	2	5	5	5	6	6	5	8
c. Mint/Print		9	2	3	2	2	2	1	5
d. Free Professions		1	1	1		1		1	7
e. Widows	2	3	2	3	3				9
Total	15	28	29	32	26	21	18	15	36
% of total	25%	30%	24%	25%	20%	16%	15%	15%	18%
Unknown	2	1	1	2	7	11	5	4	15
VII. Totals	61	93	122	130	134	135	124	121	195

Table 1 (cont.): B. The Number of New Practitioners

	1787	1790	1804	1807	1812	1823	1827	1834	1847
I. Money									
a. Exchange		3	2	1	1	0	2	1	6
b. Jewels		0	5	0	1	2	0	1	5
II. Wholesale									
a. Deliveries		2	1	0	0	1	0	0	0
b. *Grosshändler*		2	12	1	1	24	3	10	13
c. *Commis*		0	1	1	1	0			
III. Produce									
a. Leather		0	0	0	0	1	2	0	2
b. Oil, Potash		1		1	0	1	0	0	5
c. Distilling		1			1				2
d. Raw produce		1	8	0	0	0	0	2	8
e. *Gal. Sensal*			3	0	5	1	2	1	0
f. Agricultural *Sensal*						1	0	0	10
g. Horses		6	1	2	0	1	1	0	1
IV. Textile									
a. Silk		3	6	0	3	0	0	0	2
b. Wool		3	5	0	1	0	1	0	4
c. Cotton			1	0	0	0	1	2	6
d. Textiles in general		0	3	0	2	1	5	2	11
V. Manufactured goods									
			4	1	1	0	0	0	0
VI. Functional									
a. Ritual		2	17	1	0	0	0	0	2
b. Medicine		0	3	0	2	1	1	1	4
c. Mint/Print		9	2	1	0	1	0	0	4
d. Free Professions		1	1	0		1		1	6
e. Widows		1		1	0				8

These tables are based on nine lists of family heads published in Pribram, *Urkunden und Akten*. The vertical index lists professions mentioned in some of the original documents.
Table 1B includes both new "tolerees" and people who changed profession.
The totals here, for complex reasons, sometimes deviate slightly from those given by Pribram.
Note, the abrupt increase of *Grosshändler* in 1823 results from very numerous shifts in profession as well as immigration.
The early lists include the names of a small number of *Hoffaktor* widows. By 1823 these were dead; but meanwhile some 27 early tolerees had died, leaving widows very actively in charge of their firms. These women, and also toleree sons, are counted here as continuing the original "tolerance".

The story of how their wealth developed begins with what Germans call a *Gleichschaltung* of the differences at Vienna between rich Jews and rich Christians. First the restrictions on trade were relaxed. In 1764, the government allowed the Jews in Vienna to trade in domestic wares, albeit not yet to enter the import-export business. Then in the 1770s, it created for Christian businessmen a new privileged status called *Grosshändler*, or "wholesaler," which conveyed a general immunity from the restrictions on trade and enterprise which hung over the city.[22] Finally in 1781-82, Joseph II, through a well-known rescript and several patents, encouraged the wealthy Jews to make themselves over along the lines of the new, guild-free Christian upper bourgeoisie. He instructed them not only to abandon whatever special Jewish business customs they had, but also to enter all branches of trade and industry, making it now possible for them to become *Grosshändler*.

Responding to these edicts, the wealthier Jews of Vienna found themselves singularly well situated a few years after Joseph's death, when the French revolutionary wars began, to take advantage of the extraordinary economic movements of the time; and this they did in a fashion that shows up clearly in their professional composition. Even as early as 1789, a pronounced shift out of the old money-dealing mold was discernible. Among 93 family heads, sixteen still dealt in money and state loans; and thirteen still traded in jewels (of whom seven also lent money). There was now only one *Hoffaktor* (Samuel Wertheimer), whereas there were four *Grosshändler*, 29 merchants of one sort or another (wool, leather, silks, fancy goods and horses) and two agents for provincial traders. One member of the group owned a dye-factory. There were two doctors, nine mint and printing press employees, and thirteen persons who served Jewish ritual needs.[23] Excluding these last groups, which were not rich, one may observe that more than half of the wealthy in Vienna Jewry were by now officially branching out of the old professional mold. By 1812, the trend towards professional diversification had so much accelerated that out of 135 "tolerated" Jews in the city, the number of self-styled "money-dealers" was down to nine. There were still eleven jewelers and one *Hoffaktor,* but there were fifteen *Grosshändler*, also eleven merchants specializing in silk wares, another eleven in wool, cotton and leather, eleven in other raw produce, five in manufactured goods, five in textiles, one distiller and five in horses—a total of

22 See Günther Chaloupek, "Wiens Grosshandel in der kommerziellen Revolution," *Wiener Geschichtsblätter* XXXIX (1984), 105-125.

23 It may be noted that many of these *Judentraiteuren* were descendants or relatives of the really wealthy, and that often they were actually traders and money-dealers, whose declining wealth prevented them from obtaining permission to stay in Vienna in the normal way.

53 in wares; and there were also eight "Galician assessors" (commission agents for Galician merchants).

The significance of this change, which was an on-going process, lay not only in the evidence that enterprising wealthy Jews in Vienna were doing new things. It also reflected a commercial revolution. Of the new names who appeared among the tolerated between 1780 and 1810, a large percentile were from Hungary, and a large percentile of these were in the trade of wool and cotton. Their appearance reflects a boom in Hungarian agriculture touched off by Austria's resistance to Napoleon's Continental system. [24] Not only did Hungarian-origin Jews fan this boom by bringing raw-produce to Vienna; now also, Bohemian-born Jews such as Isak Löw Hofmann (an ancestor of Hugo von Hofmannsthal), invested heavily in developing silk-production in Hungary, in importing wool from Hungary for Moravian textile factories, and in importing cotton from the Balkans across the fastness of the Hungarian Great Plain for the new cotton industry at Prague. Several of the most prominent families in Vienna Jewish history made their appearance now as promoters of the Hungarian trade: Figdor, Todesco, Löwenthal, Biedermann, for example, and there were others who had transitory glory in Vienna before converting and retiring onto Hungarian estates—the Leidesdorfer, Liebmann, Kann, Lackenbacher families, for example. This Hungarian involvement had a formidable impact on the Viennese Jewish elite, as is shown clearly by the lists of *Grosshändler* firms in Vienna in the post-1815 period. In 1823 there were 118 such firms. Of these, 39 (33.9%) firms were Jewish (or of Jewish origin), and of the 39, one third (13) were Hungarian. Two more (Hofmann and Grünbaum) had exceedingly close Hungarian business connections. A decade later in 1836 there were 89 *Grosshändler* in all. Forty (45%) of them were run by Jews, or recent converts, including virtually the same strong contingent of fourteen Hungarian and Hungarian-connected firms. In 1846 there were 82 *Grosshändler* in all, 47 (57.3%) of them Jewish or of Jewish origin, and about twelve of these Hungarian.[25]

24 On this boom, see Zsigmond Pach, ed., *Magyarország Története*, 10 vols. (Budapest, 1976), vol. V/1, ch. 4.

25 The lists of *Grosshändler* are in F.B. Frey, *Allgemeine Handlungsgremial Almanach* for the years in question. I have identified Jewish firms by comparison with the lists in Pribram, *Urkunden und Akten*. Since the purpose of this counting is to trace the rise and survival of wealth, I have ignored the several conversions of wealthy Hungarian Jews out of the Jewish faith. It may be remarked that the fall-off in Christian participation in the *Grosshändler Gremium* in this period was in part attributable to the disappearance of older "foreign" (i.e. Greek and Italian) firms leading thus to a "nationalisation" of Vienna's commerce.

All told, the turn-of-the-century boom in Hungary's agricultural trade was a major source of early nineteenth century Viennese Jewry's wealth, and indeed for a half a century gave the community and its wealth its fundamental character. In the eighteenth century, Vienna Jewry had been in origin western, and especially west German, because Vienna was then essentially a *Reichsstadt*. In the first half of the nineteenth century, Vienna Jewry was Hungarian in origin, reflecting an often overlooked Hungarian character of the city's economy at that time. As late as 1870, 43.6% of the Vienna Jews were from Hungary.[26]

Meanwhile another strong economic trend was bringing Jews wealth and prominence in Vienna: this was the banking revolution touched off by the emperor Franz's repeatedly lost wars against the French. Its character is well-known and needs be only mentioned briefly here. Already in the 1790s, all the reforming efforts put into Austria's finances during the eighteenth century came to naught: a staggering inflation erupted, there was massive stock exchange speculation in the national currency and government bonds, and the government was thrown, as in Samuel Oppenheimer's day, on the mercy of its bankers. In 1811, with their connivance, it declared itself bankrupt, ruining that sector of the population which held paper money, or had invested in certain bonds. Then came further ruinous wars before the final victory of 1815.[27] This traumatic sequence of developments left the giants among the city's Christian bankers badly wounded: Fries, Geymuller and Parish were all on their way out; and no doubt many Jewish firms suffered too. One of the older Jewish banking firms, however, Arnstein and Eskeles, was immeasurably more powerful than before. Further, an array of newly immigrant Jewish banking houses from Germany were now thriving; and as is well known, in 1816, to both balance its indebtedness to Arnstein, and reinforce the then newly-organized National Bank, the government induced one of the great Jewish bankers of western Europe, Salomon Rothschild, to settle in Vienna, in this way completely transforming and internationalizing the local banking scene.[28]

One may measure exactly what the financial experience of the Napoleonic era meant for Vienna's Jewish elite. Before this banking revolution, though many Jewish bankers served the imperial government, not one of them would have

26 Israel Jeiteles, *Die Kultusgemeinde der Israeliten in Wien* (Wien, 1873), p. 55.

27 See Michael Wagner, "Zwischen zwei Staatsbankrotten," *Wiener Geschichtsblätter* XXXII (1977), 115-123; Franz Baltzarek, *Die Geschichte der Wiener Börse* (Wien, 1973), pp. 19 ff; Egon Scheffer, *Das Bankwesen in Österreich* (Wien, 1924); and Siegfried Pressburger, *Österreichische Notenbank, 1816-1966* (Wien, 1966).

28 For the circumstances of Rothschild's advent to Vienna, see Hellmuth Rössler, *Graf Johann Philipp Stadion,* 2 vols. (Wien, 1966). For the family history, see Heinrich Schnee, *Rothschild: Geschichte einer Finanzdynastie* (Göttingen, 1961); Bertrand Gille, *Histoire de la Maison Rothschild,* 2 vols. (Genéve, 1965-1967); and Egon Count Corti, *Das Haus Rothschild,* 2 vols. (Leipzig, 1927-1928).

been allowed to style himself, without conversion, as a government policy advisor. In 1823, however, when the National Bank published a long list of the 105 members of its advisory committee, sixteen unconverted Jews figured alongside seventeen from the historic aristocracy and 72 "others." One Jewish banker, Bernhard Eskeles, and one converted Jew, J. J. Löwenthal, were directors. In addition, everyone knew that another Jew advised the Government on economic policy behind the scenes. However, the name Rothschild was not mentioned on the Bank list, because its bearer, in protest against the anti-Jewish laws, had refused to accept Austrian citizenship.[29]

Nor was this the end of the banking change: in the era of European financial expansion after 1820, the Rothschilds did not long remain the only international Jewish bankers to have standing representatives in Vienna. Their cousins, the Schnappers of Frankfurt soon imitated them, as did the Königswarters of Paris and Frankfurt, the Kaullas who had a family headquarters at Stuttgart, and a whole galaxy of often converted and ennobled Jewish bankers, "visitors" from the Germanies. These people tended not only the needs of the state, but those of Austria's great aristocrats, who needed cash in the new capitalist era. Consequently, by 1836, out of 97 names on the Bank Committee, 37 were Jewish—41%, as opposed to the 14% of 1823. By the 1840s, the Bank had stopped publishing such tell-tale lists, but did not conceal the decisive weight of Baron Rothschild at the top![30]

It was not only the commercial and banking booms of the Napoleonic era, that brought Vienna Jewry decisive wealth during the half century after Joseph II. Some more gradual economic developments of the *Vormärz* period also contributed, above all the demand of the rapidly growing city for provisions. By the 1840s, when both the total population and the Jewish population of Vienna were sky-rocketing, the largest professional group among the 110 newly tolerated Jews since the last count of 1834, dealt in natural produce, most notably in grain. In some ways this was nothing new: for generations Jews had been involved in the provisioning of the capital. Since 1815, however, the business had been given over to private dealers, and a Fruit and Grain Exchange

29 So as to avoid the discriminatory Austrian laws against Jews, Rothschild claimed throughout the *Vormärz* that he was a foreigner simply visiting in Vienna. He lived there in a hotel and until his death was registered as a citizen of Frankfurt am Main.

30 The source of the lists is again Frey's *Allgemeine Handlungsgremium Almanach* for the years in question. In 1846 no Bank Committee list appeared, but the names Eskeles, Wertheimstein, Erggelet and Liebenberg, all originally Jewish, were among the 12 directors of the bank; and of the 16 members of the Discount Committee, eight (Biedermann, Elkan, Königswarter, Wertheimstein, Borkenstein, Goldschmidt, Schnapper and Wodianer) were Jewish or originally Jewish (with three of these, Wertheimstein, Goldschmidt and Schnapper, direct representatives of the Rothschild house).

had been organized on the curb near the Stock Exchange. A knowledgable observer remarked that towards mid-century the dealers were almost exclusively Jews—he could think of only a few exceptions, most of them Italians or Greeks.[31] The Jews from Hungary may have particularly thrived on this business. It has been impossible to identify the place of origin for most of the "tolerees," but among the *Grosshändler* a majority of the newcomers in the *Vormärz* were regularly from Hungary and dealt in natural produce. Ten of the new tolerees of 1847 were specifically assessors at the Grain Exchange; most were from Hungary.

Table 2: New Jewish *Grosshändler* by Place of Origin

	1787-1804	1812-1823	1827-1847	total
Vienna	6	4	1	9
Other Austria	-	-	1	1
Bohemia	5	2	4	11
Moravia & Silesia	-	1	3	4
Galicia	-	4	-	4
Hungary	2	13	13	28
Germany	3	4	2	9
Turkey	-	1	-	-
Unknown	-	1	1	2

Despite this record, it does not seem that the produce trade by itself generated great and lasting wealth among the Vienna Jews. Many Viennese Jewish produce-trader families acquired "tolerance", indicating that they were getting rich; but among them, it was primarily those who moved from trading into the processing of wool (Biedermann, for example), of oil (Leon), of hops (Mauthner-Markhof), or of leather (Pollak von Borkenau) who ended up with real wealth, and even so it was often conversion out of Judaism along the way that secured the ascent of these families. There were even many jokes at the time related to the fact that a well-known figure, Leopold von Wertheimstein, was registered with the authorities as a *Produktenhändler,* a grain-trader. Wertheimstein was actually the Rothschild firm's principal representative in public life. His wife, Josephine née Gomperz, ran a famous literary salon. In 1849, he became president of the recently re-organized Jewish *Kultusgemeinde.* A man of his immense wealth and considerable culture was clearly the antithesis of the ordinary Jewish grain-trader. Nonetheless, it may be said that produce trading was a major springboard from which *some* rich Vienna Jews leaped to

31 Sigmund Mayer, *Die Wiener Juden* (Wien, 1917), pp. 228, 231-232, 243, 267.

even greater wealth in the first half of the nineteenth century. Virtually every *Grosshändler* house did a little business in grain or produce (which, of course, is why Rothschild let von Wertheimstein list himself as a produce-trader). Indeed it became one of the peculiarities of the great Vienna banks later on that they all, because of the *Vormärz* precedents, usually did business not just in money, but also in grain, sugar and other natural produce.[32]

In the 1820s, 1830s and 1840s, Austria's growing textile business also became an important source of Viennese Jewish wealth. Textile manufactures and trading had of course always played a role in the Vienna economy, because the city's guilds had long specialized in making luxury goods and clothing for the court. From the reign of Joseph II, Jewish textile traders were important in the capital—by 1789 there were four in silk trading, six in wool trading among the tolerated Jews. In the past, however, Moravia had been the woolens manufacturing center of the Danube valley, Bohemia had been the center of the newer cotton weaving industry, and silk-weaving had usually taken place in northern Italy. Now, in the 1820s and 1830s, with the building of modern manufacturies at Vienna, and with the construction in the 1830s of the first railroads, the capital became the textile emporium of the entire Danube valley.

The shift led to a major influx of Jews into the city. In the past, Jewish traders had played a vital role in the provincial distribution of textiles—and also, it is alleged, in smuggling cloth across the empire's external frontiers, and across its internal frontier into Hungary. Now they all had to shift their attention to Vienna. Of the new tolerees of 1847, the second largest single category of new names, 23 of the 110, were those of textile merchants. Moreover, large numbers of such traders who could not afford "tolerated status" took to commuting weekly from Bratislava (Pressburg, Pozsony) and the Jewish inhabited towns of Moravia and today's Burgenland.[33]

Nor was this the whole of it. As it happened the workshops where the Vienna guilds had for generations put together fancy clothing for ladies and gentlemen alike, where they had made laces, braids, embroidered purses, umbrellas, and other luxury goods—these ateliers were in general situated in the so-called "suburbs" between the broad *Glacis*, or parade-ground around the inner city, and today's *Gürtel,* the city's outer defense line. In the period before 1858, the inner city was still walled, and communications and transport between the workshops and the downtown area were difficult. When in the 1820s and 1830s the inner city acquired its textile emporium character, the increasingly

32 Bernard, *Banques et banquiers*, pp. 28-30.

33 See Mayer, *Die Wiener Juden*, passim. An interesting case history of such "commuting" is in the biography of Arminio Cohn in Gerson Wolf, *Zur Culturgeschichte in Österreich-Ungarn, 1848-1888* (Wien, 1888), p. 128 ff.

numerous provincial and foreign buyers proved ever more loathe to wander around the suburbs looking at artisan wares. The manufacturers were correspondingly loathe to go downtown; and consequently the newly arrived Jewish textile traders were able to step in and to become the middle-men in the marketing of Vienna luxuries. Thus by mid-century, Jews had gained major entrée into the principal commerce and industries of Vienna.

As in the case of produce-trading, so here one may suggest that commerce by itself was not enough to produce great and lasting wealth. The textile-trader tolerees who rose to the top were those who diversified by becoming *Grosshändler* (above all, those like Hermann Todesco who became Stock Exchange speculators as well as *Grosshändler*); or else those who got in on manufacturing, either by establishing a factory in the Vienna suburbs, or (perhaps more frequently) by founding one in the provinces, and then retailing its produce at Vienna. At Prague, for example, all through the *Vormärz* Jews were the owners of the cotton goods plants which were spearheading the industrial revolution there. Among the tolerees at Vienna in the 1840s, these same families figured largely as owners of textile outlets, or indeed as founders of new cotton manufacturies in the city's suburbs. These families—Porges, Jerusalem, Epstein, Geiringer, Bondi, Biach and Brandeis, for example—even if they did not wholly transplant themselves to the capital, proved to be among the most lasting in terms of Viennese Jewish great wealth.

What now of those parameters of Jewish wealth that we observed in the eighteenth century: the landlessness and the "administrative" character? Of the first it must be said that on the whole it survived in the *Vormärz*, because the legal bars on Jewish land ownership were not removed in Austria until 1848 and later. There were certainly signs of approaching change. In 1833, the ban on Jewish landownership did not prevent Baron Rothschild from "renting" the iron mine and foundry on the great estate of the Archbishopric of Olmütz at Witkowitz. This foundry would become the cornerstone of the Rothschild family's heavy-industry empire later in the nineteenth century. Nor did the bar prevent Rothschild in the mid-1830s from organizing the first great Austrian railroad, the *Nordbahn*; and in 1842 the city of Vienna awarded him honorary citizenship, which gave him personally the right to own land. His formal purchase of his hotel, of Witkowitz, and of a huge hunting estate followed.

Meanwhile a number of the other leading Vienna tolerees had taken the critical step of converting so as to escape the bar on Jewish land-holding. This was true not only of some of the *Grosshändler* of Hungarian origin mentioned above—the Kaans, the Mayers von Alsó Russbach, and the Lackenbachers (who coincidentally obtained nobility as a sign of the land-lust that drove them)—but also for example, of the children of Nathan Arnstein and Bernhard Eskeles, the leading bankers of Vienna, and of Ignac Lippmann von Liebenberg and Marcus Leidesdorfer von Neuwall, and Isak Löw Hoffmann von Hofmannsthal, leaders of the Vienna Jewish religious community when it was founded in the 1820s. In addition, the ambiguities of Joseph II's legislation had enabled many enterprising Jews to control land. That emperor had strongly encouraged Jews to establish factories. Then as now, it was a rare capitalist who would build a factory on someone else's property, so there was a standing implication in the legislation that Jews might own real property if they would manufacture on it.

We may refer tangentially here to a major problem of central European Jewish economic history: the problem of why despite the imperial incentives, Jews actually entered manufacturing very unevenly. In Moravia, for example, which in the period under consideration was the manufacturing center of the whole Danubian valley and a major seat of Jewish habitation, there were practically no Jewish manufactures until the last years before 1848. Even in Vienna, the Jews who set up and stuck to factories were clearly not the common breed. In Bohemia, by contrast, there was the flowering of Jewish owned cotton manufactures, mentioned above. Whatever the explanation of this uneven pattern, however, it may be observed that by the 1840s, Lower Austria and the region around Prague were dotted with enterprises on land that was for all intents and purposes "Jewish." The landlessness of the Jews was ending.

What of the second parameter of eighteenth century Viennese Jewish wealth, its "administrative" character? In general we may say that gradually circumstances transformed it. This does not mean that the rich Jews in any way abandoned their dependence on private credit and correspondence networks. To the contrary, the *Grosshändler*, who in the main constituted the wealthy elite of Vienna Jewry throughout the period, depended, each and every one of them, on such networks, exactly as had the *Hoffaktoren* of the eighteenth century. However, in the old, still feudal world of the eighteenth century, the "differentness" of the Jewish credit networks had been very pronounced—there had been very few non-Jewish *Hoffaktoren*, and the sheer boldness required of them had been very notable. Now in the presence of early industrial capitalism, these networks, and their owners' bravery, were far less distinct. Now there were a great many Christian *Grosshändler* around, many of whom organized their businesses exactly as did the Jews, and entered professional fields that had formerly been thought of as Jewish. As Karl Marx observed in his notorious "Jewish Question" essay, in the early nineteenth century the central European Christian world was becoming "Judaized."[34]

34 A good example of a non-Jew organizing his business in a typically "Jewish" fashion was the hero of Heinrich Benedikt, *Alexander von Schoeller* (Wien, 1958).

Further, one may perceive in the toleree lists from the end of the *Vormärz* clear signs of another transformation of central Europe's business world which would soon come and make the old personalized networks a thing of the past. Three major figures on the toleree list of 1847—von Wertheimstein, Moritz Goldschmidt and Heinrich Sichrowsky—were, despite considerable wealth, not self-employed businessmen, but hirelings of Baron Rothschild. Sichrowsky was the closest to heralding the future: he was secretary general of the *Nordbahn*, a publicly-owned company. All three men were prototypes of all the wealthy stock company directors who would proliferate in the following decades. They were symbols of the de-personalized business administrations that would make the *Hoffaktoren* firms obsolete by the twentieth century.

IV

To treat the second half of the nineteenth century as just one economic period might cause any historian indigestion. Even in "backward" central and eastern Europe, the changes that occurred between 1850 and 1910 were stupendous. By 1910 Vienna had become a city of two millions, Budapest a city of almost one million, and the lesser Habsburg towns had also experienced a demographic explosion. The industrial revolution had blossomed throughout the region, today's world was born. Yet here we must treat those long decades as just one "period," for the simple reason, noted at the start of the paper, that the identification of Viennese Jewish wealth now becomes as difficult, as earlier it was easy.

To suggest the problem, let us discuss the sources we must deal with, and first of all the essential ones which identify who is or was a Jew. As it happens apparently authoritative indices exist in the lists of highest tax-payers published by the *Kultusgemeinde*. We have used two, one dating from 1870 with 1626 names and professions, the second dating from 1910 with 866 names, professions and addresses.[35] Unfortunately, when it comes to identifying the truly wealthy, these lists are in one respect largely unhelpful. 9008 Jews converted in Vienna between 1868 and 1903; many more followed just before and after the first World War;[36] and notoriously, the conversion rate was highest among the wealthy and ambitious, the very people we are after. Our *Kultusgemeinde* tax-payer lists obviously do not cover converts.

35 *Verzeichnis der wählbaren Mitglieder...der israelitischen Kultusgemeinde in Wien* (Vienna, 1870) and *Verzeichnis der im Wiener Gemeindegebiete wohnhaften höher besteuerten Wähler* (Vienna, 1910). Both lists are available in the Central Archives of the Jewish People, Jerusalem under AW/16 (11).

36 See Thon, *Juden in Österreich*, p. 9; and Rozenblit, *Jews of Vienna*, ch. 6.

To locate the converts, there is one very useful tool: the Vienna social register, the *Highlife*. This remarkable research aid lists large numbers of people all over the Austrian half of the Monarchy who felt they were distinguished; and as a rule it provides not only names and addresses, but also extensive professional information, and spouses' maiden names. From this volume it is not hard to pinpoint large numbers of converts.[37]

Supplementary are two secondary historical works which identify Jewish-owned industrial concerns in Habsburg central Europe.[38] In difficult cases—of which there are many—one may go back in Vienna to the records of deaths, which lie in the city archive; and then trace down obituaries.[39] All told, thus, while the identification of wealthy Jews and convert Jews from old Vienna is possible, it is often an arduous task.

Let us turn now to a second problem: How to pin-point the prime bearers of business wealth in the capital, and then specify how many were Jews. In the first half of the century, two neat global lists were available—the lists of the National Bank advisory committee, and the lists of *Grosshändler Gremium* members. In mid-century, however, a major institutional expansion transformed the Vienna business world. The National Bank ceased to be the sole public institution: it was flanked now by a chamber of commerce (*Handels- und Gewerbekammer*), and by an expanded and democratized stock exchange (*Börse*). Meanwhile the old *Grosshändler* firms were joined in the private wealth sector by an array of joint-stock company (JSC) banks and by a proliferation of publicly owned railroad and industrial companies. The very multiplicity of these business institutions obviously complicated the matter of counting rich people.

37 I have relied in particular on the *Highlife* volume for 1913. It is suggestive of the utility of this volume, that it frequently lists both higher educational degrees, and summer addresses. One may thus determine the educational record, and the estate-holdings of the individuals one follows.

38 Sigmund Mayer, *Die Wiener Juden*; and Gustav Otruba, "Der Anteil der Juden am Wirtschaftsleben," in Ferdinand Seibt, ed., *Die Juden in den böhmischen Ländern* (Munich, 1983), pp. 209-268.

39 The *Totenprotokkole* are in the *Stadt-Archiv* at the Vienna Rathhaus. To call them, one must know the year of death. This, as it turns out, can in many cases easily be determined by following an individual's career in the Vienna telephone books, the "Lehmann," which are conveniently shelved in the *Stadt-Archiv* reading room. When a name disappears, death is presumptive. If it disappears between 1939 and 1941, the Jewishness of a convert is to some degree presumptive. The *Totenprotokkole* give in most cases the exact date of death, the religion of the deceased, and the nearest survivor. Once the death-date is determined, it is possible to seek out obituaries in the daily press. In old Vienna, these were sometimes, albeit not always, extremely revealing. The problem here, of course, is to know which of the many prominent newspapers, carried an extensive obituary. The families of converts in particular were apt to favor a paper other than the most accessible one, the *Neue Freie Presse*.

In addition, with the blossoming of stock-holding, middle class wealth grew significantly less visible.

Theoretically, one still should be able with this new situation to get a good idea of who was wealthy by pooling the leaderships of all the new institutions. To be sure, longer lists will plague the researcher who does this—but why not? The business world was much much bigger now! When one looks at the lists even for a first sample year, 1858, however, one must retreat. Take first the *Grosshändler Gremium* list, which in the *Vormärz* provided a neat index of the Viennese rich people.[40] In 1858 one discovers that out of 93 member firms, 62 (67%) were Jewish! This seems a fascinating advance over the 45% and 57% of the 1836 and 1847 lists, until one notices that despite the economic liberalization of society in those decades, the number of Christian *Grosshändler* had kept falling off. It turns out, in effect, that the Jewish percentile of the *Gremium* was rising, because Christian businessmen had stopped becoming *Grosshändler*. Jews had continued to do so, in part perhaps because they liked the fancy title; but their practice does not make our statistic meaningful as an index of either real or relative wealth.

Table 3: Jewish Participation in Viennese Public Institutions, 1858-1913

Year	National Bank	*Handelskammer*	*Börse*	JSC Banks	% in Banks
1858	12/40	–	4/17	18/49	37%
1873	11/40	14/50	9/16	43/101	43%
1886	5/15	16/50	19/27	43/124	35%
1900	–	22/50	21/27	52/138	38%
1913	–	–	19/28	97/196	49%

When one looks at the leadership in 1858 of the newly reorganized National Bank, likewise, one encounters difficulties (Table 3). For twenty years in mid-century the bank was ruled by a governor and two vice-governors, all appointed by the emperor, by a general administrative secretary, by a twelve-man directorship, and by a 25-man board of censors. One may quickly observe that in 1858, five of the directors were Jews or of Jewish origin; and that in 1873, a second sample year, four were Jews and that, indeed, in 1873 one of the vice-governors was a converted Jew, Moritz Wodianer. The list, thus, certainly

40 This and the following lists for 1858 are from M. Heinrich, *Handels- und Gewerbe-Adressenbuch für die Kaiserthum Österreich* (Vienna, 1858).

seems to attest the existence of a growing Jewish economic strength, which one can hypothesize from other sources. The list is also very short, however; and once one looks at the much larger board of censors of the National Bank, one must recognize that the bank-leadership was no longer, as in the *Vormärz*, an index of wealth, but one of politics. In both 1858 and 1873, the board of censors was made up overwhelmingly, not of Jews, but of often insignificant Christian businessmen.

Much the same is true of the leadership of a third eminent newly reorganized institution, the *Börse* or stock exchange. In 1858, a short time before the political triumph of Austrian liberalism, the *Börse* president, vice-president, and general secretary were Christians, and of the sixteen *Börseräthe* or councilors, the four who were of Jewish origin were all converted. Technically, then, no Jews were to be found here. By 1873, however, with liberalism politically supreme, the stock exchange president was a converted Jew (Baron Wodianer), the vice-president was a Jew (Baron F. Schey), seven of the fifteen councilors were Jewish and 31 out of 42 assessors (*Sensalen*) (74%) were Jewish. Clearly enough it was not the dominantly Jewish reality of the Vienna Stock Exchange which had changed between 1858 and 1873: it was the political situation! In 1858 politics had insisted on a wholly unrepresentative, all-Catholic leadership, in 1873 politics allowed, even encouraged the revelation of a strong Jewish presence.

In later sample years, 1886, 1900 and 1910, the stock exchange leadership became an apparently useful and accurate index of Jewish influence in the Vienna business world.[41] In each year about 70% of the *Börseräthe* were Jewish. In 1900 the vice-president, in 1910 the president and vice-president were again Jewish (Leopold Lieben and Ludwig Wollheim). Alas! the stock exchange is the only such useful index. The other great business institution of late-nineteenth century liberal Vienna, the *Handelskammer* or chamber of commerce, was so organized that only politically minded, not necessarily wealthy people, were elected to representative positions. The Jewish presence in the so-called industry council of the *Handelskammer* stood at about 15% in each of the years 1873, 1886 and 1900, in its trade council the percentile crept up from 46% in 1873 to 62% in 1900, and in 1900 the president, Max Mauthner, was a converted Jew. Still, one does not find the greatest Vienna-based industrialists of the era, whether Jewish or Christian, listed here. Most of the people involved in this organization, especially on the Christian side, were distinctly petty bourgeois.

41 These lists are taken from the Austro-Hungarian *Compass* for the years in question.

When one checks the directorships of the great Vienna joint-stock company banks, whether for 1858 or later, once again one comes away unsatisfied with the emerging picture of what role Jews actually played, and of who was really important and wealthy in the late nineteenth century Vienna business world. One problem here is that, from the very start of the public-bank era, the bank organizers made strenuous efforts to recruit members of the historic aristocracy into the bank directorships. Baron Rothschild set the model when he organized the *Creditanstalt* in 1855: he made himself vice-president, appointed his two chief deputies, von Wertheimstein and Goldschmidt to the *Verwaltungsrat* (*VWR*—policy directorship) and posted five other prominent Jewish names to the masthead (Louis Haber, Jonas Königswarter, Leopold Lämmel, Eduard Wiener and Paul Schiff). But then he made Prince Schwarzenberg president and included six other aristocrats alongside the seven other Christian bankers in the leadership. One does not know exactly how many in this bank leadership were actually *Paradegoyim*, who had greater names than wealth, but unmistakably some of the great people involved were "padding". And in the following half century there were few Viennese banks which did not have such "padding" in the lead, so it is difficult to tell from the lists who actually had the money, who just a name.

Further, in the 1870s Rothschild led the way at the *Creditanstalt* in another feint—in the "Christianization" of the business world that we mentioned at the start of this paper. In 1873, 1886 and 1900 he so arranged that it seemed that only 33% of this bank's leadership was Jewish. In reality, of course, the Rothschild secretaries were always present in the *VWR*. They were Jewish, as were in 1873 the vice-president and the administrative secretaries of the bank. In 1886, 1900, and 1913 the bank's presidents (Eduard Wiener and Max Gomperz) were Jewish and the administrative secretariat was entirely staffed by Jews; and finally, in 1913, a *VWR* appeared that was openly 60% Jewish. One strongly suspects, therefore, that in this bank, despite its "Christianized" exterior, Jews were wholly in control right along.

Each of the great Vienna banks was different in its treatment of Jewishness. In no matter which year, if one aggregates the directorships, men of Jewish faith appear to have been perhaps 20% of a sample comprised overwhelmingly of old or new aristocrats, on the one hand, and of more or less wealthy Vienna Christian burghers, on the other.[42] The proportion is much, much higher, however, if one counts converted Jews—the average then is 40%. Moreover, the study suggests that in reality only one of these banks, the *Erste*

42 See the assessment in *Dr. Bloch's Österreichische Wochenschrift* XV (1898), 64. Bloch found only 22 Jews among the 124 directors of 12 banks he surveyed (18%); and 20 Jews among 142 directors of 14 railroad companies (14%).

Österreichische Sparkasse, was not dominated by Jews. In the other banks, whatever the "padding" arrangement, there was invariably a person of Jewish background in *the* most significant administrative post. At the *Escompte Gesellschaft* the key figures were in succession Daniel Eskeles, Wilhelm von Boschan, Karl Bunzl, Moritz von Borkenau and Max Feilchenfeld. At the *Anglobank* were Adolf von Seidler, Hugo Schwarz, Carl Morawitz and Siegfried Rosenbaum. At the *Bodencreditanstalt* were Adolf Schenk, Theodor Taussig, Julius Herz, Alfred Herzfeld and, last but not least, Rudolf Sieghardt. At the Union Bank from start to finish, regardless of whether a dozen Jewish nobles (as in 1886), or a dozen impeccable Christians (as in 1900) sat in the *Verwaltungsrat*, Eugen Minkus and Otto Wiedmann actually ran the business. At the particularly pious Catholic *Länderbank*, a bank which seemed in Count Taaffe's time his personal answer to the "Jewish bank" problem, whose funding came from Eugène Bontoux in Paris, the general director throughout the 1880s and 1890s was Samuel von Hahn, a confessional Jew, and the administrative directors even in 1913 under the Christian president, Eduard Palmer, were largely Jewish. At the *Wiener Bank Verein*, Adolf Ritter von Schenk, Moritz Bauer and Bernard Popper held the key offices over the period we are discussing. At the *Depositenbank*, the key figures were Hermann Grunbaum and Adolf Dessauer; at the *Verkehrsbank*, Philipp Broch; at the *Mercur Bank*, Eugen Brettauer and Moritz Pflaum. And to return to our start, even in the long lists of insignificant Christian directors which the *Erste Österreichische Sparkasse* sported, one invariably finds hidden away in some crucial corner a Wilhelm Boschan, an Arminio Cohn or a Gustav Figdor.

All told, thus, the aggregated leadership lists of the Vienna banks give a deceptive image of where in Vienna power and wealth really lay. These are not lists of leading stockholders, or of the truly rich, but often of straw men selected so as to disguise (to mix a metaphor) how the strings were actually pulled.

To round up this survey of why it is so difficult to identify and define Jewish wealth in late nineteenth century Vienna, suffice it to mention three major facts about how industry, the greatest modern source of wealth, was run in Habsburg Austria. It is crucial to know first, that despite the appearance there in the later 1850s of the characteristic modern form of industrial organization, the joint-stock company, most Austrian industries remained firmly in family hands until after the first World War. The reason for this was the tax system: the state actually discriminated against companies which went public.[43] As a result, most of Austria's industrial wealth remained well concealed from the public eye!

43 Richard Rudolph, *Banking and Industrialization in Austria-Hungary* (Cambridge, 1976), p. 103.

Whereas in other European countries economic historians can locate who the principal industrialists were, by aggregating the directorships of the leading industrial joint-stock companies, not so here!

Secondly, in those companies which did go public, the cult of aristocrats was even more pronounced than in the banks. This practice was especially true of the railroad joint-stock companies, which were set up as public companies in the *Gründerzeit* and formed the basis for the enormous stock market speculation of the 1860s. If one aggregates the directorships of the railroads for the crucial year 1873, for example, together with those of the other then extant industrial joint-stock companies, one finds stacks of titled Christian nonentities, whereas by all account it was the Richard Jeitteleses, the Jacob Jakobis, the Victor von Ofenheims and the Johann Herzes, who were Jewish, who actually ran the show. The railroad directorships simply do not reveal who had the actual wealth, much less the power; and in addition, most of these companies were removed from the public sphere in the 1880s through nationalization.

Then thirdly, in studying Austrian industrial leaderships of the late Monarchial period, one runs once again into the bankers. The most glaring demonstration of their prevalence on the industrial scene is an aggregation of 408 holders of Austrian industrial directorships listed in the the great business directory, the *Compass* of 1917, a year chosen because many industrial concerns had by then finally gone public. To compose this aggregate (Table 4), I culled the directors of all the industrial companies listed as having more than nominal investment capital. Then, in a search for "great industrialists," I determined from the *Compass* volume's index which of the 408 directors were multiple directors—in other words which held more than seven simultaneous directorships. There were 112 of these, and they held up to 45 directorships each. The schema resulting from this extensive aggregation of names proved that although Bohemia and Moravia were the industrial heartlands of the Empire, 254 of the directors lived in Vienna, as opposed to 71 from Bohemia and 17 from Moravia. Next it appeared that 79 of the 112 multiple directors lived in Vienna, as opposed to 15 and 2 respectively from Bohemia and Moravia. Finally, when the 112 multiple directors were studied in detail, it turned out that with few exceptions they were bank employees, or closely associated with the great banks.

It was nice to learn from this aggregate that Jews held 130 of the 408 industrial directorships overall in the Austrian half of the dual Monarchy, about 33% of these slots; that in Vienna they held 96 out of 254, well over 33%; and that among the multiple directors they held both overall and in Vienna about 50% of the slots. This knowledge cannot compensate, however, for the disappointment one feels on learning that truly important Jewish industrialists of old Austria, Max Bondy, the "copper king," for example, or Robert Fuchs, the paper magnate, or Fritz Mandl of the Hirtenberg Munitions factory, do not figure on the list; and that the Petschek brothers are not multiple directors. The aggregate does little more than confirm that the industrial joint-stock companies in Austria were overwhelmingly in the hands of the banks.

Table 4: Industrial Stock Company Directors, 1917

	Aristocrats	Nobles		Non-nobles		Total		Together
		Jewish	Christian	Jewish	Christian	Jewish	Christian	
A. All Directors								
Vienna	10	25	42	71	106	96	158	254
Bohemia	4	2	9	10	46	12	59	71
Moravia & Silesia	-	3	3	1	10	4	13	17
Galicia	1	1	3	1	2	2	6	8
Styria & Carinthia	2	1	10	-	8	1	20	21
Triest	-	1	2	-	7	1	9	10
Other	1	-	1	-	2	-	4	4
Hungary	-	7	5	7	4	14	9	23
Totals	18	40	75	90	185	130	278	408
B. Directors with Seven or More Directorships								
Vienna	2	10	17	27	23	37	42	79
Bohemia	1	-	6	2	6	2	13	15
Moravia & Silesia	-	1	-	1	-	2	-	2
Galicia	-	-	-	-	1	-	1	1
Styria & Carinthia	-	-	-	-	-	-	-	0
Triest	-	-	1	-	2	-	3	3
Other	-	-	-	-	-	-	-	-
Hungary	-	4	2	6	-	10	2	12
Totals	3	15	26	36	32	51	61	112

This table is based on the directorships of all the sizeable industrial JSCs listed in the Austrian *Compass* for 1917. 38 foreigners (including 25 Germans) are omitted.
Converts are listed under "Jewish".

Before concluding, let us note that we have learned one valuable thing from our discussion of all these sources: the conditions here brought to light are subtly suggestive of some important qualities of wealth, and perhaps especially of

Jewish wealth, in Vienna at the end of the imperial period. Just as in the older periods, Jewish wealth had an "administrative" parameter, so now it was exceedingly, let us say, "manipulative". We will discuss the significance of this manipulative quality at greater length below.

In general, we have learned that whoever seeks to study the Jewish holders of wealth in late nineteenth and early twentieth century Vienna will find the available sources in many ways frustrating. It is extremely difficult to pinpoint the substantial body of wealthy Jews who were converts. In addition, the public institutions of the city tended not to place rich people or Jews in their lead. The banks tended to flaunt social prominence while systematically concealing Jewish power and wealth. In the publicly held industrial companies, the actual stockholders tended to hide behind their bankers. And overwhelmingly modern industrial wealth remained concealed in private hands. These, in general, are what makes it necessary to approach our subject—Jewish wealth in Vienna in its last period—on a very broad, "macro" scale.

V

What were the peculiarities of Viennese Jewish wealth in the last seven decades of the Habsburg Empire? In the following we will report on a card-collection concerning 173 Jewish businessmen whose names appear on the directorship lists of 1913 and 1917, described in Tables 3 and 4 above. We will call it Collection B to distinguish it from another, Collection A, which includes about 300 names from the lists of 1858-1900 from Table 3, but which will not be analysed here. The Collection B cards are filled out with data about family and individual career patterns, and also property holdings, taken from obituaries, from the death and ennoblement records in the Vienna archives, and from secondary literature. The cards fall far short of providing uniform information about the people involved, but they seem sufficiently comprehensive to suggest real answers to the questions we ask. We will analyse them here in conjunction with the tabulation according to profession that the Vienna *Kultusgemeinde* published about its 866 highest tax-payers in 1910.

What were the characteristics of Jewish wealth in the city over this long period? The first and most unequivocal answer must be from start to finish, continuity through inheritance. This is not to say that there was absolute continuity. Just as by 1800 the name of Oppenheimer, the leading Viennese Jew of 1700, was for natural causes disappearing from the lists of the tolerated Jews, so one finds very few of the important names of 1800 (Leidesdorfer, Hönig and

Arnstein, for example) even on the last toleree list, published in 1846.[44] All the more rare are such names on the *Kultusgemeinde* list of 1910; nor does one find on this last list many of the Hofmannsthals, Königswarters, Wodianers and Brandeis-Weikersheims who led Viennese commerce in 1850. It is worth noting, however, that the name Wertheimer, the second great Vienna Jewish name of 1700, was present still in great strength on the toleree lists of both 1800 and 1847, and that the family did not really die out until 1908. Correspondingly, the Rothschilds were the leading Vienna Jewish family both in business and in society from 1816 until 1938. And then there were the Gomperzes.

This extraordinary family had first appeared in Vienna in the early eighteenth century. It renewed its wealth through a *Grosshandlung* at Brno during the *Vormärz*; entrenched itself in Vienna towards mid-century with marriages into the Wertheimstein, Todesco, Sichrowsky and Auspitz families, whence it gained links to the Königswarter, Lieben, Schnapper, Schey, Paul Schiff and Springer families and many others. The Gomperzes and their relatives thereupon dominated Jewish Vienna socially throughout the late-Habsburg decades. They dominated in economics also: a Gomperz was president of the *Creditanstalt* until his death in 1913; a Lieben was president of the Vienna Stock Exchange and simultaneously vice-governor of the Austro-Hungarian Bank in that year; and there were two other Liebens, an Auspitz, a Springer, several Schiffs, and a Schey very prominent in the Vienna business world in 1913.

There were other such great clans in turn-of-the century Jewish Vienna that advertised inherited family wealth, for example, the Mauthners.[45] The fact of the matter is that the old *Hoffaktoren* left their riches in part to the Viennese *Tolerierten* whom their children married. These last did the same for the wealthy *Gründer* of the 1860s, many of whose children and in-laws were still wealthy and prominent in 1918. When one studies the 173 businessmen in our "B" collection, one may observe that 16% of them can be traced directly to *Tolerierten* families. Another 20% were born in Vienna only shortly after mid-century. Further 56% of the 173 businessmen in the group were not "self-made men", but had wealthy fathers.

There were limits to this continuity of old Jewish wealth, of course. For example, on the list of highest tax payers in the *Kultusgemeinde* in 1910, as

44 Conversion was also a major cause of name disappearance, of course. Thus the name Herz disappeared from the list between 1827 and 1834 because of conversion, while the names Sinzheim, Popper and Ettinger disappeared at the same time because the families had died out. The names Arnstein, Eskeles, Österreicher, Leidersdorfer, and Neuwall disappeared between the 1834 and 1846 lists, because of conversion; but the first two shortly afterwards died out.

45 For a recent account of the Mauthners, see my *History of Habsburg Jews*, pp. 175 ff.

noted earlier, only a small number of names, some 20 out of 866 (barely 2%), recall the *Tolerierten* and many of these even are just common names, not demonstrable descendants. This contrast between the *Kultusgemeinde* and our elite group seems explicable in terms of the substantial number of converts in Collection B—33% in all. In many cases, evidently, older accumulations of Jewish wealth descended into convert hands and gradually ceased to be "Jewish." Further, everywhere in Europe, of course, the periodic financial vicissitudes of the late nineteenth century led to the erosion of accumulations of wealth in families which were unwilling to change. Vienna was no exception: the most characteristic mid-nineteenth century form of wealth in the city, the private *Grosshändler* bankhouse, was notoriously becoming obsolete as early as the 1890s.[46] By 1910 even Rothschild's private bank was having to share honors with the public banks.[47]

Table 5: Bankers and Industrialists, 1913-1917

A. Place of Origin

Total	Vienna		Bohemia	Moravia	Galicia	Other	Hungary	Germany	Unknown
	Tolerated	Other				Cisleithania			
173	27	35	28	27	3	4	16	7	26
100%	16%	20%	16%	16%	2%	2%	9%	4%	15%

B. Status

Total	Jewish	Convert	Rich parent	Ennobled	Land	House
173	112 (65%)	57 (33%)	97 (56%)	57 (33%)	45 (26%)	21 (12%)

Withall, it seems highly probable that continuity through inheritance was characteristic even of Jewish families, because as is often noted in the memoir literature, the late-Habsburg period despite its seemingly bustling political movement, basically witnessed unprecedented long-term political and social

46 See the elegant obituary of Philipp Thorsch in the *Neue Freie Presse*, 30 September 1905, p. 13; the memoir about the Thorsch family in the Hirschfeld MS conserved at the Leo Baeck Institute in New York, and Heinrich Benedikt, *Damals im alten Österreich* (Wien, 1979), pp. 55-56.

47 Cf. Eduard März, *Österreichische Industrie- und Bankpolitik in der Zeit Franz Josephs I.* (Wien, 1968), pp. 352 ff.

stability. It left contemporaries feeling that nothing ever changed.[48] It was an ideal era for the slow regular transmission of wealth from generation to generation. Moreover, one may balance one's awareness of the wealth erosion problem with further data from the "B" collection. Fifty-seven of the 173 businessmen in the collection (one-third) were ennobled by 1918; and one may look at their socially elegant marriage patterns for extensive further confirmation of how significant inherited wealth was in that old world. Since 77 persons among the 866 *Kultusgemeinde* members (9% in all) were ennobled, and thus comparably involved in the world of dynasty-building, one may deduce that wealthy confessional Vienna Jews considered the inheritance of wealth important too.

What did they inherit? Judging from our card collection "A" (which we do not fully analyse here), one of the characteristics of the wealth belonging to Viennese Jews throughout the final third of the nineteenth century was its emergence from a specific episode—or rather cluster of episodes: the great boom of the so-called *Gründerzeit*, 1855-1873, which began, as is well known, with the establishment of the joint-stock company railroads and banks in the 1850s by Anselm von Rothschild and a very small circle of colleagues. Literally within ten years the Vienna market, whose staples had hitherto been state bonds, letters of credit to aristocrats, grain and textile wares, became the scene of frenzied trading in abstract paper values. Fortunes which refused to adapt, most notably the old Arnstein and Eskeles banking fortune, were destroyed or obliged to retire. Others, which were reckless (whose owners, in other words, like Gustav Epstein, over-speculated) went under. A good part of the older Vienna Jewish elite got onto the crest of the speculative wave, however. The Gomperzes and their many relatives were especially successful in this respect, and the boom swept them to stupendous new wealth.

Further, a main phenomenon of the *Gründerzeit* episode was a vast influx from the provinces of new young and eager Jewish aspirants for wealth. Some made it—in this category fall virtually every one of the great bankers who were winding up their careers on the eve of the first World War: Julius Herz, Eugen Minkus, Karl Morawetz, Bernhard Popper, and Theodor Taussig, for example. Others did not make it, but all contributed to making stock-holdings a basic element in the wealth of the Vienna elite. The investors suffered a bitter experience at the end of the boom—the crash of 1873—and came out cautious; but stocks now for better or worse were "in," and these could be and were passed on.

48 Cf. Albert Fuchs, *Geistige Strömungen aus Österreich* (Wien, 1978), p. v.

Coincidentally with the *Gründer*'s stock boom, wealthy Vienna Jews began to acquire another new currency, as it were, which could be passed on: land. In general central European Jews acquired the legal right to buy land during the revolutions of 1848-1849. But still at the end of the 1850s there was a certain danger: shortly after 1848, for example, one of the Todesco brothers purchased an estate, yet then found his ownership challenged because in the so-called neo-absolutist decade of the fifties, in several regions of the Empire, the law on Jewish land-holding remained unclear.[49] Only after 1859 did the great political turn to liberalism put an end to the uncertainty, releasing the elastic craving for land that we have noted earlier. Just at that same time the authorities in Vienna launched a considerable boom in urban real estate by opening to development the *Glacis* between the Inner City and its suburbs. At that point virtually all the members of the Gomperz clan, and a great many of the leading stock-brokers of the day, threw themselves vigorously into the purchase and construction of palaces on the *Ringstrasse,* where they could hob-nob with the Kaiser himself and (in theory) with the aristocracy of the past.[50] Some of these same people, for example Baron Königswarter and numbers of less ostentatious Jewish speculators, went more broadly into house acquisition. Because Vienna housing was not always profitable, however, real estate may have figured less in accumulations of Jewish wealth than one might expect. Meanwhile, a number of the wealthiest Vienna Jews, following the Rothschilds, acquired provincial estates. The Biedermanns, the Springers, the Königswarters, the Oppenheimers and the Gutmanns in particular acquired huge latifundia. Other Vienna Jewish families contracted marriages with Hungarian or Moravian Jews who were buying estates for business purposes. In the 1870s and 1880s a whole cluster of such people appeared in the capital in connection with the lumber business, which fed the construction boom. Others came as representatives of the important Moravian and West Hungarian sugar-refining industry, which by 1890 had made Austria-Hungary one of the world's major sugar producers. It is suggestive of the mark these last sorts of land acquisition made on Vienna, that almost 13% of our "B" collection businessmen were involved in the sugar and wood-processing industries (Table 6).

In such fashion, estate-holding became important for Jews in Vienna. Further by 1900 it had become commonplace for Vienna Jews (like middle class Christians) to own smaller country properties, or villas at Semmering or Baden or Ischl. The record speaks for itself. Of the *Gründer* in our "A" collection,

49 See the documentation in Haus- Hof- und Staatsarchiv, KZ 1858, K-19, 3663.

50 The record of purchases on the *Glacis* is published in Franz Baltzarek, Alfred Hofmann and Hannes Stekl, *Wirtschaft und Gesellschaft der Wiener Stadterweiterung* (Wiesbaden, 1975).

virtually everyone of importance made an investment in land. Of the 173 people on our List "B", at least 26% seem to have been owners or sharers of larger

Table 6: The Banker and Industrialist Elite by Occupations, 1917

Total	Fathers	Education of Sons	Sons
Börse	13		2
Banking	9	56	75
Agricultural Trade	7		
Textile Trade	18		2
Other Trades	2		
Leather	2		
Sugar	6		13
Distilling / Oil	12		6
Paper	0		9
Glass	1		1
Chemicals	1		5
Coal	3		5
Machines	2		3
Electricity	1		3
Textile Manufacturing	25		17
Shipping	2		1
Railroads	1		1
Law	4	14	8
Engineering	0	6	
University	1	20	5
Land	1		3
Unknown	61 (35%)		0

estates. Another 12% seem to have been substantial Vienna house owners. One must be cautious in assessing the impact of real property on Jewish wealth. Of the 866 Vienna *Kultusgemeinde* highest tax-payers who listed their professions in 1910, only twelve gave their profession as "real estate," only two chose to call themselves "houseowners," and only eight flaunted their possession of estates—in all, 2.5% of the highest tax-payers (Table 7). Patently wealthy confessional Jews were not inclined then to boast of their real estate holdings, and indeed, one may doubt whether in that Christian city, Jewish landlording was all that important. But, to suggest the other side of the coin, we may repeat that 60 of those tax-payers were ennobled in Austria, and 17 others were ennobled in agricultural Hungary. Insofar as nobility still implied in 1910 at least token connection with the land, these ennoblements amounting to about 9% of the total make the minimalist real estate listings in the *Kultusgemeinde* seem deceptive.

Let us turn now to a third major element in the wealth of rich Vienna Jews in the late imperial period, the profits from industry. We may note in passing that in terms of occupation, as in the *Vormärz*, so in the *Gründerzeit*, the prime occupation of Vienna Jewry was still trade, and accumulations of wealth from trade certainly formed a significant part of what was passed from one generation to the next—and of what each new generation earned. Significantly, a major joint-stock company in 1917 was based on the great department store of the Gerngross family in the Mariahilfe Strasse. Even in the *Gründer* period, however, industry, reflecting the new capitalist era, was playing a greater role than before in the Vienna Jewish occupational picture. By the turn of the century the picture was changing rapidly. On the *Kultusgemeinde* list of 1910, 272 highest tax-payers were still in trade (31%), but 282 (32.6%) were now in industry, and it was presumptively in industry that the greatest quantities of accumulated property were now being passed on.

We may refine this generalization. As in western Europe, so in Austria throughout the eighteenth and early nineteenth centuries, textiles were the leading sector in the rapidly advancing industrial revolution. First the woolens manufacturies at Brno in Moravia, then the cotton industry of Prague and the Sudetenland, finally the clothing industry at Vienna were the bases whence industrialization overflowed into other branches of manufacturing.

We have earlier noted the beginnings of the Jewish involvement in Austrian textiles: Jews had even in the eighteenth century been important in the commerce, as opposed to the manufacture of textiles. In the early nineteenth century Jews were pioneers in the development of cotton manufacturing at Prague. In the *Vormärz* when the textile emporium shifted to Vienna, Jews there increasingly found it possible to move into manufacturing. Indeed, as we have noted, those who rose from agricultural or textile trading to real wealth were usually those who took to operating a factory, and most often a textile factory. In the *Gründerzeit,* when so much wealth was being formed in railroads and construction companies, the Gomperzes themselves, and large numbers of the speculators who came to Vienna from the Bohemian Crownlands, were still making their money substantially through textile manufacturing, and actually came to the capital because it was a textile emporium. After 1870 they made Vienna the center for the whole Monarchy's clothing manufacture (though of course textiles were by now only one among several leading branches of Austrian industry). By the turn of the century some of the greatest figures in Austrian textile manufacturing were Jews: Leopold Pollack von Parnegg, for example, and Max Mandl, Isidor Mauthner, and the Brunner family of Trieste.

Table 7: Highest Taxpayers in the *Kultusgemeinde*, 1910: Professional Composition[51]

Property	
Privatier	72
House-owner	2
Real estate	12
Estate owner	7
Land renter	1
total 10.9%	*94*
Money	
Insurance	10
Bank official	31
Private banker	39
Grosshändler	18
Bookmaker	3
Börse	21
Prokurist	1
Apothecary	5
Commis	8
Agent	1
total 15.2%	*132*
Manufacture	
Industrialist	12
Coal	9
Iron/Steel	7
Machines	3
Oil	8
Sugar	15
Mill	6
Distiller	14
Wood processing	19
Construction	14
Textiles	102
Clothing	13
Leather	14
Chemicals	9
Electricity	7
Glass	6
Baskets/Umbrellas	5
Food processing	12
Publishing	7
total 32.6 %	*282*

Professions	
Military	1
Medicine	12
Law	1
Judge	1
Architect	2
Art/ Music	2
Writer/Journal	2
Academics	17
Public Administration	2
Engineer	5
Railroad official	1
Student	1
total 9.9%	*86*
Trade	
Metal/Iron	9
Trade in general	1
Spediteur	14
Antiquities/Art/Photo	4
Coal	7
Tailor	2
Machinery	1
Colonial wares	1
Textiles	33
Leather/Feathers	13
Manufactured wares	9
Wood	20
Sugar	20
Wine	6
Produce	46
Tobacco	4
Livestock	5
Clothing	40
Rugs	1
Furniture	2
Books	2
Pianos/Clocks	5
Rubber goods	5
Restaurant	2
Jewels	18
Vienna goods	16
total 31.4%	*272*
Grand total	*866*

51 Based on *Verzeichnis der im Wiener Gemeindegebiete wohnhaften höher besteuerten Wähler* (Wien, 1910).

One may easily observe the impact of this involvement in the textile industry on the wealth of rich Jews in Vienna. It seems significant, for example, that the largest single category of the fathers of our earlier twentieth century elite, at least 25% were in the textile business, and at least 14.5% were actually textile manufacturers. (These are uncertain figures, of course, because paternal occupation is known in only 65% of all cases; see Table 6.) Of the business elite itself, 10% were textile manufacturers. In the 1910 *Kultusgemeinde*, 13.2% of the higher tax payers were in textile fabrication (Table 7). This was the largest single professional category by far in the *Kultusgemeinde*. Another 8% were in the commerce of textiles and clothing. Obviously textile manufacturing had made and was making an important contribution to the wealth of Vienna Jewry.

One may make an important further distinction here, however. The wealthy Viennese were involved in the furthering of the textile industry not just in and around their own city, and in the provinces, but in certain provinces. Whereas in mid-century their factories had dotted Hungary as well as in the Austrian Crownlands; and whereas back then people like the Goldbergers, the Kanitzes and the Kerns, who manufactured textiles in Pest, were eagerly coming to establish their sales outlets in the Empire's leading city; now the Hungarian connection had lapsed. The explanation is obvious: since the Austro-Hungarian *Ausgleich* in 1867, Budapest had become first a political, then an economic rival of Vienna in so far as the development of Greater Hungary was concerned.

Here we may observe for the first time the extent to which Vienna Jewry, over 40% Hungarian in origin in the 1870s, had become by 1900 a "merely Cisleithian" Jewry in its interests and wealth. It is indicative of this new relationship that of our 1917 Jewish "industrial" elite, only 9% were born in Hungary, in contrast to the 31% from the Bohemian Crownlands. In the Vienna *Kultusgemeinde* in 1910 only 7.7% gave their *"Heimat"* as Hungary, as opposed to the 63.4% from Lower Austria and the 21.4% from the Bohemian Crownlands.[52] All in all these figures confirm the probability that towards the end of the monarchial era, Vienna Jewry's wealth, whether derived from textiles or otherwise, was much more distinctly Cisleithian than before.

Once we leave the textile industry, and turn to the other great branches of industry which flourished in Austria towards the start of this century, to iron and steel and weapons, to glass and chemicals and oil, we find a different record of Jewish involvement from that in textiles. The machine industries in particular were overwhelmingly in "Christian" hands. Further, the greatest figures in Austrian industrial history, from Schoeller in the *Vormärz* to Skene and Miller von Aichholz in the *Gründer* period, and to Skoda towards the end, were all

52 See the figures in Rozenblit, *Jews of Vienna*, p. 20.

Christians. Karl Wittgenstein, the "Jew" who became towards the turn of the century Austria's steel magnate, was born of convert parents and owed his success in industry, probably, to the team of Christian collaborators which he drew together.

This is far from suggesting that there were no Jews in the history of Austrian industrial development outside textiles: to prove the contrary, one needs only mention the role of Rothschild in the financing, and of many other Jews in the construction of the railroads; the pivotal importance within the iron and steel industry of the Rothschild industrial complex at Witkowitz, and within the coal mining industry early on of the Gutmann and later of the Petschek family enterprises. When it comes to generalizing, however, one may recognize that Jewry's involvement in Austrian industry outside of textiles was much less a matter of direct participation, than of indirect control through the great banks, which we have encountered before.

As others have very competently recounted, these banks were founded in the 1850s and 1860s, and initially involved themselves extensively in industrial enterprise.[53] However, burned by the great stock market crash of 1873, they tended during the critical last three decades of the nineteenth century to abstain from industrial activity. This was surely not just because the bank directors were archly conservative and distrustful of innovation, but also because of the sheer limitations in Europe's age of imperial capitalism, of the Vienna capital market. Withall, the bankers' policy had notable effects. On the one hand, it struck many observers (for example, Wittgenstein) as a strangling factor that held back the industrial growth of the Cisleithian lands. On the other hand, it contributed to the emergence of a strong alternative industrial center in Hungary; for paradoxically, the banks were willing to trust the Budapest government, and government-backed Hungarian industrial concerns. Perhaps the restrictive policy contributed also to the emergence of a Czech national economy alongside the under-financed German-Austrian industrial economy in the Bohemian Lands. Thereupon, after 1900 with the entire great Habsburg imperial order fractured, some of the great banks went to an opposite extreme. They turned to encouraging new industries adventurously.

Throughout the half century of their existence, whether strangling industry or over-encouraging it, these banks had an unusually close, paternal relationship with those industrial concerns which they did help. They did not just lend money against guarantees so that others might use it: when they made a loan, they

53 See in particular the lucid account in Richard Rudolph, *Banking and Industrialisation*, ch. 5. Compare März, *Österreichische Industrie- und Bankpolitik* and most recently David Good, *The Economic Rise of the Habsburg Empire, 1750-1914* (Berkeley, California, 1984).

supervised it—in other words they became deeply involved in industrial management itself. The bankers in Vienna to a large degree took over, cartelized and manipulated the firms in which their investments were placed. This was what led to the anomalous situation that interests us here, and which we have already encountered in the previous section of this paper. By the turn of the century, the leading industrial directors of the Empire turned out to be above all Vienna bankers, and among them above all Jewish bankers. Typically, of the 173 Jewish businessmen in our "industrial" elite group of 1910-1917, 43.3% were bankers, whereas only 36% were directly in industrial management.

Who were these Jewish bankers? Were they really rich, or were they just bureaucrats acting not just in the name of, but at the behest of wealthy stockholders? One can only give a mixed answer. Some of them, like the various Vienna leaders of the Rothschild house, or like Max Gomperz were clearly rich in their own right. Others, like Theodor Taussig or after him Rudolf Sieghardt of the *Bodencreditanstalt* came from the lowest social orders. It is relevant that 35% of our group simply failed to leave any public record of who their fathers were.[54] But however humble their beginnings, and however most of them lived out lackluster lives working their way up the hierarchy of just one employing institution, they all became well-to-do, because Vienna bankers, once they approached the top, were eminently well paid. Further, thanks to the paternal relationship of the banks to the objects of investment, all these men dealt not just in money, but in power. They all controlled a great deal more property than they owned, particularly industrial property. Though they were employees, though they were on salary, even the most bureaucratically minded of them had at his disposition manipulative instruments that would have been the envy of the Oppenheimers of the past.

They all, thus, manifested the final characteristic we will attribute here to Jewish wealth in Vienna early in this century. This wealth involved access to power over broad areas of Austria's new industrial complex, which Jews did not actually own.

VI

To sum up, Jewish wealth in Vienna changed very considerably over the two centuries we have surveyed in this paper. Initially it was held by a very small number of people who came above all from the German *Reich*. This wealth was built initially and most adventurously by the Court factors of the late seventeenth century, and was maintained through money lending. It was the wealth of the

54 Cf. the findings of Michel Bernard, *Banques et banquiers*, pp. 314 ff.

landless, and involved considerable "administrative" element and these Jews possessed the private credit and the executive relations capable of meeting great administrative tasks.

Later on, in the first half of the nineteenth century, Jewish wealth in Vienna became in many ways Hungarian: an increasingly important number of its bearers came from Hungary and made their leap upwards through business relating to the agrarian Hungarian Great Plain. *Reich* Germans continued to arrive, particularly after the banking boom of the Napoleonic era. Bohemians and Moravians came with the emergence of Vienna as a textile emporium. Still, it was the Hungarian connection that then gave the wealth of the Vienna Jews its élan. Moreover, in this period the landlessness of the past gradually began to change, and the special administrative skill required of the *Hoffaktoren* ceased to set Jews apart.

Thereupon in the final period of the Monarchy, the wealth of the Vienna Jews settled down to become very nearly the opposite of what it had been at the start. Now to a significant extent it became inherited wealth, with real property playing a substantial, though hardly dominant role. It had many modern aspects, deriving as it did from the speculative boom of the 1860s and the steadily blossoming textile sector of Austria's industrial revolution. It was much more narrowly focused, however, less Hungarian, less German, much more Cisleithian in terms both of its bearers and its investments. The great private administrative networks once possessed by the wealthiest Vienna Jews now gave way to the great public power instruments represented by the Vienna great banks which were controlled by Jews.

Two recently published memoirs suggest how these mighty changes affected the fate of the wealthy Jews of Vienna in the twentieth century. The first was written by Valentin Sobotka, the scion of a prosperous Bohemian malt-producing family that lived in Vienna from the 1880s until the 1940s.[55] It tells above all of the impact of World War I, which through taxation, inflation and administrative collapse wiped out a great deal of the money that central European Jews had accumulated during the preceding century. By 1920, Sobotka tells, his family had literally nothing to eat. Yet like so many of the people we have surveyed, this family possessed land: an estate with summer villas in western Austria, factory properties in Lower Austria and Bohemia, houses in Vienna and apartments. And on the basis of this real property, which contrasted so with the mobile wealth of the Jews of the *Hoffaktor* past, the Sobotkas not only survived, but when political conditions settled down, prospered again. Because they had land, they were able to weather the first great central European

55 Valentin Sobotka, *Ways and Issues Retraced* (Berkeley, California, 1980).

catastrophe of the twentieth century and to remain middle class. Perhaps this was true of a great deal of Vienna Jewish wealth during and between the wars

The second memoir is actually a novel written by an Englishman, David Pryce-Jones,[56] but the author is the great-grandson of Baron Gustav Springer, one of the major figures of Vienna's *Gründerzeit*, and the book, while not strictly family-biographical, is based on highly interesting, insider research into the Springer family history. To a considerable extent it underlines the lessons of Sobotka's story. Old Ellingen, as the family-founder is called in the book, started as a penniless orphan who quite fortuitously managed to go to school. Adopted by a prominent Vienna *Grosshändler* he entered the stock market in the 1860s, bought a locomotive factory cheap after the crash of 1873, and made millions. He then purchased land in Upper Austria on which to expand the factory, in the *Wienerwald* on which to build an extravagant villa, and in Hungary on which to breed his racehorses and spend the summer. He trained his spinsterly only daughter to succeed himself as head of the firm, and bought her a wealthy French homosexual husband to produce him an heir. Then in 1916, apprehending his coming end, he patriotically, though irrationally converted his large horde of Swiss Franks into Austrian currency. He died coincidentally with Franz Joseph, leaving the daughter to watch the money become utterly worthless.

Ellingen's daughter had quite as much success as did the Sobotka family in surviving the postwar crisis. She had land all over the place and a factory: by the mid-1920s she was wealthy again. Then came the crunch of 1938. She was travelling abroad when the *Anschluss* came, so she did not have to buy her life. No matter. The factory was in the hands of its bank-director shareholders. The Nazis removed the Jews among them, and suddenly she was almost as superfluous as they were to the functioning of the industrial machine.

Like so many of the wealthy Jews in early twentieth century Vienna, the Ellingens were immensely vulnerable once they and their friends lost command of the bank administrations. These modern tools were not their property, and bring to mind a sad contrast. In 1683, Samuel Oppenheimer was let out of prison as the Turks approached Vienna, because Kaiser Leopold abruptly recognized that he, the Emperor, had no one else on whom to rely for the administration of the war. Unlike the administrative apparatus of the Ellingens, Oppenheimer's was his own; and he survived, whereas they did not.

56 David Pryce-Jones, *The Afternoon Sun* (New York, 1986).

The Occupational Structure of Hungarian Jewry in the Eighteenth and Twentieth Centuries

László Katus

Really reliable and detailed data about the occupational and social structure of Jews in Hungary can be found only in the censuses of the twentieth century from 1900 to 1930. But already the censuses of Jews (*Conscriptiones Judaeorum*) in the eighteenth century attempted to register the occupational distribution of the Jewish families living in Hungary. Consequently, we can essay a comparison of these two periods and suggest some of the factors which would explain the particular occupational structure of Hungarian Jewry.

I

Table 1 shows the results of the census of 1768, which covered the whole territory of Hungary proper, excluding Croatia, Transylvania and the Banat. This census registered 5440 Jewish families in 35 counties of Hungary.[1] The census of 1768 gives useful data about the occupational distribution of 3754 Jewish families. The numbers show that 48.2 percent of the Hungarian Jewish families derived their living from different branches of trade. But only in the case of 803 out of 1809 trading families does the census go into detail about the kind of merchandise they specialized in. The majority of these merchants traded in several kinds of goods. The number of Jewish itinerant pedlars was also large. Most of the specialized traders dealt in leather, wool, textiles and clothing. Innkeeping and distillery were also characteristic Jewish occupations: nine and seventeen percent of Jewish families respectively were engaged in these activities, mostly in the northern and eastern counties of Hungary.

The number of artisans altogether did not exceed that of the distillers; the majority of them were butchers and tailors. Besides trading, distilling,

1 *Magyar-Zsidó Oklevéltár* [Monumenta Hungariae Judaica], 18 vols., ed. by Sándor Scheiber, vol. XVI (Budapest, 1974), pp. 19-20.

innkeeping and craftsmanship, the main source of income for the Jewish families was leasing certain rights from the landlords. The landlords held the monopoly on milling the peasants' corn; distilling strong liquors, brewing beer and selling these beverages at the local tavern; as well as retailing their own wine throughout the year. In many cases these rights were leased to Jews.

The census of 1768 shows that in eighteenth century Hungary, Jews were free to enter only certain branches of the economy. They were, as a rule, forbidden to reside in the royal free cities, to own landed property and to practice many occupations. Consequently, Jews were not to be found in the main sector of the traditional Hungarian economy, agriculture, which provided about 90 percent of total employment and about 80 percent of the national product.

On the other hand, they played a great role—in the second half of the eighteenth century already a leading role—in trading in agricultural products and later in their industrial processing. In the last third of the eighteenth century, they gradually took over the place of the so called "Greek" merchants in the commerce of Hungary. In the county of Sopron, for example, the number of the non-Jewish merchants did not reach half of the number of Jewish traders.

The census of 1768 indicates that the majority of the Jewish families lived in the western and northwestern counties of Hungary (Nyitra, Pozsony, Trencsén, Mosony, Sopron, Vas, Veszprém). The reason for this regional distribution was due to immigration: Jews came to Hungary mainly from Bohemia, Moravia and Germany. We can observe some differences in the occupational structure of the Jewish families living in the western and in the eastern counties of Hungary. Those living in the West were mainly traders and artisans. The Jews in the East, on the other hand, were mostly distillers and innkeepers.

Comparing the 1768 census with the censuses of 1900 and 1910 we can see that significant changes occurred during those 140 years in the number of Jews, their territorial distribution and their occupational structure.[2]

Between 1785 and 1900 the number of Jews increased from roughly 80,000 to 831,000, from 1% to 5% of Hungary's population. Their geographical distribution also changed significantly. In 1768, 70 percent of the Jewish families lived in Transdanubia and in northwest Hungary. In 1900, however, we find only 20 percent of the Jewish population in these regions. Forty percent lived in the eastern and northeastern counties and 30 percent resided in Budapest

2 *A magyar szent korona országainak 1900. évi népszámlálása* [The Census of 1900 in the Lands of the Hungarian Crown]; *A népesség foglalkozása az anyanyelvvel és a hitfelekezettel egybevetve* [Occupations related to mother tongue and denomination] (Budapest, 1906); *A magyar szent korona országainak 1910. évi népszámlálása* [The Census of 1910 in the Lands of the Hungarian Crown], vol. IV, (Budapest, 1915).

Table 1: The Occupational distribution of Jews in Hungary in 1768
(without Croatia, Transylvania and the Banat)

Occupational groups	number of families	%
Tradesmen (*quaestores*) in specified goods		
in leather	228	6.07
in textile	55	1.47
in wool	53	1.41
in articles of clothing	37	.99
in tobacco	38	1.01
in flour and foodstuffs	19	.51
in wine	12	.32
in live-stock	7	.19
in small wares	348	9.27
in other articles	6	16
Total tradesmen with specified goods	803	21.39
Tradesmen in unspecified goods	393	10.47
Merchants (*mercatores*)	308	8.20
Pedlars (*quaestores pagatim ambulantes*)	305	8.12
Total tradesmen and merchants	1809	48.19
Lessees, licensees (*arendatores*):		
of village inns	104	2.77
of distilleries	59	1.57
of breweries	47	1.25
of butcheries	30	.80
of other unspecified leases	98	2.61
Total lessees and licensees	348	9.27
Innkeepers	291	7.75
Artisans (*artifices, opifices*):		
butchers	204	5.43
tailors	182	4.85
furriers	88	2.34
glaziers	52	1.39
shoemakers	15	.40
other artisans	114	3.04
Total artisans	655	17.45
Distillers	639	17.02
Total Jewish families	3754	100.00

and its environs. In the nineteenth century, the majority of Jews came to Hungary from Galicia. They first settled in the northeastern counties and towns and later moved westwards. By 1910 more than half of the Hungarian Jewry lived in towns, constituting 12.4 percent of the urban population. In the rural population, on the other hand, their share was only 3.1 percent. (These data relate to Hungary proper and exclude Croatia-Slavonia).

The most important changes in the occupational structure of the Jews were due to the abolition of the former prohibitions and restrictions. In the second half of the nineteenth century, as a consequence of emancipation, they appeared in agriculture as big landowners, capitalist lessees and bailiffs, and in a considerable number of free professions. The rapid economic growth, the modernization and industrialization of Hungary's economic and social structure, opened before Jews new fields of activity in various sectors of modern capitalist economy: in large-scale industry, in railway construction, in trading companies, in joint stock banking.

Despite all these changes, the "traditional" Jewish occupations of the eighteenth century—trading, innkeeping, craftsmanship—were still able to maintain their leading positions in the beginning of the twentieth century, although, of course, in forms adapted to the developing and industrializing modern economy.

II

The great amount of information provided by the censuses of 1900 and 1910 makes it possible to examine the occupational and social structure of Hungarian Jewry from different aspects. First, we can analyze the occupational structure of the Jews as a separate social group itself. Then we can make comparisons with other social groups living in the country, with the non-Jewish population or with different ethnic groups. Thirdly, we can examine the participation of Jews in each of the occupational and social groups. This share could be expressed in percentages or in the form of the so-called "index of participation". Fourthly, the data of these censuses covering the whole territory of historical Hungary before World War I allow us to trace the tendencies of change over time. The results of these different approaches are shown on the tables included in this paper. They speak for themselves and do not require much comment.

Table 2: Distribution of Jewish Population in Hungary by Social Groups in 1900 and 1910 (excluding Croatia)

	Active Population			Total Population		
	1900	1910	Index	1900	1910	Index
Landowners						
with 1000+ *hold*	322	315	98	948	926	98
with 100-1000 *hold*	1,971	1,956	99	6,225	5,641	9
Lessees with 100+ *hold*	2,897	2,515	87	9,745	8,431	87
Small landowners under 100 *hold*	16,102	11,063	69	46,823	31,525	67
Self-employed						
in industry	48,843	54,869	112	169,205	188,832	112
in trade and transport	62,684	71,708	114	234,257	259,428	111
Public officials and free professions	17,770	24,512	138	48,748	61,222	126
Clerks and employees in agriculture, industry, trade and transport	27,529	44,885	163	67,879	100,555	148
Army officers	259	263	102	584	605	104
Office attendants	3,288	3,143	96	13,215	12,627	96
Non-commissioned officers	1,262	891	71	2,095	1,588	76
Workers						
in agriculture and forestry	6,201	4,009	65	16,850	11,992	71
in industry	49,308	57,107	116	77,162	95,451	124
in trade and transport	38,012	39,993	105	56,786	61,376	108
Day laborers	8,469	5,057	105	23,932	15,015	63
Domestic servants	7,739	6,184	80	8,152	6,490	80
Soldiers	3,419	2,463	72	3,425	2,464	72
Rentiers and pensioners		12,225			25,960	
Others	15,190	3,598	24	45,131	21,099	47
Total	311,265	346,756	111	831,162	911,227	110

1 *hold* = 0.575 hectares = 1.43 acres

Table 3: Distribution of the Jewish Population in Hungary by Main Occupational Groups, 1900-1910 (excluding Croatia)

	Active Population			Total Population		
Occupational groups	1900	1910	Index	1900	1910	Index
Agriculture, forestry	30,212	22,504	75	89,837	67,064	75
Mining	220	382	174	617	971	157
Industry, manufacturing	105,140	126,224	120	261,317	314,526	120
Commerce and banking	108,859	128,246	118	302,384	346,067	114
Transport	9,438	11,064	117	31,725	35,529	112
Public service and free professions	21,058	27,655	131	61,963	73,849	119
Day laborers	8,469	5,057	60	23,932	15,015	63
Rentiers and pensioners		12,225			25,960	
Domestic service	7,739	6,184	80	8,152	6,490	80
Defence	4,940	3,617	73	6,104	4,657	76
Others	15,190	3,598	24	45,131	21,099	47
Total	311,265	346,756	111	831,162	911,227	110

Table 4: Occupational Structure of the Jewish and Non-Jewish Population in Hungary, 1900-1910

	Jews		Non-Jews	
Occupational groups	1900	1910	1900	1910
A. Active population				
Agriculture, forestry	9.71	6.49	68.28	62.57
Mining	.07	.11	.74	.89
Industry, handicraft	33.78	36.40	13.01	16.63
Commerce and banking	34.97	36.98	1.38	1.98
Transport and communications	3.03	3.19	1.59	2.36
Public service and free professions	6.77	7.98	2.40	3.02
Defence	1.59	1.04	1.55	1.60
Day laborers	2.72	1.46	3.74	2.67
Domestic service	2.49	1.78	4.93	4.86
Rentiers and pensioners		3.53		2.43
Others	4.88	1.04	2.39	.96
Total	100.00	100.00	100.00	100.00
B. Total population				
Agriculture, forestry	10.81	7.36	69.37	65.30
Mining	.07	.11	.95	1.07
Industry, handicraft	31.44	34.52	13.47	16.25
Commerce and banking	36.38	37.98	1.35	1.85
Transport and communications	3.82	3.90	2.32	3.13
Public service and free professions	7.46	8.10	2.89	3.21
Defence	.73	.51	.80	.81
Day laborers	2.88	1.65	3.64	2.53
Domestic service	.98	.71	2.47	2.30
Rentiers and pensioners		2.85		1.73
Others	5.43	2.32	2.75	1.78
Total	100.00	100.00	100.00	100.00

Table 5: Social Structure of the Jewish and Non-Jewish Population in Hungary, 1900-1910

A. Active population

	Jews		Non - Jews	
Social groups	1900	1910	1900	1910
Landowners with 100+ *hold*	.74	.66	.24	.25
Lessees with 100+ *hold*	.93	.73	.03	.04
Small landowners under 100 *hold*	5.18	3.19	41.23	38.18
Self-employed				
in industry	15.69	15.82	4.65	5.21
in trade and transport	20.14	10.68	.78	.92
Public officials and free professions	5.71	7.07	1.74	2.12
Clerks and employees in agriculture, industry, trade, banking and transport	8.85	12.94	.68	.99
Army officers	.08	.08	.11	.13
Office attendants	1.06	.94	.65	.90
Non-commissioned officers	.41	.26	.28	.32
Workers				
in agriculture and forestry	1.99	1.16	26.63	23.99
in industry	15.84	16.47	8.94	12.05
in trade and transport	12.21	11.53	1.80	2.71
Day laborers	2.72	1.46	3.74	2.67
Domestic servants	2.49	1.78	4.93	4.86
Soldiers	1.10	.71	1.17	1.16
Rentiers and pensioners		3.53		2.43
Others	4.88	1.04	2.39	.96
Total	100.00	100.00	100.00	100.00

Table 5: Social Structure of the Jewish and Non-Jewish Population in Hungary, 1900-1910 (continued)

B. Total population

	Jews		Non - Jews	
Social groups	1900	1910	1900	1910
Landowners with 100+ *hold*	.86	.72	.29	.28
Lessees with 100+ *hold*	1.17	.93	.04	.05
Small landowners under 100 *hold*	5.63	3.34	41.67	40.26
Self-employed				
in industry	20.36	20.72	6.64	7.01
in trade and transport	28.18	28.47	1.04	1.27
Public officials and free professions	5.87	6.72	2.04	2.17
Clerks and employees in agriculture, industry, trade, banking and transport	8.17	11.04	.82	1.00
Army officers	.07	.07	.18	.10
Office attendants	1.59	1.39	.85	1.04
Non-commissioned officers	.25	.17	.18	.21
Workers				
in agriculture and forestry	2.03	1.32	27.17	24.57
in industry	9.28	10.47	7.61	10.12
in trade and transport	6.83	6.74	2.18	3.12
Day laborers	2.88	1.65	3.64	2.53
Domestic servants	.98	.71	2.47	2.30
Soldiers	.41	.27	.53	.49
Rentiers and pensioners		2.85		1.73
Others	5.43	2.32	2.75	1.78
Total	100.00	100.00	100.00	100.00

III

If we compare the occupational and social structure of the Jews with that of the non-Jewish population, we can notice two radically different social patterns (Tables 4 and 5). The occupational distribution of the non-Jewish population suggests a traditional agrarian society: 65 percent derived their living from agriculture with 40 percent being small and dwarf-holding peasants. Mining and industry provided the livelihood of only 17 percent and only 5 percent lived on commerce and transportation. The distribution of the Jewish population, on the other hand, was very different. The overwhelming majority, 77 percent, were engaged in the modern non-agrarian sectors of the economy: industry, trade, banking and transport. Thirty-seven percent of the Jews lived on industry and the same number on trade and banking. Only 7 percent earned their living from agriculture.

Among the Jews engaged in agriculture, there were two groups which played an important role in the capitalist development of agriculture. On the one hand, the big landowners and the big lessees (the Jewish share was respectively nine and more than fifty percent!), and on the other hand, the bailiffs, the managers of big estates.

Comparing the occupational structure of Jews with that of the non-Jews reveals two radically different, but actually complementary and interdependent substructures within the same national economy and the same national society. The second half of the nineteenth century was a period of rapid economic growth and structural change in Hungary. Between 1860 and 1914, Hungary was one of the most rapidly developing countries of Europe. But the traditional Hungarian social structure was rigid and unprepared for modernization and capitalism, and its reaction was hesitating and inelastic to the challenge of economic growth. Consequently, immigrant Jews found a great variety of jobs and positions in the new developing sectors. All the more, since a number of these jobs and positions had been held by Jews already before 1848 within the framework of a traditional, feudal society. To these traditional positions in commerce, money-lending, private-banking acquired in the eighteenth and in the first half of the nineteenth centuries, came new ones in railway construction, large-scale industry, joint-stock banking, etc. in the second half of the century.

IV

These statements can be corroborated by a second approach, by analysing the share of Jews in the main occupational categories and social groups. The result of the examinations can be illustrated by so called *indices of participation*. We arrive at this index by relating the percentages of Jews in each of the occupational groups to their percentage in the total population of Hungary (4.6 percent in 1900 and 5 percent in 1910). The numbers in tables 6 and 7 show that the share of Jews was extraordinarily high among the self-employed merchants, technical and commercial employees and clerks, the so-called white collar workers, and in agriculture among the big lessees of land. In these groups more than half of the number employed were Jews.

The index of participation of Jews was also high among industrial entrepreneurs and self-employed craftsmen, and in the free professions among lawyers, doctors, veterinary surgeons, pharmacists, private engineers, journalists and artists. In industrial occupations, Jews had a leading part in printing and the catering trade, but their share was also high among the butchers, bakers, tailors, barbers and shoemakers (Table 8).

Table 6: Share of Jews in the Main Occupational Groups of the Active Population of Hungary in 1900 and 1910

Main occupational groups	Share of Jews in %		Index of Participation	
	1900	1910	1900	1910
Agriculture, forestry	.61	.48	12	10
Mining	.41	.58	8	12
Industry, handicraft	10.07	9.30	204	186
Commerce and banking	52.25	46.63	1059	935
Transport and communications	7.61	5.95	154	119
Public service and free professions	10.82	11.00	219	221
Defence	4.23	2.96	86	59
Day laborers	3.04	2.49	62	50
Domestic service	2.13	1.69	43	34
Rentiers and pensioners		6.34		127
Others	8.10	4.82	164	97
Total	4.13	4.47	84	90

Table 7: Share of Jews in Selected Occupational and Social Groups of the Active Population, 1900-1910

Occupational and Social groups	Share of Jews in % 1900	1910	Index of Participation 1900	1910
Big landowners with 1000+ *hold*	18.4	19.2	373	385
Landowners with 100-1000 *hold*	10.9	10.1	220	202
Lessees with 100+ *hold*	55.3	48.6	1120	974
Small and dwarf landowners under 100 *hold*	.5	.4	11	8
Self-employed				
in commerce	58.6	54.1	1173	1084
in industry	12.7	12.5	257	250
in transport	20.7	20.9	420	429
Bailiffs and estate managers	21.7	23.2	439	465
Clerks and employees				
in trade and banking	57.9	53.3	1173	1069
in industry	38.9	42.7	787	856
in transport	13.4	13.0	271	260
Doctors	48.3	48.9	978	980
Lawyers	34.1	45.2	691	906
Journalists	30.7	42.4	622	850
Veterinarians	24.8	40.0	502	802
Private engineers	23.8	37.6	482	754
Actors	16.5	22.6	334	453
Pharmacists	7.7	14.5	156	291
Teachers	11.9	9.6	241	193
Administrative officials	4.7	5.2	95	105
Office attendants	6.5	4.5	132	90
Non-commissioned officers	6.0	3.6	121	73
Army officers	3.3	1.4	66	29
Workers and servants in agriculture	.3	.2	6	4
Workers				
in trade	42.7	34.9	865	699
in industry	7.7	6.4	155	129
in transport	3.5	2.4	71	48
in mining	.1	.1	3	3
Day laborers	3.0	2.5	62	50
Domestic servants	2.1	1.7	43	34
Soldiers	3.9	2.8	79	56
Rentiers and pensioners		6.3		127

Table 8: Share of Jews in Selected Trades in Hungary, 1910

Trades	Number of Jews		Share of Jews	
	self-employed	employees	self-employed	employees
Typographers	554	2,813	57.05	18.37
Catering	14,419	9,101	41.31	15.54
Butchers	3,199	2,230	23.62	12.03
Bakers	1,238	1,831	22.85	12.41
Tailors, needle-women	13,231	13,868	20.90	19.94
Barbers	1,430	387	12.03	3.00
Shoemakers	5,462	3,507	8.91	5.55
Furriers	274	324	6.03	8.94
Millers	482	441	4.10	1.62
Joiners, carpenters, cartwrights	13,339	1,949	2.44	2.22
Smiths, locksmiths	791	3,296	2.14	3.19
Weavers	66	147	1.13	.80
Masons	103	100	.61	.16
Others	12,269	17,027	10.39	5.20
Total	54,857	57,021	12.47	6.44

It is well known that the Jews constituted the majority of Hungary's economic elite. But we must not forget about that there was an important Jewish working-class composed of industrial and commercial workers.

Summing up the lesson of our tables, we can say that about 54 percent of Hungarian Jews were self-employed in agriculture, industry, trade and professional occupations; 18 percent were white collar workers, that is clerks and employees in agriculture, industry and trade; and 22 percent were registered in the contemporary censuses as "other auxiliary personnel", that is as hired workers.

This picture can be complemented by data compiled from contemporary school statistics.[3] In the field of secondary schools it is interesting to see that "only" 18-19 percent of the students of gymnasiums were Jews (index: 380), but in the *Realschulen,* the share of Jewish students was around 35-36 percent. Jews constituted 52 percent of the students at the Faculty of Medicine, whereas their percentage was 24 at the Faculty of Law and 36 percent at the Faculty of Pharmacy. The share of Jews among the law students was decreasing between 1895 and 1914, but it increased among the students at the Faculty of Arts (from 14 to 19 percent) as well as among the students of Pharmacy (from 15 to 36

3 *Magyar statistikai évkönyv* [Hungarian Statistical Yearbook] (1872-1914).

percent). In 1871, only 10 percent of the students at the Technical University were Jewish, by 1890, their share had grown to 40 percent. One must also take into account that many Hungarian Jews studied abroad, especially in German, Austrian and Swiss universities and colleges.

V

Our third task is to examine the changes over time in the occupational and social structure of Hungarian Jews in the first decade of the twentieth century. To be sure, ten years is too short a time to make statements about the trends of structural changes. However, I would like point out certain tendencies. The most obvious change is the increasing number of commercial and technical clerks and employees, the so-called white collar workers. The increase can be noticed in their number and in their percentage as well. Looking at the professional occupations such as doctors, pharmacists, journalists, etc., we observe the same trend. However, although the absolute number of the Jews self-employed in industry and trade increased, their percentage and share decreased during this decade. The number of Jews engaged in agriculture decreased in every occupational group between 1900 and 1910.

It is well known that Hungary lost two-thirds of her former territories and population after 1918 and that the number of its Jews decreased by a half. We have to transform the data of the 1910 census to the territorial basis of Trianon Hungary to get further information about the development of the occupational structure of the Jewish population. Although the figures we get are rough estimates, the tendency of the changes can be traced quite well. The basic trends observed between 1900 and 1910—mainly the growth in the number and percentage of private employees—continued after the First World War. The only difference is that the number of Jews in professional occupations did not increase between 1910 and 1930 and even showed a slight decrease, as a consequence of the changed situation of Jews in interwar Hungary.[4]

4 *Az 1930. évi népszámlálás* [The Census of 1930], vol. IV, *Magyar statisztikai közlemények* [Hungarian Statistical Publications] no. 96 (Budapest, 1936).

Table 9: Occupational Structure of the Active Jewish Population on the Territory of Trianon Hungary, 1910 and 1930

Occupational groups	1910	1930
Agriculture, forestry	2.78	2.71
Mining	.15	.13
Industry, handicrafts	37.54	34.63
Commerce and banking	39.53	42.23
Transport and communications	3.34	1.93
Public service and free professions	8.37	8.14
Rentiers and pensioners	3.79	7.23
Day laborers	.59	.41
Domestic service	1.44	.85
Defence	.95	.07
Others	1.53	1.66
Total	100.00	100.00

Table 10: Social Structure of the Active Jewish Population on the Territory of Trianon Hungary in 1910 and 1930

Social groups	1910	1930
Landowners with 100+ *hold*	.52	.36
Lessees with 100+ *hold*	.57	.42
Small landowners under 100 *hold*	.81	1.07
Self-employed in industry	13.81	11.20
Self-employed in commerce and transport	19.89	18.51
Public officials and free professions	17.17	20.90
Office attendants	7.78	7.29
Workers and servants in agriculture	.32	.43
Workers in mining and industry	18.21	16.67
Workers in commerce and transport	12.02	12.07
Day laborers	.59	.41
Domestic service	1.44	.85
Rentiers and pensioners	3.74	7.23
Soldiers	.95	.07
Others	1.59	1.66
Total	100.00	100.00

Jewish Leaseholders in the Course of Agricultural Development in Hungary, 1850-1930

Julianna Puskás

One of the most exciting and interesting questions in the history of Jewish Hungarians has hardly been touched upon, namely: How and to what extent did the social and physical environment play a part in their remarkably rapid social mobility and integration?

I would like to provide a brief overview of the history of the system of landleasing and highlight the part played by Jews in the development of this system by introducing several sources and making a few general observations. From an historical point of view it is important to consider how features of feudal commodity production which were unique to Hungary prepared the way for the part played by Jewish tenants in capitalist agriculture.

It is known that in Hungary from the second half of the eighteenth century onwards, Hungarian nobles interested in increasing their production for the market tried to establish profit-yielding manorial economies. Struggling with the problems of selling their products, they supported the settlement of experienced Jewish businessmen and merchants on their properties in the interest of getting their raw material to the market. The activities involved in the expansion of market-production therefore became an incentive for Jewish mass immigration.

From the beginning of the nineteenth century the nobility and the Jews were drawn even closer together through their common economic interests. The nobility's increasing need for money on the one hand and restricted income on the other, led Jewish merchants to offer the financially pressed landowners advances on their products. Thus the landowners tended to turn to them more and more in order to acquire loans and capital. This, in turn, expanded cooperation in other areas as well. Landowners began to employ Jewish overseers and farm managers for their estates. The renting of the so-called *regale*—for example inns and butcheries—was undertaken by Jews. Occasionally land was included along with these leaseholds. These *regale* represent early examples of land rental by Jews.

Legal barriers which prevented Jews from renting or owning land in Hungary were gradually abolished from the late eighteenth century onwards. The first step in this process was Emperor Joseph II's decree in 1783 which allowed Jews to rent property. In 1818 Emperor Franz I again forbade Jews to accept the estates of nobles as collateral or to take a loan on their estates. This decree, however, soon proved anachronistic in the face of increasing need for capital and loans; thus in 1819 it fell into disuse, a full two decades before it was repealed altogether.

In Hungary the economic mobility of the serfs—who were obliged to pay tithes and to perform *socage* for their feudal landlords—was rather restricted. With the enlargement of the market-oriented manorial economy, earlier leases of the serfs on the whole, began to fall into disuse. This was not the pattern of development experienced in western Europe and as a result the growth of market-production did not create a mass of peasant leaseholders—as in England for example—who would have been able to become capitalist tenants through the transformation to a capitalist economy. It was the Jewish *regale* tenants who were the forerunners of capitalist tenants in Hungary. From the turn of the nineteenth century it was not uncommon to find noble estates being rented by Jewish wholesale dealers of agricultural products and moneylenders as collateral on debts. In some cases these represented the leasing out of an entire estate (for example the Grassalkovich estates in Gödöllö and Hatvan and the Bretzenheim estate in Sárospatak). In this way wholesalers such as Mór Ullmann, Samuel Wodianer, Selig Mandel, Samuel Hirsch, Moses Goldner and Salamon Strasser of Pest (just to name the best known) acquired manorial leaseholds. This type of enterprise merely represented a side-line to the primary economic activities of these merchants. For the most part, they did not plan to enter long-term farming.

Before the 1850s, farming by tenants was characterized neither by innovation nor by significant investment. Legal limitations discouraged such practices. Jews, like serfs, were forbidden to own land, they were not permitted to acquire the land they rented. And for the same reason the safety of the lease was also unstable in that it could always be contested on the grounds of entailment. Consequently, these forerunners of capitalist landleases were really based on the exploitation of the land in the quickest and most profitable manner. Only now and then were there attempts at a more rational organization of serf-labor on these estates.

From the early decades of the nineteenth century, a crisis situation emerged from the untenability of the traditional economic system. This crisis, along with the lure of greater opportunities created by capitalist development in western Europe, encouraged reformers among the nobility to dismantle feudal institutions in 1848. The desire to follow the western model focused attention already in the 1840s on the English system of land leasing as a practical economic form. The establishment of 300-500 *hold* (600-1000 hectare) leases on large estates was increasingly put forth as the ideal for the economy of the future by agricultural experts (Korizmics, Letenyey).

What happened after the emancipation of the serfs? The 1850s and 1860s were marked by a whirlwind of successes and failures as agriculturists tried to accommodate to the changed conditions. After the abolition of serfdom, the question of "how and where" became all the more important in the farm economy. The lands which had earlier been used in the form of manorial economy became the property of the former landlord while the copyhold became the property of the peasants. This method of land division created a polarized distribution of property which was unique in Europe. There were on the one hand, landowners possessing vast amounts of property, and on the other, peasants with small parcels of land and masses of landless agricultural laborers. With the abolition of the peasants' obligations, the former landlords lost their free labor force. At the same time, the introduction of general taxation caused an increase in their cost of production while their constant lack of money forced them further and further into debt. These forces provided the impetus in the 1850s for the first great wave of property buying and selling, as well as land leasing. As one contemporary author put it, "Even the better landowners have been forced—while others have chosen, convinced of its expediency—to lease out at least part of their land.... The amount of land being leased out, both by estate owners and by the owners of medium-sized holdings, has increased considerably."[1]

How did the advantageous position of the Jews in the competition for leaseholds come about? Tenants were recruited from a wide range of social strata in the period immediately following the abolition of serfdom. These included impoverished members of the lesser nobility, overseers and peasants bound to the land whose lack of capital had already restricted their opportunities. Soon, however, the Jewish *regale* tenants and wholesale dealers in agricultural products (who from this time began to show increased interest in acquiring leases) came to dominate. One writer (Károly Mészáros) for the journal *Village Farmer* made the following bitter complaint in 1858: "What kind of leasing system is now in vogue in Hungary? None in the legal sense—all there is anymore is the Jewish lease."[2]

1 Károly Galgóczy, *Magyarország, a szerb vajdaság és temesi bánság mezőgazdasági statisztikája* [The agrarian statistics of Hungary, the Serb Voivodina and the Banat of Temes] (Pest, 1855), pp.176-177.

2 *Falusi Gazda* [Village Farmer] (1858), p. 355.

Most of these Jews had previously been business partners of the big landowners, either as *regale* tenants or as wholesale merchants of agricultural products. Among these tenants were those who either had substantial amounts of capital available or could raise it to rent large tracts of land. They were able to offer a half year advance in rent as security which was exactly the kind of money landowners needed at the time. Not only did this enable the continuation of the nobles' extravagant lifestyles but it also paid the annuity and covered the interest on the increased loans. These sometimes represented such a burden that they would even threaten to discontinue agricultural activity altogether. Yet, even if someone with lesser debts wanted to outfit one of his properties he would have to sell or lease out another to pay for it. Whenever possible, the landowners opted for the latter, clinging to their land as the source of their wealth and status. They were uneasy about allowing peasants to rent the land in small parcels even though the rent such a system offered would have been higher. They felt that such leases posed a threat to their ownership.

At the same time Jewish merchants who had business contacts with agricultural operations and market conditions, realized that renting large tracts of land would offer excellent returns on capital investment. In this they were able to rely on business experience and an extensive network of personal contacts as well as on capital accumulated mostly through trade. Since it was precisely this sort of capital and business ability which landowners lacked at the time, victory in the competition for leases was assured for the Jewish entrepreneurs.

Inseparable from the remaining feudal social and property structures was the form of rent called *General Pachtung*. This system of large leasing became more and more popular in the 1850s and 1860s on the very largest estates. Individuals from the same family or families organized themselves into tenant partnerships, or financial consortiums and rented 40,000-60,000 *hold* (20-30,000 hectares) areas, establishing connected chains of main and subsidiary tenants. One leaseholder was Ferenc Schöberl who, in 1848, established a private land renting venture as a joint stock company and as its director, managed some fifty thousand *hold* (one hundred thousand hectares) of agricultural land in western Hungary (in Komárom, Fehér, Baranya and Somogy counties). In 1861 under the *General Pachtung* system the entailed property of the princely branch of the Eszterházy family came up for lease. This property represented the largest latifundium not only in Hungary but throughout the whole of the Austro-Hungarian Monarchy. As soon as the form and conditions of the leasing out of the more than 600,000 *hold* (an amount which represented thirty estates) became public there was a tremendous outcry particularly among those landowners and agriculturists who had missed out on this, one of the greatest business opportunities of that time. Arguments and counter-arguments were extensively published, there were legal actions, and challenges and modifications of the original rental contracts.

Today we know in more detail—from the writings of one of the farm managers—the history of the rental conditions as contained in the contracts relating to the 47,000 *hold* entailed Ozora estate and of the tenants' agricultural activities. Changes in the directions and forms of ventures can be traced over the course of some eighty years. For example, in time, the system of *General Pachtung* and extensive agricultural economy was succeeded by individual leases and intensive agricultural farming.

Accompanying these was a decrease in the areas of rented farms and changes in the types of tenants. In 1861, four families formed a tenant partnership to rent a 47,000 *hold* (25,000 hectare) estate: the Bischitz brothers (David and Salamon); Strasser and König; Károly König and Jakab Lányi. They were all relatives, business partners as well as wool and grain merchants. The Bischitz and Strasser company became one of the largest grain suppliers in the Monarchy. Soon the tenant partnership split into four chief-tenancies of approximately the same size and in 1889 when the contract came up for renewal it split into eight tenant groups. Among these groups the management of the five thousand *hold* Majsa estate remained within one family for three generations, until the end of the 1930s. One descendant of the Bischitz family, who were among the first renters, received the highest degrees in economics in Vienna. He was known and respected for his well-managed farming.

Within the tenancy, both parties consistently attempted to advance their own interests. Under such conditions the materially less well to do owners of middle-sized estates who had entered into rental agreements while heavily in debt succumbed in a relatively short period of time. The income they gained through leasing out their properties was not enough to cover the expense of maintaining the lifestyle of the nobility to which they had become accustomed. The agricultural magazine *Village Farmer* described their fate as follows: "Owing to their difficult circumstances, the landowners often let out their lands under disadvantageous terms. The rents are collected and consumed ahead of time, they go into debt, and fall into the tenants' web as they watch their lands slowly slipping away from them and passing into the tenants' hands."[3]

To some landowners the leasing out of their land merely represented one phase of a process under which they lost their rights of ownership, one which often coincided with tenants becoming landowners. This process is not merely restricted to a few scattered instances: even a selective analysis of the Registers of Landowners demonstrates that a substantial number of tenants became

3 *Ibid.*

owners. This tendency is also suggested by the fact that this process became the constant theme of periodicals and appeared in fiction as well.

Between the 1850s and 1870s, the period of transition to capitalist economy, there was a great amount of turnover among the tenants. Land leases were, for the most part, based on short-term contracts: renters tried to keep their capital as mobile as possible and owners resisted committing their properties for longer periods of time. From the 1870s, once Jews were emancipated and could acquire property, the time was ripe for consolidating rental conditions as well as long term capital investment in leased farms. The way in which farm lease activity was still in some cases a sidebranch of commercial activity—or at least subordinate to it—can be seen in the 1897 *Register of Landowners*. Terms such as "produce merchant", "wool merchant", "wine merchant" and "grocer" appear more than once as the main occupations of tenants. Their innovative activities were not so much directed at the improvement of production as at market organization and sales.

The crisis in agriculture brought the momentum of land leasing to a halt. There were some who were drawn away from renting land by the prospects of greater profits to be found in enterprises in other branches of the economy. But there were others, too, who became landowners at this very time.

What quantitative data exists showing the spread of leaseholds and the social structure and farm economies of the renters from the 1890s? Unfortunately statistical sources, from which the quantitative aspects of the development of the landleases can be studied are only available for the 1890s onwards. The first source is the agricultural operations statistics of 1895.[4] From this we know that at that time some 19% of the total agricultural area of Hungary was leased, although in the main agricultural regions of the country the percentage was as high as 25-28%. The proportion of such leaseholds among peasants with less than 100 *hold* (50 hectare) was minimal; most of the leased lands were estates of over 100 *hold*. More than half the total area of leased estates belonged to farms over 1000 *hold*.

According to data gained from the 1911 *Register of Landowners*,[5] 36.8% of the area of the land owned by aristocrats was leased. Figured on the base of cadaster net income, it represented 47.7 % of the assessed value of the land.

4 The agrarian statistics of 1895 is the first to provide data on the landleases.

5 List of name, occupation, address, property or tenancy by villages is given in the Registers of Landowners (*Gazdacimtár*).

The important part played by Hungarian Jews in tenant farming can be seen in the 1900 and 1910 censuses as well.[6] Out of all tenants renting more than 100 *hold* (50 hectares) of land, 49.5% were Jewish. If we exclude the area between the Danube and Tisza rivers where the proportion of peasants among those renting over 100 *hold* (50 hectare) of land was significant, the majority of large tenants were Jewish. There was no separate listing in the censuses for tenants with over 1000 *hold* (500 hectare) of land. Based on a study of the names listed in the 1911 *Register of Landowners* it can be stated with a high degree of certainty that tenants with more than 1000 *hold* of land were—with few exceptions—almost all Jewish. The proportion of Jewish tenants renting over 100 *hold* of land varied from region to region. The percentage is not highest in western Hungary (the Dunántúl)—as one would have thought—even though they represented the majority there, but rather in eastern Hungary (the Tiszántúl) and in particular, in Szabolcs and Zemplén counties in the northeast.

By 1910, the percentage of Jewish owners of large land had become significant. Of the total number of landowners with over 1000 *hold*, 20.6% were Jewish; and of the total owning between 200 and 1000 *hold* 18.1% were Jewish. These numbers are truly remarkable when we take into account that it was only as late as 1867 that Jews in Hungary acquired the unlimited right to obtain and use agricultural property (article 17 of the 1867 Law). These figures are well known. What is not so well known is another statistic; of the total number of farm managers in Hungary, 26.6% were Jewish.

From all these statistics we can conclude that Jews in agriculture were part of a peculiar occupational structure. Table 1 shows data pertaining to the breakdown of Jews and non-Jews in the population of agricultural occupation. In 1910, 7% of all Hungarian Jews were engaged in agriculture, 23.1% of these either owned or rented more than 100 *hold* of land. As far as I know nowhere else in East-Central Europe did Jews make up such a large proportion of the large landowners and tenants. In addition, the proportion of large landowners and tenants among Jews engaged in agriculture in Hungary is much higher than in any other East-Central European country.

The stratification of Jewish agriculturists varied greatly from region to region: 66.3% of the Jewish small landowners and small renters with less than 10 *hold* of land lived in the two north eastern counties, Máramaros and Bereg and 84.7% of their total number lived in the area comprising northeastern Hungary and the Tiszántúl. The expansion of rented agricultural land in Hungary was rather the product of the transition to a capitalist economy; this can

6 The censuses of 1900 and 1910 give information of the religion of the population, too. I based my study of the occupational distribution of the Jewish and Christian agrarian population on these data.

also be seen from the census data. Between 1900 and 1910 the total number of tenants renting more than 100 *hold* of land hardly changed at all. However, figures fell in Hungary's most advanced region, the Dunántúl in the west of the country. A noteworthy increase was shown in those regions where modernization began later—Transylvania and the area between the Tisza and Maros Rivers.

What was the difference between owner-managed and tenant farming? The 1895 agricultural statistics suggest, though imperfectly, the advantages of tenant farming over farming by estate owners. We can compare the livestock and machine supplies as well as the division of the land farmed by the owners and the tenants according to the lines of cultivation. In the course of comparison the relatively better provisions of the rented farms becomes evident—less in livestock but noticeably more so in the use of more modern equipment. In terms of farming, the proportion of the area under cultivation was far higher on rented farms than on owned ones.

Other data regarding capitalization—for example, the level of development of agricultural technology, as well as the role and proportion of the basic elements of capitalist economy, capital and wages—could not be gleaned from farm statistics. Unfortunately, the few monographs dealing with the history of farming activity on large estates which have been published over the last 15 years do not provide much help either. It seems that, in respect to the use of paid work, there was not much difference between owner and tenant operations. Payment in kind and share-cropping were practiced on the big leaseholds too.

Up to 1914, the economies of both the big estates and the leases was geared toward the secure market of the monarchy and the export of grain and live-stock into the Austrian and Bohemian provinces. In the struggle for the safety of these markets, with the help of protective tariffs in the so-called "agrarian movement", the tenants fought on the same side as the owners.

What characteristics of renting in Hungary can be emphasized in comparison with other countries? In the Prussian areas of Germany, where the process of capitalization in agriculture had been undertaken by the landowning Junkers, about one-quarter of the total amount of farm land had been leased out by the end of the nineteenth century. Thus, the biggest difference does not appear in the proportion of leased land, but in the types of leases. In Germany, on the majority of rented land, middle- or smaller-sized businesses were set up in the hands of peasants (this is reflected by the 1892 German farm statistics). In Hungary, on the other hand, the majority of rented land was concentrated in the hands of big tenants. Hungarian agriculture, therefore, is not only characterized by its great estates but also by great leaseholds covering thousands of *hold*. The typical big tenants were Jewish entrepreneurs.

During the same period very different sorts of large leaseholds developed in Romania beginning in the 1870s through Jewish agricultural activity. Following the dismantling of feudal systems, the landowning nobles, the *boyars* of this country also retained their economic and political power and they opposed the emancipation of Romanian Jews vehemently. The parliament only granted citizenship to a Jew as a special privilege based on individual consideration. The hazards and restrictions caused by this uncertain legal status determined the scope of Jewish economic activity. Thus, they were restricted to lending money at very high rates of interest and to those kinds of investments which could be easily mobilized.

Thus, when Romanian large landowners—because of their lack of capital, credit and entrepreneurial spirit—wanted to make money by leasing out their lands, a handful of Jewish merchant families in the form of a so-called "tenant trust" undertook to rent the estates. They controlled 56% of the total leased land and established a speculative form of *General Pachtung*. The source of their profit was the sub-leasing of the land they themselves had rented (rather cheaply) to the peasants at a higher price. The Fischer brothers, in this way, had 56,000 peasant families renting land from them. When the rent contracts expired in 1906 and the main tenants again wanted to raise the sublease fees, the peasants revolted. Since the revolt began on Fischer leaseholds, it took on an antisemitic cast. The peasants' revolt was not just against the big Jewish renters, it also spread to lands which the aristocracy itself controlled.

Characteristic economic and social conditions can be seen in the various types of large leaseholds. In this case, it was the backwardness of Romania which was reflected in the state policy toward the Jews and which also held back enterprise that would have promoted modernization and the development of the middle class.

What was "modern" and what was "traditional" in leaseholds in Hungary? The influence of the entrepreneurial activities of Jewish large leaseholders was also felt in the fairly rapid rate of growth in Hungarian agricultural production. The part they played in the process of transforming feudal agriculture—often as merchant, creditor and leaseholder all in one—still cannot be interpreted in terms of a "traditional" versus "modern" linear model. New ways, as well as adaptation and conservation of old traditions were employed simultaneously on Jewish leaseholds. Meanwhile, tenants "managed" the feudal estates within a system of capitalist agriculture and by this not only modified traditional property relations but also consolidated them along with accompanying social tensions. On the great estates and manors there developed a "double rule"—that is, of the owner and the renter—which contained advantages for both. The renters also strove to acquire land. Whether the reason for this was profitability or the desire to imitate large landowners is not clear. "Within the Monarchy, a tremendous market has opened for Hungary," Bischitz's grandson wrote to their former farm managers. "My grandfather's principle was to farm more and more land, as much as possible." There were big tenants whose territory was established in such a way that they rented land from more than one owner at the same time.

The impoverished owners of middle-sized estates, however, were unsuited for this "double rule" and many of them were squeezed out from land ownership altogether. Those landowners who had suffered economic and social decline—especially the conservatives among the gentry—began to organize into a political party in the 1880s under the banner of antisemitism. Among the economic ramifications of the so-called "Jewish question" great emphasis was placed on the assertion that the Jews had reduced the remaining elements of the Hungarian nation to ruin through the acquisition of land that had been owned according to "ancient right". Antisemites for the first time began to record data on how Jews acquired property.

The "new" Jewish landowners—though tenants as well—took on a number of the elements inherent in the behavior and value system of the "old" landowners. Examples appear in Hungarian literature, novels, family histories, autobiographies and other writings (such as the works of Lesznai, Hatvani, Bauer and others).

The successes achieved through the combination of "modern" and "traditional" in the course of this agricultural transformation tended to overshadow the so-called "land or peasant question". One shortcoming of the economic policy at the time was that it ignored the peasantry not only as a social group but as farmers as well. The growing peasant population began to feel more and more strongly that the economic basis of its existence was becoming restricted. Stubbornly, each of them tried to acquire pieces of the large estates. It happened more than once that a Jewish renter who acquired property from a large estate, would not always keep it, but rather planned to sell it to the peasants. The method of property exchange based on a property structure of feudal origin, however, did not change in essence. In this way, hemmed in by the large landowners and large leaseholds, bogged down by traditional means of production and gnawing with hunger for land, the resentment of the peasants increased against both the old and the new landlords.

It is difficult to follow the process after World War I because of the changes in the territory of Hungary. The state of affairs in 1930 can be seen on Table 4 and 5. The proportion of Jews among owners of more than 1000 *hold* land was 9.3% (in 1910 it was 20%).The picture is significantly different from 1910 as regards the big landleases. Among the tenants who leased more than 200 *hold* land the proportion of Jews was 35.4%. Among those who rented more than 1000 *hold*, 35.2% were Jewish. If we add to this the leases rented by corporations the rate increases to 47.7%.

Further research is needed to give an answer to the question as to how much of these striking changes can be explained by former Jews who converted in the meantime, by the changed position of the market for agricultural products, by the changes of the territory of the country and by the changes in the political climate. The result of the research will also show the relative importance of each of these causes.

In 1935, 23% of land on estates of over 100 *hold* was leased. What is significant is not so much that changes took place in the size of the land being rented as much as in the persons who rented it and in the types of tenancies. In 1935, the land of four leaseholds exceeded 1000 *hold*. These were corporations, concerns of banks or enterprises of agricultural industries. The number of landleases of over 1000 *hold* was 40, managing a total of 240,000 *hold*. Their farming was generally linked vertically to industrial activities, e.g. to the sugar industry. On the other hand, the leasing activity on the part of Jews individually or in family enterprises decreased. In many villages where big leaseholders' names appeared in 1911, landowners' names can be seen in 1935 or the land is managed by small tenants. Some estates decreased in size, while others disappeared entirely from the category of properties over 100 *hold*. Further research, and, not least of all, a methodological review of the full content of the *Registers of Landowners* would make it possible to describe these changes in a more exact way. It is not likely, however, that this would show any change in the indicated trends.

When I undertook to report on the leasing of land in Hungary and the historical perspective of the role played by Hungarian Jews in such activity, I did not realize how difficult it would be to write about this subject. This is not just because this is a relatively new field of study and therefore we can only make tentative statements, but also because the role of the Jews in agriculture has always been a very sensitive question in Hungary. The contemporary sources quoted in the paper indicate the type of hostility which was directed against Jewish land renting in the nineteenth century and, if I might add, in the 1930s as well. A reluctance to avoid entanglement in debates over antisemitism may explain the tendency of the few scholarly studies which do consider Jewish participation in agriculture, to concentrate on the role of Jews as innovators, without due consideration for the broader national milieu in which they operated. This approach saves the historian from having to consider such difficult issues as the nature of the relations between gentile landowners and

Jewish tenants, or between Jewish tenants and gentile peasants. Yet such an approach is distorting. It ignores the interaction between Jewish enterprise and the character of Hungarian social and economic structures. Yet it appears that just such a combination of traditional social and agricultural structures, favorable natural resources for agricultural production, good soil and relative proximity of western markets provided the kind of environment which could explain the remarkably fast integration and mobility of the Jews in Hungary. In order to show the uniqueness of the Hungarian case, a comparison with the process of modernization in agriculture in other east-central European countries would be required.

Table 1: Jews within each Stratum of the Agricultural Population, 1910
(based on male earners)

a. Number

Occupations	Total	Jews	Non-Jews
Landowners over 1000 *hold*	1,439	296	1,143
Owners of medium-sized land			
200-1000 *hold*	5,493	992	4,501
100-200 *hold*	10,761	741	10,020
Tenants with over 100 *hold*	4,863	2,405	2,458
Owners or tenants of			
50-100 *hold*	45,911	1,065	44,846
20-50 *hold*	277,523	1,745	275,778
10-20 *hold*	517,468	1,774	515,694
less than 10 *hold*	1,341,373	4,060	1,337,313
Share cropper, shepherd	27,701	42	27,659
Independent gardener	4,675	11	4,664
Farm officials	9,611	2,553	7,058
Farmhand,worker	1,435,606	3,019	1,432,587
Forestry, other agricultural workers	51,236	495	50,741
Total in agriculture	1,733,660	19,198	3,714,462

b. Percentage

Occupations	Share of Jews in Total Agricultural Population	Distribution of Population Jewish	Non-Jewish
Landowners over 1000 *hold*	20.6	1.6	0.0
Owners of medium-sized land			
200-1000 *hold*	18.1	5.2	0.1
100-200 *hold*	6.9	3.9	6.9
Tenants with over 100 *hold*	49.5	12.5	0.0
Owners or tenants of			
50-100 *hold*	2.3	5.6	1.2
20-50 *hold*	0.6	9.1	7.4
10-20 *hold*	0.3	9.3	13.9
less than 10 *hold*	0.3	21.2	36.0
Share cropper, shepherd	0.1	0.0	0.7
Independent gardener	0.2	0.0	0.1
Farm officials	26.6	13.3	0.3
Farmhand,worker	0.2	15.7	38.6
Forestry, other agricultural workers	8.9	2.6	1.4
Total in agriculture	0.5	100.0	100.0

Source: *A magyar szent korona országainak 1910. évi népszámlálása*, part IV, pp. 308-309.

Table 2: Jewish Landowners and Tenants of Large and Medium Estates (over 100 *hold*) According to Regions, 1910 (based on male earners)

	Agricultural Population		Number of Jewish		
	Total	*Jewish*	*landowners*		*tenants*
			1000+ *hold*	100-1000 *hold*	100+ *hold*
a. Number					
Hungary	3,733,660	19,198	296	1,733	2,405
SW (Dunántúl)	674,501	1,390	30	142	351
NW	414,503	2,042	16	240	447
Between Danube and Tisza	579,173	1,457	113	280	267
NE	319,297	4,715	25	278	453
East (Tiszántúl)	588,715	7,954	85	592	642
Between Tisza and Maros	507,653	380	15	147	62
Transylvania	649,238	1,259	12	54	183
b. Percentage					
Hungary	100.0	100.0	100.0	100.0	100.0
SW (Dunántúl)	18.1	7.2	10.1	8.2	14.6
NW	11.1	10.6	5.4	13.8	18.6
Between Danube and Tisza	15.5	7.6	38.2	16.2	11.1
NE	8.5	24.6	8.4	16.0	18.8
East (Tiszántúl)	15.8	41.4	28.8	34.2	26.7
Between Tisza and Maros	13.6	2.0	5.1	8.5	2.6
Transylvania	17.4	6.6	4.0	3.1	7.6

Source: *A népesség foglalkozása a főbb demográfiai adatokkal egybevetve; föld és házbirtokviszonyai: A magyar szent korona országainak 1910. évi népszámlálása*, (Budapest, 1915), part IV, pp. 308-309.

Table 3: Regional Variations in the Percentage of Jews within Various Agricultural Occupations, Hungary 1910 (based on male earners)

Occupations	Hungary	SW	NW	Center	NE	East	SE	Transylvania
Landowner								
1000+ *hold*	20.6	14.0	14.0	24.0	16.0	35.0	15.0	8.0
100-1000 *hold*	10.7	9.0	22.0	5.0	25.0	20.0	8.0	2.0
Tenant 100+ *hold*	49.5	53.0	74.0	20.0	82.0	64.0	22.0	43.0
Owner-tenant								
50-100 *hold*	2.3	1.3	4.4	0.5	8.2	6.4	0.3	1.7
10-50 *hold*	0.4	0.1	0.4	0.1	1.5	1.6	0.0	0.2
less than 10 *hold*	0.3	0.0	0.1	0.0	1.2	1.1	0.0	0.0
Farm official	26.6	18.0	33.0	26.0	37.0	42.0	11.0	11.0
Farm worker, laborer	0.2	0.0	0.0	0.0	0.2	0.7	0.0	0.1

SW = Transdanubia; Center = Between Danube and Tisza; East = Tiszántúl; SE = Between Tisza and Maros

Source: *A magyar szent korona országainak 1910. évi népszámlálása*, pt IV, pp. 308-309.

Table 4: Proportion of Leases and Properties over 100 *hold*, 1911 (based on the Registry of Landowners)

	Plowland	Garden	Vineyard	Meadow	Pasture	Forest	Marshland	Fallow	Total
Communal group	8.2	2.2	0	3.5	4.5	6.3	0.6	4.9	5.6
Village	35.9	6.1	40.5	28.6	15.5	13.6	30.2	15.4	16.7
Company	25.6	35.0	4.3	12.9	32.4	11.3	2.9	19.5	16.4
Association	28.1	24.1	33.3	23.5	12.9	18.9	10.8	10.9	15.5
Ecclesiastical body	43.6	28.7	27.7	36.4	40.0	18.6	48.8	28.2	31.0
State	14.9	15.8	30.3	7.5	13.7	8.7	3.2	12.1	9.6
Foundation	77.0	45.9	66.3	55.7	72.8	29.2	66.0	72.0	57.9
Legal entity	38.6	14.3	26.3	25.2	15.1	11.4	33.0	16.3	16.1
Aristocrat	46.6	32.9	37.6	41.9	39.8	25.6	40.7	41.5	36.8
Commoner	25.4	24.0	14.7	22.7	25.1	14.8	22.7	32.1	22.9
"Natural person"	34.1	27.7	22.2	31.5	32.0	21.6	33.6	37.8	29.9
Total	34.9	23.5	22.9	29.8	22.1	15.5	33.4	24.3	23.6

Source: Tibor Kolossa and Julia Puskás, "A 100 kat. holdon felöli birtokterület tulajdoni és birtokkezelési struktúrája Magyarországon 1911-ben," *Agrártörténeti Szemle* XX (1973), 444-480.

Table 5: The Agricultural Population 1930 (based on male earners)

a. The Number of Jews within Each Stratum

	Total	Non-Jewish	Jewish
Landowners over 1000 *hold*	463	420	43
Owners of 100-1000 *hold*	6,054	5,478	576
Tenants with 1000+ *hold**			
Tenants with 200-1000 *hold*	1,002	647	355
Owners or tenants			
100-200 *hold*	1,064	970	94
50-100 *hold*	16,349	16,039	310
20-50 *hold*	91,226	91,038	188
10-20 *hold*	170,122	169,772	350
5-10 *hold*	215,041	214,777	264
less than 5 *hold*	371,508	371,206	302
Farm officials	4,941	4,054	887
Farm workers	212,455	212,156	299
Agricultural workers	424,587	424,249	338
Total in agriculture	1,514,812	1,510,806	4,006

b. The Distribution of Jews within Each Stratum

	Percent of Jews in the Total	Agricultural Population Non-Jewish	Jewish
Landowners over 1000 *hold*	9.3	0.0	1.1
Owners of 100-1000 *hold*	9.5	0.4	14.4
Tenants with 1000+ *hold**			
Tenants with 200-1000 *hold*	35.4	0.1	9.0
Owners or tenants			
100-200 *hold*	8.8	0.1	2.3
50-100 *hold*	1.9	1.1	7.7
20-50 *hold*	0.2	6.0	4.7
10-20 *hold*	0.2	11.2	8.7
5-10 *hold*	0.1	14.2	6.6
less than 5 *hold*	0.8	24.6	7.5
Farm officials	17.8	0.3	22.1
Farm workers	0.1	14.0	7.5
Agricultural workers	0.08	28.0	8.4
Total in agriculture	0.3	100.0	100.0

* In this grouping of the statistical data there is no information on the tenants who rented more than 1000 *hold* of land. In another table we find that the total of those who rented more than 1000 *hold* was 321, out of whom 113 were Jewish (35.2%).

Source: *Az 1930. évi népszámlálás*, Vol. IV, *Magyar statisztikai közlemények* no. 96 (Budapest, 1936), pp.81-103. The occupation of the population was related to the major demographical data.

Bibliography

Sources

Magyar Király Központi Statisztikai Hivatal. *Magyarország mezőgazdasági üzemstatisztikája* [Agricultural Statistics of Hungary] Vol. 2: *Gazdacimtár* [Register of Landowners]. Budapest, 1897.

Magyar Király Központi Statisztikai Hivatal. *Magyarország földbirtokosai és földbérlői (Gazdacimtár)* [Owners and Tenants of land in Hungary (Register of Landowners)]. ed. Gyula Rubinek. Budapest, 1911.

Magyar Király Központi Statisztikai Hivatal. *Magyarország földbirtokosai és földbérlői (Gazdacimtár)* [Owners and Tenants of Land in Hungary (Register of Landowners)]. *A 100 kh-as és ennél nagyobb földbirtokok és földbérletek az 1935. évi adatok alapján.* [Property and Tenancy of 100 *hold* and over According to Data of 1935] Budapest, 1937. pp. 504-514.

Magyar Király Központi Statisztikai Hivatal. *A népesség foglalkozása a föbb demográfiai adatokkal egybevetve; föld és házbirtokviszonyai* [The Occupation of the Population Related to the Major Demographical Data and the House- and Land Relations] *A magyar szent korona országainak 1910. évi népszámlálása* [The 1910 Census of the Crown Lands of Hungary], (Budapest, 1915), Part IV, pp. 308-309.

Magyar Király Központi Statisztikai Hivatal. *Az 1930. évi népszámlálás* [The Census of 1930]. Part I. Demographical data. Budapest 1932. [= *Magyar Statisztikai Közlemények*, Uj sorozat (New series) Vol. 83, p. 29*.

Magyar Király Központi Statisztikai Hivatal. *Az 1930. évi népszámlálás* [The Census of 1930]. Part II. Occupational data. Budapest 1934. Vol. 86. p. 23*. Part III. Occupation of population in detail - corporation statistics. [= *Magyar Statisztikai Közlemények*, Uj sorozat (New series), Vol. 94.] Budapest, 1935.

Studies

Gaál, László. "Az Eszterházy hercegi hitbizomány gazdálkodása 1930-1940" [Farming on the entailed estate of Prince Eszterházy, 1930-1940] *Agrártörténeti Szemle* XVIII (1971).

Galgóczy, Károly. *Magyarország, a szerb vajdaság és temesi bánság mezőgazdasági statisztikája* [The agricultural statistics of Hungary, the Serb Voivodina and the Banat of Temes]. Pest, 1855.

Gunst, Péter. *A magyar mezőgazdaság története 1919-1939* [History of the Agriculture of Hungary]. Budapest 1970.

Hayami, Vujiro and Vernon W. Ruttan. *Agricultural Development in International Perspective*. Baltimore, 1971.

Kolossa, Tibor. "Adatok az agrárnépesség összetételében az Osztrák-Magyar Monarchiában 1900 körül" [Data on the division of the agrarian population of the Austro-Hungarian Monarchy, around 1900], *Agrártörténeti Szemle* IX (1962).

Kolossa, Tibor and Julia Puskás. "A 100 kat. holdon felöli birtokterület tulajdoni és birtokkezelési struktúrája Magyarországon 1911-ben" [Ownership and farming structure of the properties over 100 *hold* in Hungary in 1911], *Agrártörténeti Szemle* XX (1973).

Mészáros, Károly. *Falusi Gazda* (1858).

Mészáros, Károly. *Herceg Eszterházy jószágai bérleteinek története* [The history of the tenancies on the properties owned by Prince Esterházy] Pozsony, 1866.

Oláh, József. *Az akasztó-vésztői uradalmak gazdálkodása a XIX-XX. század fordulóján* [Farming on the Estates of Akasztó-Vésztő at the Turn of the nineteenth century]. Budapest, 1975. [=*Agrártörténelmi Tanulmányok*].

Petrassevich, Gusztáv. *Zsidó földbirtokosok és bérlők Magyarországon* [Jewish landowners and tenants in Hungary]. Budapest, 1904.

Puskás, Julia. "A tőkés nagybérletek a 19. századvégi Magyarországon az 1895-ös mezőgazdasági statisztika adatai alapján" [Capitalist large landleases in Hungary at the end of the nineteenth century on the basis of the agricultural statistics of 1895], *Történelmi Szemle* (1959).

Puskás, Julia. *Die kapitalistischen Grosspachten in Ungarn am Ende des 19. Jahrhunderts (Auf Grund der Landwirtschaftsstatistik des Jahres 1895)* [=*Studia Historica* 51]. Budapest, 1961.

Puskás, Julia. "Die Trend und Wachstumsraten des ungarischen Feldbaus von 1869-1913," *Acta Historica* (1981).

Puskás, Julia. "Die Entwicklungstendenzen der landwirtschaftlichen Produktion in Ungarn von der zweiten Hälfte des 19. Jahrhunderts bis zum ersten Weltkrieg," *Jahrbuch für Wirtschaftsgeschichte* (1972).

Puskás, Julia. "Die Trends und Wachstumsraten des Ungarischen Feldbaus von 1869-1913: Demographie, Bevölkerungs- und Agrarstatistik." Budapest, 1981 .

Puskás, Julianna - Scott Eddie - Margit Lánc. "Adatbázis az 1911. évi Gazdacimtár adataiból a gazdaság- és társadalomtörténeti kutatások számára. (Módszertani tanulmány)" [Data-base from the data of the Register of Landowners of 1911 for Research on Economy and Sociology], *Történelmi Szemle* (1976).

Ungár, László. "A magyar nemesi birtok eladásodása 1848 elött" [Indebtedness of the Hungarian estates of noblemen before 1848], *Századok* LXIX (1935).

Szabad, György. *A tatai és a gesztesi Eszterházy uradalom áttérése a robotrendszerröl a tőkés gazdálkodásra* [The Changeover from Socage into Capitalist Farming on the Estates of Eszterházy at Tata and Gesztes]. Budapest, 1957.

Varga, János. "A bihari nemesség hitelviszonyai a polgári forradalom előtt" [The position of the credit of the nobles in Bihar before the bourgeois revolution]. *Történelmi Szemle* (1958).

Végházi, [Stephen] István. "The Role of Jewry in the Economic Life of Hungary." In: *Hungarian Jewish Studies*, Vol. I, edited by Randolph L. Braham. New York, 1969.

Vincze, László. "Egy dunántúli tőkés nagybérlet gazdálkodása (Maisa, 1861-1941)" [The Farming of a Capitalist Large Land-Lease in West Hungary, Maisa, 1861-1941], *Agrártörténeti Szemle* XXIV (1982); XXV (1983); XXVI (1984).

III

Demographic Aspects

The Standard of Living of Jews in Austria-Hungary: The Anthropometric Evidence, 1860-1920

John Komlos

Until fairly recently, the income and wealth of Jews in the Habsburg Empire have not been the subject of serious analysis. Generally, Jews are thought to have prospered during the economic expansion that lasted until the outbreak of the First World War.[1] Impressionistic evidence on the business elite is sometimes used to support the notion that the Jews fared well relative to their Christian compatriots. Yet, evidence from the extreme right tail of the income-distribution curve can hardly be indicative of the relative socio-economic position of a group whose diversity must have been similar to that of the other elements in the society. The occupational structure of the Jews no doubt diverged in significant ways from that of the rest of the population, but this difference need not have been translated into a financial advantage. Nevertheless, many commentators on the subject suggest, on the basis of these two kinds of evidence, that the economic mobility of the Jews was above average. Thus, according to Arthur J. May, Hungarian Jews "obtained a controlling influence in industry, banking, commerce and the press."[2]

In short, the impression is often generated that the Jews controlled practically all of Austro-Hungarian economic life. By implication, they must have enjoyed a higher standard of living than the rest of the population, because their "control" of the economy could not have been for altruistic purposes. Such generalizations should be regarded with some skepticism, however. While emphasizing the concentration of Jews in certain occupations, scholars have tended to overlook their lack of representation in others. There may have been

1 David F. Good, *The Economic Rise of the Habsburg Empire 1750-1914* (Berkeley, 1984) and John Komlos, *The Habsburg Monarchy as a Customs Union: Economic Development in Austria-Hungary in the Nineteenth Century* (Princeton, 1983).

2 Arthur J. May, *The Habsburg Monarchy 1867-1914* (New York, Norton, 1968), p. 243 (first published in 1951.) See also Andrew C. Janos, *The Politics of Backwardness in Hungary 1825-1945* (Princeton, 1982), p. 113 and Istvan Deak, "The Convert," *New York Review of Books* 34 (1987), no. 4, p. 41.

many Jewish lawyers, for instance, but there were few Jewish law professors at the universities. Moreover, it is dangerous to make inferences from occupational structure to the distribution of income and wealth, because the relationship between the two has not been adequately explored. The Jewish population, too, had its underclass, whose omission from the analysis prevents us from acquiring a complete picture of the standard of living. This notion is vividly reinforced by the visual evidence of Roman Vishniac's photographs,[3] which reveal the existence of a broad stratum of Jews living near the very bottom of the income distribution. In short, we do not know how well the Jews fared financially relative to their Christian compatriots, because this question has eluded rigorous examination. From a theoretical point of view, the problem is hardly intractable. It cannot, however, be tackled unless one has a broad random sample of the population at large, representing the full range of incomes. Then one could calculate the mean per-capita annual income of the Jews and compare it with the societal average. One could use probate records to make a similar comparison for assets.

In this study I attempt to illuminate these issues by using anthropometric evidence to develop a set of proxy measures for income. Economic historians have recently begun to explore the ways in which biological, economic, and demographic variables interacted in the eighteenth and nineteenth centuries, using nutritional status as a crucial link among these processes.[4] Human stature plays an important role in this research because data are plentiful and because their use allows one to quantify nutritional status, something hitherto unfeasible. A population's nutritional status—that is, the quality and quantity of nutrients it consumes, less the nutrients lost to work and disease—has a major influence on stature at a particular age, on the annual growth rate, on the timing and intensity of the adolescent growth spurt, and on the age at which final height is reached.[5] The nutritional status of a population depends mainly on its food intake, which, in turn, depends on a wide variety of factors, such as the relative price of food, family income and therefore the occupation of the head of household, and the distribution of wealth. More formally, the demand for food F is a function of

3 Roman Vishniac, *The Vanished World* (New York, 1983).

4 Robert W. Fogel, "Nutrition and the Decline in Mortality since 1700: Some Preliminary Findings," in Stanley Engerman and Robert Gallman, eds., *Long-Term Factors in American Economic Growth* [National Bureau of Economic Research, Studies in Income and Wealth, vol. 51] (Chicago, 1987); John Komlos, *Nutrition and Economic Development in the Eighteenth-Century Habsburg Monarchy: An Anthropometric History* (Princeton, 1989) and John Komlos, "The Height and Weight of West Point Cadets: Dietary Change in Antebellum America, 1820-1880," *Journal of Economic History* (December, 1987), 897-927.

5 J. M. Tanner, *A History of the Study of Human Growth* (Cambridge, 1981).

real income Y, the price index of a typical basket of food products P_F relative to all other prices P_{AOG} and tastes T. Let P_F/P_{AOG} be designated by Z. Then

$$F_t = (f_1, f_2, ..., f_n) = q(Y_t, Z_t, T) \qquad (1)$$

where f_i is the quantity of the ith foodstuff. The vector F_t is determined by utility maximization. The ith foodstuff has a caloric content c_i and price per unit p_i. The total caloric intake C is given by:

$$C = j(f_1, f_2, ..., f_n) = j(F_t) = f_1c_1 + f_2c_2 + ...+f_nc_n \qquad (2)$$

The consensus among biologists is that the terminal height of a population, H, must be between the genetically determined minimum H_{min} and maximum H_{max}. The degree to which H exceeds H_{min} is determined by the caloric intake C above the requirements of basic metabolism, the work effort, and the nutrients claimed by diseases. Let these claims on the nutrients be designated by W. Then

$$H = H_{min} + \int_{-1}^{30} [h(C_t - W_t, t)]\, dt \leq H_{max} \qquad (3)$$

where h is the instantaneous growth rate and t designates time. The integral is from -1 to 30 in order to signify, on the one hand, that to some extent nutritional status is hereditary, i.e., that intrauterine nutrition also influences nutritional status, and, on the other hand, that growth cannot continue past age 30. From equations (1), (2), and (3) we obtain:

$$H = H_{min} + \int_{-1}^{30} [g\,(Y_t, Z_t, T, W_t, t)]\, dt \leq H_{max} \qquad (4)$$

If Z, T, and W remain constant, there is a positive correlation between Y and H. Moreover, if one studies ∂H, the change in stature over time, the genetic component of stature, H_{min}, drops out of equation 4. The correlation between ∂H and ∂Y has been amply documented.[6] In France, draftees who could afford to pay for a substitute to take their place in the army averaged one centimeter taller than those who replaced them.[7]

Research has also supported the notion of a strong correlation between social status and stature, presumably because family income correlates positively with

6 Richard H. Steckel, "Height and Per Capita Income," *Historical Methods* 16 (1983), 1-7 and John Komlos, "Stature and Nutrition in the Habsburg Monarchy: The Standard of Living and Economic Development in the Eighteenth Century," *American Historical Review* 90 (1985), 1149-1161.

7 Emmanuel Le Roy Ladurie and N. Bernageau "Étude sur un contingent militaire (1868): Mobilité géographique, delinquance et stature, mises en rapport avec d'autres aspects de la situation des conscrits," *Annales de démographie historique* (1971), 311-37.

social status. Thus in Germany the sons of titled nobles were on average 4 centimeters taller than the sons of the lower aristocracy in the 1760s. The latter, in turn, were about 3.5 centimeters taller than the sons of middle-class families, who were 4.5 centimeters taller than lower-class boys.[8] Thus there was a 12-centimeter gap between the height of the upper and lower classes in eighteenth-century Germany. In the 1790s, boys in the London slums were so malnourished that they were shorter than boys living in practically any society of today, and a full 20 centimeter shorter than their gentlemanly contemporaries attending the Sandhurst Military Academy.[9] Class distinctions in America also translated into differences in stature, although they were not as large as in Europe. American slaves were only about 2.5 centimeters shorter than their masters.[10] Cadets at the West Point Military Academy whose fathers had blue collar occupations were 1.1 centimeters shorter than those whose fathers were professionals.[11] Thus it has been amply demonstrated that there is a strong and persistent correlation in historical populations between human stature and socio-economic variables such as status and income. This is particularly the case if the groups that are compared face the same relative prices for foodstuffs. Whenever income has been found not to correlate positively with stature it is because food prices varied across space or time.[12] This does not pose a problem in this study of Viennese Jews, because they faced the same food prices as their fellow countrymen.

I therefore compare the stature of Viennese Jews with that of the rest of the population in order to ascertain whether their standard of living in the late nineteenth and early twentieth centuries was above average. The data were obtained from the Viennese *Kriegsarchiv* (*Stellungslisten* 1873-1914).[13] Only those Jews who were born in Vienna were sampled for the purposes of this study. Given the large number of lower-class Jews who migrated to Vienna from Galicia, it is clear that the average income of all Jews was less than that of

8 John Komlos, "Height and Social Status in Eighteenth-Century Germany," *Journal of Interdisciplinary History* 20 (1990).

9 Roderick Floud and Kenneth Wachter, "Poverty and Physical Stature, Evidence on the Standard of Living of London Boys 1770-1870," *Social Science History* 6 (1982), 422-452.

10 Richard Steckel, "Slave Height Profiles from Coastwise Manifests," *Explorations in Economic History* 16 (1979), 363-380; Robert Margo and Richard Steckel, "Heights of Native-Born Northern Whites during the Antebellum Period," *Journal of Economic History* 43 (1983), 167-74; Richard Steckel, "A Peculiar Population: The Nutrition, Health and Mortality of American Slaves from Childhood to Maturity," *Journal of Economic History* 46 (1986), 721-742.

11 Komlos, "The Height and Weight of West Point Cadets."

12 Komlos, "Stature and Nutrition in the Habsburg Monarchy."

13 Vienna, Kriegsarchiv. *Stellungslisten*, Niederösterreich. 1873-1914.

those in the sample. Consequently, the standard of living of all Jews who resided in Vienna will be overestimated.

Table 1: Height of 21- and 22-Year-Old Recruits in the Austro-Hungarian Army (cm)

Place of Birth	Vienna				Lower Austria	
	Jews		Non-Jews		Non-Jews	
Decade of Birth	N	X	N	X	N	X
1860	41	167.6	345	167.5	276	166.1
1870	1055	166.8	1589	167.4	521	165.4
1880	1154	167.1	1525	167.6	544	165.9
1890	727	167.8	1192	168.7	229	166.1

N=Number of observations X=mean value

Source: *Stellungslisten*, 1873-1914

Jewish recruits born in Vienna were consistently shorter at age 21 and 22 than their non-Jewish Viennese counterparts (Table 1). The birth cohorts of the 1870s were 0.6 centimeters shorter; by the 1890s the difference was 0.9 centimeters. Viennese Jews were between 1.4 and 1.7 centimeters taller, however, than the recruits born in the rural districts of Lower Austria. A similar pattern emerges among 19- and 20-year-old birth cohorts of the 1890s. The 19- and 20-year-old Jews (N=351) were 1.6 centimeters shorter than non-Jews born in Vienna in the same decade (N=654), but they were 1.2 centimeters taller than 19- and 20-year-old Christian men born in the rural areas of Lower Austria. This result is confirmed by examining the change in stature between the birth cohorts of the 1870s and 1890s. During these two decades the height of the 21- and 22-year-old Jewish recruits increased by 1.0 centimeter, while the height of the Christian recruits born in Vienna increased by 1.3 centimeters. In contrast, recruits born in Lower Austria grew only 0.7 centimeters in this period. Hence the economic position of the Viennese Jews improved by more than that of the Lower Austrians, but by less than that of the Viennese Christians.

Because stature is a cumulative measure of nutritional status, it reflects the individual's well-being prior to reaching terminal height. Hence the height of the recruits is actually a proxy for family income. On the basis of this evidence it appears that Jewish family income was not extraordinarily high by any stretch of the imagination. In fact, in Vienna they appear to have enjoyed a lower standard of living at the end of the nineteenth and beginning of the twentieth centuries than the rest of the urban population, even leaving out of consideration those poor Jews who had recently migrated into the city from Galicia.

Table 2: Distribution of Recruits' Occupation by Birth Decade

Occupation	Jews 1860s*	Jews 1870s	Jews 1880s	Jews 1890s	Non-Jews 1890s
A Student	2.8	11.9	18.7	43.3	17.3
B Bureaucrat	3.3	10.1	14.2	12.5	9.2
C Commercial employee	34.3	18.9	17.2	10.6	3.6
D Clerk	17.4	24.7	18.0	9.2	11.4
E Professional	8.9	7.5	4.8	6.2	5.8
F Blue Collar/Unskilled	1.4	10.4	9.2	5.7	13.3
G Technician	2.8	4.2	6.6	5.2	5.9
H Artisan	13.6	4.7	2.8	2.1	13.1
I Salesman	5.6	2.1	2.0	1.9	0.6
J Performing Artist	0.5	2.1	1.6	1.4	2.4
K None	0.0	1.8	1.9	1.2	1.5
L Blue Collar	9.4	1.5	2.6	1.1	15.9
Number of observations	213	1101	1053	1677	667
1 Student	2.8	11.9	18.7	43.3	17.3
2 Professional	12.2	17.6	19.0	18.7	15.0
3 Third Sector/Other	57.8	47.8	39.0	23.1	18.0
4 Unskilled Worker	1.4	10.4	9.2	5.7	13.3
5 Skilled Worker	25.8	10.4	13.0	8.4	34.9

*Includes the birth cohorts of the 1850s
Source: *Stellungslisten*, 1873-1914

Note: Classification includes the following occupations:
A Hochschüler, Gymnasiast, Handelsakademiker
B Beamter, Privatbeamter
C Kommis, Handelsangestellte
D Kontorist, Korrespondent, Praktikant, Buchhalter
E Mediziner, Jurist, Ingenieur, Chemiker, Apotheker, Lehrer
F Gehilfe, Hilfsarbeiter, Geschäftsdiener, Fabriksarbeiter, Manipulant, Lehrling, Taglöhner
G Techniker
H Bäcker, Bildhauer, Photograf, Weber, Schneider, Taschner, Glaser, Schlosser, Installateur, Uhrmacher, Goldschmied, Porzellanerzeuger, Buchbinder, Bürstenbinder, Maler, Schuhmacher, Fleischhauer, Friseur
I Kaufmann, Reisender, Vertreter, Agent, Händler
J Schauspieler, Künstler, Musiker, Sänger, Tänzer
K Privat, Ohne Beschäftigung
L Goldarbeiter, Elektromonteur, Mechaniker, Steinschleifer, Metalldreher

1 = A; 2 = B; 3 = C, D, J; 4 = F; 5 = G, H, L.

The military data can also be used to explore the occupational distribution of the recruits and the dynamics of economic change. During the approximately half a century under consideration, there was a large increase in the share of students and bureaucrats among the Jewish recruits, but a significant decline in the number of artisans, lower-level clerks, and blue-collar workers. The evidence also confirms the hypothesis of a segmentation of the labor market (Table 2). Among the birth cohorts of the 1890s, that is, those who reached young adulthood just prior to the outbreak of World War I, many Christians, but few Jews, entered blue-collar occupations (e.g., mechanic) or became artisans. Whereas almost half the Christians were blue-collar workers, only 14 percent of the Jews were. Another major difference is that a large number of Jewish youth decided to postpone their entrance into the labor force. While 43 percent of the Jewish birth cohorts of the 1890s were students in their early twenties, only 17 percent of the Christians followed the same life-cycle pattern. While this is an indication of differences in both labor-force participation rates and of labor-market segmentation, these differences apparently did not translate into higher average nutritional standards for the Jews.

Differences in occupational distribution are also evident among women. This is clear from the protocols of one of the public welfare clinics in Vienna where expectant mothers who were unable to pay for a midwife came to deliver at government expense. The women were generally lower class and unmarried. While half of the Jewish women had semi-skilled occupations, such as seamstress, almost all of the Christian lower-class women were unskilled, primarily domestics (Table 3). The nutritional status of the women can be inferred from the age at which they reached menarche, a biological variable influenced by nutritional intake during childhood and adolescence. Among Vienna-born women, Jews reached menarche at age 15.4 (N=41), while Christians reached menarche at age 15.1 (N=453), that is, 3.6 months earlier. By contrast, Christians born in Lower Austria reached menarche at age 15.8 (N=531). These data indicate that the nutritional status of Viennese lower-class Jewish women during childhood was similar to that of Jewish men: inferior to that of Christians born in Vienna, but better than that of those born in Lower Austria.

In conclusion, this preliminary study on the standard of living of Viennese Jews indicates that the issue is much more complex than the stereotypical view would lead one to believe. Certainly much more research needs to be done before we can more fully understand this question. One should be careful not to confuse the situation of a few business leaders at the top of the social pyramid with that of the Jewish masses. The data on recruits into the Austro-Hungarian army and on lower-class women giving birth at the Viennese *Allgemeines Krankenhaus* confirm the hypothesis of a segmentation of the labor market while showing that on average this segmentation did not provide an advantage to the Jewish members of the society. While the standard of living of Jewish men and women born in Vienna was below that of the Christians born in the city, it was above that of the Lower Austrian population. Even from this preliminary research, it is quite clear that it is dangerous to draw inferences about the distribution of income and wealth from occupational distributions.

Table 3: Occupational Distribution of Lower-Class Viennese Women, 1907-1908

Occupation	Jewish	Non-Jewish
A Domestic	7.2	7.6
B Maid	24.6	63.7
C Seamstress	39.1	4.7
D Blue-collar unskilled	15.9	24.1
E Commercial	10.1	0.0
F Student	1.4	0.0
G Prostitute	1.4	0.0
Number of Observations	69	278
1 Servants	31.6	71.3
2 Unskilled worker	17.3	24.1
3 Skilled worker	49.2	4.7
4 Student	1.4	0.0

Source: *Protokollbücher*, 1907-08.

Note: Classification includes following occupations:
A Bedienerin
B Magd
C Schneiderin, Näherin, Strickerin
D Büglerin, Gehilfin, Tageslöhnerin, Arbeiterin, Lehrling
E Kontoristin, Verkäuferin, Hausiererin, Floristin
F Schülerin
G Prostituterte

1=A,B; 2=D,G; 3=C,E; 4=F

Hidden Urbanization: The Birth of the Bourgeoisie in Mid-Nineteenth Century Hungary

Peter I. Hidas

From an economic perspective, Hungarian society during the past 150 years can be seen, in the words of W. W. Rostow, "as lying within one of five categories: the traditional society, the pre-conditions for take-off, the take-off, the drive to maturity, the age of high mass-consumption."[1] The application of this Rostowian model to Hungarian society, i.e., the discovery that developments in East Central Europe followed the pattern of other societies studied by Professor Rostow, can facilitate a re-examination of mid-nineteenth-century Hungary.

Hungary was dominated by a traditional agricultural society for some eight hundred years. The "pre-conditions for take-off", the focus of our investigation, existed from the 1820s to the 1870s. According to Rostow, "the beginning of take-off can usually be traced to a particular sharp stimulus."[2] The constitutional compromise of 1867, struck between Franz Joseph and Hungary's political leaders, provided this stimulus. The drive to maturity lasted until the mid-twentieth century. Today Hungarian society is on the threshold of the age of high mass-consumption.

During the pre-take-off period the Hungarian nobility underwent the necessary preparation, both by their own efforts and under the influence of external forces such as the Vienna government and the local Jewish community, for sustained economic growth. The Magyar political elite turned its attention to the Hungarian nation and to larger international issues. One powerful force motivating the transition was nationalism, a reaction against intrusions by the more advanced Austrian economy and against regional interests; burgher and gentry, aristocratic and conservative that strove to establish an independent modern state. Before 1848 the Hungarian political leadership "wanted the fruits of modernization, but it was in fact weighted too heavily with interests and

1 W. W. Rostow, *The Stages of Economic Growth: A Non-Communist Manifesto* (Cambridge: Cambridge University Press, 1967), p. 4.

2 *Ibid.*, p. 36.

attitudes from the traditional past to do the things that needed doing to make a modern society."[3] The mistakes of 1849 led the nation to the tragic defeat at Világos, to Magyar isolation in a Slavic milieu, and to increased peasant docility despite emancipation. "Then finally, there came into power, in a second transitional phase... a generation of men who were not merely anxious to assert national independence but were prepared to create an urban-based modern society."[4] By the 1860s the Magyar elite, taking advantage of Austria's international difficulties, accepted the progressive social, economic and cultural reforms of both the neo-absolutist regime and of the independent Hungary of 1848-49, without the former's authoritarianism and the latter's revolutionary posture. Thanks to an economic alliance forged by the old nobility with a new economic elite, the Jewish middle classes, the Compromise of 1867 could usher Hungary into the take-off stage.

The preconditions stage had been spawned, four decades earlier, by the impingement of economically more advanced societies rather than endogenously. These external influences, such as the rapid growth of the Hungarian Jewish community, the arrival of various commercial and industrial specialists and adventurers, the influx of Western ideas of progress, and the news of the first results of the Industrial Revolution, upset the traditional Magyar society, both rural and urban, and initiated its unravelling. The idea spread "not merely that economic progress is possible, but that economic progress is a necessary condition for some other purpose, judged to be good: be it national dignity, private profit, the general welfare or a better life for the children."[5] New types of entrepreneurs came forward, Jewish merchants in the private sector, reform-minded Magyars and liberal Josephinist civil servants in the government sector, who were willing to mobilize savings and take risks in pursuit of profit or modernization. Banks and other capital-mobilizing institutions first appeared in Hungary in the 1830s. Foreign investment increased, notably in transport, communications, and mining. The scope of trade, both foreign and domestic, widened in direct proportion to the consolidation of the new middle class. After the Jewish entrepreneurs accumulated enough capital from commerce to take advantage of new opportunities and local talents, modern manufacturing enterprises began to appear on the scene. But all this activity proceeded at a limited pace, within an economy and a society still dominated by traditional low-productivity methods, by old structures and values, and by regionally based political institutions.[6]

3 Professor Lawrence Barss, quoted in *ibid.*, p. 30.
4 *Ibid.*
5 *Ibid.*, p. 6.
6 *Ibid.*, p. 7.

Nevertheless, surplus disposal income, until then concentrated in the hands of the land-owning classes, began to find its way into the hands of those who spent it in a productive manner, either through re-investment in the economy or through applying state resources to building roads, railroads and schools. The former was done by the Jews of Hungary, the latter by the Vienna government. A substantial part of the surplus income from agriculture was transferred to the modernizing sector, out of the hands of those who would squander it on prodigal extravagancy, the nobility, and into the hands of the new productive middle class, who invested it in the modern sector and then regularly plowed back their profits as output and productivity rose.[7] Investment rate gradually outstripped population growth. Starting in the 1860s risk capital became available for industry and for cost-reducing inventions, especially in the milling industry. At the same time, the members of the disintegrating guilds and freed peasants provided a docile labor force. The rapidly growing mining industry and tax revenues from the nobility (heretofore exempt) provided a good base for servicing the new infrastructure. Rising rural incomes and a prospering middle class contributed to the growth of the domestic market. The modernization of Hungary began.

As already noted, the pre-conditions for take-off were created by reformist Magyar nobility, Austrian civil servants led by the Franz Joseph's liberal ministers, and the new Hungarian middle class, which was predominantly Jewish. The essence of this process, the birth of a commercial class, its penetration into every corner of the country and takeover and rapid development of commerce in the towns of Hungary, in short, urbanization, can be demonstrated quantitatively. Despite the restrictions imposed by the limited demographic data, a statistical analysis can clearly show the validity of our model. The other two features of Hungarian capitalism, the role of the Magyar and Viennese political elite, have been amply demonstrated by historians and require no repetition here.

Occupational Profile

Even a cursory examination of the demographic data for the period under consideration reveals Jewish migration to the towns. But can this development be equated with modern urbanization? If it can be demonstrated that the Jews of Hungary were primarily a merchant community, one may assume that their influx into towns would signal a corresponding increase in commercial activity.

7 *Ibid.*, p. 19.

According to the census of 1857, 1.37% of the population of Hungary were traders. By 1869 the figure had risen to 1.57%.[8] Nationwide figures for the Jewish community are not available, but samples are. In Pest in 1846, 59.50% of the Jewish breadwinners were traders, 18.05% were craftsmen and manufacturers, 9.41% were professionals, and 13.04% were laborers. In the same year, the proportion of merchants was 65% in Buda, 32% in Óbuda, 70% in Székesfehérvár, 45% in Komárom, 63% in Szabadka, and 51% in Szeged. In the counties the proportion was as follows: Túróc, 37%; Nógrád, 54%; Somogy, 42%; Szepes, 29%; Bereg, 9%; Borsod 52%.

A decade earlier, according to Bácskai and Nagy,[9] who examined 58 market centers, 34% of the Jewish households were supported by trade; however, they categorize 50% of the Jewish households as "occupation unknown." Many heads of family in this category may have been engaged in commerce and/or commerce-related occupations. Innkeepers, 3% of the Jewish households, should also have been included in the business category. In the same 58 towns, 3.4% of the non-noble population (who composed the vast majority of the urbanites) were engaged in trading. In 1827, 19% of them were Jewish. In certain categories of towns, according to Bácskai and Nagy, more than half the merchants were Jewish. Jews were particularly prominent in the grain trade (47%) and the leather trade (67%). Some 90% of hawkers were Jewish. Bácskai and Nagy's data show the importance of Jews in commerce in the late 1820s and demonstrate tendencies in the occupational profile of Hungarian Jewry. Their calculations, in conjunction with the data provided by the *Jewish Calendar of 1848* (see Table 1), indicate, if they do not yet prove, the correctness of our original assumptions.

Since no reliable and comprehensive information is available on the occupational profile of non-Jews, we are forced to use an indirect approach, the statistical method of correlation, to strengthen or weaken the original hypotheses. If we can establish a positive correlation between the merchant profession and the Jewish community and a zero or negative correlation between the Gentile population and the urban traders of Hungary, and if, at the same time, we can demonstrate a significant increase in the Jewish urban population,

8 *A magyar korona országaiban az 1870. éve elején végrehajtott népszámlálás eredményei a hasznos házi állatok kimutatásával együtt* (Pest: Az Országos Magyar Kir. Statisztikai Hivatal, 1871); hereafter *Census 1870*.

9 Vera Bácskai and Lajos Nagy, *Piackörzetek, piacközpontok és városok Magyarországon 1828-ban* (Budapest: Akadémiai Kiadó, 1984). With the kind cooperation and permission of the authors I was able to use the original manuscripts. See also their "Piackörzetek a XIX. század elejei Magyarországon," *Ethnográphia* 89, No. 2 (1978), pp. 217-230; English version: "Market Areas, Market Centers and Towns in Hungary in 1828," *Acta Historica* 26 (1980), pp. 1-26.

Table 1: Occupational Profile of Hungarian Jews in 1846

	Commerce	Industry	Agriculture	Professions	Workers	Total
Counties						
Túróc	70	48	47	25	0	190
Nógrád	547	174	85	109	91	1006
Somogy	435	278	21	63	251	1048
Szepes	127	83	148	78	0	436
Bereg	122	270	708	77	209	1386
Borsod	663	331	105	146	33	1278
Bihar	296	197	170	82	14	759
Csanád	240	70	20	40	0	370
Torontál	319	79	39	43	0	480
Krassó	105	50	4	21	0	180
Verőce	12	12	6	7	0	37
Szerem	56	1	2	3	0	62
Zágráb	85	30	4	29	0	148
Varasd	34	12	16	9	0	71
Total	3111	1635	1375	732	598	7451
%	41.8	21.9	18.5	9.8	8.0	100.0
Towns						
Pest	1948	591	0	308	427	3274
Buda	207	84	0	25	4	320
Óbuda	176	344	3	21	0	544
Székesfehérvár	37	10	0	6	0	53
Komárom	87	62	1	45	0	195
Szabadka	149	54	10	24	0	237
Szeged	117	63	3	18	27	228
Total	2721	1208	17	447	458	4851
%	56.1	24.9	.4	9.2	9.4	100.0

	Commerce	Industry	Agriculture	Professions	Workers	Others	Total
Hungary	66,788	588,283	2,267,877	162,147	1,141,164	649,713	4,875,972
1857	1.4	12.1	46.5	3.3	23.4	13.3	100.0
Hungary	119,305	746,853	3,690,509	167,143	2,512,387	384,118	7,620,315
1869	1.6	9.8	48.4	2.2	33.0	5.0	100.0

Sources: Henrik Pollák, "Adatok a magyar izraeliták statisztikájához," *Első magyar zsidó naptár és évkönyv 1848-ik szökőévre* (Pest, 1848), pp. 111-112, 124-125 (hereafter *Jewish Calendar of 1848*). The 1857 and 1869 figures are from *Census 1870*.

then, in the absence of any other universally applicable factor, increased commercial activity in the towns can be explained by the presence and especially the influx of Jews.

Correlation Analysis

Scattergram and Pearson's r

The statistical method of bivariate correlation, which will be employed here, yields a single number that summarizes the relationship between two variables. This number, called the correlation coefficient, indicates the degree to which variation (change) in one variable, such as religious affiliation, is related to variation in another, such as occupation. A correlation coefficient not only summarizes the strength of association between a pair of variables, it also provides an easy means for comparing the strength of the relationship between two different pairs of variables.[10]

Scattergrams and the Pearson product-moment correlation *(r)* produce a clear picture of such relations. A scattergram is a graph of data points based on two variables, where one variable defines the horizontal axis and the other defines the vertical axis. The values of the variable for any given case serve as the coordinates of a point representing that case. Scattergrams, however, often suffer from excessive detail. One way to reduce the detail is to draw a straight or curved line through the scattergram in such manner that it approximates the pattern of points.[11] The line of best fit (the "regression line") is the one for which the vertical distances of all the points from the line are at a minimum.[12]

In social-science research it is unusual to find a straight regression line which perfectly fits the data. Occasionally, the true relationship does not quite fit the curve being drawn or there are errors or imprecision in the data collection. A measure of the "goodness of fit" of the regression line is used to compensate for these errors. The Pearson product-moment correlation coefficient *(r)* serves this purpose for linear regression. When there is a perfect fit (no error), r, the regression coefficient, has the value +1 or -1. A negative r does not mean a bad fit, but rather denotes an inverse relationship: as x becomes larger y tends to become smaller.

The correlation coefficient can be determined through the use of Pearson's r. Pearson's r serves as an indicator of the "goodness of fit" of the linear

10 Norman H. Nie et al., *SPSS: Statistical Package for the Social Sciences* (New York: McGraw-Hill, 1975), p. 276.

11 *Ibid.*, p. 277.

12 *Ibid.*, p. 278.

regression and also indicates the degree of association in the linear relationship between the two variables. If the value of r approaches +1.0 or -1.0, one can assume the presence of a strong linear relationship. By squaring the Pearson's r one gets another statistical measure that is easier to interpret. The result indicates the degree of relationship (r^2) rather than the direction of the relationship (r); r^2 is a measure of the proportion of variance in one variable "explained" by the other. Variance is usually defined as a measure of the variability or lack of homogeneity.[13]

Partial-Correlation Analysis

Partial correlation provides the researcher with a single measure of association which describes the relationship between two variables, such as occupation and religious group, while adjusting for the effects of one or more additional variables, such as other religious groups, through the use of control variable(s).[14] Partial correlation can help a researcher understand and clarify relationships among three or more variables. It also helps uncover spurious relationships and locate intervening variables. A spurious correlation is defined as a relationship between specific values of two variables, e.g., Catholics and merchants, in which the ostensible correlation between Catholics and merchants is solely the result of the fact that membership in the merchant class actually varies with some other variable, such as Jewishness. In this case, once the effects of Jewishness are held constant, the correlation between Catholics and merchants disappears.[15]

Graphical Analysis

In the absence of annual population totals for the towns of Hungary, a plot of absolute birth and death figures will be used for interpretation. It will be assumed that, within a reasonable time period, aggregate birth figures for a given community are reliable indicators of population changes. If, during such a time period, the crude birth rate CBR (the number of births/total population) and the crude death rate CDR (the number of deaths/total population) of a community remain stable, any population increase or decrease will be due to net migration and can be determined, for any given year within the period, from the corresponding absolute birth figures. Major changes can be pinpointed within two years. Since the number of births in a given community cannot double

13 *Ibid.*, p. 279.
14 *Ibid.*, p. 302.
15 *Ibid.*, p. 303.

Graph 1: Increase in Births among Roman Catholics and Jews in Miskolc, 1836-1870

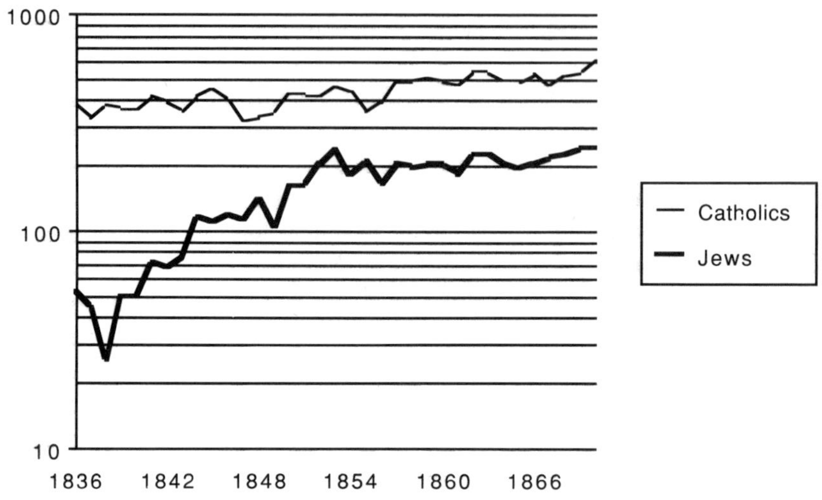

or triple without a corresponding increase in the number of women of childbearing age, the new population must be the result of immigration. On the other hand, when the number of births decline drastically, the explanation is to be sought in out-migration and/or the aging of the population. Since population totals, in addition to births and deaths, are available for 1836 and 1869, we can compute the average natural birth and death rates and net migration. For example, the CBR of Borsod-Abauj-Zemplén counties was stable between 1836 and 1900. The number of births per thousand in 1836 and in four census years were as follows:[16]

Year	1836	1870	1880	1890	1900
CBR	41.86	42.55	40.49	43.04	40.43

Over the 64-year period the deviation from the mean is less than five per cent. Therefore, any increase in annual births—as for example in the city of Miskolc between 1836 and 1870 (see Graph 1)—must be attributed to immigration.

16 *A népmozgalom főbb adatai községenként 1828-1900; VI. kötet: Borsod-Abauj-Zemplén megye, Miskolc, Heves Megye*, ed. András Klinger (Budapest: Központi Statisztikai Hivatal, 1979).

Degree of Urbanization

Urbanization can be defined as the elimination of the rural and agricultural character of a population and also as the growth of the urban component at the expense of the rural. Urbanization closely parallels and is a direct consequence of a growth in the GNP.[17] The difficulty is finding a generally accepted definition of "town" or "city." In this study three different definitions will be used: the legal definition, as employed by Ludovicus Nagy in 1827; a modified legal definition of the so-called royal free cities; and a modern definition by two contemporary Hungarian scholars. For "degree of urbanization" we use a simple formula: urban population/rural population x 100.

Table 2 presents the degree of urbanization by religion for Hungary in 1827, using the legal definition of "city", "town" and "village" adapted by the nineteenth-century statistician L. Nagy. Thus 30% of the Roman Catholics and Uniates (Greek Catholics), 22% of the Greek Orthodox, 34% of the Protestants, and 46% of the Jews of Hungary lived in towns. Despite the legal exclusion of Jews from many royal free cities and the doubtful urban character of many "towns" using Nagy's definition, the difference in the degree of urbanization between the Jewish and Gentile is significant. For the larger market towns, often the centers of commerce, the Jewish : Gentile ratio is around two to one, except for the Protestants who held onto a strong second place. According to the census of 1869, the degree of urbanization in Nagy's "town" category, the only one for which data are available, increased from 8% to 9% for Catholics, decreased from 5% to 3% for the Orthodox, and increased from 6% to 7% for Protestants, an average decrease from 6.22% to 6.19% for all Gentiles. In the same period Jewish urbanization doubled, from 4.3% to 9%. Consequently, the conclusions of a recent study by Yehuda Don and George Magos, namely, that there was rapid urbanization in Hungary between 1825 and 1869, require revision.[18]

17 P. Bairoch, "Urbanization and Economic Development in the Western World: Some Provisional Conclusions of an Empirical Study," *Patterns of European Urbanization Since 1500,* ed. H. Scham (London, 1981), pp. 61-75.

18 "A magyarországi zsidóság demográfiája," *Történelmi Szemle* 28 (1985), p. 445.
The name of towns: Dunaföldvár, Sopron, Pozsony, Nagyszombat, Nagy Kanizsa, Keszthely, Veszprém, Pápa, Gy.őr, Szombathely, Körmend, Székesfehérvár, Esztergom, Komárom, Paks, Balassagyarmat, Losonc, Galgóc, Vágujhely, Nyitra, Sasvár, Érsekújvár, Zsolna, Besztercebánya, Sátoraljaújhely, Homonna, Ungvár, Huszt, Mármarossziget, Rimaszombat, Rozsnyó, Gyöngyös, Eger, Késmárk, Bártfa, Eperjes, Arad, Temesvár, Kassa, Nagyvárad, Vác, Szatmárnémeti, Nagykároly, Nyíregyháza, Zombor, Újvidék, Baja, Gyula, Szeged, Kecskemét, Debrecen, Miskolc, Pest, Buda, Versec, Csakova, Lugos, Nagyszentmiklós.

Table 2: Urbanization and Religion in Hungary in 1827

	Catholics	Greek Orthodox	Protestants	Jews	Total
Royal Free Cities	410,840	45,370	127,683	15,754	599,647
Market Towns 2,000+	782,578	140,014	526,300	55,653	1,504,545
Market Towns 2,000-	314,288	24,551	90,326	16,896	446,061
Villages 2,000+	500,773	241,850	300,479	17,456	1,060,558
Villages 2,000-	3,067,906	519,993	1,123,438	85,721	4,797,058
Total	5,076,385	971,778	2,168,226	191,480	8,407,869

Distribution in Percentages

	Catholics	Greek Orthodox	Protestants	Jews	Total
Royal Free Cities	8	5	6	8	7
Market Towns 2,000+	15	14	24	29	18
Market Towns 2,000-	6	3	4	9	5
Villages 2,000+	10	25	14	9	13
Villages 2,000-	60	54	52	45	57
Total	99	101	100	100	100

Source: Ágnes B. Lukács, *Magyarország népessége törvényhatóságok szerint az 1820-as években* (Budapest: KSH, 1979).

Using a combination of corrected sources, from Elek Fényes's volumes of the 1830s to the official census of 1869, the following results emerge: The population of Hungary, without Transylvania and Croatia-Slavonia was 8.1 million in 1836, 8.9 million around 1847 and 10.1 million in 1869. From the 1830s to 1847 urbanization increased by 10% and from 1847 to 1869 by 14%. The increase in urbanization for the entire period was 26%. The change in the urban population of the 58 towns selected by Bácskai and Nagy is shown in Table 3. If we discount Jewish internal migration, there was proportionally little urban growth in Hungary outside Pest. As a matter of fact, the Gentile urban population, excluding Pest, grew 3% slower than the Hungarian population as a

Table 3: Urban Population, 1830s-1869

	without Pest	with Pest	increase in percentages without Pest	increase in percentages with Pest
		Total		
1830s	714,831	781,619		
1840s	770,183	856,983	8	10
1869	941,979	1,142,267	20	32
1836-1869			32	46
		Gentiles		
1830s	684,671	745,428		
1840s	735,652	816,412	7	10
1869	845,264	1,006,356	17	27
1836-1869			23	35
		Jews		
1830s	30,160	36,191		
1840s	34,531	40,571	14	12
1857	62,661	76,502	81	89
1869	96,715	135,911	54	78
1836-1869			221	276

whole (10%) between the 1830s and 1840s. But since these towns actually grew 32% between 1830s and 1869, a substantial part of the increase had to come from Jewish newcomers. The Jewish population in the towns of Hungary almost tripled from the late 1840s to 1869. The growth was fastest in Pest, but there was also a tendency to move from smaller to larger towns.

Yet another method demonstrating Jewish urbanization is to examine the major and minor market towns identified by Bácskai and Nagy (Table 4).

In 1836, there were no Jews in 12 of the 42 towns counted (out of 58). By the end of our period, all of these towns had Jewish inhabitants of their own.

There was a dramatic decline in the number of towns where the proportion of Jews was below the national average (3-6%). In the major market towns the proportion of Jews surpassed the national level and the number of minor towns where the percentage of the Jewish population was below the national average, dropped from 15 to 2. After 1857, the minor towns' largest communities began

Table 4 : Distribution of Jews in Market Towns
According to their Proportion in the Population, 1830s-1869

no Jews	major towns	minor towns	total
1830s	4	8	12
1840s	3	8	11
1857	0	1	1
1869	0	0	0
1% to 2%			
1830s	1	7	8
1840s	1	7	8
1857	1	3	4
1869	0	2	2
3% to 6%			
1830s	3	7	10
1840s	3	7	10
1857	5	6	11
1869	4	6	7
7% to 15%			
1830s	6	1	7
1840s	3	2	5
1857	4	2	6
1869	6	4	10
16%			
1830s	0	5	5
1840s	1	5	6
1857	2	8	10
1869	2	4	6

to decline, but now there were two major towns with very large Jewish communities. In comparison the Gentile community showed little growth.

The revolution and civil war of 1848-49 interrupted the process of urbanization in Hungary. Budapest continued to register moderate growth; suddenly, however, and presumably for political reasons, the Gentile population abandoned the major market towns in large numbers, to be replaced by Jews.

By 1857 seven out of every hundred Jews lived in these towns, as opposed to four per hundred in 1828 (Table 5). By 1869 the proportion of Gentile urbanites had increased by only 0.6% since 1828. The Jewish population in 17 major market towns quintupled between 1828 and 1869; by 1869 over nine per

Table 5: The Degree of Urbanization in Budapest and in the Major and Minor Market Towns, 1828-1869

	1828		1857		1869	
	Gentile	Jewish	Gentile	Jewish	Gentile	Jewish
Budapest	85,876	8,264	186,945	21,661	225,795	44,702
	1.0%	4.3%	2.0%	5.6%	2.2%	8.6%
Major (17)	284,378	8,318	182,093	28,331	397,772	46,801
	3.3%	4.3%	2.0%	7.3%	3.8%	9.1%
Minor (36)	269,090	12,953	296,799	29,450	286,173	43,602
	3.1%	6.8%	3.2%	7.6%	2.7%	8.4%
Total urban	639,344	29,535	665,837	79,442	909,740	135,105
	7.4%	15.4%	6.5%	20.5%	8.3%	26.1%
Hungary	8,609,780	191,475	9,191,262	388,374	10,408,637	517,066
Total	8,801,255		9,579,636		10,925,703	

cent of Hungarian Jews made their homes in them. The small Hungarian towns changed little in the 1830s and 1840s, and the events of 1848-49 had no major impact on their growth. By 1870 they were growing more slowly than the country as a whole. Many Gentiles left these towns and were replaced by about the same number of Jews. Over a period of 40 years, the urbanization of the Gentile population in the 53 Hungarian market towns remained stationary. The growth of these towns was due entirely to the rapid urbanization of the Jewish community. During this period the urban population of Hungary did not grow faster than the rest of the country, but urbanization did take place. It was a hidden urbanization, manifesting itself through a restructuring of the social structure of the towns.

There were major population shifts within the Jewish community starting in the late 1840s. Pest attracted the largest number of Jews. All commercial centers attracted the Jews, who tended, especially after 1857, to leave the smaller centers for larger ones and traditional communities for the towns. Some families stayed less than a decade before moving on to a still-larger community. A study of the "royal free cities" with a population of more than 2000 in 1869 supports the above findings.

Table 6: Average Proportion of Population Engaged in Commerce by City Size and Percentage of Jews, 1869

% of Jews	Size of Royal Free City			
	2,000 to 6,000	6,000 to 20,000	above 20,000	average
less than 5%	.73%	.88%	1.44%	.91%
number of cities	8	7	3	18
more than 5%	1.40%	1.48%	2.08%	1.74%
number of cities	5	5	9	19
average	.99%	1.13%	1.92%	1.32%
number of cities	13	12	12	37

Statistical analysis indicates that both city size and the proportion of Jews have a highly significant effect on the proportion of people in commerce ($p<.0001$).[19] Approximately 46.5% of the variation in the proportion of people engaged in commerce can be attributed to the presence or absence of Jews in the Royal Free Towns in 1869.

The Merchants of Hungary

The occupational profile of the Jewish community is available for the years before 1848, but not for later periods. Although it is unlikely that the economic profile changed significantly, change is always possible. Furthermore, hardly any information is available about the social, ethnic, or religious origins of various occupational groups in mid-nineteenth century Hungary. The Austrian and Hungarian governments, the Roman Catholic Church, and individual statisticians did, however, collect data about religious, ethnic, and occupational affiliation. Since in the early nineteenth century there was often a close link between one's religion, ethnic origin and profession, investigation of the relationship between religious affiliation and occupation may yield useful indirect evidence concerning the social origins of capitalism in Hungary.

The investigation focused on the major religious communities of Hungary—Roman Catholic, Calvinist, Lutheran, Uniate, Greek Orthodox, and Jewish—and on those employed in commerce and industry in the 1830s, 1840s, 1857

19 The analysis of variance F statistic of 28.7555 (for the effect of Jews) can be converted to an equivalent t statistic of 5.362 (at 33 df), which, in turn, yields $r = 0.682$ and $r^2 = 0.465$.

and 1869. The research dealt with Hungary as a whole, its economic regions, and its towns. The methodology has already been summarized.

No relationship was established between any religious group and urban *craft* or *industrial* occupation. This does not mean that no such relationship exists, merely that such relationship cannot be demonstrated with our statistical method. Small groups from a particular community may have dominated the upper echelons of some industrial sector. Since the pace of industrial development quickened in the early 1860s, it is also possible that the correlation is delayed.

For *commercial* occupations, however, the picture is different. A study of 58 towns indicated substantial correlation between the presence of Jews and merchants: r^2 is .61 for the 1830s, .76 for 1857 and .92 for 1869, with 0.00000 significance (chance of error).[20] The correlation was the highest for 1869 when 92% of the presence of merchants can be explained by the presence of Jews. Similarly, a study of 31 counties found substantial correlation in 1857 and a high correlation in 1869 when 56% of the presence of merchants can be explained with the presence of Jews.

For eleven Transdanubian counties, scattergrams show a negative correlation of commercial occupations and Calvinists in 1836. In 1847 Jews and Lutherans seem to have equal influence on the size of the merchant community. By 1869, however, only Jews and Catholics dominate. In the northwestern counties, Catholics and Jews dominated the merchant community, but the r value for the Jews increased from .6 in 1836 to .93 by 1869. The Great Plain counties show the same Jewish-Catholic domination, with some Lutheran input in 1857 and Greek Orthodox input in 1869.

Scattergrams yielded the following meaningful results in the case of towns (see Table 7): For the major centers in 1836, the merchant-Catholic correlation is 64%, the merchant-Jewish correlation only 32%. In 1857 and 1869 there seems to be a positive correlation only for Catholics and Jews. In the minor centers, the scattergrams indicate some influence of the Greek Orthodox in 1836 and 1869 and some Catholic influence in 1869.

20 r^2, or the coefficient of determination, gives the proportion of variation in Y values that is determined, "explained by," or "caused by" the variations in x values. If r^2 is between .00 and .19, the correlation is negligible;
.20 and .49, the correlation is substantial;
.50 and .64, the correlation is high;
.65 and .80, the correlation is very high;
.81 and 1.00, the correlation is extremely high.

Table 7: Correlation between Merchants and Religious Affiliation in Towns

Religious group	Date	Correlation	r^2
Jews	1836	high	.60985
Roman Catholics	1836	high	.61575
Jews	1857	very high	.76337
Roman Catholics	1857	substantial	.45544
Uniates	1857	substantial	.49328
Jews	1869	extremely high	.91686
Roman Catholics	1869	very high	.68615

In the towns of southeastern Hungary, scattergrams for 1836 show extremely high correlation between merchants and Greek Orthodox, but by 1869 the only correlation is between Jews and merchants (96%). On the Great Plain, Jews and Catholics are the most influential in 1836 and 1869, but there seems to be some Orthodox and Uniate influence in 1857. In Transdanubia there are Catholic and Jewish influences, but only in 1869. In the Northeast, Catholics, Jews and Calvinists are to be found in the merchant communities of at least four towns.

Scattergrams established interrelationships mainly among merchant, Jewish, and Roman Catholic presences in towns. To refine the investigation, the method of zero-order partial correlation was used. The temporary removal of the Jews from the triangular relationship eliminated the correlation between merchants and Catholics in 1847 (3 towns), in 1857 (16 towns) and 1869 (20 towns). This was not the case in 1836, when the absence of Jews simply reduced the influence of Catholics from 66% to 37%.

The same method suggested that the correlation between merchants and all the other religious groups except Calvinists, in both the counties and the towns, was spurious. Calvinists did have some influence on the size of the merchant population, according to the zero-order correlation method, at least in the countryside as late as 1869.

Thus by 1857 the presence of merchants and the presence of Jews in the towns of Hungary became completely interdependent. In the 1830s and the 1840s there was already a connection between the variables, but the presence of other groups, especially Catholics, shows moderate correlation. There are regional differences also. The towns of the Great Plain show faster-growing Jewish-merchant correlation than do other regions. Fourteen towns have an 84% correlation in the 1830s. In the southeast and in Transdanubia the

Table 8: Zero-Order Correlation of Jews and Merchants in Towns

Year	no.	controlling for Roman Catholic	Calvinist	Lutheran	Greek Orthodox	Uniate
1836	47	.4578	.5983	.5942	.5119	.6011
1857	16	.9454	.9696	.9629	.9683	.9942
1869	19	.9650	.9935	.9840	.9928	.9942

correlations do not appear until 1869, but by then they are 98% and 96%, respectively. For the northeast, the correlation increased to 82% in 1869, up from 68% in the 1830s. Finally, there is a stronger correlation between Jews and merchants in the major market towns than in the minor market towns.

Conclusions

Between 1830 and 1870 Hungary entered the track of rapid urbanization. The process was not restricted to the largest Hungarian town, Pest, but also encompassed the other major and minor urban centers. Except for Pest, the total population of the towns grew slowly, if at all. The increase was frequently less than the growth of the country as a whole. Nevertheless, urbanization did take place. Since it is not self-evident from general demographic data, it may be labelled "hidden urbanization".

Hidden urbanization meant a fundamental change in the social makeup of the towns. Some groups abandoned the towns and were replaced by a prominent Jewish community. This community became the yeast for capitalist development, because the majority of its breadwinners were free merchants, and the others pursued mainly urban-type occupations. The change was a rapid one, taking place in the 1850s and intensifying in the 1860s. No other group participated in this development except for Jews, whose role in the commerce of Pest further strengthens our thesis. The Jewish community played a fundamental, if not exclusive, role in the general urbanization of Hungary and, at the same time, provided the economy with the most important source of domestic capital accumulation—commerce. When the Hungarians regained control of their own affairs after 1867, they had in their midst a new middle class with whom they stood a chance to build a modern economy.

Statistical Sources

Bácskai, Vera and Lajos Nagy. *Piackörzetek, piacközpontok és városok Magyarországon 1828-ban*. Budapest: Akadémiai Kiadó, 1984. Supplementary source for size of merchant communities.

Bárándy, János. ed. *A Magyarországi városok népessége átnézete vallásra és nyelvre tekintven és legujabb polgármegyei összeirások szerint*. Second Edition. Wien: Raffelspereger Ferencz, 1843. The main source for towns in the 1840s.

Bevölkerung und Viehstand von Ungarn (Sämmtliche fünf Verwaltungsgebiete nach der Zählung vom 31. Oktober 1857). Wien: Herausgegeben vom k. k. Ministerium des Inneren, 1859. The basic source for 1857.

Czoernig, Karl, Freiherr von. *Statistisches Handbüchlein für die österreichische Monarchie*. Wien, 1861.

Fényes, Elek. *Magyarország geográphiai szótára mellyben minden város, falu és puszta, betürendben körülményesen leiratik*. 3 vols. Pest: 1851.

Fényes, Elek. *Magyarország statistikai, birtokviszonyi és topográphiai szempontbol*. I. Pest: Ráth Mór, 1860.

Fényes, Elek. *Magyarország 1859-ben statistikája, birtokviszonyi és topographiai szempontbol. Részletes és kimeritő leirása az egyes vármegyéknek, s azokban a 100 holdnál többet bíró birtokosok*. I. Pest: Boldini nyomda, 1859.

Fényes, Elek. *Az ausztriai birodalom statistikája és földrajzi leirása*. 2 vols. Pest: Heckenast, 1857.

Fényes, Elek. *Magyarországnak és a hozza kapcsolt tartományoknak mostani állapotja statistikai és geográphiai tekintetben*. 6 volumes. Pest: Trattner-Károlyi, 1836-1840. The basic source for town statistics in the 1830s.

Fényes, Elek. *Magyarország leirása*.. 2 volumes. Pest: Beimel, 1847. The main source for the counties, 1840s.

Frater, Zsuzsa J. ed. *Az 1855. évi kolerajárvány Magyarországon. Történeti Statisztikai Füzetek* 5. Budapest: Központi Statisztikai Hivatal - Országos Levéltár, 1980.

Hornyánszky, Victor. *Geographisches Lexikon des Königreichs Ungarn und der Serbischen Woiwodschaft mit dem Temescher Banate*. Pest: Heckenast, 1858. A supplementary source for religious affiliation.

Pinkas Hakehillot: Hungary. [Encyclopedia of Jewish Communities] (Hebrew) Jerusalem: Yad Vashem, 1976.

Pinkas Hakehillot: Rumania. [Encyclopedia of Jewish Communities] (Hebrew) Jerusalem: Yad Vashem, 1969.

Appendix 1: Statistical Correlation: Scattergram

	Year	no.	r^2	correlation
1. Counties, Northeast (12): merchants and...				
Catholics	1830s	12	.36	substantial
Catholics	1840s	12	.80	high
Calvinists	1840s	12	.27	substantial
Orthodox	1840s	12	.35	substantial
Jews	1857	8	.42	substantial
Calvinists	1857	8	.39	substantial
Jews	1869	12	.67	very high
Uniates	1869	12	.27	substantial
2. Counties, Transdanubia (11): merchants and...				
Calvinists	1830s	11	.29	negative
Jews	1830s	11	.29	substantial
Lutherans	1840s	11	.31	substantial
Jews	1869	11	.53	high
3. Counties, Northwest (11): merchants and...				
Jews	1830s	11	.37	substantial
Catholics	1830s	11	.43	substantial
Jews	1840s	11	.60	high
Catholics	1840s	11	.64	high
Jews	1857	6	.70	very high
Catholics	1857	6	.77	very high
Jews	1869	11	.86	extremely high
Catholics	1869	11	.77	high
4. Counties, Great Plain (10): merchants and ...				
Jews	1830s	8	.61	high
Catholics	1830s	8	.88	extremely high
Jews	1840s	10	.62	high
Catholics	1840s	10	.68	extremely high
Jews	1857	5	.79	very high
Catholics	1857	5	.70	very high
Lutherans	1857	5	.73	very high
Jews	1869	10	.62	high
Catholics	1869	10	.68	very high
Orthodox	1869	10	.30	substantial

	Year	no.	r^2	correlation
5. Towns: merchants and ...				
Jews	1830s	58	.61	high
Catholics	1830s	58	.62	high
Jews	1857	58	.76	substantial
Catholics	1857	58	.46	substantial
Uniates	1857	58	.49	substantial
Jews	1869	58	.92	extremely high
Catholics	1869	58	.69	very high
6. Towns, Great Plain (14): merchants and ...				
Jews	1830s	14	.81	extremely high
Catholics	1830s	14	.72	very high
Jews	1857	6	.97	extremely high
Orthodox	1857	6	.65	very high
Uniates	1857	6	.55	high
Jews	1869	8	.99	extremely high
Catholics	1869	8	.71	very high
7. Towns, Northeast (14): merchants and ...				
Jews	1869	4	.83	extremely high
Catholics	1869	4	.93	extremely high
Calvinists	1869	4	.95	extremely high
8. Towns, Northwest (11): merchants and ...				
Jews	1830s	11	.68	very high
Catholics	1830s	11	.81	extremely high
Lutherans	1830	11	.87	extremely high
Jews	1857	3	.99	extremely high
Jews	1869	3	.99	extremely high

Appendix 2 Statistical Analysis: Partial Correlation (0 order)

1. 1830s

Merchants and Catholics in the towns (54)
with Jews, Calvinists, Lutherans, Orthodox, and Uniates

	r	r^2	correlation
Catholics	.8138	.6623	very high
Jews	.6846	.4687	substantial
Lutherans			nil
Orthodox			nil
Uniates			nil
Merchants and Catholics but controlling for Jews:	.6116	.3741	substantial

Note: The presence of Jews reduces the correlation between merchants and Catholics from very high to substantial in the towns of Hungary in the 1830s.

2. 1857

Merchants and Catholics in the towns (16)
with Jews, Calvinists, Lutherans, Orthodox and Uniates

	r	r^2	correlation
Catholics	.6862	.4709	substantial
Jews	.9675	.9361	extremely high
Uniates	.7337	.5381	high
Orthodox			nil
Uniates			nil
Catholics and merchants but controlling for Jews:			nil

Note: The correlation between Roman Catholics and merchants is a spurious one because it is wiped out once we ignore the presence of Jews. This is not the case when we control the other religious groups.

3. 1869

Merchants and Catholics in the towns (20)

with Jews, Catholics, Lutherans, Orthodox and Uniates

	r	r^2	correlation
Catholics	.8436	.7117	very high
Jews	.9919	.9839	extremely high
Uniates			nil
Orthodox			nil
Calvinists			nil
Catholics and merchants but controlling for Jews			nil

Note: There is no real correlation between Roman Catholics and merchants in the 20 towns. There is only a spurious relationship which is due to the presence of Jews.

4. 1830s

Merchants and Jews in the towns (52)

with Catholics, Calvinists, Lutherans, Orthodox and Uniates

	r	r^2	correlation
Jews	.7946	.6314	high
Catholics	.8285	.6864	very high
Jews and merchants but controlling for Catholics:	.5545	.3075	substantial

Note: In the early 1830s the presence of Catholics reduces the correlation of Jews and merchants from high to substantial.

5. 1857

Merchants and Jews in the towns (16)

with Catholics, Calvinists, Lutherans, Orthodox and Uniates

	r	r^2	correlation
Jews	.9675	.9362	extremely high
Catholics	.6862	.4709	substantial
Uniates	.7337	.5384	high
Calvinists			nil
Orthodox			nil
Lutherans			nil

Jews and merchants but controlling for any other: remains extremely high

Note: In the 16 towns examined the presence of merchants can be explained with the presence of Jews in over 95% of the cases.

6. 1869

Merchants and Jews in the towns (19)

with Catholics, Calvinists, Lutherans, Orthodox, and Uniates

	r	r^2	correlation
Jews	.9919	.9839	extremely high
Catholics	.8436	.7117	very high
Uniates			nil
Calvinists			nil
Orthodox			nil
Lutherans			nil

Jews and merchants but controlling for
Catholics: .9650

Note: By 1869 in 98% of the cases the presence of Jews explain the presence of merchants in at least 19 Hungarian towns.

IV

Religion and Economy

Religious Divisions, Socio-Economic Stratification and the Modernization of Hungarian Jewry after the Emancipation

Victor Karady

This paper is an attempt at an overall evaluation of the socio-economic foundations of the religious schism that followed the Jewish Congress of 1868. Since there are no reliable studies of the socio-economic peculiarities of the three networks of Jewish communities that emerged after the schism—to the extent that I could not even lay hands on a detailed list of communities with a precise indication of their affiliation with the Orthodox, Status quo ante, or Neolog organization under the Dual Monarchy—the present paper must be limited to an exploratory probe of a vast area that must be studied with a much more refined methodology, especially that of local social history. Let me start by summing up the major methodological obstacles I encountered, which largely determined the methodological options I adopted.

• Formal religious divisions, even if they could be fully identified, do not express the totality of individual or collective religious options in terms of practice, belief, or the attitude towards the religious heritage. In most places—cities, villages, community sectors—there was only one established community, whose members evinced a vast array of religious attitudes. In Neolog cities, small Orthodox or even Hasidic prayer houses attempted to formally establish a parallel community of Orthodox or Status quo ante persuasion.

• As mentioned before, there is no reliable list of individual communities (since archival data on the period of the Dual Monarchy are not accessible).

• Even if the affiliation of each community could be verified, there is no hope at present of finding other indicators of the socio-economic status, modernity, or degrees of assimilation characteristic of each individual community.

Hence we have the option to draw upon aggregate indicators on the level of the county or autonomous city, which can be obtained in relatively large numbers from the published data of the 1910 census, and on this basis identify each county or city, by its presumed dominant religious character, as Orthodox,

Status quo ante, or Neolog. But we cannot deny that such use of aggregate indicators tends to blur the picture and muddle some of the correlations that a more precise analysis could reveal concerning economic stratification, social mobility, assimilation, and modernist attitudes. Still, observed co-variations of religious persuasion and sets of socio-economic and attitudinal factors objectified in social statistics present such patently different patterns as to suggest that community types (and types of religious persuasions) in the Dual Monarchy were even more clearly correlated with the professional and economic as well as the psycho-sociological make-up of local Jewish groups than is hinted by our overly general indicators. This leads me to a short exposition of the historical problem with which I am attempting to deal here. It can be summarized in three sets of logically interrelated hypotheses:

1. Jewish religious divisions—inasmuch as they imply a measure of religious innovation and modernization or, on the contrary (in the case of Orthodox Jewry), the rejection of such—can and must be linked with innovative or modernist attitudes and behavior in other fields of public or private activity. Hence it is worthwhile to examine differences between Orthodox, Status quo ante, and Neolog communities with regard to their attitude to social change in general.

2. The intensity of such societal change was a general feature of the Dual Monarchy after (and even somewhat before) Emancipation. The period following the recovery of Hungarian political independence in 1867 was one of rapid modernization, economic growth, and institutional innovation. Modernization was consistent with the policies implemented by the liberal Magyar elite, which also aimed at the fullest possible social integration and national assimilation of the ethnic minorities who, including the Jews, actually constituted a majority of the population. Avenues of socio-economic mobility, even status mobility (within the rigid status system dominated by the gentry and clergy) were opened up before Jews, who were offered a veritable assimilationist social contract:[1] protection against political anti-semitism and free access to instruments of social mobility and progress (in terms of state credits, access to public schooling, legally guaranteed religious equality) as well as an unprecedented measure of social integration was offered in exchange for loyalty to the national state, political support of its power elite, cultural Magyarisation, and acceptance of a degree of social assimilation presupposing the discarding of various Jewish cultural, behavioral, and even denominational "peculiarities." In

1 With regard to the "assimilationist social contract," see my recent study in Hungarian: "Zsidó identitás és asszimiláció Magyarországon" [Jewish identity and assimilation in Hungary], *Mozgó Világ* 1988, no. 8, pp. 26-49, and no 9, pp. 44-57, especially no. 8, pp. 30ff.

this context it is worth exploring which sections of Hungarian Jewry accepted the terms of this contract, and to what extent, seeing that it involved a collective challenge, an opportunity, and a risk of historically unique dimensions.

3. If existing religious streams were sensitive to the possibilities of social change, innovation, and modernization, it is worth exploring aspects of the collective experience of modernization in the light of religious divisions. I will attempt this in three interrelated fields: economic and professional stratification (providing clues about differential patterns of social mobility); degrees of social integration and cultural "assimilation"; and modernist attitudes in private or public conduct, as visible through objective social indicators.

First, though, we must examine the geography of Jewish religious divisions.

Geographic Dimensions of Religious Fragmentation

To understand what follows, we must sketch a broad picture of the distribution of the three community networks on the map of Hungary in the early twentieth century, even if—as we shall see below—affiliation with one or another of these streams did not have precisely the same meaning in different geographic and social environments.

Broadly speaking, we can describe the major religious split in Hungarian Jewry by drawing a diagonal line across the country from northwest to southeast, that is, say, from Pozsony to Brassó. Most of the regions south of this line were dominated by Neolog Jewry; those to the north by the Orthodox. Status quo ante communities, a minority, were much more diverse and cannot be strictly defined in this framework.[2]

2 Contemporary statistics supply only indirect indications about the size of the three community networks, especially in terms of the number of children born, marriages celebrated, rabbis and other religious personnel, etc. The best data, published in 1897, are:

	Congress (Neolog)	Status quo ante	Orthodox	Total
children born	50.3	9.5	40.2	15,233
boys circumcised	49.0	9.8	41.2	8,092
marriages	55.7	11.2	33.2	4,286
number of communities	24.0	10.8	65.2	2,395
number of religious staff	25.0	10.2	6.5	1,602

Source: *Magyar statisztikai közlemények* (1897) pp. 366-367. (I gratefully acknowledge my debt to Michael Silber for this source.)

More specifically, Transdanubia was mostly Neolog, except in the northwest, including parts of Győr, Moson, and Sopron counties. The Central Plain, between Tisza and Danube and also between Maros and Tisza (with the exception of Bihar county) was predominantly Neolog. Budapest was of course a Neolog stronghold with, nevertheless, the largest concentration of Orthodox Jewry in any one place (the local Orthodox community had approximately 50,000 members)[3]—one-fourth of the capital's Jewish population. All except three of the largest provincial towns (Miskolc, Pozsony, and Debrecen) were Neolog centers. The most prominent among these urban Neolog centers, sometimes located in rather traditionalist counties, were Kassa, Pécs, Szeged, Nagyvárad, Arad, and Temesvár.

The rest of the country was Orthodox or Status quo ante (which, to all practical purposes, was a milder form of Orthodoxy). Orthodoxy was particularly concentrated in the northwest and northeast (Slovakian and Ruthenian areas) as well as in the eastern parts of the Plain and in the High Tisza region. Transylvania was mostly Orthodox, with several smaller Neolog cities, but with a Jewish population of limited size.

This summary, based on several religious indicators (such as the nature of individually identified communities according to the *Magyar Zsidó Lexikon*, declared Sabbath observance in 1926, the actual identification of individual communities in 1941), reveals a broad geographic dichotomy among Hungarian Jewry: a southwestern and a northeastern type.[4] This simplistic perception of

The data suggest that, in demographic terms, the Neologs by the end of the nineteenth century constituted a clear-cut majority, with something more than half the Jewish population, the other half being divided unequally between the Status quo ante and Orthodox communities. Neolog communities must have been much larger on the average and much less densely staffed than the Orthodox communities, due mainly to the urban-rural division.

3 For Budapest there are no reliable data concerning the size of the two types of communities (one Orthodox and four Neolog). The size of the Orthodox was sometimes estimated at around one-fourth of the total (with a strength of approximately 50,000 at the turn of the century), but this is not confirmed by observed demographic data. One study sets the proportion of births in the Orthodox community at only 2.9% of all Jewish births in the years 1886-1889. See Anikó Prepuk, "A területi átrétegeződés vizsgálata Pest orthodox kereskedői között (1873-1895)" [A Study of the Territorial Reorganization among Orthodox Jewish Merchants in Pest (1873-1895)], *Magyar Történeti Tanulmányok XXI* (Debrecen, 1988), pp. 41-55, esp. p. 44. This small proportion is probably due to the irregular registration of Orthodox births. The true size of the Orthodox community must have been somewhere between the two estimates.

4 The map and figures in Gyula Zeke, "Szakadás után..." [After the Schism], in *Hét évtized a hazai zsidóság életében* [Seven Decades in the Life of Hungarian Jewry] (Budapest, 1990), pp. 145-161 offer a good estimate of regional divisions among Hungarian Jewry, showing a decisive Orthodox dominance in the northern and eastern districts and Neolog dominance in the Central regions, including Budapest and the south-central counties.

religious divisions can be overcome and corrected by further analysis, which will demonstrate fundamental differences between urban and rural Neolog Jewry and also between regionally distinct behavioral patterns of Orthodox Jewry. The latter contrasts Western and Eastern Orthodoxy versus Magyarized Orthodoxy and those remaining, even in the early twentieth century, within the Yiddish or German cultural orbit.[5]

Religious Fragmentation, Economic Stratification and Social Mobility

It is well known that onerous residential and professional restrictions were imposed upon the Jewish masses, most of whom entered the country starting in the last decades of the eighteenth century. Until the mid-nineteenth century they were excluded from agriculture and urban handicrafts (reserved for members of craft guilds). This explains the almost exclusive concentration of Jews in trade, petty banking, and small industry producing for home consumption and rural markets. The progressive abolition of professional restrictions after 1840 opened up new avenues for economic success, especially in agriculture, industry, and banking, as well as in new middle-class fields (the liberal professions, intellectual semi-public occupations like teaching, and even in the civil service). The regional differences of social stratification that emerged by 1910 give us a clue as to the preferential directions of professional mobility. Table 1 provides a rather broad overview of this.

Agriculture is important only in the eastern, northern, eastern central regions, that is, in strongholds of Yiddish- or Magyar-speaking Eastern Orthodoxy. In Orthodox counties about one-sixth of the active Jewish population are concentrated in farming. Closer scrutiny shows that this rather limited group consists mostly of farmers with substantial holdings, often veritable "landed bourgeoisie," especially in the west and south, while their counterparts in the east are typically small farmers or even landless farm laborers. In Transdanubian counties like Fejér, Baranya, Komárom, and

Neolog dominance in the west (Transdanubia) is much more qualified. The data draw upon the late nineteenth-century statistics referred to in note 2 above.

5 These divisions were already clearly demonstrated in the votes cast in the 1868-69 Jewish Congress, as shown in the maps and figures elaborated by Michael Silber in a 1988 lecture concerning the religious affiliation of the deputies attending the Congress. (The map is on display at the Diaspora Museum exhibition on Hungarian Jewry at the Goldmark auditorium in Budapest). Here too northern Orthodoxy is clearly distinct from the southern Neolog regions. The division of Orthodoxy into a Western and an Eastern section is also demonstrable, since the two are separated by a number of relatively Neolog-minded counties north of Budapest (such as Árva, Hont, Zemplén, and Zólyom). Southern Transylvania also belonged to the Neolog orbit during the Jewish Congress.

Veszprém, the majority of those engaged in agriculture belong to this propertied class. The situation is quite similar in western Slovakia, especially in Árva and Turócz counties. The contrary prevails in the east, where small farmers and even farm hands make up the majority. In Bereg, Ugocsa, Ung, and Máramaros (where the proportion of the agricultural population in the region as a whole is well over 20%), and to a lesser degree in Szilágy, Szabolcs, and Szatmár counties (with an agricultural population of around 15%) small farmers are a majority and farm laborers (10% of the active population in Máramaros) are far from uncommon. Given that merchants, craftsmen, and industrial managers also frequently invested in rural property—typically in the east—one arrives at the conclusion that, after the Emancipation, agriculture became a major path of socio-economic diversification and mobility in some sections of traditional Jewry. Here one can mention another typical pattern in the move towards rural bourgeois status, involving either the management of rented property or salaried managerial status on large estates. This pattern is best demonstrated in western Slovakia, but can also be found in Magyarized tradition-bound regions like Szabolcs county, where, out of the 14.8% of the population engaged in agriculture, the land-owning class with over 50 *holds* accounted for 6.6% and estate managers for 3.5%.

In 1910, trade was still the largest individual profession. The proportion of self-employed traders was between 20% and 30% outside Budapest. This surviving traditional occupation still engaged—together with commercial workers and manual laborers—approximately one-third to one-half of active Jewry. All the same, the internal stratification varied significantly from one region to another.

In Budapest as many persons were commercial employees as were self-employed, and the manual labor force in trade was almost the same size. This demonstrates the considerable capital intensity of commerce, that is, the importance of wholesale dealers and large trading companies. This pattern is that of urban Jewry in general, although it was somewhat more accentuated in Neolog towns than in Orthodox ones (see Table 2). By contrast, the poverty of commercial capital investment among Eastern Jewry is striking. The relative scarcity of commercial employees is particularly remarkable in Máramaros, Bereg, Ung, Ugocsa, Szatmár, and Szilágy counties, where the number of employees and executives in trade is less than one-tenth the number of independent traders. This is a sign of under-capitalized, underdeveloped, personalized commercial services. In some sectors of traditional Jewry business and trade represented a sort of economic conservatory, a locus of social immobility, and, at the same time, a cultural hothouse, wherein social reproduction remained confined to the traditional professional framework. In cities, on the other hand—especially in Budapest—the accumulation of trading capital permitted a high degree of mobility in business (from retail to wholesale trade) and also presumably from trade to banking and to industry; hence the low proportion of self-employed merchants in the capital city. A more detailed analysis would find significant differences in the internal structure of the profession as well—rural trade being largely limited to traditional grocery stores, taverns, door-to-door sales, peddling, etc., while urban trade was much more specialized as to the range of products, especially imported wares.

A quite similar interpretation of the Jewish industrial population can be attempted. Since by 1910 there were more Jewish industrial workers (46% of the total) than commercial workers, and given the original professional set-up, heavily dominated by trade, there must have been from the pre-industrial period on a major transfer of the employed Jewish population towards industrial occupations. Since premodern times Jews had a share in industrial crafts, especially among the self-employed (tailors, tanners, goldsmiths, shoemakers, etc.). Twentieth century censuses of the industrial self-employed lumped these together with industrial entrepreneurs, although the number of large-scale entrepreneurs could not have been very great. Here again the relative number of employees and workers vis-à-vis the self-employed is an indicator of the importance of industrial investment and modernization. Regional and community-based differences are quite similar to those in trade, although their scale is even greater. While in the underdeveloped eastern and northeastern regions (e.g., Máramaros) the combined size of the categories of industrial employees and workers falls short of those self-employed, in more developed regions, in the Central and South-Eastern Plain and even in Transylvania they exceed it considerably. In Budapest, industrial executives and employees are almost as numerous as the self-employed, and the industrial proletariat is two-and-a-half times larger still. In comparisons of the western and eastern regions and of Neolog and Orthodox towns and counties, there is a clear opposition between the predominance of the larger industrial enterprises and that of small industry and individual craftsmen. In counties like Abauj-Torna, Bereg, Borsod, Sáros, Ung, Zemplén, Hajdu, Máramaros, Szatmár, Szabolcs, Szilágy, and Ugocsa, industrial executives make up a mere one percent or even less of the labor force. In this eastern and traditional sector of Hungarian Jewry professional mobility in industry remained embryonic and, unlike the situation in the western and central regions of the country, could not contribute significantly to social mobility.

A parallel study could be made concerning the distribution of the educated middle classes, that is, of those professional clusters—the intellectual and liberal professions, the public and the semi-public professions (including clerics, teachers, etc.)—that owe their positions to their educational qualifications. These qualifications are themselves the direct outcome of the new social mobility, since

Jews had formerly been denied access to formal education (in Hungary, at least until the Edict of Tolerance of Joseph II) and excluded from secular, public intellectual professions.

The overall proportion of the educated middle classes hovered around the nationwide average of 6.1% except in some eastern and northeastern regions, like Bereg, Ung, Máramaros, Ugocsa, Beszterce, Csík, Maros-Torda, Szolnok-Doboka, and Udvarhely counties, where it hardly exceeded half that value. This absence of the intellectual middle classes is all the more notable considering that some of these found in the above-mentioned counties must have originated in more developed counties: the professions, including clerics and civil servants, displayed much greater geographical mobility than did other occupations. Despite the obviously unsatisfied demand for professional services, in many eastern Orthodox communities there was a marked deficit of intellectuals. This is also reflected in the extremely low number of secondary school graduates there (Table 3), who accounted for less than 3% of the population in Bereg, Ung, Hajdu, Szatmár, Szilágy, Ugocsa, Beszterce, Kolozs, and Szolnok-Doboka, and as little as 0.7% in Máramaros county—as against a national average of 10%.

Having noted this, we must add that the internal stratification of this educated middle class seems to have varied significantly by region and community affiliation (cf. Table 4). In the cities—whether Neolog or Orthodox (most of them were Neolog)—more than two-thirds (73% in Budapest) of the cluster belong to the freelance liberal professions that tend to require advanced degrees (doctors, engineers, actors, journalists, lawyers); this is the case in Neolog counties too (60%). In other Jewish sectors, such distinctly modern middle-class brackets make up hardly one-half of the cluster. Typically, in Orthodox counties there is a high proportion of rabbis, private and public teachers, and midwives (about 40%), all of these belonging to the traditional Jewish clerical and non-clerical service class. In both eastern and western Orthodox counties, rabbis and clerics, together with (presumably mostly religious) private teachers, make up one-fifth or more of the educated middle class. This is true of counties like Győr, Moson, Sopron, Pozsony, Abauj-Torna, Bereg, Borsod, Sáros, Ung, Zemplén, Ugocsa, Bihar, Hajdu, Máramaros, Szabolcs, Szatmár, Szilágy, Beszterce, Csík, Kolozs, Maros-Torda, and Torda-Aranyos. We can state that in Orthodox regions, especially in eastern Orthodoxy, traditional occupational categories tend to predominate even within the educated intellectual professions.

Special mention must be made of data concerning the proportion of Hungarian civil servants within the educated cluster. Paradoxically, the civil service seems to be strongly represented in Orthodox counties, which might indicate a high degree of social integration by this section of the middle class.

Closer scrutiny shows that civil servants in Orthodox counties were heavily concentrated in administrative positions, as heads of village administrations. In northern and eastern Hungary Jews were often entrusted with such positions in rural settlements with a Jewish majority or a strong Jewish minority.

We can state, then, that Orthodoxy of all sorts was linked with a measure of socio-professional immobility, at least in the long run, and especially when compared with Neolog Jewry. The latter is clearly marked by a high degree of radical social mobility, that is, by a trend of rapid transfer to modern, expanding economic and professional sectors that often demanded large investments in economic and/or educational capital.

Assimilation, Integration and Religious Divisions

This is not the place to elaborate a theory of social integration, let alone of assimilation—a highly controversial issue indeed. I have attempted to sketch out such a theory elsewhere, demonstrating that Jewish "assimilation"—as it occurred in Hungary—can by no means be reduced to a unilateral process of Jews coming closer to Gentiles in terms of their manners, culture, daily language, etc.[6] Instead, it must be seen as a creative process that engendered a new cultural system (in the anthropological sense of the term), one in close contact with Gentiles—especially those of Magyar and German stock. In the course of this process, Jews adopted a number of non-Jewish cultural traits, but also served as cultural innovators and even assimilators when it came to the manners, economic habits, and intellectual behavior of the new middle class. Assimilation was thus not only "assimilation" proper, but also a multi-faceted venture of collective action and change. Nevertheless, indices of "assimilation" do permit a clear-cut opposition between the collective attitudes and achievements of the traditional and more or less "modernized" sectors of Hungarian Jewry.

This is obviously the case with use of the vernacular. It is well known that the Magyar ruling elite exerted considerable pressure on minority groups to learn Hungarian and use it as a general means of communication. Schooling was often forcibly Magyarized (for instance, the abolition of Slovakian gymnasia in 1874); Magyar-language schooling was promoted through special financial incentives and by administrative pressure. Aggregate census data show that Magyarisation made more decisive and rapid progress in the late nineteenth and early twentieth century among the Jews than among any of the other ethnic minorities. All of these, with the exception of some German and Slovak groups, mostly in urban

6 See my article cited in *Mozgó Világ*, p. 41ff.

environments, adamantly resisted linguistic assimilation. Thus the linguistic Magyarization of Hungarian Jewry was an exceptionally successful but rather unique phenomenon.

But there was great inequality in this respect among the various Jewish sectors. Neolog Jewry became deeply Magyarized, so much so that by 1910 Hungarian had become the language of sermons in most Neolog synagogues, while this remained a rarity in Orthodox houses of worship.[7] But linguistic Magyarization in everyday life—accompanied by bilingualism (Yiddish or German remaining the language of the older generation or of the synagogue)—gradually took root in many sectors of Orthodox Jewry too, especially in the cities and in ethnic Magyar milieus. This situation is broadly presented in Tables 3 and 5. Eastern regions, both the northeast and east-central, appear to be more thoroughly Magyarized than the national average. In Máramaros, Bereg, Szepes, Ung, Sáros, and several Transylvanian counties (such as Brassó, Fogaras, Beszterce, and Hunyad), where Jews lived among non-Magyars, Magyarization was slow and very limited; but in Magyar-populated counties in the same geographic region, such as Csík, Háromszék, and Udvarhely (in Transylvania), and, more importantly, in Borsod, Hajdu, and Szabolcs counties, not to speak of east-central cities like Miskolc, Debrecen, and Szatmárnémeti, Magyarization was almost complete (over 90%) by 1910. Yet urban and even small-town Jews were much more Magyarized than their rural co-religionists. Thus the Orthodox-Neolog opposition was not expressed simply in terms of the degree of Magyarization. On the contrary, some Neolog sections (most conspicuously in some Transdanubian counties—like Vas or Baranya—where little more than 50% of the Jews spoke Hungarian) remained relatively untouched by the language change. In addition to a Magyar environment, the factors correlated with such a change were the intensity of public schooling, the importance of the network of Jewish public schools, and other miscellaneous factors of social integration that will be considered below.

Let us stress here only one such factor, education, which was also an essential component of both modernization and assimilation. Since most schools at all levels were conducted in Hungarian, especially at the secondary level and exclusively so thereafter, it is understandable that the number of years of schooling was correlated with the penetration of the Magyar tongue among the Jews. This was obviously the case in the cities, but it also held in Magyar-

7 All the same, Magyarization affected the synagogues of all persuasions. A comparison of data for 1903 and 1912 shows that the proportion of synagogues where the sermon was delivered in Hungarian rose from 78% to 88% among the Neolog, 59% to 68% among the Status quo ante, and from 9% to 13% among the Orthodox. See *Magyar statisztikai közlemények*, 1912, p. 458 and *ibid.*, 1903, p. 403.

populated areas where public primary schools tended to have a monopoly in the educational market. It is remarkable that the proportion of illiterates in general, and particularly of those aged six and above, was extremely high in counties with a majority of Yiddish speakers (Bereg, Máramaros, Ung, and Ugocsa), while it was correspondingly low (less than 15%) in highly Magyarized Orthodox counties (Hajdu, Borsod, Szabolcs, Csík, and Háromszék). Still, the correlation between Magyarization and basic education was not always unambiguous: western Orthodoxy (in Moson, Pozsony, Nyitra, Trencsén, Turócz, Zólyom, and Liptó) had excellent basic educational scores even while it held fast to German (or western Yiddish). This fact can be attributed to a number of independent circumstances, including the density of the school network; the frequency of non-Magyar schools (especially high in the northeast and even in Transdanubia); the presence of strong Western-type educational models—such as German Lutheranism in Transylvania, Transdanubia, and the northwest; the attraction of Austrian and German universities for those interested in pursuing advanced studies; and, most importantly, a higher degree of social mobility towards new middle-class occupations, which could stimulate educational propensities even without a corresponding degree of Magyarisation.

The general correlation between a strong Magyar linguistic bias and a significant educational propensity was much more typical of urban Jewry, and particularly of Neolog Jewry. The correlation is particularly strong between Neology and advanced secular education, since the latter presupposed long-term integration in the secular school system, including the values it conveyed, the common and denominationally neutral socialization it offered, the preeminence of secular knowledge it inculcated, and the importance it gave to the view of national history imposed by the ruling Magyar elite. To continue religious schooling in a more advanced setting in yeshivot, customary in Orthodox Jewry, was to some extent at cross purposes with the pursuit of post-compulsory secular education. This is why the proportion of secondary-school graduates in eastern Orthodox regions was only one-third to one-half of that in Neolog regions. There was a significant difference in this respect between western and eastern Orthodoxy. The proportion of Jewish male secondary-school graduates in northwestern counties like Árva, Nográd, Trencsén, Turócz, and Zólyom exceeded the nationwide average (10%), showing the pervasive character of the Western educational pattern even in some relatively tradition-bound sectors of non-Magyarized Jewry.

Other indicators of social integration, too, demonstrate the major differences between Neolog and Orthodox Jewry, as well as between various sections of Orthodoxy, especially eastern and western Orthodoxy.

Mixed marriages are obviously a case in point. For reasons of space, I must refer the reader to the substantial theoretical interpretation of the social and demographic incidence of this phenomenon that I have suggested elsewhere.[8] Here let us simply note that Jewish-Gentile marriages were effectively proscribed in the region of eastern Orthodoxy and in some of the western counties of Orthodox persuasion (such as Nyitra, Liptó, and Hont). Still, the occurrence of mixed marriage was not insignificant in some other western Orthodox counties, like Moson, Sopron, Trencsén, and Turócz, and even in Orthodox-dominated cities such as Sopron and especially Pozsony (the rate here—above 13% around 1910—which far exceeded the national average, may be due to the presence of a sizable Neolog community alongside the Orthodox majority). While all Neolog counties evinced a generally high rate, the zenith was reached in the central southeastern region, between Tisza and Maros, where the proportion of mixed marriages in cities such as Nagyvárad, Arad, Temesvár, and Szeged often exceeded that in Budapest. In these places, roughly one-fifth of all marriages involving Jews were arranged with non-Jewish partners. Studies of local conditions must account for the specific factors facilitating intermarriage, including the strength of the local Jewish bourgeoisie, the degree of mixing in other arenas of socialization and self-assertion (such as schooling, sports, youth movements, etc.), the ratio of the sexes among young Jewish adults, religious indifference, the frequency of isolated Jewish men or women (possibly isolated immigrants), and so forth. A detailed socio-demographic study of the intermarried in the above-mentioned cities, in which I am currently engaged,[9] will provide more precise information for a thorough analysis of the factors contributing to intermarriage.

Paradoxical as it may seem, the proportion of illegitimate births can also serve, at least in borderline cases, as an indicator (mostly negative) of social integration. The much stronger community control to which Jews were subject, the scarcity among them of sexually free groups (domestic servants, migrant laborers), as well as the pervasive effect of bourgeois morality, considerably reduced the proportion of illegitimate births among Jews vis-à-vis Hungarian Gentiles. Still, it was precisely in the socially most homogeneous sections of traditional Jewry that an astonishingly high proportion of illegitimate births were

8 See my study, "Vers une théorie sociologique des mariages interconfessionnels: Le cas de la nuptialité en Hongrie sous l'ancien régime," *Actes de la recherche en sciences sociales* 57-58 (juin 1985), pp. 47-68.

9 A survey of all Jewish-Gentile marriages between 1896 and 1940, based on public records, has been completed for Nagyvárad (Oradea), Arad, Temesvár (Timisoara), Kassa (Košice), and Szeged, which were the major provincial melting pots. A similar survey is being carried out for the fifth district of Budapest. The first elaboration of the findings will appear in my forthcoming book, *Zsidóság és Magyarság a 20. században. Tanulmányok az asszimilációról* [Jewry and Magyardom in the Twentieth Century: Studies on Assimilation].

regularly recorded: over 15% in Bereg and Beszterce counties, and as much as 45% in Máramaros county. Elsewhere, especially in Neolog cities, illegitimate births were regularly more numerous than among rural Neolog Jewry. To sum up, we can distinguish two independent causes for a relatively high illegitimate birth rate. In urban Jewish environments such as Budapest, but also in cities like Kassa and Kolozsvár, the factors that led to the relative frequency of illegitimate births were similar to those prevailing among Gentile urban groups, and involved the relaxation of family ties and the loosening of collective control over sexual behavior. Even there, though, the rate of Jewish illegitimacy remained far below that of the rest of urban population, specifically because of the low incidence of prostitution and the rarity of floating female domestic servants—the two being statistically interrelated.[10] In the strictly Orthodox eastern counties, similar relaxation of sexual control was of course out of the question. Here illegitimate births must have been more generally connected with the frequent neglect of civil-marriage formalities, which automatically defined as illegitimate all children born of a marriage celebrated only before a rabbi. The frequency of the failure to register a civil marriage can obviously also serve as an indication of the measure of social isolation vis-à-vis the Gentile establishment and as a mark of disrespect or ignorance of the administrative rules, by which civil marriage was made compulsory in 1896.

Modernity and Religious Divisions

All the indicators and processes referred to hitherto, including group-specific patterns of socio-professional mobility, are strongly related to those more-or-less rational attitudes to the life cycle in general and to individual or collective futures in particular that are usually categorized as "modern." In traditional society, the prevailing rules of behavior are stringently defined by tradition and do not encompass a quest to improve living conditions by rational planning and, more generally, by maximizing the profits deriving from economic and social activities. To be sure, there was necessarily always a measure of rationality in

10 The scarcity of uncontrolled female domestic servants among the Jews must have been a major factor in this respect. While in 1910 Jews represented 5% of the economically active population, their share among domestic servants was as low as 1.6% nationwide, and even in Budapest (where Jews constituted 23.1% of all workers) only 2.6%. The corresponding figures, though always less than the percentage of Jews among the working population, were significantly higher in the easternmost counties, the home of the most traditional and poorest sections of Hungarian Jewry—Bereg (14% of Jews among domestic servants), Máramaros (14.8%), and Ugocsa (11.9%) counties, and in the city of Szatmárnémeti (11.9%). Cf. *Magyar statisztikai közlemények* 64 (Budapest, 1920), pp. 278-279.

Jewish economic attitudes, to compensate for the system of legal restrictions and constraints that Jews had suffered in pre-Emancipation times; but an attitude of rationality in matters that were not strictly economic developed differentially in Jewish circles according to their respect for religious tradition or degree of secularization. This is why we can find considerable differences among various sections of Jewry in the non-economic social indicators of modernity. Most of these indicators are of a demographic nature, since demographic data were among the most reliable collected by old-regime statisticians.

The fall of birthrates was one of the earliest and most distinctive indicators of modernity in non-traditional circles, probably because it was closely linked with conscious efforts at improvement of one's children's prospects of socio-economic mobility. Active birth control increases along with the per capita income of the family, permitting a corresponding growth in the family investments devoted to each child—in financial, affective, emotional, and practical terms—in formal education, in child-rearing services, etc. This is why, in early modern times, mobile groups tended to the systematic practice of demographic Malthusianism, especially when schooling became an essential asset of social mobility. The impact of regional and group-specific differences in this respect are most patent in Tables 3 and 5. While traditional Orthodox Jewry, especially in the east, maintained a quasi-natural rate of fertility—with 35 or more births pro mil in Bereg, Máramaros, Ugocsa, Ung, Hajdu, Szabolcs, Szatmár, Syilágy, Háromszék, Beszterce, Hunyad, Kisküküllő, Szolnok-Doboka, and Torda-Maros counties—in western Jewry, even in Orthodox counties like Trencsén, Turócz, Moson, Sopron, Árva, Nyitra, and Bars, birthrates tended to drop below the national average. By the early twentieth century, Neolog counties and urban Jewry—especially in Baja, Újvidék, Kecskemét, Baranya, Pécs, Arad, Temesvár, Pancsova, and Versec—the birthrates hardly reached the replacement level. The behavior of the Neolog Jewish community of Budapest must have been similar, though it cannot be statistically demonstrated because of the relatively high fertility of the local Orthodox community. Between the two world wars the demographic crisis of the entire Jewish population of the capital was obvious.

If migration trends do not intervene, low fertility automatically results in an aging of the population, while there is a surplus of the younger age groups in communities with a high birthrate. The latter structure can be observed in eastern Orthodox Jewry, including Transylvania. The former trend prevailed in the west and in the cities, where the proportion of the young—those under 7 years of age—tended to approach that of the over-60 group. This was typically the case in Transdanubia and in the Tisza-Maros region. In Budapest both the young and the old were under-represented. This peculiarity was probably due to the presence of many young adult immigrants, especially males of working age.

Mortality also presents significant, though not so sharp, regional and group-specific patterns. Differences in deathrates started to appear in the nineteenth century, largely because of the unequal availability of medical care in different regions and among different social groups; but since the medical science of those days—even at the highest level—was still largely impotent in the face of many infectious and other diseases, most conspicuously tuberculosis (the most common cause of death before the age of 50) differences in mortality rates were due essentially to living conditions and welfare, which is why the urban population with its poor housing suffered in particular. This is why observed differences in deathrates are much smaller than those in birthrates. Nevertheless they remain highly significant. In many eastern Orthodox regions, four out of ten children died before the age of seven; in most other western and Neolog regions the incidence was much less, though never negligible. Paradoxically enough, the lowest death rates (around 20%) were registered in counties of northwestern Orthodoxy, like Moson, Liptó, the city of Pozsony, Trencsén, Turócz, and Zólyom. This reminds us once again of the unique traits of western Orthodoxy, marked not only by a rationalist rabbinical tradition (and by the complete absence of Hasidism), but also by a degree of embourgeoisement in a number of small or large cities (Pozsony, for one) and by the direct influence of western Jewry (in Vienna, Brünn, or Prague) in terms of life style, economic attitudes, and conscious investment in medical services.

Divorce rates can also serve as an indication of modernity, if we consider that the propensity to divorce expresses a rational attitude towards marriage, including the acceptance of its break-up in the case of personal incompatibility between the partners. It is certainly an index of a more secular approach to marriage, even though Jewish religious law recognizes the right to divorce. The proportion of divorces could not have grown very much by 1910, since at that time the civil law concerning divorce—which served as a basis for contemporary statistics on the matter—dated back for only fifteen years. Still, the contrast between urban and rural Jewry was dramatic. While Budapest and the south-central regions exceeded the national average, the rest of the country, especially the easternmost regions had far fewer divorces. The divorce rate in traditionalist Máramaros county was barely one-third the national average and less than one-fifth that of Budapest.

The level of women's education is another indicator of modernity, inasmuch as it is heavily dependent on the move towards women's emancipation and on non-traditional conceptions of the women's role as a wage-earner and autonomous personality worthy of educational investments comparable to those made for males. Investment in formal education for women was typical only of the most secularized middle-class circles among both Jews and Gentiles. It is most remarkable that in many provinces the provision of relatively advanced schooling for women (4-6 years of high school) exceeded or equalled that of the capital. This was the case in many Neolog cities, but also, and more importantly, in rural regions of western Orthodoxy, such as Liptó and Zólyom counties, and in some smaller but highly modern southern Transylvanian communities, such as Brassó, Temes, and Háromszék counties. This fact once again attests to the importance of the secular educational model in the West, which was also found in Transylvania among German Lutherans as well as among Jews originating from Western countries in general, whether they sided in religious matters with the Orthodox or the Neolog.

Conclusions

The social indicators of modernity clearly divide Hungarian Jewry into two major sectors which broadly correspond to the Orthodox-Neolog division. Still, the main conclusion of this investigation—which I believe will be more confirmed by a statistical factor analysis, currently in preparation, of all interrelated indicators dealt with above, should stress the importance of secondary divisions cutting across the Neolog-Orthodox divide. Several essential principles of such secondary divisions can be clearly discerned within both the Neolog and Orthodox camps. One of these principles is obviously related to selective urbanization and economic development. To be sure, urbanization per se, the mere concentration of a large Jewish population in administratively autonomous centers, is by no means a condition of modernization. In the northeast the reconstruction of traditional *shtetl* culture is well attested in large semi-rural townships such as Máramarossziget, Ungvár, Munkács, etc. In order to produce deep-reaching cultural change, urbanization must be combined with rapid economic development. This happened most conspicuously in Budapest and in some provincial cities in the west, but even more markedly in the southeast. The major centers of Jewish modernization emerged in rapidly developing towns along the main routes of inter-regional and international trade, like Pozsony (where the large Orthodox community coexisted with a smaller Neolog community) and, more importantly, in Nagyvárad, Arad, Temesvár, and Szeged. This raises the question of selective migration trends, that is, the self-selection of the more enterprising sectors of Jewry—who also appear to be more inclined to attitudinal change and to religious modernity and secularization—in these emerging centers of economic development. Local history should focus upon how the economic development there attracted mobile Jewish groups, which in turn substantially strengthened the trends of economic development, a clearly circular causal relationship. The institutional and social conditions of this process should also be more closely studied, especially the availability of schools—particularly secular secondary gymnasia—and the local ethnic and socio-economic structure of the Gentile environment and its attitude towards the Jews. The centers of Jewish modernization mentioned above were also to some extent serving as melting pots for the social integration of Jewry—at least during the Dual Monarchy.

The ethnic origin of the Jews and the ethnic composition of the local host society are major factors in this respect. The East-West division of Orthodoxy largely corresponded to the contrast between Jews of Galician, Bukovinian, and Moravian (Austrian and German) extraction, and had to do with initial levels of literacy, with the nature of the rabbinic tradition, with differential access to and influence of the Jewish *haskalah*, with initial life styles—especially the absence of an integrated *shtetl* culture in the West—with the degree of early embourgeoisement, and, last but not least, with the presence of Hasidic communities. Thus the pervasive opposition between Eastern and Western Jewry, going well beyond ethnic origins, can be formulated in sociological terms.

Ethnic environment was a major watershed within eastern Orthodoxy itself. In a Magyar environment, the eastern parts of the Central Plain, a rapid and thorough process of Magyarization had been completed by the early twentieth century. The switch to the vernacular went hand in hand with a far-reaching political identification with Hungarian nationalism, with loyalty to the State and government, and with social symbiosis with the Gentile rural environment. In non-Magyar environments, such as Ruthenia, linguistic Magyarization and other aspects of assimilation (except perhaps political allegiance) remained quite limited. A similar division can be observed in western Orthodoxy too. Generally speaking, local observations, especially those concerning mixed marriages, show that integration was easier in a Magyar environment than among non-Magyar ethnic groups. Cultural as well as social assimilation was preferentially directed towards the Magyar elite and ethnic Magyar marriage partners. This raises the problem of the differential social acceptance of Jews in Magyar and non-Magyar environments and the factors that played a role in the acceptance process: the attitudes to Jewish integration held by various ethnic groups (the "assimilationist" contract proposed by the liberal political elite), the nature of the school system as an agency of cultural assimilation and social integration, the socio-economic composition of ethnic partner groups, etc.

When all of these factors have been considered, one can arrive at a much more complex image of Hungarian Jewry than that suggested by the Orthodox-Neolog division. Within Orthodoxy, western Jewry must be distinguished from both eastern Yiddish-speaking and eastern Magyar-speaking communities; within the Neolog sector, urban-modern Jews must be distinguished from their rural and relatively traditional brethren. Other secondary divisions could and should be made according to the place of Jews in the local social and political power structure—which was important in most Neolog urban centers and quite limited elsewhere.

Appendix: Regional Categories Used

A. Geographic Divisions By Counties (Modification of Historic Regions)

Northwest (Western Slovakia)
Sopron, Győr, Moson, Komárom, Esztergom, Pozsony, Nyitra, Hont, Bars, Nógrád, Turócz, Zólyom, Trencsén, Liptó, Árva
Transdanubia
Fejér, Veszprém, Vas, Zala, Somogy, Tolna, Baranya
Northeast (Eastern Slovakia and Ruthenia)
Szepes, Gömör, Abauj-Torna, Sáros, Zemplén, Ung, Bereg, Ugocsa, Máramaros
East-Central (High Tisza region, Eastern Plain)
Borsod, Heves, Hajdu, Szabolcs, Szatmár, Bihar, Szilágy
Central Plain (between Danube and Tisza)
Pest-Pilis-Solt-Kiskun, Bács-Bodrog
South-Central Plain (between Tisza and Maros)
Jász-Nagykun, Csongrád, Békés, Csanád, Arad, Temes, Torontál, Krassó-Szörény
Transylvania
Hunyad, Kolozs, Torda-Aranyos, Alsó-Fehér, Szeben, Kis-Küküllő, Nagy-Küküllő, Fogaras, Szolnok-Doboka, Beszterce-Naszód, Maros-Torda, Udvarhely, Brassó, Háromszék, Csík

B. Religious Divisions*

Budapest
Liberal-dominated cities
Pécs, Szabadka, Zombor, Újvidék, Baja, Szeged, Arad, Nagyvárad, Kolozsvár, Temesvár, Kassa, Selmecbánya, Székesfehérvár, Kecskemét, Hódmezővásárhely, Brassó, Versec, Fiume
Orthodox-dominated cities
Miskolc, Márosvásárhely, Szatmárnémeti
"Mixed cities"
Debrecen, Sopron, Győr, Pozsony
Liberal-dominated counties
Arad, Bács-Bodrog, Baranya, Békés, Csanád, Csongrád, Fogaras, Jász-Nagykun, Krassó-Szörény, Pest-Pilis-Solt-Kiskun, Somogy, Torontál, Zala
Orthodox-dominated counties
Bereg, Borsod, Gömör-Kishont, Hajdu, Hunyad, Kolozs, Máramaros, Maros-Torda, Moson, Nagy-Küküllő, Pozsony, Sáros, Sopron, Szabolcs, Szatmár, Szepes, Szilágy, Szolnok-Doboka, Ung, Zemplén
"Mixed counties"
Abauj-Torna, Brassó, Esztergom, Fejér, Győr, Heves, Hont, Nyitra, Nógrád, Tolna, Trencsén, Vas, Veszprém

* Some counties, unidentified by religious status, have been omitted.

Table 1: Socio-Professional Stratification of Hungarian Jewry By Regions , 1910 (%)

	Agriculture	Industry and Transport			Trade and banking			Civil service and professions	Total	Jewish Population
		Employees & executives	Self-employed	Manual workers	Employees & executives	Self-employed	Manual workers			
Transdanubia	5.1	3.8	18.6	13.6	6.2	30.3	15.2	6.6	100	90,075
Northwest (Western Slovakia)	7.2	5.0	22.5	16.3	4.3	24.9	13.6	6.2	100	87,360
Central plain (between Danube & Tisza)	0.9	9.1	12.5	27.4	11.9	16.7	10.3	6.5	100*	294,254
Northeast (Eastern Slovakia)	13.7	2.3	22.8	18.4	3.2	22.4	11.9	5.1	100	122,286
East and Central East (High Tisza region)	17.1	2.1	20.3	17.5	4.0	22.8	11.1	2.8	100	197,384
Between Tisza and Maros	3.5	7.2	13.8	12.7	10.4	29.6	12.8	9.5	100	34,098
Transylvania	7.2	4.7	21.7	22.2	3.9	22.0	12.1	5.3	100	64,074
Hungary outside Croatia	6.7	6.0	17.9	20.6	7.8	22.1	12.0	6.1	100	911,227
Máramaros	33.3	0.7	19.5	15.7	1.4	19.2	8.0	1.9	100*	65,694
Budapest	0.5	10.6	12.3	28.9	14.0	14.0	10.0	6.4	100	203,687

* Approximate data only.

Table 2: Socio-Professional Stratification of Hungarian Jewry by Residence and Estimated Community Affiliation, 1910 (%)

	Budapest	Liberal towns	Liberal counties	Mixed towns	Mixed counties	Orthodox towns	Orthodox counties	Others
Agriculture	0.5	1.4	4.4	3.5	7.3	1.7	17.6	6.8
Industry, mining:								
Employees & executives	8.9	6.5	3.7	5.9	3.3	2.6	1.3	4.7
Self-employed	12.3	16.2	16.4	15.4	21.3	18.6	21.9	17.7
Manual workers	23.7	18.0	15.8	17.7	14.0	23.1	16.4	18.3
Trade, banking:								
Employees & executives	14.0	12.4	6.9	11.2	4.5	8.8	2.2	7.6
Self-employed	14.0	22.7	29.2	22.0	27.4	22.5	23.3	21.9
Manual workers	10.0	12.4	13.8	15.0	13.1	14.7	11.5	11.9
Transport								
Employees and workers	6.9	3.2	2.4	2.4	2.2	2.8	1.5	3.7
Civil service, liberal and intellectual professions	6.4	8.2	7.5	7.7	6.9	6.4	4.2	6.0
Total	96.7	101.1	100.0	100.0	100.0	101.2	100.0	98.6

Table 3: Indicators of Assimilation and Modernity in Hungarian Jewry by Region, 1910 (%)

	Transdanubia	NW	Central Plain	NE	E & CE	Between Tisza &Maros	Transylvania	Hungary without Croatia	Budapest	Máramaros
Birthrate	21.6	23.9	20.4	34.5	37.4	19.5	34.1	27.7	19.2	42.4
Illegitimate births	1.2	9.6	7.0	8.2	20.1	2.7	8.2	10.1	9.4	45.1
Child mortality (under 7)	28.7	26.9	29.3	36.4	41.7	32.5	35.9	34.9	27.3	40.9
Elderly (over 60)	10.4	10.0	7.1	7.2	5.8	8.7	5.5	7.4	6.5	4.5
Young (under 7)	13.9	14.8	12.4	20.0	20.5	12.8	18.9	16.2	11.0	23.9
Married	41.5	39.4	39.1	36.5	36.2	42.8	37.6	38.3	38.2	33.8
Divorcees	0.6	0.7	1.6	0.5	0.7	1.1	0.9	1.0	1.9	0.4
Mixed marriages (1909-11)	7.9	4.5	16.8	2.2	2.6	18.9	6.7	9.4	18.4	0.2
Graduates of 8 years of secondary school										
men	8.9	8.9	17.4	4.6	3.9	13.8	6.2	10.1	20.3	0.7
women	1.2	0.9	3.2	0.5	0.5	1.6	0.7	1.5	4.1	0.1
Graduates of 4 or 6 years of secondary school										
men	12.4	14.2	16.7	6.7	5.6	17.5	9.7	11.7	8.2	0.9
women	12.4	14.7	21.6	6.4	5.7	20.2	9.0	13.2	24.0	0.8
Illiterates (all ages)										
men	15.8	17.2	13.2	29.2	38.0	14.1	28.1	22.2	11.5	64.7
women	18.7	19.8	16.3	35.5	45.9	18.0	35.3	27.8	14.8	71.9
Illiterates (over 6)	6.1	6.7	4.6	18.4	29.8	5.8	18.4	13.2	4.0	60.4
Magyar mother tongue	75*	32.4	80.8	53.0	61.6	22.0	33.9	44.1	84.8	14.7

*Approximate data only

Table 4: Socio-Professional Stratification of Hungarian Jewry within the Intellectual Professions by Residence and Estimated Community Affiliation, 1910*

	Budapest	Liberal towns	Liberal counties	Mixed towns	Mixed counties	Orthodox towns	Orthodox counties	Others
Civil service	8.0	14.7	15.7	10.4	15.3	13.0	18.1	13.9
Lawyers and employees of lawyers	37.8	39.3	27.6	38.4	28.6	36.2	21.9	31.0
Doctors, veterinaries, pharmacists	18.8	22.0	28.5	21.8	23.9	19.9	18.5	21.5
Engineers	6.6	1.2	1.2	0.8	0.5	1.3	0.7	2.6
Schoolteachers and professors	10.7	8.3	12.7	12.5	14.4	9.4	11.5	11.6
Rabbis and clerics	0.7	1.9	3.8	3.9	5.8	3.8	9.7	3.9
Private teachers	6.0	2.8	3.9	3.1	6.2	3.3	9.9	6.1
Actors	3.0	4.4	1.8	5.5	0.8	7.7	1.1	2.6
Journalists	6.3	2.8	1.1	1.8	0.8	2.3	0.3	2.7
Midwives	2.2	2.7	3.7	2.9	3.6	3.1	8.3	4.1
Total	100.1	100.1	100.0	101.1	100.0	99.9	100.0	100.0

* % of all those employed in the civil service, the liberal and the intellectual professions.

Table 5: Indicators of Assimilation and Modernity among Hungarian Jewry by Residence and Estimated Community Affiliation, 1910 (%)

	Budapest	Liberal towns	Liberal counties	Mixed towns	Mixed counties	Orthodox towns	Orthodox counties	Others
Birthrate	19.3	21.1	23.5	24.3	23.7	29.7	37.0	27.7
Illegitimate births	9.4	5.8	2.5	4.5	10.6	4.4	15.4	10.0
Illiterates (over age 6)	4.0	6.6	6.6	5.1	7.2	8.3	26.7	13.3
Illiterates (all ages)								
men	11.5	15.0	17.6	?	17.5	18.4	36.1	22.5
women	14.8	19.1	20.3	?	20.2	24.3	43.2	27.9
Graduates of 8 years of secondary school								
men	20.3	14.2	9.3	12.0	9.3	8.6	3.2	10.0
women	4.1	2.4	1.2	1.2	0.9	1.5	0.3	1.5
Graduates of 4 or 6 years of secondary school								
men	8.1	17.7	12.6	16.3	13.4	13.1	5.0	11.7
women	23.9	21.6	12.8	9.5	14.3	14.0	4.5	13.1
Divorcees	1.85	1.17	0.87	1.1	0.7	1.0	0.5	1.0
Mixed marriages 1909-1911	18.5	15.0	12.7	11.8	4.3	5.8	2.0	9.3

V

Politics and Economy

Mór Wahrmann: A Jewish Banker in Hungarian Politics in the Era of the Dual Monarchy

Károly Vörös

Complicated economic and social processes can be understood not only by examining them at the level of large social groups but also by tracing the careers of prominent individuals. Such biographical studies can answer questions about social processes that cannot be understood solely through analysis of large social groups. By way of example, the history of Hungary's Jews under the Dual Monarchy can be brought into sharper focus by examining the career of Mór Wahrmann (1832-1894), a Jewish politician from an upper-middle-class Budapest family.[1]

1 The following works were used when writing this study: On the history of the Jews in Hungary: Lajos Venetianer, *A magyar zsidóság története a honfoglalástól a háború kitöréséig* [The History of Hungarian Jewry from the Conquest of the Country to the Outbreak of the War], (Budapest, 1922); György Szalai, "A hazai zsidóság magyarosodása" [The Magyarization of the Jews of Hungary], in *Világosság* XIV (1977), 216-223; Károly Vörös, "Ungarns Judentum vor der bürgerlichen Revolution," in *Studies in East European Social History*, ed. Keith Hitchins (Leiden, 1981), vol. II, pp. 139-156. On Budapest: János Kósa, *Pest és Buda elmagyarosodása 1848-ig* [The Magyarization of Pest and Buda to 1848], (Budapest, 1937), pp. 93-131. On the Wahrmann family: Ede Vadász, "Adalékok a Wahrmann-, Szófer- (Schreiber-), gorlicei Weiss- és Fischmann-családok származási adataiból; a családok kiválóbbjainak életrajzaihoz is" [Contributions to the origins of the Wahrmann, Szófer (Schreiber), Weiss of Gorlitz and Fischmann families, as well as the biographies of the most outstanding members of these families], *Magyar Zsidó Szemle* XXIV (1907), 313-341. Biographies of Mór Wahrmann: A scholarly biography of Mór Wahrmann, utilizing sources accessible at the time, is Gyula Mérei, "Mór Wahrmann," *IMIT Évkönyve* (Budapest, 1943), pp. 313-343. A popular biography is Andor Kellér, *Mayer Wolff fia* [The Son of Mayer Wolff: A Biography of Mór Wahrmann], (Budapest, [1947]). Short biographical summaries include: *Vasárnapi Újság* (1878), no. 51 and (1892), no. 49; *Ország Tükre* (1865), no. 37; *Magyarország és a Nagyvilág* (1869), no. 27; Dr. Constant von Wurzbach, *Biographisches Lexikon des Kaisertums Österreich* (Vienna, 1885), vol. 52, p. 147 and pp. 144-146 (the biographies of Israel Wahrmann and Jehuda Wahrmann); József Szinnyei, *Magyar irók élete és munkái* [Lives and works of Hungarian writers] (Budapest, 1914), vol. 14, columns 1397-1398 and columns 1395-1397 (the biographies of Israel Wahrmann and Jehuda Wahrmann).

The scope of this study does not extend to a detailed description of the Jewish impact on Hungarian history. The basic features of this contribution are well known, although many details are only now coming to light. As feudalism waned in Hungary, Jews (including the first Wahrmanns) began to play an increasingly active role in the economic and social development of the new Hungary.

We do not know where the Wahrmann family originated or when it migrated to Hungary. The first member of the family known to us, Israel Wahrmann, was born in Old Buda in 1755. As a young man he studied at various yeshivot, first in Hungary in Kismárton (Eisenstadt), then in Pozsony (Pressburg) and later in Prague. He returned home from Prague in 1781 after marrying a girl from a wealthy family. Israel's plans to become a rabbi pleased his father-in-law. By becoming a rabbi he took his first step up the Jewish social ladder (it was not only among Christians that the clergy enjoyed a favoured status). His career was successful. He became an assistant rabbi in Posen and was later elected rabbi in the Hungarian community of Keresztur. In 1796 the Jewish community of Pest invited him to become their rabbi. He accepted and remained there until his death in 1826. In 1814, against considerable conservative opposition, he founded the congregation's first modern school, basing it upon models in Amsterdam and Kassel. Thanks to his efforts, in 1825 the Chancellery passed a decree mandating one hour of religious studies a week for Jewish secondary-school students (later broadened to include Jewish university students), a requirement that implied an unprecedented toleration of Judaism by the non-Jewish educational institutions. (There were as yet no Jewish secondary schools.) He remained a strictly orthodox Jew, yet he believed that religious and secular studies could be combined.[2]

Israel's children embarked upon a variety of careers. Of his five sons (he also had four daughters) two became rabbis, while the other three chose business. His first son, David Joseph Wahrmann (1793-1852), graduated from the Piarist gymnasium and took a liberal-arts degree at the University of Pest before moving to Galicia. In 1826 he turned down an offer to replace his father as rabbi in Pest. Later, however, he accepted the rabbinate of Nagy Várad where he served from 1842 until his death ten years later. He was a master of rhetoric and hermeneutics and an outstanding rabbinical scholar. In 1847, he welcomed the Palatine Archduke István to his town on behalf of his congregation, speaking in Latin because he regarded German as inappropriate and his own knowledge of Hungarian as inadequate. He ran his congregation skillfully and became very popular. Israel's third son, Jehuda Wahrmann (d. 1868), attended the same Piarist secondary school and went on to the university in Pest, where he studied

2 On Israel Wahrmann, see Ignatz Reich, *Beth-El* (Pest, 1859), vol. I, esp. p. 124.

philosophy with the enlightened Lajos Schaedius. He, unlike his older brother, already learned Hungarian. He continued his Judaic studies in Prague and after his first essays in exegesis he returned to Pest. Here in 1836 he published his works on the system of tropes in the Bible and later, in poetry and prose. As a consequence of his marriage he too moved to Galicia in 1833, but because of the increasingly oppressive situation there, he returned to Hungary, first to Miskolc and then to Pest. In both places he engaged in various business enterprises, but with no great success. He also took on the duties of the principal of the Jewish school in Óbuda: perhaps this also played a role in his bankruptcy in 1848. His father's community decided to appoint him as a *dayan*, an assistant rabbi, a position he continued to fill until his death. In 1861-1862, he wrote excellent German textbooks on religion for Jewish students.

Israel Wahrmann's second son, Mayer Wolf (1795-1859), departed from the careers chosen by his brothers, and became a successful textile merchant. After he took the business over from his father-in-law, he moved its location several times, first from the present-day Anker palace to 10 Gyula Alpári Street and later to what is today 5 Akadémia Street. As a member of the royal and imperial privileged wholesale merchants' association, he was moving closer and closer to the busy, elegant center of town then under construction. Less is known about Israel's other two sons: Abraham Solomon became chief cantor in Óbuda, while Ezekiel also embarked on a business career.

Mór Wahrmann was born in Pest in February, 1832 to Mayer Wolf and Regina Weiss, the daughter of a wealthy Galician merchant. His father provided him with a thorough education. Mór belonged to the third Pest generation of the Wahrmann family. He graduated from the Lutheran gymnasium and Pest University (where he studied liberal arts). But already in 1847, when Mór was only 15, his father began to employ him in the textile factory. Five years later he became manager and in 1858, a partner in the firm. During this time the family dealings branched out into banking. After his father's death in 1859, Mór Wahrmann became sole proprietor of the *Wahrmann and Son Bank*, licensed to operate in both Buda and Pest. By the early sixties Wahrmann had become a successful businessman, well-known in both cities. One of the reasons for his success may have been his ability to look beyond the confines of business; he had a good understanding of the wider social-political environment.

Mór Wahrmann brought his family into the political arena, adding a new role for a clan already prominent in religion and business. He accurately foresaw the rapid growth of an independent Hungarian economy (despite Vienna's centralized economic policy), where Pest-Buda, at the center of a rapidly growing rail network, would play the key role in trade and banking. In the early 1860s Wahrmann wrote newspaper articles about ways to make Hungary financially independent of Austria. The articles attracted the attention of the faction aligned with Ferenc Deák, which was at the time drafting the Compromise (which in 1867 restored Hungary's constitutional rights). The Deák camp had long regarded the establishment of a separate Hungarian national economy as an important step towards loosening the political ties with Austria. More than the Compromise was needed to achieve this. The Hungarian economy had to become part of the mainstream of the *Gründerzeit*. But the Deák group was also aware of the need for financial support from leading Hungarian and Viennese businessmen. The Jews constituted the most significant group among them; hence a great effort was made to win them over.

In 1867, almost on the morrow of the enactment of the Compromise, Article XVIII was enacted granting the Jews full emancipation. Among other rights, Jews were guaranteed direct and indirect suffrage (naturally subject to the limitations imposed upon other Hungarian citizens).

Mór Wahrmann became the first Jew to sit in the Hungarian Parliament. He was brought in at the recommendation of Ferenc Deák, who believed that Jewish interests coincided with those of the capitalist merchants and, by and large, with those of the liberal nobility too.[3] Wahrmann represented Budapest's modern business center, Lipótváros, a constituency whose electorate was composed mostly of upper-middle-class Jews. First elected in 1869, he served eight terms, until his death in 1894. Only once was his election contested. Until the very end he remained a member of the Liberal Party, although he bolted the party for a few months in 1878 in protest over the occupation of Bosnia-Herzegovina, because he regarded the cost of the action to be unwarranted.

Even before he became a parliamentarian, Wahrmann was concerned with the problems of Jews and their position in the Hungarian economy. At the time, the Jews of Hungary were sharply divided and not only along economic lines. Traditional Jewish ways of life were being challenged by the demands of a society undergoing rapid change. Neolog Judaism—a mild variation of the German Reform movement—was beginning to view Orthodoxy as ever more alien and anachronistic vis-à-vis Hungary's new economic and social conditions, which were characterized by a rapid growth of the middle class and a new industrial base. Their outlook came into conflict with Orthodoxy from the early 1840s on. The line dividing the two camps was their attitude towards bourgeois development and a specific (or at least so perceived) Jewish identity expressed in a conservative religious value system.

In the immediate years following the Compromise, the conflict errupted when the Hungarian government, following the precedent set for Protestant denominations, called for the establishment of a national organization for Jewish

3 Mérei, "Mór Wahrmann," 321.

congregations. Until then, Jewish congregations had been completely independent of one another and there was no central organization to represent national interests. One of the government's aims was to facilitate direct communication with Hungary's Jewish congregations. A congress was convened to establish such a national organization. Its president was Ignác Hirschler, a renowned eye doctor; Wahrmann served as its vice-president. Despite initial agreement that the Congress was not to discuss religious issues, the sessions were occasionally disturbed by religious disputes. The final result of the 81-day Congress was the division of Hungary's Jews into three groups: the Neolog (Congress), the Orthodox and the Status quo organizations. The Congress's discussions reflected the tensions that existed in the Jewish community at large.[4] Although genuinely loyal to their nation, Hungary's Jewish population was still strongly influenced by certain positive and negative experiences acquired over the generations in a variety of host societies. This complex background unavoidably influenced the Jews' struggle to determine norms of behavior compatible with their religious traditions. Considering that Wahrmann came from an upper-middle-class family and (with justification) expected to play a significant role in national politics, it is not surprising that he joined the Neologs. In 1881 he became the president of the Pest Neolog community, succeeding Ignac Hirschler. The religious split among the Jews of course had nothing to do with a change in their traditional livelihoods. Yet Jewish tradesmen and professionals were becoming increasingly influential in developing Hungary's market economy and in contributing to the momentum towards urban dominance. Their impact was especially felt in Budapest, which had become Hungary's economic center. Here Jews constituted 25% of the city's population throughout the Dual Monarchy period. Hence it is not surprising that in 1872 it was Mór Wahrmann along with Ferenc Házmán (representing a Buda district) who submitted the bill to unify Pest, Buda, and Óbuda.

Wahrmann was one of the most influential and certainly one of the most durable figures in Hungarian politics. Until the very end he was a member of the Hungarian Delegation to the Austro-Hungarian Monarchy's Joint Committee and served on the finance committee in the House of Representatives. As the Liberals' financial expert, his opinion carried decisive weight during budget negotiations. In 1875, he was actually nominated for the post of Finance Minister and apparently only his failing eyesight prevented his appointment.[5]

4 On the 1868-69 congress of Hungarian Jews (with a bibliography), see: Thomas Domján, "Der Kongress der ungarischen Israeliten 1868-69," *Ungarn-Jahrbuch* I (Mainz, 1969), 139-162.

5 Mérei, "Mór Wahrmann," 321.

But above all he was known for his affluence. We do not know exactly where his wealth came from. Especially in the early seventies he figured in a number of industrial and financial ventures. His bank was still a registered firm in 1888. The best guess is that his enormous wealth originated from skillful trading on the stock exchange. His contemporaries testified to his outstanding talent, saying that before the first morning reports arrived from the exchange he could predict what was going to happen during the day's trading. He is said to have made fantastic profits by buying gold very cheaply at the time of the *baisse* and selling them after their value had gone up considerably. He was known to have good contacts with brokers. His contemporaries also knew that the Wahrmann banking house almost collapsed during the Vienna Stock Exchange crash of 1873: the firm was saved only through the intervention of the finance minister, Menyhért Lónyay, who was later to become a count and prime minister. In gratitude, Wahrmann became a loyal supporter of Lónyay's. Wahrmann lived in high style, displaying his wealth in his luxurious apartment on the first floor of the Tänzer House (today, 3 Akadémia Street), where he kept his important art collection.

Wahrmann was a popular figure in Parliament: "He never left home without his glasses and wit," said Kálmán Tisza. He was short, myopic, and not particularly handsome, with a large bald head, and a sharp tongue. Mikszáth, who covered Parliament for decades, depicted Wahrmann as one of that body's most enduring characters. Others painted a less favorable picture. As he grew older, Wahrmann became more bristly and sullen. A particularly negative portrait was depicted by Ignaz Goldziher, already then a world-renowned Orientalist and a corresponding member of the Academy from 1875, who served as the general secretary of Pest's Neolog community. In Goldziher's diaries, Wahrmann, the president of the community, looms as a threatening figure constantly humiliating and scolding (in public, if possible) his unfortunate underling, deprecating his worth not only as a scholar but as a man as well. To be fair, however, it must be pointed out that Goldziher himself appears throughout his diary as a person difficult to get along with, extremely touchy and (albeit with some justification) fairly vain.[6]

A speech delivered to his Lipótváros constituents on 27 May 1884 gives a glimpse of Wahrmann the politician. On this occasion Wahrmann described the current state of Hungarian liberalism and presented his own opinion on the subject. He also gave his views on the other important Hungarian political parties and their policies. It had been only two years since the Tiszaeszlár anti-Jewish trial had stirred up popular antisemitism. In 1884, there were only a few

6 For Goldziher's hostile remarks, see Ignaz Goldziher, *Tagebuch*, ed. by Alexander Scheiber (Leiden. 1978), pp. 96-98, 141, 155-156.

survivors of the two liberal generations that of the pre-1848 Age of Reforms and of the framers of the 1867 Compromise. The Hungarian political scene was undergoing significant changes, turning towards new and not exactly liberal ideals.

It was these very changes and dangers that he warned about in his speech. On the right, "reactionary forces" were threatening "individual and political freedoms" and pushing for radical economic changes. Socialists and anarchists menaced on the left. Wahrmann argued that the threats from both right and left had to be taken seriously, since they jeopardized not only individuals and society but perhaps the very existence of the Hungarian state. In 1867 there had been a consensus in support of liberal, democratic development. It included followers of "Lajos Kossuth, the nation's greatest patriot, and Ferenc Deák, its sage," and even received the support of the center-left and ethnic minorities. After that, however, this general agreement dissolved as the government spent its funds to maintain the state and came to be viewed by the public as a haven for opportunists. Special-interest groups concerned only with their own selfish goals came into being, and the political parties were no longer able to curb them. After seventeen years of such corruption, the reactionary forces could openly advocate the overthrow of parliamentarism and liberalism, in favor of a revival of the old feudal system. This brand of reaction came from Germany: its program advocated agrarian interests, opposition to parliamentary government, curbing freed industry, antisemitism, and feudalism. The reactionaries were willing to make compromises even with the social democrats, playing them off against the liberals. But whereas in Germany the reactionary forces were recruited from the upper class, and the middle class was able to resist its pressure, in Hungary it was the other way around: the hotbed of reaction was found in the middle class, which was backward, lazy, and unable to take action on its own.

Here it was the upper class, chiefly its representatives in the government and the Liberal party, that stood up to the reactionaries. In his Lipótváros speech Wahrmann advocated making new alliances and compromises, even with the conservatives, as long as the new allies were willing to commit themselves to "conserve" and protect existing institutions against radicalism. Wahrmann also discussed the economic results of the Liberal government and gave his views on the relationship with Austria. "Today, too, my unchanged conviction is that radically changing our laws and relationship with Austria cannot be carried out at present without causing great upheaval. Any attempt to do so would arrest our nation's development, risk what we have achieved so far, and might prove fatal for Hungary itself." Although in principle he supported the aims of the so-called "48-ers" who demanded greater independence for Hungary, he cautioned that the situation in Europe made the peaceful separation of Hungary from Austria unimaginable. Even if this were possible,

> could Hungary, with its many centrifugal minorities, vulnerable geographical position, and lack of powerful allies maintain its independence and territorial integrity? In view of these real dangers is it not much wiser to maintain the links connecting us to Austria as being in the interest of the country and to preserve the rule of law?... I strongly believe that the reactionaries will not be satisfied with erecting walls between the classes and the evil forces once released will prove impossible to contain....Every retrograde theory is immediately embraced by those in the Party of Independence, especially by its provincial press, in spite of Lajos Kossuth's noble proclamations and letters![7]

In the Upper House, those opposing popular rights had succeeded in blocking a marriage law reform. In such a political climate, it is understandable why Wahrmann remained a supporter of Deák.

Further research is needed to understand Wahrmann's contributions during his more than quarter-century service as a representative and delegate and his general conception of liberalism. His views generally reflected those of the Jewish upper middle class, especially during the 1870s and 1880s. The first steps towards understanding Wahrmann's role were taken in a brief biography written by Gyula Mérei (1943). Further results are promised by Tibor Frank, who is conducting research for a monograph on Wahrmann. Some of Wahrmann's views are already well known, however. As shown in the excerpts from his Lipótváros speech, he had many reasons (especially economic ones) for advocating unconditionally the maintenance of the Dual Monarchy. To this end he was even willing to form alliances with the conservatives. At the same time, he was a firm advocate of the economic and political independence of Hungary within the Monarchy. He wanted the Hungarian market within the Monarchy to be founded on a parity basis, and warned the Austrians against alienating the Hungarian economy and thereby possibly damaging the market for their own goods in Hungary. He interpreted liberalism in its classic form, rejecting all state interference in the economy and championing free competition. He firmly believed that this program would produce a productive, strong, and stable Hungarian state. His passion for this goal led him at times to become, in the words of one of his admirers, an "unenthusiastic supporter" of Kálmán Tisza. He believed that a strong Hungary had to develop markets in the Balkans

7 Mór Wahrmann's speech is summarized in the study, *A Lipótvárosi választókerület polgáraihoz Wahrmann Mór beszéde 1884. május 27-én* [Mór Wahrmann's speech to the citizens of Lipótváros constituency on May 27 1884], (Budapest, 1884).

and give preferential treatment to heavy industry, including legal and tariff protection. Although more research is needed for a complete picture of Wahrmann's activities and recommendations, the main contours of his career are quite clear.[8]

I will close with a quick sketch of Wahrmann's private life. He married only once and his wife died four years after their marriage, leaving him with a daughter and two sons. His daughter Renée first married a nobleman, Izidor Krausz of Megyer, who owned a large factory in Újpest (the dowry was reportedly two million forints).The marriage was dissolved after 12 years. Her second marriage was to the Imperial-and-Royal Chamberlain Endre Beretvás. Renée underwent baptism for the sake of the marriage. After the death of her second husband she remained in the same social milieu by marrying another Imperial-and-Royal Chamberlain, a Count Fay. (In these two matches, Renée's estate of approximately 10,000 *hold* in Szabolcs and Szatmár counties probably played a role). Wahrmann's two sons, Richard and Ernő, were completely alienated from their father. After their father's death they too converted to Christianity. That act, however, was only one example of how they differed from their father. The two young men managed quickly to go through a fortune estimated at 12 million crowns, including cash, securities and the banking business itself, mainly by gambling it away at cards. One of Richard's enormous card debts was allegedly paid by Franz Joseph's court treasury out of respect for his father's good name. But such help could not save Ernő who committed suicide and was soon followed to the grave by his brother.[9]

After Mór Wahrmann's death a street in Lipótváros was named for him. At the end of 1944 the Arrow-Cross Party removed the street signs from the houses. After Hungary's liberation from the Germans, Wahrmann's name was not reinstated, and the street was renamed after Victor Hugo. At present the municipal council refuses to restore the old name. We are trying to have a memorial plaque placed on the wall of his last home, to commemorate Wahrmann as one of those who helped create a united Budapest out of what had been the separate cities of Pest, Buda, and Old Buda.

8 On the member of parliament, see Kálmán Mikszáth's parliamentary sketches written over two decades, available in various editions. His speeches and activities in parliament can be found in the parliamentary diaries. For other arenas, see the daily press as a subject for further research. For example, *Wahrmann Mór képviselői jelentése az 1869-1872-ki országgyűlésről* [Mór Wahrmann's Report on the 1869-1872 Parliament as a Member of Parliament] (Pest, 1872) which also appeared in German and *Wahrmann Mór Pest belvárosi képviselői beszéde a január 13-an este 7 órakor a Redout terméiben tartott választási értekezleten.*

9 On the fate of his children, their baptism, Renée's marriages, and Ernő's suicide, I used the data published in 1907 by Vadász, "Adalékok."

Manfréd Weiss
The Profile of a Munitions King

László Varga

As feudalism waned in Hungary, no urban bourgeoisie developed that could have become a vehicle for capitalist transformation. The guild-burgher invested his capital in accordance with the old traditions. His very position proved an obstacle to any effort on his part to expand commodity production: he remained rigidly attached to his familiar ways and retained the feudal disdain for the emerging forms of commerce and trade, which, despite its peddling character, was based on a modern buying-up pattern.

The Jews, who provided one of the bases for the new capitalism, had always been relegated to the periphery of society. Along with other, non-Magyar tradesmen, they virtually monopolized the buying-up trade. The eighteenth century saw a remarkable surge of Jewish immigration, initially from the more highly developed provinces of the Habsburg empire. Joseph II's 1783 decree permitted wealthy Jewish tradesmen to settle in the cities. During the Napoleonic wars this trading bourgeoisie, radically different from the guild-bourgeoisie both in the solidity of their capital and in their mentality, gained considerable strength. Because its members had no hope whatsoever of penetrating the social elite, the profit motive was their primary motivation. Due to the insecurity of their situation, they were always ready to change the forms and scope of their activities. This flexibility proved to be a decisive factor in their rise. The basic pattern was to progress from the grain trade to the milling industry and thence to the various branches of the economy. Each career had its individual shape—but there were common characteristics as well.

According to family legend, Manfréd Weiss's grandfather was a humble villager who made pipe-bowl lids. It is a fact, however, that already at the start of the nineteenth century he had a shop in Pest, in Rumbach Sebestyén Street. Half-craftsman, half-tradesman, he had presumably arrived in Hungary from Bohemia, as suggested by his business connections with that land. His son, born in 1807, made a good match in 1839, marrying into the respected Kánitz family of Óbuda.

Baruch Weiss's economic activities barely extended the traditional limits. A truly modern business policy was implemented by his sons, Arnold and Adolf. They began by trading in the famous Bohemian slivovitz and augmented their business with the grain trade, but also by buying and selling anything that promised a profit. When his sixth and last child was born in April, 1857, Adolf Weiss was already a well-known trader. By the beginning of the sixties his property was estimated at around 250,000 forints. His eldest son, Berthold (born 1845), studied economy and law after finishing the commercial academy and then joined father's business. Soon, though, he decided to set up business for himself.[1]

As their commercial transactions became more diverse, the Weisses were bound to turn up in the extraordinarily lucrative milling industry, too. Adolf Weiss had a share in establishing the First Budapest Steam Mill Corporation *(Első Budapesti Gőzmalom RT);* Arnold personally directed the foundation of the Erzsébet Steam Mill; Berthold was involved in establishing the Király Steam Mill and later became a member of the Concordia's board of directors.[2]

Berthold Weiss was representative of the Hungarian commercial bourgeoisie. In the second half of the 1870s he was regarded as a prosperous grain trader, visiting the Stock Exchange once or twice a month, subscribing to the Pester Lloyd and the Pester Journal, and with a taste for good cigars.[3] His mother tongue was German, but elements of "Hungarianism" and "monarchism" were mingled in his way of thinking. In this spirit he undertook public roles and represented the interests of the Hungarian economy, among others in his books, published both in Hungarian and in German.[4] His developed closer and closer economic ties with the largest customer in the Dual Monarchy: the imperial army.

It was Manfréd Weiss's accession to the family business that brought about a qualitative change in its policies. After finishing the commercial academy in 1873 he spent the next four years in Hamburg, where he ended up as executive manager of a firm trading in colonial goods. In the summer of 1877 he returned home because of his father's progressive illness (Adolf died in October of that year) and joined his brother's business. Whereas Berthold Weiss did no more than continue the activities of his father's generation, the entry of the younger brother signalled a new attitude. His abilities first became widely known in Hungary during the occupation of Bosnia and Herzegovina.

1 Magyar Országos Levéltár [OL]. Filmtár 3567/68; Vilmos Balla, *A vadember* (Budapest, 1923), pp. 68-72; *Budapesti Közlöny,* 16 November 1870; Cégbíróság Cg. 32438.

2 Emma Lederer, *Az ipari kapitalizmus kezdetei Magyarországon* (Budapest, 1952), p. 220.

3 OL Weiss Manfréd Könyvelőség 1875-1876 Napló.

4 See for instance *Közgazdasági és közegészségügyi állapotok tekintettel Pestre* (Pest, 1869) and *A jegybankügyi reformja* (Pest, 1870).

The occupation of those provinces opened up new prospects for the Weiss firm to carry out further significant transactions with the imperial army, in addition to expanding their grain trade. Thus, in August 1878—in cooperation with several other trading houses—they undertook to build a 300,000 forint hospital in the occupied territories. At the same time, the War Ministry commissioned them—along with two other firms—to organize all military deliveries to Bosnia. Yet another contract with the War Ministry involved the commercial exploitation of the Bosnian Railway. Thirty years later the War Ministry still esteemed Manfréd Weiss's activities during this period. The occupation accelerated remarkably the Weiss family's accumulation of capital and strengthened their business contacts.[5]

Manfréd Weiss's rise in the business world also meant the entry of a second generation. He had not yet become an industrial capitalist; he merely complemented the relatively "clean" grain trading with newer enterprises, risky but all the more lucrative. This, in turn, speeded up the circulation of the family's capital. When all was said and done he remained a tradesman to the very end. Due to the appearance of American wheat on the market and the resultant wheat crisis and fluctuation in prices, by the beginning of the eighties the grain trade had lost much of its attraction, and army contracts could not compensate for the loss. The profitability of investments in the milling industry also fell below the levels of the previous decades.

These developments alerted the Weisses and spurred them to search for newer and more effective avenues of investments. In practice, this cautiousness meant preserving their capital, ideally by investing in land. The bankruptcy of the *Baugesellschaft* provided a favorable opportunity. The last *Baugesellschaft* property, a section of Andrássy Avenue between Gyár Street and Nagymező Street (the most valuable plot of land in the Terézváros), was purchased by the Weiss brothers, together with Haggenmacher, a well-known figure in the milling industry. They bought several other properties as well, some on the Pest embankment, as well as a hotel in the city. The largest plot (about 60 acres) in their possession was situated in Angyalföld. Their best acquisition, however, was undoubtedly the so-called *Újvilág* (New World) complex, on the right side of the later *Ring* between the Margit bridge and the Víg theater. Although at that time still on the edge of town, it carried the promise of a new world—*nomen est omen*. Soon after the Margit bridge was constructed and the capital's main thoroughfare, the Budapest *Ringstrasse*, developed. The Weisses were said to

5 Kriegsarchiv Vienna [*KA*] KM 1879 5A 6-30/105, 12A 60-1/47; 1880 8A 50-1/47; 1909 Praes 5-48/20.

have spent no more than 190,000 forints to purchase all these properties, whose value soon exceeded a million forints.[6]

Thus, at the beginning of the eighties the Weiss brothers invested most of their wealth in real estate, thereby safeguarding their capital and increasing their wealth. By its nature, the safeguarding of capital—actually verging on land speculation—went together with exploring new ways of its profitable utilization and investment. Manfréd Weiss had no doubts that it was industry which had the largest potential.

In his industrial ventures, Manfréd Weiss had two prime considerations. First, since in Hungary the function of the milling industry—and, more widely, the food industry—paralleled that of the textile industry in other countries (especially Western Europe), the direction of his industrial ventures was obvious. His second consideration followed from the nature of the imperial army orders. According to the economic agreement between Austria and Hungary, all imperial institutions were obliged to purchase in Hungary in proportion to her contribution to the Dual Monarchy's common expenses.

As a start, the Weiss brothers decided to establish their own factory; but they could not agree about what to manufacture and even considered splitting. Given their rather limited experience and ignorance of marketing possibilities, a food-processing plant seemed to be the best bet. The initiative of the War Ministry was also of decisive importance. While Berthold nursed the idea of a biscuit plant, Manfréd favored building a canning factory. This was how the first cannery was established in Hungary.[7]

Following his business method, within two months of the decision and long before the production facilities were ready—even where the cans would be produced was still undecided—Manfréd Weiss sent a sample of his canned goulash to the War Ministry in Vienna. Eventually, the cannery was put into operation near the slaughterhouse, with an initial investment of 60,000 forints. In the middle of the eighties the factory employed 600 workers in peak season, but only 30 out of season. They were manufacturing their own cans; this metallurgic production, their only continuous activity, formed the most solid basis for further development. In 1887 they began manufacturing cartridge cases for the imperial army, soon followed by the manufacturing of cartridge boxes. They started off with a high rate of rejects, but the initial losses were amply made up for by the profitable canning operation. By this time they were

6 Balla, *A vadember,* p. 85; Fővárosi Levéltár Tan. Központi Irattár III. 1855/1884, 1433/1884, 1938/1884, 2012/1884, 2146/1884, 66/1885, 642/1885, 2214/1885, 164/1886, 808/1887, 825/1887, 2414/1888, 808/1889; Cégbiróság Cg. 2691.

7 *Ibid.*; OL PM Általános Iratok 1889-35578/2078, 1884-50610/1060, Kereskedelmi Minisztérium VI. 1891-2-43093/46808, 59046, 64161, 79821; BKIK Általános Iratok 1891-2-43033; KA KM 1887 7A 1-1/61.

exporting canned goods to Germany and Italy, while 34 percent of all imperial army provisions came from the Weiss's cannery. In addition to canned meat, they were making canned soup, vegetables, and coffee (12 grams of sugar and 12 grams of coffee to be dissolved in hot water). In ten years their canning capacity increased forty-fold and was supplemented by increasing production of metal products for the military.[8]

The first decade of the canning factory's operation accurately reflected Manfréd Weiss's business strategy. He aimed at market breakthrough by whatever means possible and with a relatively small capital investment. This breakthrough was facilitated by the Austro-Hungarian economic agreement. All he had to do was to pick out a product with which he could dominate the Hungarian market; then, having gained strength, he could meet the challenge of his Austrian competitors. In turn, the combined Austro-Hungarian market provided a solid foundation for becoming an important actor in the European market.

Manfréd Weiss's crisis strategy was unique. He realized that during an economic crisis (such as the second half of the eighties), traditional production can no longer be expanded and new products must be found. The initial losses coincide with the unavoidably critical period; later, though, when the economy is again on the move, he could offer new products that were truly competitive, with the initial difficulties behind him. Weiss always adjusted production capacity to potential rather than actual demands—a requirement of the War Ministry as well.

The success of their own industrial activities confirmed the Weisses in their belief in the expedience of industrial investments. Berthold Weiss became a founder, then a director, and ultimately, from 1890, deputy chairman of the First Hungarian Weaving and Knitting Mill in Vác *(Első Magyar Szövő- és Kötőgyár)*. The Weiss brothers took a prominent role in the Hungarian Industry and Trade Bank *(Magyar Ipari és Kereskedelmi Bank)*, established in May 1890 under the chairmanship of István Tisza, the future prime minister. The brothers also had a six percent share in the Danube Shipyard and Machine Works Corporation *(Danubius Hajó és Gépgyár RT)*, formed with a starting capital of one million forints. In 1891, under the management of the Industry Bank, the Arms and Machine Factory Corporation *(Fegyver és Gépgyár RT)* was established. Manfréd Weiss had a considerable share in this; according to government circles, "the construction and operation of the factory...would never have become feasible without his initiative." It was mainly in placing the arms factory on a firm footing that Manfréd Weiss became the greatest figure of the Hungarian arms industry. It is fair to add that the arms factory was very

8 *Ibid.*, 1884 12A 12-1/1-3, 1886 12A 22-1/1-6, 1909 Praes 5-48/20.

generous in return for these services. In 1901, for instance, the bonus paid to its elected directors approached 50,000 crowns.[9]

Business talent and expanding capital were not enough to guarantee success, though. The right connections were a prerequisite. The Weiss brothers had solid business contacts in both parts of the Monarchy, and were further strengthened by their family ties. In 1877, Berthold Weiss married Hermine Blau, daughter of one of his clients, who brought a dowry of 60,000 forints. His brother-in-law, Móric Eisler, was also a business connection, as was his other brother-in-law, Ede Machlup. Manfréd Weiss married Alice Wahl, daughter of General Superintendent Albert von Wahl.

Starting from the grain trade, the Weiss brothers penetrated the most influential circles of industrial capital. Their position was now secure. Their careers, however, soon diverged. Manfréd Weiss repeatedly proved his exceptional commercial abilities. For him, the basic issue always remained what products could be marketed; he never left a single opportunity unexploited. He was always ready to take risks and put up with temporary difficulties. He always stayed one step ahead in a given situation, thus becoming a major influence in the economy himself. His reaction to the unexpected was prompt, and this promptness had much to do with his success. Berthold Weiss, on the other hand, became increasingly distracted from his business ventures as he became involved in public life.

By the beginning of the nineties the Weiss brothers had a new project: as the next stage in their cartridge manufacturing they planned to make ball cartridges. The dangerous nature of the munitions plant as well as the shortage of space on the site of the canning factory, once considered oversized, demanded new grounds. Thus at the turn of 1892-93 they founded on Csepel Island what later became the largest industrial plant in the country. Again they were lucky in their site selection: Csepel had all the advantages of Budapest or the already industrialized Újpest, but land was still inexpensive and labor (mostly unskilled labor) was available in abundance. In the first few years the Csepel Works lagged well behind the canning factory in importance. For more than a decade the growing Weiss empire continued to be directed from its original headquarters.

Within three years the initial staff of 30-40 increased tenfold. In the meantime, the Weiss brothers, together with the well-known Austrian textile manufacturer, Isidor Mauthner, established the country's largest textile mill in Rózsahegy, the Hungarian Textile Industry Corporation *(Magyar Textilipari*

9 Hadtörténeti Levéltár [HTL] 1890. eln. 6048a; Cégbiróság Cg. 2192; OL Király személye körüli miniszter 1896. eln. 1044; *Magyar Pénzügy* (1901), no. 14.

RT), with a capital of 3 million crowns.[10] By the middle of the nineties, the two brothers had reached the top and the gates of the traditional Hungarian gentry opened before them, in accordance with the liberalism of the age. It was then that they arrived at a crossroads. The political elite made the decision easier for both of them with a spectacular gesture. Following the millennial exhibitions in 1896, which demonstrated the unprecedented prosperity that followed the 1867 compromise, Franz Joseph elevated Manfréd Weiss to the nobility. Contrary to common belief, Manfréd Weiss did not buy his title; he was even exempted from paying its regular fee.

Only forty, Manfréd Weiss accepted this highest of honors, but without foregoing his bourgeois consciousness, as is proved by the coat of arms he had designed. None of the heraldic devices are missing that the traditions of the age required: a golden shield, a river (the Danube) with some green in the middle (Csepel Island), a black lion, a knight's helmet, an eagle's wing, etc. However, this lion is rampant on a cog-wheel, holding a shuttle in one paw (Rózsahegy) and a smoking bomb in the other (Csepel). The lion is flanked on both sides by a six-pointed star: the star of David.[11]

Almost at the same time that Manfréd Weiss was ennobled and accorded the noble predicate *csepeli*, Berthold was elected to Parliament for Székelyföld on the government platform. Since joint ventures were under direct control of the Treasury, at the end of 1899 Berthold Weiss chose to withdraw from the firm. The company, now under the sole control of the younger brother, came to be known as Manfréd Weiss's First Hungarian Canning and Metal Works *(Weiss Manfréd Első Magyar Konzerv és Ércárugyára)*. While a member of parliament, Berthold preserved his former positions: leader of the Pester Lloyd Society and of the National Pension Association of Private Office Employees *(Magántisztviselők Országos Nyugdíjegyesülete)*, established on his initiative.

With upper-middle class consciousness, Berthold represented the interests of Hungarian big industry in every possible forum. On one occasion, when someone interrupted him, saying that "Berthold Weiss acquired millions with his private economic morality," he nobly assumed responsibility for the millions. "I am proud of my private economic morality," he replied.

> I am proud of the economic activities I have pursued while I was in business. It is well known to all that I broke off these activities as soon as I became a member of the Honored Parliament—a turn I considered a great boon and honor—gaining a seat in the Honored House as a merchant and industrialist. As a result of these activities, as well as of my keeping this

10 OL KM. Ipar és Belkereskedelemi szakosztály. 1899-2-86979.

11 OL Királyi könyvek, vol. LXX, pp. 123-128.

> economic morality always in view, factories were established in various parts of the country, where now thousands of workers can earn their living. Largest in size and greatest in significance is the one on Csepel Island, which came into being on my initiative in 1893, and which I handed over to my brother in 1896, wholly and completely, with all its legal consequences. I do believe, Honored Gentlemen, that this activity did no harm whatsoever to the nation.[12]

An extensive and qualitative change in the development of the Csepel Works took shape in the wake of a slowdown in Hungarian economic prosperity at the turn of the century. In the countries of the Dual Monarchy, an initial decrease in industrial investments was soon followed by a grave credit crisis, leading eventually into a crisis of overproduction. This dragged on until 1905, considerably restraining the development of heavy industry and being especially marked in the production of war materials. Not surprisingly, for Manfréd Weiss the crisis meant yet another breakthrough: the unique "Weiss crisis strategy" was put in operation again, and Csepel underwent enormous change. During the years of the recession Manfréd Weiss expanded his production range (the first step was to create the largest rolling mill in the country); he broadened his product line and began manufacturing artillery shells and field ovens. With this the metalworking center was transferred from the canning factory to Csepel, making it the country's largest privately owned manufacturing plant.[13]

After the turn of the century, foreign commissions played an increasingly important role in the development of the factory. From this time on there was hardly an armed conflict in the world in which at least one of the adversaries did not use Manfréd Weiss's munitions. In answer to a conservative attack in 1906, Secretary of State József Szterényi went to great lengths to elaborate on the significance of the Csepel Works:

> Manfréd Weiss's manufacturing plant is one of Hungary's largest and internationally most well-known industrial works, which won [a commission for] a hundred million cartridges only last year, beating the German and Austrian rivals, and gaining, I believe, great honor for Hungarian industry. This factory has 7,400,000 crowns invested in it, employs 1800 Hungarian workers, and has an annual turnover of 17,500,000 crowns. It has an office staff of 72.[14]

12 *Képviselőházi Napló* 21 November 1901.

13 For more details on the development of the factory, see László Varga, "A csepeli gyáróriás kialakulásának története," *Századok* 116 (1983).

14 *Képviselőházi Napló* 23 October 1906.

After the turn of the century Manfréd Weiss's various initiatives became part of a unified and ambitious concept. Whereas before 1900 his primary aim was to invest his money in the best possible way, now his name turned up only where truly essential issues were at stake. He withdrew from the Hungarian Textile Industry Corporation and gave up land transactions. In 1902, however, he was one of the initiators of the National Association of Industrialists *(Gyáriparosok Országos Szövetsége, GyOSz),* which was the first capable representative of large Hungarian industry; he later became its deputy chairman. Three years later he was elected to the board of directors of one of the two leading national banks, the Trade Bank, becoming one of the most influential figures of the financial bourgeoisie. It was almost unparalleled for an industrialist to penetrate the banking world.

Manfréd Weiss became a board member of several industrial companies and joined the management of important corporations. A decisive role in his personal career should be attributed to the economic underpinning provided by his own companies. Moreover, changed family circumstances also multiplied his economic power. As a result of Berthold Weiss's illness he had to take over his brother's economic posts and through his daughters' marriages he created alliances with the Chorins, the Kornfelds and the Hatvanys.

In the first decade of this century Manfréd Weiss earned fame for his philanthropic endeavors as well. He was deputy chairman of the National Child Welfare League and was responsible for the establishment of the Alice Weiss Maternity Home of Csepel, named for his wife, who had died several years earlier. The inauguration of this unique institution in 1910 was attended by the Prime Minister himself, representing the government. Manfréd Weiss took an active part in the Jewish community's charity work, donating to the victims of the Messina earthquake and to military aeronautics, contributing generously to the economic fund of the imperial army, and the Non-commissioned Officers' Fund of the Hungarian territorial army *(A magyar honvédség altiszti alapja).*[15]

He was lauded in a statement by the War Ministry in 1909. "Manfréd Weiss is an extraordinarily firm, energetic, and absolutely reliable industrialist, whose practical generosity is entwined with an active patriotism and a noble way of thinking." Ten or fifteen years earlier Manfréd Weiss would not have cared for this sort of recognition. Over the course of time, however, he had gradually conformed to his surroundings. Though he never gave up his pride and principles, he had endeavored to meet the traditional requirements of the gentry. His charity may have been partly rooted in his religion, but more and more it

15 *Városatyák Lapja* (1910), nos. 14 and 15; *Magyar Gyógyászat* (1936), pp. 205, 237; *Magyar Zsidó Almanach* (1911), p. 240; *Magyar Gyáripar* (1911), no. 17; KA KM 1908 Praes 65-8/1; 1909 Praes 5-48/20; 1911 Praes 65-6/1.

was dictated by his status as a member of the *haute bourgeoisie*. Whereas he had initially accepted his ennoblement with the mindset of a bourgeois, now he expected (but never initiated) official recognition. In 1901 he was awarded the Order of the Iron Crown for his successes at the Paris World Exhibition. In 1907 it was still his industrial activities which earned him the gold medal of the Industry League *(Iparegyesület)*. In 1910, however, the generals of the imperial army recommended him for the order of the Franz Joseph Crown "in recognition of his generosity to the charitable institutions of the defense forces and of his services in the interest of the war stores."[16]

Yet again, it was Manfréd Weiss who was among the first to realize that the flourishing prosperity of the first decade of the century was doomed to an early decline. In accordance with his crisis strategy he had a new, ambitious project, surpassing all former investments: the establishment of a steel mill. Even given Manfréd Weiss's dynamism, the project seemed excessive. He could not hope for the usual state support (tax benefits and government orders), because his enterprise threatened the interests of his major rival in Hungary, the Diósgyőr State Iron Works. Besides, the Diósgyőr Works was controlled by the Finance Ministry, instrumental in the award of benefits and promotions. A tough fight ensued between the two giant companies, lasting for several years. Whereas Diósgyőr could count on the support of the financial administration, Manfréd Weiss's Hungarian supporters—like the Ministry of Trade and Industry—could not risk open confrontation. Yet his promptness and reliability payed off: the imperial War Ministry in Vienna came to succor its more reliable supplier.

For the Diósgyőr State Iron Works, the future Csepel steel mill meant a challenge not only in steel production but also in the manufacture of large-caliber bullets. This was because the two were inseparable for Manfréd Weiss: the steel mill's profitability depended on his being his own biggest customer. The manufacture of large-caliber bullets was more profitable than that of other war matériel, and also safer—at least until Manfréd Weiss's appearance on the market. According to an agreement between Austria and Hungary, fully half of the imperial army orders were to be filled by Hungarian industry in compensation for its lack of gun manufacture.

The conflicting ministerial patrons resulted in a stalemate. Manfréd Weiss got a leg up only when he concluded a contract with the Witkowitz Works, which belonged to the Rothschilds. The Witkowitz people were willing to impart their production experience to Csepel and even to broker orders by the imperial navy, in return for a fairly large commission. Manfréd Weiss did not hesitate to use any means to attain success. Stealing away talent from competitors—even from Witkowitz—and bribery—two cases came to light and were smoothed over

16 *Ibid.* 1909 Praes 5-48/20, 1910 Praes 5-80/7-1, 2.

only with difficulty—were both employed. After much effort, the Csepel Steel Works began operation in May, 1912, and the mass production of large-caliber bullets was launched.

The mammoth plant, as though directed by prophetic vision, was waiting in preparation when the First World War broke out. Although no more than one-third of its products were of a military nature, the entire factory could be easily switched over to war production. On the eve of the world war Manfréd Weiss was the largest canner in the Dual Monarchy, he held a monopoly with his so-called "service vehicles", and, with the completion of his steel works, he could now go into full scale production. Having become the economic miracle of its age, Csepel's future was ensured by the coming war.

This unique story of economic development was made possible by Manfréd Weiss's ability to synthesize fundamentals and reconcile seemingly conflicting influences. Supported by the Hungarian ministerial bodies and the so-called joint delegation (a sort of joint parliament of the two halves of the monarchy), he succeeded in winning all the War Ministry's Hungarian orders for infantry supplies. He fought a long but ultimately victorious battle—actively supported by the War Ministry—for the artillery shells market against the Diósgyőr State Iron Works, which was backed by the Hungarian ministries. With his new products (field ovens, cooking boxes, field kitchens, and various kinds of ammunition), he anticipated the demands of the army and thereby shaped them himself. Added to all this was his familiar crisis strategy.

The history of the Weiss Works was determined by three major stages and developments: the introduction of metallurgy in the second half of the eighties (still on the premises of the canning factory); the establishment of the metal works at the turn of the century; and finally the establishment of the steel works at the beginning of the second decade. All three events coincided with recessions, proving that in his major investments Manfréd Weiss was not merely expanding production but, by choosing the right time, taking advantage of it so as to counteract the recession.

In periods of crisis—unlike so many others—he never withdrew his capital from Csepel. On the contrary, he wound up or limited his other concerns for the sake of its further development. Introducing new branches of production resulted in initial losses in any case—regardless of the actual economic situation. Thus Manfréd Weiss took advantage of periods of economic crisis, which would have made the expansion of traditional products impossible in any case, in order to bridge over initial hardships. In parallel, he set about to explore appropriate marketing possibilities—first of all in the War Ministry in Vienna. This transition was promoted by the internal needs of the Csepel plant, ensuring the profitability of new investments as a matter of course. With this method,

Manfréd Weiss managed not only to survive the crisis but also to shorten it for himself by expanding the scale of production.

By the time the representative of the Viennese artillery arsenal turned up in Csepel to observe preparations for the war, Weiss had already doubled his staff. The major plants—cartridge manufacturing, munition manufacturing, joinery, rolling mill—were operating around the clock. Nevertheless, the existing equipment still proved insufficient to meet the demands of the army, and Manfréd Weiss had to use every means to expand. In the first years of the war he invested 13 million crowns in the Csepel Works. (By way of comparison, the government granted no more than 3 million crowns to develop the two state iron works, one in Budapest and the other in Győr.)

Now came the time when the energetic expansion, considered obsessive and exaggerated by many, bore fruit. The Csepel Works were operating and yielding profits on a scale undreamed of before. According to official balances (which can hardly be regarded as reliable), the first three years of the war netted a profit of 55 million crowns. (To compare again: the Diósgyőr Works closed the first two years with a loss.) By the end of the first year of the war, four times as many workers and employees were generating profit for Manfréd Weiss than in the last year of peace.

Former Prime Minister István Tisza reportedly paid a high tribute to the merits of Manfréd Weiss. "Only two things have worked: our boys' heroism and Manfréd Weiss's efficiency. If only our High Command and our public administration and diplomacy had developed with such perfection."[17] Whether Tisza said it or not, one thing is certain: Manfréd Weiss became a topic of general conversation. If nothing else, his fabulous fortune gave rise to legends. In 1917, he paid a tax of 34 million crowns, from which it was safe to conclude that his wealth was around 400-500 million. According to the estimate by the Generali Insurance Company, the Csepel Works were worth 100 million crowns; its own management stated a value of 137 million—exclusive of raw materials and semi-finished and finished products. During the war years, Weiss purchased Count László Károlyi's huge estate at Derekegyháza—about 14,000 acres. Within a half year in 1917, he bought various shares and stocks valued at more than 70 million crowns.[18]

He was not short of official recognition for his activities. At the end of 1915, he became a member of the Upper House. On this occasion, *Magyar Ipar* celebrated him as "the greatest industrialist and greatest organizer in the country." In 1918 he was made a baron. The Presidential Council proposed that

17 Andor Kun, *Úttörők: A magyar gazdasági élet pionirjai* (Budapest, 1933), p. 79.

18 Nándor Kozma, *Hadimilliomosok: Karrierek a háború aranyhegyén* (Budapest, 1918), pp. 21-22; *Népszava* 23 September 1917.

he get the title free. King Karl, however, considered this excessive, and in spite of Minister Zichy's intervention he had to pay the fee.[19]

Sándor Bródy, the noted Hungarian writer, spent two entire days interviewing him; the result most remarkably was that he could hardly get him to speak. Manfréd Weiss left no memoirs or private letters. He lived a self-contained life, inaccessible to outsiders. He liked music—he himself played the violin—and was keen on the fine arts. He even endowed an arts award. He was self-conscious and never sought the friendship of the great men of his age, even though he mixed in their company day to day. Bródy called him patriarchal, jovial, and intelligent. In his business correspondence and his rare public appearances he was brief and to the point. This, in fact, was the core of his personality. He was a pragmatic businessman, refusing to confront the consequences of his war-centered industry. Bródy asked about the somberness of his occupation. "This is my trade," was the answer, "and I have no other concern than to carry on with it in the most perfect way possible."[20] It may sound cynical, but it was not intended to be. Manfréd Weiss did not and could not allow this central issue to intrude upon his conscience. He never asked himself how many death's were caused by the products of his factory. His obsession carried him to the peak—and the same obsession helped him evade the thought of death. Yet when in 1919 the Hungarian Soviet republic nationalized his empire he tried to kill himself. His unsuccessful suicide answered the question Bródy had posed three years earlier. The Works was not his trade—it was his life.

He had no reason to fear revenge; he lived to a peaceful old age, surrounded by his grandchildren. He enjoyed the loyalty of his employees: at the time of his attempted suicide, the workers of the canning factory sent for a doctor; the Csepel workers, too, were shocked to hear the rumor of his death. Although Manfréd Weiss survived the grave toxicosis due to the prompt medical aid he received, this was nevertheless the end of his life—if only symbolically. His family took the critically ill man to Vienna—presumably without his knowledge and against his will. Manfréd Weiss returned to the Csepel Works only in 1920, after the political situation had stabilized. Following his recovery, while still in Vienna, he embarked upon new enterprises and started new businesses. But the collapse of Csepel was disastrous. Instead of the tens of thousands working there during the war, no more than a few hundred were left.

On his return, Manfréd Weiss produced his miracle once again. He employed his crisis strategy, this time even more drastically than before. He transformed the plant, which had been the most up-to-date and best-organized in

19 OL Király személye körüli miniszter 1918 eln. 31.

20 Sándor Bródy, *Fehérkönyv* (Budapest, 1918).

the country, into a gigantic workshop, manufacturing everything his machines were suitable for—from horseshoe nails to milk cans. Thanks to this, Csepel managed to survive the most acute crisis of its history until 1945. He did not live to see its most flourishing period when economic stabilization was reached. He died on Christmas, 1922.

The Search for an Urban Alliance: The Politics of the National Association of Hungarian Industrialists *[GyOSz]* before the First World War

George Deak

Contemporary antisemites and modern historians largely agree about the preponderance of Jews among the founders and leaders of large industry in Hungary at the beginning of the twentieth century. We may take as our starting point that Jews composed a large majority among the industrial elite of Hungary at the turn of the century. The Jewish industrialists had, however, a much less significant voice in the politics of the country than their economic power would suggest.

By the outbreak of the First World War, Hungarian industry had become an important factor in the economic life of the country. While some sixty percent of the work force was still employed in agriculture in 1910, as opposed to 18.3 percent in industry and mining, large industry had been the engine of economic growth for most of the previous quarter century. But the men who directed the industrial enterprises in the country, most of whom were of Jewish origin, had considerably little influence in national politics. The National Association of Hungarian Industrialists played an important part in the attempt by the industrial leadership to redress this imbalance. The opinions voiced and the actions described in the publications of this organization and in the writings of its directors provide us with a glimpse into the sometimes surprising political orientation of the Hungarian industrial elite. Though strong upholders of the capitalist order, they chafed at the conservatism with which the Hungarian nobility tried to maintain its landed wealth and political hegemony. Their cultural propensities as well as the weakness of their own political situation prompted the men in charge of Hungary's large industry to support some of the reform movements of other urban groups.

The National Association of Hungarian Industrialists *(Magyar Gyáriparosok Országos Szövetsége*, or, as we shall refer to it hence, the *GyOSz)*, was formed in 1902 by a handful of the leaders of Hungary's largest industrial concerns. Chief among the founders were Ferenc Chorin, president of the Salgótarján

Coal Mines and of the Hungarian National Association of Mines and Forges (founded in the previous year) and Sándor Hatvany-Deutsch, whose family owned Hungary's largest sugar refineries and who was himself the founder and president of the Hungarian Association of Sugar Manufacturers (founded in 1894). Both of these men were Jews. Two gentiles also played a prominent role—Ferenc Aich, president of the Association of Brewers, and Nándor Fórster, president of the Association of Iron and Machine Manufacturers. It should be made clear at the outset that the *GyOSz* did not represent Jewish industry but Hungarian large industry in general. Still, of the fifty founding members, roughly sixty percent were Jews or converted Jews.[1]

The organization was established because of the growing size and maturity of the industrial elite as well as in response to the divergence between their economic interests and those of the large agricultural producers. By the turn of the century, the arrangement between industry and government that had existed through much of the second half of the nineteenth century had begun to come undone. According to this arrangement, the Magyar nobility and the largely foreign or Jewish middle class cooperated in the industrialization of the country; the nobility saw its role as the creation of a modern state bureaucracy and of a liberal social and legislative climate, and the modernization of agriculture, while the middle class was given free reign in the private sector. Government and the private sectors of commerce, finance, and industry had cooperated closely in the creation of a transportation network, direct government subsidies, and a tariff policy that favored the growth of industries based largely on agriculture. The cooperation broke down, however, when industry expanded beyond these traditional branches and the food-processing branches themselves developed to a far greater extent than the agriculture whose products they were supposed to process. The productivity of the large estates fell far behind that of American, Australian, and other producers; Hungarian mills found that they could make handsome profits by buying foreign wheat and re-exporting it in the form of flour, much to the chagrin of Hungarian landlords.

The career of Ferenc Chorin exemplifies the forces at work in the above-mentioned division of labor between the nobility and those Jews who aspired to prominence. Chorin was the grandson of the reformist Rabbi Aron Chorin, who had migrated to Hungary from Moravia and settled in Arad in 1789. The rabbi's son became a doctor; the latter's son, Ferenc, born in 1842, studied law in Vienna and was attracted to a political career. He founded and edited a Kossuthist newspaper in Arad and entered parliament as a member of the

1 For a fuller discussion of the *GyOSz*, see the author's "Industry and Politics: The National Association of Hungarian Industrialists, 1902-1914," (unpublished Ph.D. dissertation, Columbia University, 1980).

opposition in 1869. By 1890, however, Chorin had made the transition from politics, where his success was limited, to business, where, as executive director of Hungary's largest coal mine, he was at the pinnacle of the economic elite. One suspects that there was as much push as pull in this transition. By temperament, Chorin seems to have been more a politician than a businessman; the *GyOSz* provided him—and perhaps Hungarian industry in general—with an outlet for political ambitions.

The tension between agriculture and industry spurred the spread of the neo-conservative ideology of agrarianism among a portion of the Hungarian nobility. This movement had a distinctly modern character in that it sought to enlist the masses in the opposition to Jewish "mobile capital." Though by the 1890s it had abandoned some of its strident antisemitism, by the turn of the century agrarianism had made inroads in both major political parties and had gained a number of victories in economic policy, such as the restrictions on the milling transit trade and higher tariffs on agricultural goods (1906). Agrarianism's major political victory was the 1901 Law of Incompatibility, which effectively excluded from the lower chamber of Parliament those engaged in large industry and was an extremely sore point with the *GyOSz* throughout the period under discussion. This loss of political influence, moreover, coincided with a moderate recession, making the experience all the more painful.

In February of 1902, the 50 founding members of the *GyOSz* published an appeal for new members, declaring that "Hungary's industrialists deserve to be heard and respected by the nation and given a position in public life commensurate with their economic importance." By May, the organization had recruited 245 firms; it had grown to about 1000 firms by 1914. About seventy percent of the upper half of joint stock companies registered in Budapest were members. While smaller firms composed a majority, it was the large firms that provided most of the organization's leadership and financing. They also seem to have provided most of the progressive elements, though this question deserves further study. Many of the demands of the *GyOSz* involved economic issues: tariffs, rail rates, and, perhaps most frequent of all, government contracts. But the organization participated in several of the key political debates of the time, adopting a more progressive position than the established political parties did.

Social Clubs and Freemasonry

Before examining the political debates in which the *GyOSz* was involved, mostly after 1906, let us look at the proto-political milieu of the social clubs to which *GyOSz* members belonged.

Despite the cooperation between the Jewish bourgeoisie and the nobility in many areas during the early period of the Dual Monarchy, the two groups were on the whole socially segregated. The bourgeoisie had never been accepted into the nobility's social clubs (casinos). The oldest and most prestigious bourgeois casino, Lipótváros, generally tended to imitate the customs of its noble counterparts.[2] After the turn of the century, however, the clubs multiplied in the bourgeois districts of Budapest and a change may be discerned in them. Their stated goals bore distinct signs of an emancipation from the coattails of the nobility. The Erzsébetváros casino, founded in 1905, declared its aim to be "the concentration of the bourgeoisie of Budapest's largest district into a prestigious club dedicated to supporting the spirit of good companionship, developing the conscious cooperation of the bourgeoisie, and increasing its weight as a factor in society." The casino worked towards the solution of certain "social, cultural, and economic questions in the spirit of the Enlightenment, progress, and civil equality." Its first officers included Zsolt Beöthy, a university professor, the retired general József Debiecky—both gentiles—and the Jewish Dr. Adolf Kohner, a member of the *GyOSz* executive.[3]

Members of the *GyOSz*, especially its leaders, also played important roles in Hungarian Freemasonry. Twenty of the 104 industrialists who were members of the *GyOSz* leadership in 1903 were also Masons at the time, the proportion being higher among the higher officers of the *GyOSz*.[4] The Grand Master of Hungarian Masonry, Marcell Neuschloss, was a *GyOSz* member. His brother Ödön, who reportedly shared his older brother's views, was a founding member of the *GyOSz*. The Grand Master, who died in 1905, was remembered by the industrial publicist Mór Gelléri as a man of advanced social views who had worked for legal recognition of the right to strike (though he himself was the employer of several thousand workers), initiated the establishment of day-care centers for the children of workers, and founded several important charities.[5] Some of the Masonic lodges with which *GyOSz* members were affiliated—*Demokrácia, Haladás, Neuschloss, Eötvös, Galilei, and Comenius*—were also heavily influenced by the "bourgeois radicals." According to Marcell Benedek, the last Grand Master of Hungarian Masonry (which was dissolved by the Communist regimes in 1919 and again in 1947) the members of the upper bourgeoisie, however uncomfortable they may have felt with the radical connections of Masonry, "always had their pocketbooks open"

2 Péter Hanák, ed., *Magyarország Története, 1890-1918* [History of Hungary, 1890-1918], 2 vols., (Budapest: Akadémiai Kiadó, 1978), vol. I, p. 406.

3 *Fővárosi Szemle*, 1915, advertisement, n.p.

4 József Palatinusz, *A szabadkőművesség bünei* [The Sins of Freemasonry] (Budapest, n.d.).

5 Mór Gelléri, *Ipartörténeti vázlatok* [Sketches from the History of Industry], (Budapest, 1906), pp. 737-46.

for the cultural, social, and even some of the political activities inspired by the radicals.[6]

Neo-Liberal Ideology

The ideological orientation of the organization can be judged by the politics of its executive directors. In the period under discussion, the managing directors were Ámbrus Neményi (1902-1905), who was Jewish, Lóránt Hegedüs (1905-1912), and Gusztáv Gratz (1912-1917). Miksa Fenyő, a converted Jew, was appointed the fourth director in 1917, but he had been on the *GyOSz* staff since 1904 as editor of the *Közlemények* and the *Magyar Ipar*.

Neményi was a Liberal member of the Lower House and a journalist. Trained in economics, he had been a strong supporter of the industrialization policies of the Liberal governments of the late nineteenth century. The choice of Neményi for the post was a reflection of the cautious attitude characteristic of the first four years, during which the *GyOSz* limited itself to demands for a favorable economic policy without in any way challenging the political structure based on the rule of the nobility.

Neményi's successors, starting with Hegedüs, represented a break with this passive attitude. Hegedüs, Gratz, and Fenyő all had ties of varying strength with the so-called "second reform generation," which manifested broad discontent with the political and cultural life of the country. When Fenyő founded the modernist literary magazine *Nyugat* (West), its major shareholders included founders of the *GyOSz* (Sándor and Béla Hatvanyi-Deutsch, Manfréd Weisz, Leo Goldberger, and Alfréd Brüll), and sons of *GyOSz* founders—Ferenc Chorin, Jr. and Lajos Hatvanyi. Hegedüs was an admirer of the avant-garde poet and radical social critic Ady, whom he praised to Tisza in 1913. Hegedüs reports that Tisza replied that Ady was a "vermin on the palm leaf of Hungarian culture"—a compliment that Ady no doubt returned.[7] Both Hegedüs and Gratz published articles in the critical sociological review *Huszadik Század* (Twentieth Century). Gratz was a member of the executive of the League for Universal Suffrage during the Fejerváry period (1905-1906).

In their writings in *Huszadik Század*, both Hegedüs and Gratz recognized the deep-seated problems facing Hungarian society and expressed impatience with the attempts by the major political parties to ignore or repress them. They both had faith in the capacity of capitalist industrialization to raise the general

6 Zsuzsa L. Nagy, *Szabadkőművesség a XX. században* [Freemasonry in the Twentieth Century] (Budapest: Kossuth, 1977), pp. 27-28.

7 Lóránt Hegedüs, *Ady és Tisza* [Ady and Tisza], (Budapest: Nyugat, n.d. [1936?]), p. 51.

standard of living and, coupled with liberalism, to reduce social conflict. Hegedüs was optimistic about the future of liberalism on the international scene and expected the socialist menace to fade away; pointing to the example of the United States, he noted that "all the conditions for socialism are present, only socialism is nowhere in sight." Declaring himself a liberal, he called for the end of the feudal spirit that tolerated old wealth regardless of its magnitude but envied and scorned the newly rich and those who tried to get ahead. He saw this prejudice operating not only against industrialists but also against the peasantry and small businessmen. He called upon liberalism to work to reform the institution of *mortmain*, the tax system, public administration, and those social values that obstructed the advance of talent.[8] Hegedüs, in an insightful 1905 study on the causes of emigration, widely held to be a national disgrace, voiced similar views. He attributed the problem not so much to the peasants' poverty, though this, he admitted, was widespread, but to the barriers to social mobility, whose causes lay in the feudal mentality and privileges of the Church and nobility.

Like Hegedüs, Gratz declared himself a liberal, but objected to identifying liberalism with the programs of the actual "Liberal" parties operating in Hungary and elsewhere. These, he claimed, had not tried to fulfill the true liberal program, which he defined as the guarantee of complete political equality and the right of every group to struggle for its interests within limits permitting the same right to every other group. He saw liberalism as a political framework; its content depended on social policies determined by the free interplay of all groups. Gratz pointed out that the ameliorative demands of the Social Democratic Party could be supported by liberals dedicated to the maintenance of the capitalist order. On a pessimistic note, Gratz predicted the emergence of some socialist regimes in Europe, though he did not hold this to be inevitable. He deplored this development on the grounds that state ownership of all means of production would constrict the scope for human freedom even more than was the case under the existing rule of liberal parties.[9]

Political Action

The years following the founding of the *GyOSz* were marked by debates and "crises" in the Hungarian parliament over the finer points of Hungary's constitutional relation with Austria. This issue had little to do with the major

8 *Huszadik Század*, 1904, No. 2, pp. 490-98.

9 For Gratz's writings, see *Ibid.*, pp. 615-32; *Huszadik Század*, 1905; and *Huszadik Század*, 1906, No. 8, 130-49.

social conflicts brewing in the wings: the demands of the nationalities for greater autonomy, the peasants' hunger for land, the political and social demands of the working class, the frustrations of the growing numbers of small craftsmen with their worsening lot, and the intelligentsia's demands for a more modern and just society. But the parliament of the nobility tried to ignore or suppress these issues. This state of affairs was changed when the Fejérváry government, appointed by the monarch against the wishes of parliament, sought to reach over the heads of the nobility and raised the possibility of reforming the suffrage. Until the resolution of the constitutional crisis and the re-establishment of parliamentary rule under the Coalition, the *GyOSz* kept out of most of the debates, both on constitutional questions and on suffrage reform. The *GyOSz* had little sympathy with the largely symbolic "national" demands of the opposition parties—though it did come out in favor of a separate customs area. This was an obsession of Chorin and probably of some of the smaller firms in the *GyOSz*, though not shared by other leaders, such as the Hatvanyi-Deutsches and the Weiszes. To have joined the suffrage-reform movement encouraged by the Fejérváry government would have invited charges by the nobility of treason and the hostility of the large part of nationalist opinion that the ruling class had been able to mobilize. The threat that Vienna might impose universal suffrage was sufficiently frightening for the nobility to backpedal on its national demands. The monarch could thus return the country to parliamentary rule in April 1906, under the leadership of the "Coalition." The three-and-a-half years of the Coalition's rule were a watershed for cooperation between the *GyOSz* and other urban movements, including the protests over aspects of the Wekerle Government's tax reform proposals, the movements demanding relief from the rise in the cost of living, and the movement for suffrage reform.

Tax Reform

During his first term as prime minister (1893-95), Sándor Wekerle had advocated reforms that would have substituted a progressive income tax for many of the sales taxes that were the mainstay of the largely outmoded revenue system. This would have shifted some of the fiscal burden from the lower classes to the wealthier landholders and bourgeoisie. The attempt had nearly cost Wekerle his political career. When he returned to power in 1906 he made allowances for what he saw as the prime immovable of the Hungarian political landscape, namely, the power of the agrarian interests. The proposals he submitted in early 1908 left intact the principle of self-taxation for agriculture, whereby committees elected by the landowners would make only minor "adjustments" to the thoroughly outdated assessments compiled in 1875. The rate on these holdings would be reduced from 25.5 percent to 20 percent; according to the official calculations submitted with the draft law, this would decrease the direct taxes paid by landowners, albeit in a way most favorable to the smallest owners. In contrast with the self-monitoring of the landholders, the corporate income taxes would come under close—and unwelcome—government scrutiny. Incomes above 600 crowns (K) would be taxed at a rate progressing from 0.7 to 5.0 percent, with the highest bracket beginning at 200,000 K.

The true economic effect of these reforms on the urban classes cannot be determined, because they were never implemented. The political effect, however, was to stir up a protest movement that united the large and small bourgeoisie and even enjoyed the support of the Social Democrats. The focal points of the movement were municipal governments and economic interest organizations, such as the National Association of Hungarian Merchants *(OMKE)*, the Chambers of Commerce and Industry, the National Association of Industry *(OIe)*, and the *GyOSz*. But it also included generally meek groups like the National Association of Civil Servants, which submitted a list of grievances to the Ministry of Finance and objected to being treated less favorably than those engaged in agriculture.

Protest meetings were organized in Budapest and most other cities. A joint conference of representatives of municipal governments and of various interest groups, including the *GyOSz*, met at the end of February, 1908. The conference declared the proposals "unacceptable both from the point of view of the finances of the local authorities and from the situation of the taxpaying population." The *GyOSz* noted that although all members of parliament from urban districts had been invited, only eight or ten actually attended; this gave a clear indication of the legislative underrepresentation of the urban middle classes.[10]

The *GyOSz* submitted a separate memorandum to the government, protesting aspects of the reform that would affect mostly the highest income brackets and corporations. But it also demanded that the minimum taxable income be raised from 600 K to 800 K, a measure that would have benefitted both the working class and those who employed them.

The unexpected vehemence of the urban protests forced Wekerle to withdraw his proposals and to invite the representatives of the urban interest groups to a discussion in March. At this meeting, the *GyOSz* demanded that in view of the rapidly increasing cost of living, and as an immediate emergency measure, the lower classes in both industry and agriculture be exempted from the occupational income tax.[11] The revised draft law, submitted to parliament in November, left the distribution between agriculture and industry intact but made

10 *Magyar Ipar*, XXIX, No. 9 (1908), 230-40.
11 GyOSz, *1908. évi jelentés*, p. 129.

the progressivity even steeper by raising the minimum taxable income to 800 K and lowering the threshold of the highest bracket to 120,000 K. The protest movements went into action again. Although the bill was passed into law largely unchanged in March, 1909, the sections applying to the urban classes were not implemented before the outbreak of World War I. The experience of the tax reform movement demonstrated to the *GyOSz* the potential benefits that could accrue from a self-consciously urban political force united in its opposition to the dominance of the landowners.

Protests over the Cost of Living

A similar constellation of groups formed in the years of Wekerle's government to protest the rise in the cost of living. As in most of the industrialized world, prices, which had been falling since 1873, began to rise in Austria-Hungary in the mid-1890s. Between 1896 and 1908 prices rose by 32 percent, with the steepest increases occurring after 1903.[12] The price increases that were of most concern to the urban population were for rent and food, especially meat. The trade policies of Hungary, supported by the Agrarians, could be clearly seen as contributing to the rise in food prices. In the late 1890s Hungary had become a net food importer, including grain and meat. The agricultural interests in Hungary and Austria took advantage of this to raise agricultural tariffs. The duty on wheat was nearly doubled in 1906 and rose again under the Coalition in 1907. The effect of these high tariffs was further exacerbated by the promotion of agricultural exports through premiums. Moreover, starting in 1906 Hungary conducted a highly visible customs war with Serbia, and later with Romania—both important sources of livestock.[13]

Complaints about the cost of living were expressed in the daily press, in the statements, resolutions, and petitions of the urban economic and professional interest organizations and of political parties, as well as through government inquiries. The *GyOSz* was an active participant in the last. Its concern with the issue was understandable. Most importantly, the rising cost of living sparked labor unrest and demands for higher wages. Furthermore, the customs wars with the Balkan states had led to the closing of their borders to Hungarian industrial products. Here again the *GyOSz* found that its interests coincided with those of other urban groups. At an inquiry held by the government at the beginning of March, 1908, the *GyOSz* demanded an end to the customs war

12 Magyar Királyi Központi Statisztikai Hivatal, *Árstatisztika* [Price Statistics], *Magyar Statisztikai Közlemények*, no. 44, n.s. (Budapest, 1913), pp. 406-407.

13 Hanák, *Magyarország Története, 1890-1918*, pp. 621-23, 774-76.

with the Balkan states, the easing of agricultural protectionism, the elimination of export premiums on agricultural goods, and the restoration of the milling transit trade.[14] In response to the complaints that the working class was not represented at an inquiry that concerned it more than any other group, the *GyOSz* suggested that a permanent committee, comprising representatives of all major interest organizations, including those of the workers, be set up to advise the government. As a further remedy the *GyOSz* demanded that the institution of *mortmain* be abolished immediately, at least within the vicinity of Budapest, so that better use could be made of the land for supplying food to the capital.

Suffrage Reform

The area in which the *GyOSz* went the furthest in demonstrating its political liberalism and its search for allies among the urban population was suffrage reform. Having been tantalized by the Fejérváry government's proposals in 1904 and having witnessed the actual introduction of universal secret manhood suffrage in Austria, the Social Democrats and the radical intelligentsia placed universal secret suffrage at the top of their agenda. The frustration of the proponents of universal suffrage mounted as the Coalition government, which had promised suffrage reform both to the nation and to the monarch, tried to procrastinate, once installed in power. The existing franchise, encompassing only about five percent of the population and based on inherited feudal privilege or wealth, was the sole albeit precarious foundation of the rule of the Magyar nobility. The frustrations of the urban classes concerning tax reform and the increasing cost of living only added to the pressure.

Having achieved some success in cooperating with urban movements in the previous year, the *GyOSz* joined the fray in January 1909 by organizing a conference of urban interest groups to discuss the possibility of forming a League of Industrial and Merchant Voters. Chorin defined the aim of the League as improving the representation of the urban productive classes and intelligentsia in the legislative process by organizing support for those parliamentary candidates who were deemed to be reliable supporters of urban interests, irrespective of party. Chorin spoke of the ground that had been lost to agrarianism in the last ten years. He claimed that the Agrarians had come to "dominate the legislature, influence the government, and direct the structure and thinking of society." In a statement that could serve as a motto for the emerging "urbanist" ethos of the upper bourgeoisie, Chorin declared that "we can no longer stand idly by while the cities, the repositories of the great cultural and

14 GyOSz, *1909. évi jelentés*, 132-34.

economic interests, are relegated to the role of a Cinderella in our legislative process. We want [the League] to document the strength existing in the cities, on which the present Hungarian culture is built; we want to make that strength felt and respected in all its manifestations."[15] Though the call to form the League was more an attempt to bring about the fall of the Coalition than an endorsement of suffrage reform, the Social Democratic *Népszava* welcomed the "awakening of the bourgeoisie."[16] In response to the criticism that it was difficult to understand why a "league" and not a party was being formed, the *GyOSz* responded that a purely bourgeois party could not win a strong position in the next election, whereas "a handful of brave, determined men" within the existing parties could have a decisive influence on policy. Clearly, the *GyOSz* favored a peaceful evolutionary reform, which they believed should be accomplished from within the existing political order.[17]

By 1909, the Coalition had not only alienated the urban interests, it has also disappointed its supporters' nationalist aspirations vis-à-vis Austria. The monarch judged the time to be propitious for the restoration of the forces committed to maintaining the constitutional arrangements of 1867. The *GyOSz* hoped to be included in the regrouping of parties that was taking place. Although the League it had proposed earlier in the year was never formed, the leading members of the *GyOSz* made significant contributions to the discussions and to the coffers of the forces, later to be known as the Party of National Work, that were organizing around István Tisza. The prospects for the representation of industrial interests seemed to have improved with the appointment of the Khuen-Héderváry government in January, 1910. Yet the *GyOSz* was to be disappointed in this regard, for the Party of National Work sought primarily to maintain the status quo not only constitutionally, but, above all, socially. It had no intention of favoring industrial interests over agrarian ones. The complaints of the *GyOSz* about the railroad rate policies of the Khuen-Héderváry government were typical of its mood.

> How glad we were when the Coalition era was over. And individually we are still glad.... But as a body of industrialists we are aggrieved that the present government, our government, the foundations of which, the Party of National Work, we helped to build with all our might, puts us aside, while even the Coalition, which stood miles from us in sentiment, listened to our pleadings.[18]

15 GyOSz, *Közlemények*, no. 48 (1908), 11.

16 "Az ébredező burzsoázia" [The Awakening Bourgeoisie] in *Népszava*, 1908, No. 266, p. 3.

17 GyOSz, *Közlemények,* no. 48 (1908), 6.

18 Endre Scheiber, "A GyOSz, a kormány és az összeférhetelenség" [The GyOSz, the Government and the Law of Incompatibility] in *Magyar Ipar*, II. no. 2 (1912), 3.

The differences between the *GyOSz* leadership and the Tisza-dominated party were not confined to issues of economic policy; they extended to the broader ideological issue of suffrage reform. Hegedűs, in his *Ady és Tisza*, remembered that "during the preparatory stages of the organization [of the Party of National Work] I often argued with Tisza because I wished to place the new party on a broader basis by having it support the introduction of universal suffrage. Thus, from among Tisza's followers, Ferenc Herczeg [the novelist and Liberal politician] and I joined the League for the Right to Vote while at the same time campaigning for Tisza."[19]

Like its predecessor, the Khuen-Hédervány government recognized that at least the promise of suffrage reform was unavoidable in order to maintain social peace. Hence soon after assuming power it requested proposals from various organizations. The *GyOSz* was specifically asked to define the limitations that should be placed on the suffrage of the industrial working class. In its memorandum to the government the *GyOSz* declared that "economic and social reasons make it absolutely necessary that the right to vote be extended to the industrial classes and the industrial labor force.... In respect to the suffrage of these classes the Association does not consider the setting up of special restrictions as justifiable."[20] The qualifications deemed necessary by the *GyOSz* were that voters be male, at least 24 years old and demonstrate a certain "permanence"—by possessing an independent hearth, or residing in one place for two years, or being a permanent member of the National Workers' Health and Accident Insurance Fund. The *GyOSz* rejected the notion current in the government that suffrage be based on a minimum tax payment and plural voting. It objected most vehemently to the government's proposal that a worker be employed by the same firm for a given period.[21] In the cities, the *GyOSz* favored the secret ballot. While falling short of the demands of the Social Democrats and the bourgeois radicals, the demands of the *GyOSz* were in line with contemporary standards in central Europe. Had the proposals been adopted, they would have enfranchised about 500,000 workers, or about one half of all males employed in industry.

Not all members of the *GyOSz* agreed with the organization's position on this question. The National Association of Iron Works and Machine Factories dissented from what it felt was "following fashionable radical slogans";[22] the

19 Hegedűs, *Ady és Tisza*, 48.
20 GyOSz, *1911. évi jelentés*, 170.
21 *Magyar Gyáripar*, III, No. 1 (1913), 1-2; GyOSz, *1913. évi jelentés*, 164-72.
22 *Magyar Gyáripar*, III, No. 7 (1913), 3-4.

Szeklér branch of the *GyOSz* would have restricted the suffrage to those able to read and write Hungarian.[23]

Nevertheless, the *GyOSz* as a whole remained outspokenly in favor of the stance it had taken until the passage of a considerably narrower reform in 1913. When bloody clashes took place in front of parliament between a crowd of 100,000 demonstrators and the police, in May, 1912, the *GyOSz* defended the right of workers to organize. It wrote:

> Having no representation in parliament, all the passion that would otherwise have been spent there flooded the streets—let us add, in all its awesomeness.... [After these events] we have become all the more convinced that just as the productive working of a turbine transforms the destructive energy of water, so must we transform through intelligent and benevolent laws that harmful and destructive awesomeness into national energy placed in the service of national production.[24]

When Khuen-Hédervány's successor, Lukács, criticized the suffrage proposals of the *GyOSz* as perhaps serving the cause of industrial peace but harming the national interest, the *Magyar Gyáripar* wrote:

> It is not a "calm" through a law against strikes that we want—we have rejected such experiments on numerous occasions in the past. We want a parliament and a public opinion filled with a sense for the economy, with a capacity to recognize its future great interests which depend, in the first place, on the development of factory industry. It would be useless for us to expect this "calm"—in the higher sense of the word—from today's parliament. This is why we strive—in honorable conviction—for a different parliament. The interests of the country and, as with the interests of the country, the interests of industry cannot be secured by "special" measures.[25]

The protests of the *GyOSz* and other urban groups, both within and outside the political establishment, helped to bring about a suffrage reform law in March, 1913. Although it was far from what had been demanded by the Social Democrats and also less than had been proposed by the *GyOSz*, it was more than what Khuen-Hédervány's successor, Lukács had submitted to parliament in December, 1912. According to the calculations of the *Magyar Gyáripar*, the law increased the number of enfranchised citizens from about one million to about 1,800,000. The number of enfranchised industrial workers rose to a quarter million, half of what the *GyOSz* had proposed but still a significant advance. In

23 GyOSz, *1913. évi jelentés*, 171-72.

24 *Magyar Gyáripar*, II, No. 11 (1912), 2.

25 *Ibid.*, III, No. 2 (1913), 1-2.

addition, the law instituted the secret ballot in Budapest and 25 other cities, though not in the countryside.[26] The true effect of the law cannot be judged, however; no elections were held after the outbreak of war in 1914—though this in itself is an indication that the ruling nobility feared its potential.

The franchise law was one of the factors that led to a split in the coalition of urban forces that had started to emerge after 1906. A number of deputies, including Pál Sándor, president of the *OMKE*, and Ferenc Székely, who had fought for wider suffrage, quit the Party of National Work in protest. Chorin also quit in September, 1913 and joined the National Constitution Party of Gyula Andrássy, whose policies differed from those of Tisza more in style than in substance. Most deputies close to the *GyOSz*, however, such as Hegedüs and Gratz, did not quit the Party of National Work. They felt that the extended suffrage should be given a chance.

The *GyOSz* did not exhibit any serious reformist drive in the last year of peace. The recession that began in 1913 sharpened the conflict between labor and capital. Moreover, the country's military spending was on the rise. The *GyOSz* turned its attention from politics at large to procuring military orders for Hungarian industry. In January, 1914, we still find the *Magyar Gyáripar* criticizing the "bagatelle" concerns of parliament as compared to the real work performed by Hungarian industry; but the effect of the criticism was blunted by its occasion—the launching of the battleship St. Stephen, built for the Austro-Hungarian Navy by the Ganz-Danubius Shipyards.[27]

Conclusion

It would be a mistake to interpret the politics of the Hungarian industrial elite, as represented by the statements and actions of the *GyOSz*, to have been that of a doctrinaire progressivism. Nor should we condemn the builders of Hungarian industry as diehard reactionaries, as they have often been portrayed in the past. Culturally and economically, they felt themselves to be a part of a different Hungary than that represented by the ruling nobility—an emerging urban society in which they often found, or hoped to find, more common ground with other city dwellers than with the feudal upper classes. The propensity for collaborating with other urban groups in restructuring political life was there; it found expression, mostly between 1908 and 1913, in the various movements we have traced. This propensity may have been strengthened by the Jewish origins of many industrialists, who, despite the conversion of many to

26 *Ibid.*, III, No. 7 (1913), 3.
27 *Ibid.*, IV, No. 2 (1914), p. 2.

Christianity and their assumption of noble titles, could never fully assimilate socially or politically into the "historic" nobility. But as the examples of Hegedüs and Gratz illustrate, the neo-liberal politics of the *GyOSz* were not limited to the Jewish bourgeoisie. Further study is required, though, to advance our understanding of this question.

In the last year of peace the industrial elite was diverted from its active pursuit of reforms or urban alliances and we know little of its activities in this area during the war and the subsequent revolutions. Nevertheless, in the political orientations and reformist activities that we have described one can see the precursors of the bourgeois liberal opposition that emerged in the 1920s under the Horthy regime.[28]

28 Zsuzsa L. Nagy, *Bethlen liberális ellenzéke (A liberális polgári pártok 1919-1931)* [Bethlen's Liberal Opposition (The Liberal Bourgeois Parties 1919-1931)], (Budapest, 1980).

VI

Exclusiveness and Mobility in the Interwar Period

Hungarian Banking and Business Leaders Between the Wars: Education, Ethnicity and Career Patterns

György Lengyel

This paper deals with the social composition of two Hungarian economic elites in the period between the two world wars, namely, the leaders of large banks and of large business enterprises. To keep within the purview of this conference I shall focus on their ethnic background and mobility, education, and career pattern.

If by "economic elite" we mean those individuals who have power and influence over economic decisions, legislation, and ideology, then, for the period in question, representatives of employers' associations, landowners and the wealthy also belong to this group.[1]

Unless otherwise indicated, the findings presented here are based on the results of an empirical historical and sociological study in the course of which we analyzed, by two-step institutional sampling, the data of 314 prominent Hungarian economic leaders who held three or more elite positions in three selected years (1927, 1937, 1943). I refer to them as the apex—roughly the tenth decile—of the economic elite, conspicuous by their accumulation of posts as the "multipositional" elite. The social indicators for this narrow group were gleaned from public and archival sources as well as from interviews.[2]

1 I have discussed the problems of sampling in a preliminary paper on methodology, "Some Remarks on Research into the Hungarian Economic Elite" (manuscript, 1979) and surveyed the literature on the subject in a paper entitled "Economic Elite," Workshop of Value Sociology and Social Science Analyses, Hungarian Academy of Sciences (Budapest, 1982).

2 Besides the annuals, lists of civil servants, directories, and telephone books for the years in question, we have also gone through the material in the relevant volumes of Dezső Zentay's series, *Beszélő számok* [Talking Numbers] (vols. II-XIII, Budapest, 1934-1945), as well as parliamentary almanacs and lists of estate owners.
The most important biographical dictionaries we used were: *Magyar zsidó lexikon* [Hungarian Jewish Lexicon] (Budapest, 1929); *A magyar társadalom lexikona* [Lexicon of Hungarian Society] (Budapest, 1930); *A magyar állam élete* [The Life of the Hungarian

Thus in a broad sense this investigation has the same basis as that of a previous study of mine.[3] There I compared leaders in the economic control sphere with those in the private economy, whereas now I seek to explore two groups in the private sphere against the background of public statistics wherever possible.

Let us start our comparison with a well-known statistical source: the *Hungarian Statistical Yearbook* for 1935. It contains serviceable summaries of some social attributes of economic leaders, including their educational background. We find (see Table 1) that the great majority—around two-thirds—had some sort of secondary education; 35% had a high-school diploma. One-fifth of them attended institutions of higher education.

With regard to education, two subgroups–owners and managers– can be clearly differentiated. While only 40% of owners were high-school or university graduates, nearly three-fourths of the managers finished high school, and 30% of them completed college as well. At the other extreme, while over one-fourth of the owners had no more than an elementary-school education, the corresponding figure for managers is a mere 6%.

State] (Budapest, 1932); *A magyar legujabb kor lexikona* [Lexicon of Contemporary Hungary], (Budapest, 1932); *Ezer kortárs* [One Thousand Contemporaries], (Budapest, 1936); *Ki kicsoda? Kortársak lexikona* [Who's Who? A Lexicon of Contemporaries] (Budapest, 1937); *Keresztény közéleti almanach* [Christian Almanach of Public Life] (Budapest, 1940); Gulyás Pál, *Magyar írók élete és munkái. Új sorozat* [Lives and Works of Hungarian writers], vols. I-VI (Budapest, 1939-1944).

From among journalistic portraits, we used: Béla Kornitzer, *Apák és fiuk* [Fathers and sons] vols. I-II (Budapest, n.d.); Miklós Kósa, *A pénz urai* [Lords of money] vols. I-II (Budapest, 1922); idem, *Arany-emberek* [Golden men] (Budapest, 1927); idem, *Közgazdasági képeskönyv* [A Picture Book of the Economy] (Budapest, 1940); József Radnóti, *Akikről a pénz beszél* [Whom Money Speaks About] (Budapest, 1923); idem, *Pöröly és pult* [Hammer and Counter] (Budapest, 1925); idem, *Pesti pénzoligarchák* [The Plutocrats of Pest] (Budapest, 1929); Miklós Vécsey, *Száz értékes magyar* [A Hundred Worthy Hungarians] (Budapest, 1931); László Kügyi Virágh, *A city urai* [The Lords of the City], (Budapest, 1930-1934).

We have also examined the relevant material in the Gulyás estate, preserved in the manuscript collection of the Hungarian Academy of Sciences (brought to our attention by János Viczián), the relevant items among copies of registration certificates in the Hungarian National Archives, the credit records of the Hungarian National Bank, the Interior Ministry's list of freemasons, applications for ennoblement, documents of political screening committees in the Municipal Archives of Budapest, and research into foreign registers and interviews. I was greatly assisted in exploring the material by István Gajáry and Zoltán Földi.

3 György Lengyel, "The Ethnic Composition of the Economic Elite in Hungary in the Interwar Period," in Yehuda Don and Victor Karady, eds., *A Social and Economic History of Central European Jewry* (New Brunswick, NJ, 1990), pp. 229-247.

Table 1: Level of Education of Owners, Lessees and Managers of Industrial Enterprises, 1935 (%)[4]

Level of Education	Owners, Lessees	Managers
College Graduate	10.4	30.1
Secondary School with Diploma	29.9	43.3
Secondary School without Diploma	32.6	20.5
Elementary School	27.1	6.1
Total	100.0	100.0
Number	1986	2161

This difference existed in other countries as well.[5] If we take a representative sample from the *Hungarian Biographical Dictionary*, we find that in the nineteenth and early twentieth centuries around half of the owners had practical training and about one-third had higher education, while the percentage of managers with higher education was 87%.[6]

The obvious explanation is that the mechanism of recruitment was different for the two strata: schooling was a primary criterion for salaried managers, while wealth and social origin remained the most important criteria for owners.

In our case, however, there is another explanation, related to the concentration of enterprises. The 1935 statistics encompass the entire circle of business management; the approximately 4,000 leaders also include the heads of enterprises employing fewer than 20 workers. More than half belonged to this category, which employed only 8% of all industrial manpower and produced 15% of the total value of production. There were only 70 large enterprises with over 500 employees each, but they concentrated 35% of the industrial labor force and 29% of the produced value.

Because the overwhelming majority of large enterprises were joint stock corporations, whereas most individual owners and lessees were affiliated with small enterprises, the difference in educational level correlates with the type and

4 *Magyar Statisztikai Évkönyv 1935* [Hungarian Statistical Yearbook 1935] (Budapest 1936), p. 137.

5 Hartmut Kaelble, "Long-term Changes in the Recruitment of the Business Elite: Germany Compared to the USA, Great Britain and France since the Industrial Revolution," *Journal of Social History* (1980), 404-423.

6 I have discussed some findings of this research in "The Recruitment and Level of Education of the Hungarian Business Elite in the 19th and the First Half of the 20th Centuries," in Rudolf Andorka and László Bertalan, eds., *Economy and Society in Hungary* (Budapest, 1986), pp. 117-138.

Table 2: Religion of Owners, Lessees and Managers of Industrial Enterprises, 1935 (%)[7]

Religion	Owners, Lessees	Managers
Roman Catholic	33.9	36.5
Calvinist	7.6	11.4
Lutheran	7.4	9.1
Jewish	50.8	41.7
Other	0.3	1.3
Total	100.0	100.0
Number	1986	2126

size of the enterprise. More or less the same situation prevails with regard to the religious and ethnic affiliation of business leaders (Table 2).

As we can see, Jews constituted the largest group among both owners and managers (actually even a small majority in the former category). If we take into consideration that in 1937, 45% of the "multipositional" business elite and 37% of the "multipositional" banking elite were Jews, the difference is more striking. The higher percentage of Jews among small entrepreneurs seems at first glance to support the thesis of peripheral Jewish business activity rather than Jewish dominance. (The former holds that Jews concentrated in those branches where the individual risk is higher and the social prestige lower than the average.) In fact, though, Jews were overrepresented among the leaders of both large and small business, and the business leaders were segmented by ethnic relations as well as by relations of wealth and influence. The Jews were more divided than the other ethnic groups: the dichotomy of many small entrepreneurs vis-à-vis a small economically powerful elite was more acute than might be supposed on the basis of the contemporary stereotype, which obviously tended to emphasize the difference among ethnic groups.

There was a group of small-scale entrepreneurs, particularly in non-capital-intensive, dynamically growing industries (rather than in the peripheral branches), whose business success rested on their risk-taking ability and expertise or inventions. Their careers typically began with a workshop, initially set up for the production of a single article, which later grew and diversified and occasionally became a joint stock corporation. Examples include the chemical works founded by Rudolf Balló, a professor-turned-entrepreneur who was the

7 *Magyar Statisztikai Évkönyv 1935* [Hungarian Statistical Yearbook 1935] (Budapest 1936), p. 136.

Table 3: Educational Level of Technical and Commercial Clerks in Industrial Enterprises, 1935 (%)[8]

Level of Education	Technical Clerks	Commercial Clerks
College Graduate	44.7	6.6
Secondary School with Diploma	16.6	45.4
Secondary School without Diploma	35.6	43.1
Elementary School	3.1	4.9
Total	100.0	100.0
Number	4619	17,947

first to manufacture plastics in Hungary, or the small-motor factory stemming from the workshop of János Csonka and his sons. The development of the pharmaceutical ventures of Leó Egger and of Gedeon Richter was similar. Theirs, however, is not the dominant type of small-scale entrepreneurship: their professional prestige exceeded their capital and numerical importance.

Viewed from the side of production, the high level of education must be attributed to the emergence of large hierarchical and specialized enterprises. They employed a significant proportion of the technical clerks, 45% of whom had college degrees (Table 3).

By contrast, fewer than 10% of the commercial clerks finished university. Still, most of the latter did have high-school diplomas, which—as will be explained later—can be ascribed to the peculiarities of the Hungarian educational system and the role assigned to the commercial academies.

Is the 20% share of high-school graduates among business leaders high or low? Compared to the population as a whole, even the 10% among the owners is high. Among the entire population over 20, a mere 1.6% finished high school in 1930, while 11% were illiterate.[9] On the other hand, when we juxtapose the figures for all business leaders to those for the economic elite, it certainly seems low. During the interwar years 79% of the "multipositional" elite had a university education, rising from 67%-70% in the twenties and thirties to 86% in 1943. The data mentioned above reveal that in the nineteenth and early twentieth centuries 71% of the best-known industrial leaders had a higher education. For the third generation, which was active mostly in the interwar period, the corresponding figure was as high as 90%.

8 *Ibid.*, p. 137.
9 *Ibid.*, p. 13.

Table 4: Children of School Age and School-children by Religion (1900)[10]

	RC	Calv	Luth	Jew	Other	Total	N
School age children	48.9	14.1	7.7	5.0	24.3	100.0	2,929,102
School-children	52.6	14.6	8.5	5.0	19.3	100.0	2,288,452
Civil population	48.7	14.4	7.5	4.9	24.5	100.0	16,721,574

With regard to the "multipositional" business elite, the following structural changes took place: between 1927 and 1943 the proportion of engineers grew from 12% to 20%; the proportion of commercial academy graduates shrank from 25% to less than 10%; graduates in law, composed nearly half of the business elite (45%) in 1943, after an initial decline. This tendency was considerably shaped by the different patterns of education among various ethnic groups and by the changing of the guard.

If we examine Hungarian educational and religious statistics from the 1890s (a relevant decade for the educational background of the interwar business elite) we will find some highly characteristic tendencies. With regard to children of school age versus children actually attending school, the ratio among the Jews did not vary from the general figure. It was the "other" religions (mostly Greek Catholic and Greek Orthodox) that were underrepresented in school enrollments (Table 4).

In many respects, the first real watershed was the choice of a secondary school. Some 90% of secondary-school students had an upper- or middle-class background, and over 80% attended a gymnasium. But while the children of middle-class gentry and professional families were overrepresented in the gymnasia, those from a bourgeois background were overrepresented in the *Realschulen*.[11]

Jews were overrepresented in both types of schools; more than two-thirds of them attended gymnasia. But whereas they accounted for nearly 40% of the students at *Realschulen*, they constituted only 18% of gymnasium enrollment (Table 5).

There is a similar trend among university students, more than 25% of whom were Jewish. The Jewish enrollment ranged from 22% of law students and 13% in the humanities, to 41% in the medical and technical faculties. That is, while

10 *Magyar Statisztikai Évkönyv 1901* [Hungarian Statistical Yearbook 1901] (Budapest 1902), pp. 17, 316.

11 *Ibid.*, p. 342.

Table 5: Students in Secondary Schools by Religion (1891-1900) (%)[12]

	RC	Calv	Luth	Jew	Other	Total	N
Gymnasia	44.5	15.9	10.0	18.0	11.6	100.0	41,475
Realschulen	40.0	6.0	11.0	38.2	4.8	100.0	8,855
Total	44.0	14.2	10.1	21.6	10.1	100.0	50,330

one-third of all university students were in the medical and technical faculties, of the Jews, almost half (48%) were enrolled in these faculties (Table 6). These statistics reveal two characteristics of Jewish educational attainments: Jews had a higher-than-average level of education, and they were more practically oriented.

Nevertheless, the first characteristic seems to be inconsistent with our picture of the education of the business leaders. In that case, there was a correlation between their lower educational level and the Jewish overrepresentation among them. Furthermore, among the "multipositional" elite the Jews were less educated than the non-Jews (18% with only a secondary education versus more than one-third of the entire elite). Interestingly enough, an empirical study of the American business elite found a similar tendency. While the Jewish business leaders had a lower educational level, the ratio of those who had a more traditional, "family-made man" career pattern was significantly higher among them.[13]

Table 6: University Students by Religion (1891-1900) (%)[14]

	RC	Calv	Luth	Jew	Other	Total	N
Law	43.7	17.3	8.8	21.8	8.4	100.0	3,879
Humanities	46.8	20.2	13.3	12.5	7.2	100.0	667
Medicine*	31.3	11.4	9.4	41.2	6.7	100.0	1,093
Technical	35.0	7.7	6.6	40.9	9.8	100.0	993
Total	40.1	15.6	9.7	26.9	7.7	100.0	6,632

*including pharmacology

12 *Ibid.*

13 Suzanne I. Keller, "The Social Origins and Career Lines of Three Generations of American Business Leaders," (Ph.D. thesis, Dept. of Political Science, Columbia University, 1953), pp. 159-168.

14 *Ibid.*, p. 348.

How can we explain this striking inconsistency? For Hungary, one possible interpretation is that the two characteristics of the Jewish educational model become contradictory at a certain point. Precisely with regard to economic education, the higher level and the practical orientation of their education clashed. Until 1920, the dominant institutions of economic education in Hungary were the commercial academies, practical secondary schools whose students had only limited possibilities for continuing on to post-secondary education. We cannot generalize about all the commercial academies, however, for there were clear differences among them. Here we can compare the academies of Budapest and Kolozsvár. Approximately 40% of the students at the Budapest Commercial Academy were born in Budapest, whereas almost two-thirds of the students at the Kolozsvár Commercial Academy came from outlying regions in Transylvania. More than 90% of the graduates of the Budapest Commercial Academy found jobs in private firms (and nearly half of them became proprietors or managers), while more than 40% of the Kolozsvár graduates went into the civil service.[15]

The average level of education among "multipositional" bankers was somewhat below that of business leaders; for the period under study, 74% had a university education. Though startling at the first glance, this phenomenon is easy to explain: the initially high—nearly 30%—proportion of commercial academy graduates among bankers decreased far less drastically (in 1943 it was still 16%), due to the nature of their work, than it did among business leaders. On the other hand, the proportion of law graduates, which rose from 52% to 58%, was significantly higher among bankers than among businessmen. This is all the more remarkable considering that there was frequent overlapping between these two groups of the "multipositional" elite.

The question arises whether the dichotomous educational structure of owners and managers can be demonstrated for the elite as a whole. Since most of the firms in question were run as joint stock corporations, the owners remained in the background. The explicit documentation refers mainly to board chairmen and members. Here too there is a certain difference, but it is the polar opposite of what we found for the industrial leadership as a whole: the educational level of board chairmen and members with proprietary rights is higher, both in banks and commercial firms, than that of managers. The

15 János Balázs and György Lengyel, "A közgazdasági és műszaki pályák elterjedése Magyarországon" [The spread of economic and technical professions in Hungary], in: Ildikó Hrubos, ed., *Közgazdász és mérnök generációk társadalmi helyzetének néhány jellemzője* [Some Characteristics of the Social Position of the Economist and Engineer Generations] *[= Marx Károly Közgazdaságtudományi Egyetem Szociológiai Mühely Tanulmányok]* (Budapest, 1986), pp. 1-38.

proportion of university graduates among the former is four-fifths, among business managers only three-fourths, and among bank managers nearly two-thirds. But the stockholders' representatives do not form a homogeneous group either: in the case of board chairmen the ratio of law graduates strongly exceeds the average in both types of institutions.

Thus the educational structure of the elite reflected the structure of the institutional hierarchy. It stands to reason that these three categories of leaders were also characterized by different career patterns: board members were chiefly recruited from among experts produced by influential institutions in the same sphere, whereas more chairmen followed the career pattern of the politician-state administrator, and more managers stuck to the private sector.

The single largest group among both bankers (37%) and business leaders (34%) were those who began their careers as private officials. In most cases this meant starting as a junior clerk and gradually becoming acquainted with several functional areas. Another group of 11%-13% started out in managerial posts. If we add to them those who started their careers as freelancing intellectuals, we may conclude that nearly two-thirds of business and financial leaders began their careers in the private sector. It also means that the proportion of leaders who began their careers as landowners or civil servants (generally fourth-class clerks in government ministries) was also far from negligible.

Among the Jewish bankers and businessmen, the proportion of those who began their career in the private sector was conspicuous. Those with a background in a family business were also significantly overrepresented.

A comparison of career patterns and the nature of positions can clarify these assumptions. Among managers, the predominant subgroup includes not only those who began in the private sector, but even in the same type of institution: 52% of bank managers started as tellers, and 40% of business managers began as commercial clerks. We see that in this group, loyalty and practical expertise acquired by routine were important criteria of recruitment.

In industrial joint stock companies, those whose first job was in the civil service were heavily overrepresented, as were those who started out as managers and landowners. The largest single group among board members were trained in institutions of the same nature; one-fourth began as bank tellers.

The case of the board members of banks is different; they had a strong tendency to have begun their careers in public administration or managerial posts. The common view that this should be attributed to the social prestige of board membership or bank chairmanship can be verified only partly. It seems evident that Albert Berzeviczy and Vilmos Nagybaczoni Nagy were appointed to leading economic posts by virtue of their social prestige rather than their professional competence. This, however, is not true of Frigyes Fellner or János

Bud, who met both criteria and whose knowledge and skills in financial and economic policy were significant.

Our investigations have revealed a professionalization process among the business elite. One sign of this is that, as time passed, the average age at which both the first job and the first managerial position were occupied rose perceptibly. Another sign is that, in the short run, the proportion of high-school graduates and then of engineers and lawyers increased, as did the proportion of office careers.

As far as the correlations among ethnic affiliation, education, and career patterns are concerned, there are some peculiar features. While the Jewish population was more educated than the average, the educational level of Jewish business leaders was below the national average, and those with a more traditional career pattern were overrepresented among them. The dichotomy between small-scale entrepreneurs and members of the elite seems to be more striking among the Jewish leaders than for other ethnic groups.

All of these phenomena suggest that the criteria of recruitment to the Jewish elite were more traditional, underlining wealth and social origin alongside education and bureaucratic experience. We must avoid the pitfalls of an oversimplified contrast, for these differences came to the fore rather gradually. Nevertheless, the Jewish elite seems to have been at a disadvantage, not only because of the obvious effects of the different forms of antisemitism and the changing of the guard, but also because of slower adaptation to the professionalization process.

Interwar Antisemitism in the Professions: The Case of the Engineers

Mária M. Kovács

This paper addresses the Jewish role in the Hungarian economy and interwar antisemitism from the viewpoint of the country's technical elite, the ten-thousand strong group of university-trained engineers.[1] The problem of interwar Jewish segregation is discussed with regard to a vocational group which owed its rise to the technological enthusiasm of the *Gründerzeit* and was, therefore, not only largely indifferent to the anti-modernistic pessimism of more conservative circles but which also, with its mixture of Magyars, Jews, and Germans, had remained immune to the ethnic hostilities of the pre-World War I era.

It is against this background that the sudden outbreak of antisemitism in the post-war period has to be understood. In the interwar period, university-trained engineers constituted the professional group that implemented the most stringent anti-Jewish policies, especially the *numerus clausus* law that limited the proportion of Jews entering the professions to six percent. In no other learned profession was the decline in Jewish membership as swift and massive as it was among engineers, where, by 1937, the proportion of Jews had dropped from a pre-war 40 percent to less than 16 percent.

This strict application of antisemitic measures required, to some extent, the active participation of the non-Jewish segment of the profession. Yet the antisemitism of Hungarian engineers was not only an expression of their interest

1 For an overview of the corporate life and politics of the two other major professions, the legal and the medical, see my "Luttes professionelles et antisémitisme: Chronique de la montée du fascisme dans le corps médical Hongrois, 1920-1944," *Actes de la recherche en science sociales* 56 (March 1985); *The Politics of the Legal Profession in Interwar Hungary, Institute on East Central Europe* [= Istvan Deak, ed., *Columbia University Studies in Hungarian Social History*, no. 2] (New York, 1987) and "Lawyers against the Current: Anti-Semitism and Liberal Response in Interwar Hungary," in Yehuda Don and Victor Karady, eds., *A Social and Economic History of Central European Jewry* (New Brunswick, NJ, 1990), pp. 249-256.

in taking over the powerful and lucrative positions held by their Jewish colleagues, although this motive also played a conspicuous role in their behavior. But they also had other, perhaps less self-seeking motives—aspirations that could be described, with a slight anachronism, as technocratic, motivated by a kind of technological radicalism and even idealism. This technological idealism held a bright promise for the larger community, such as catching up with the technological leaders of the world and restoring the rightful place of pauperized Trianon Hungary in Europe. Another motive was the anticipated harmony between industrial workers and their natural leaders, the engineers, a harmony ostensibly disrupted by the nonproductive, capitalist captains of industry, who were mainly Jews.

This curious blend of motives was, after the brief interlude of the 1919 Bolshevik revolution, held together by the glue of antisemitism. The elimination of the Jewish competitor, both the engineer and the capitalist, promised an instant utopia wherein the *raffendes*, that is, parasitic Jewish capital, would be overcome by the *schaffendes*, that is, creative Hungarian or Christian capital.[2] But in a protracted process of learning the Hungarian engineers came to realize that the elimination of Jewish competition could neither solve their personal problems nor fulfill their corporate aspirations. This in turn led them, by the 1930s, to a home-grown version of technological totalitarianism, which, despite its amateurish character, was at times more straightforward than its Italian and German models. It is in the context of this learning process that I shall try to analyze the problem of antisemitism among engineers in its broadest outlines.

By way of introduction, it is worth remembering that the technocratic-utopian aspirations of engineers had made their first appearance in a quite different political context, during World War I. This is one of the reasons why a considerable part of the profession, Jews and non-Jews alike, lent their enthusiastic support to the Bolshevik experiment in 1919. Irrespective of their ethnic background, nearly half of all Hungarian engineers took part in the socialist organization of engineers and helped the revolution take command of industrial production.[3] Their activism anticipated the strong appeal of anti-liberal ideologies to this profession. The engineers who supported the revolution came mainly from the larger industrial plants, including their leader, Gyula Hevesi who, before he had even heard of socialism, had nourished the naive

2 It is hardly an accident that the dichotomy of *raffendes* versus *schaffendes* capital was first developed by a German engineer in the interwar period. For a stimulating account of the emergence of the Right in the German engineering profession, see Jeffrey Herf, *Reactionary Modernism: Technology, Culture and Politics in Weimar and the Third Reich* (Cambridge, 1984).

3 György Péteri, *A magyar tanácsköztársaság irányítási rendszere* [The Administration of the Economy under the Hungarian Bolshevik Revolution] (Budapest, 1979).

technocratic dream of setting up a clandestine international information agency of engineers to prevent industrial proprietors from monopolizing the innovations of their employees.[4]

Although the collapse of the Revolution put an abrupt end to the first radical experiment to transform the economic system, the engineers were by no means ready to surrender their illiberal vision of a state-dominated national economy. On the contrary, the post-war crisis only reinforced such visions because it was expected that economic reconstruction would be carried out by a strong nation-state that would break with the traditions of *laissez faire* and use its powers to release technological modernization from the constraints of domestic and international finance. This illiberal vision of an orchestrated policy of industrial reconstruction accounts for the astonishing speed with which the political Right was able to win over a substantial following among Hungarian engineers.

The first rightist organization of engineers, formed in late 1919, was the Christian Association of Builders and Engineers, whose membership was recruited from well-established, non-Jewish private practitioners, mainly architects. This elite association demanded preferential treatment for non-Jewish engineers by the elimination of free competition for public commissions.[5] Through its highly placed allies in the state administration, the Association was instrumental in securing commissions for its membership; moreover, by 1923 it had convinced the government to set up an official Chamber of Engineers, which was fully under the control of the rightist Association, with compulsory supervisory powers over all self-employed practitioners, both Jewish and non-Jewish.[6]

But the antisemitism of these twin organizations, the Association and the Chamber, was definitely exceeded by that of another, more militant rightist Union of Engineers, the *Hungaria*. Born in the turmoil of the early twenties as a paramilitary student organization at the Technical University, the Union grew to exert a great influence on non-Jewish engineers in industrial employment and the civil service. From the outset, the Union combined agitation against Jewish colleagues with a crusade against what it called "the financial swindles of Jewish capital." The spirit of Jewish capital was to be fought on several fronts. To begin with, Jewish engineers were to be excluded from both the civil service and industry. Second, the *Hungaria* kept a watchful eye on strict observance of the *numerus clausus* law, even at times when some other professions were more

4 Gyula Hevesi, *Egy mérnök a forradalomban* [An engineer in the Revolution], (Budapest, 1959), p. 71.

5 Cf. *Magyar Mérnökök és Építészek Nemzeti Szövetsége, Titkári jelentés* [National Association of Hungarian Engineers and Architects, Report of Activities] (Budapest, 1921-1944).

6 *Magyar Mérnökök és Építészek Nemzeti Szövetsége, Titkári jelentés* (1924).

relaxed in its application. Third, the Union staged a series of confrontations with the Bethlen government on account of the latter's mercantile stabilization policies. In this, the Union was supported by the academic elite of the profession. When, in the early twenties, the government proposed integrating a commercial faculty into the Technical University, the Union rejected the plan in the name of safeguarding the pure spirit of technical education and rallied the support of academic leaders to frustrate the idea.[7]

In this atmosphere, and with the uncompromising observance of the *numerus clausus*, the segregation of Jews within the profession followed a clear pattern. Jewish beginners were, in fact, practically excluded from the civil service, and their opportunities were not much better in industry. In any case, the industrial demand for engineers was declining steadily, so it was precisely in this field that the competition for positions was most bitter. In this group, held in highest esteem by the profession, the proportion of Jewish engineers declined from roughly 40 percent in the prewar period to 18 percent by 1937, with this 18 percent consisting mainly of the older cohorts of the prewar generations.[8]

The shrinking group of Jewish engineers, numbering around 2500 by the thirties, were increasingly drawn into private practice, mostly into architecture and construction, fields in which engineers were still predominantly self-employed. By 1937, more than half of all Jewish engineers worked in architecture, many of them in offices established well before the war. Thus, despite the sharp decline of Jewish membership in other fields of engineering, Jews retained their prewar positions in private practice throughout the interwar period; as late as 1937 they still made up 38 percent of the total. By contrast, in sectors operating on a corporate basis, such as industry or civil service, their presence diminished continuously: throughout the interwar period not a single Jew entered mining, metallurgy, or forestry.

This dual process of segregation—segregation with regard both to specialization and form of employment—reinforced the image of the Jewish engineer as a proponent of individualism and free competition. Furthermore, it was precisely the construction trade—which still had a large contingent of Jewish engineers—that tended to pull through, with fair success, all the major structural transformations in industry and continued to flourish even when other

7 The activities of the union were regularly reported in the journal *Technikus* [Technician] throughout the period. The union published an exclusive journal from 1934 to 1944, entitled *Hungária*.

8 OL [Hungarian National Archives] P 1070/8. Data on the distribution of engineers are computed on the basis of the 1937 register.

industries suffered serious setbacks.[9] For example, the machine industry, which had traditionally employed a large number of engineers, ceased to expand, while other industries, such as the dynamically growing textile industry, required few university-trained experts. Thus, despite the lessening of Jewish competition among industrial engineers, in the entire decade of the twenties the number of openings for engineers in industrial plants did not exceed the number of university graduates in a single year.

As a last resort, the government came to the rescue of the swelling profession: by the 1930s, 5000 out of Hungary's 10,000 engineers were employed in government and municipal administration. But the enormous 40 percent rise in the number of civil service positions was hardly a fulfillment of technocratic aspirations. Most civil-service engineers were employed in poorly paid, subordinate positions, with very little hope of rising to the status of officials with a legal education. On top of that, the exclusion of Jewish engineers from the civil service brought very little psychological comfort to the anti-Jewish radicals: Jewish engineers, now concentrated in private practice, did not seem to be at a disadvantage in adapting to the changes in the economy.

It comes as little surprise, then, that by the late twenties Hungarian engineers affiliated with the rightist organizations were more or less disillusioned with the policies of the prime minister, Count István Bethlen. On the one hand, his economic policies defied early post-war expectations of an *orchestrated national policy* of technological reconstruction which, in turn, would have created new opportunities for the profession. On the other hand, despite its undeniable economic successes, the Bethlen government was viewed as having misused its powers by subordinating technological concerns to commercial interests, even at the price of frustrating the more modern potentials of Hungarian industry.

Hence the fall of Bethlen, the Depression, and the rise of the Gömbös government marked a new phase in the radicalization of the profession. The diffuse sentiments of antisemitism, and anti-liberalism in general, now converged into a coherent program for fundamental reform of the economy. This program, entitled "Country Building," was announced at the engineers' 1933 national convention.[10] Its contents attest to the strong appeal of totalitarian concepts: the program anticipated an economy in which the role of commerce would be reduced to a minimum, while the country's resources were allocated to a *unified national program* of technological modernization. The fact that these

9 For a general overview see Iván T. Berend and György Ránki, "Gazdasági stabilizáció és fejlődés a 20-as években" [Economic stabilization and development in the twenties] in: *Magyarország története 1918-1945* (Budapest, 1978), pp. 488-501 and 504-508.

10 *Az országrendezés mérnöki megvilágításban a nemzeti munkaterv alapján* (Budapest, 1933).

radical proposals were supported even by the most moderate leaders of the Chamber of Engineers and by the academic elite demonstrates that this moderate group was uneasy about the anti-industrial and anti-modernistic attitudes of both the conservative and the populist right.

Great hopes accompanied the creation, in 1935, of a separate Ministry of Industry, led by the engineer Géza Bornemissza, the one-time founder of the radical rightist union of engineers, the *Hungaria*. In professional circles, Bornemissza was simply referred to as the Minister of Engineers.[11] At about the same time, the last psychological and mental barriers to translating the radical proposals into more systematic anti-Jewish demands eroded under the impact of events in Hitler's Germany. For the time being, the racist organizations of engineers demanded centralized political control over the flow of Jewish capital and monitoring of the investment and innovation policies of Jewish industrialists. As for more immediate results, Jewish capitalists were to be obliged to hire Gentile engineers.

To this end, a detailed register of all the engineers in the country was prepared by the Chamber in 1937, broken down by religion (including conversions), field of specialization, place of employment, and earnings. Already at this point, however, the comprehensive survey indicated the fragility of the conspiratorial theory of Jewish overrepresentation among engineers, even in Jewish-owned enterprises. A comparison of the survey with data on the proportion of Jewish industrialists indicated that by this time the distribution of Jewish engineers did not even remotely correspond to the distribution of Jewish property. Even in such fields as the chemical industry, where 64 percent of medium-to-large-sized firms were in Jewish hands, the proportion of Jewish engineers was only 15 percent; the figures were similar in the textile, paper, and machine industries. To give a few further examples: in mining the proportion of Jewish engineers was 0.5 percent, in metallurgy 1.2 percent, and in forestry zero. Apart from construction, the only field in which there was still a considerable Jewish presence (22 percent) was mechanical engineering. In the machine industry, these Jewish engineers, usually over the age of fifty and with the strikingly high figure of 30 percent Christian converts among them, worked in such large firms as Ganz and Company and the Manfréd Weiss Works, side-by-side with a much larger contingent of Gentile engineers.

In short, the findings of the 1937 survey help us understand why the introduction of anti-Jewish legislation in 1938 had a somewhat sobering effect on the Gentile majority within the profession. On the one hand, they came to realize that the exclusion of Jewish entrants or even of established Jewish

11 "Itt a technikus minisztérium" [Finally a Ministry of Technology] *Hungária*, August 15, 1935.

colleagues would hardly open up a considerable range of new opportunities for non-Jews. But more than that, anti-Jewish legislation brought little if any change in the eyes of those Gentile engineers who had been attracted to the rightist radical organizations by their demands for overall economic reform. Discounting the unprecedented wave of corruption involving Gentiles who lent their names to Jewish firms, the coming years saw no sign of a breakthrough towards any systematic reform.

Adding to their bewilderment was the growing opposition of non-Jewish private practitioners to an *étatist* reform. Although they were still a small minority within the profession, it was this group for whom the anti-Jewish legislation opened up new prospects by eliminating competition from their Jewish colleagues. Trying to secure a greater foothold in the market, they threatened to disrupt the *étatist*-technocratic consensus within the Gentile sector of the profession.[12]

All in all, the six years during which anti-Jewish legislation was in force saw growing confusion in the behavior of the profession as a whole. While discrimination against Jewish engineers never stopped, it never attained the blind fury characteristic, for instance, of the medical profession, whose Chamber submitted to the army meticulous lists of Jewish doctors to be sent away to forced labor. When, in early 1942, the government requested each Chamber to give its views on the total elimination of Jews from all professions, the Chamber of Engineers officially rejected such a measure.[13]

At the same time, the Chamber and the rightist associations flooded the government with a new wave of proposals about an inevitable, overall reform of the economy. A leader of the Chamber expressed their attitudes in Parliament in 1941 as follows:

> It is the conviction of our profession that anti-Jewish legislation had conceptually been mistaken already at its genesis. Instead of trying to deliver Jewish capital and property into Christian-Hungarian hands, which merely

12 Perhaps the most publicized case of the *volte-face* by some Gentile engineers was that of the most talented architect of the "Hungarian Bauhaus," Molnár Farkas. Once a member of the Communist Party, he and his group were attached to the small, liberal organization of private architects *[Tervezők és Magánépítészek Országos Egyesülete]* throughout the 1920s and 1930s. In response to the anti-Jewish law of 1938, Farkas left the liberal association, joined the Arrow-Cross, and aggressively demanded measures in favour of private entrepreneurs with political support from the Arrow-Cross. Cf. József Saád, "Építtetőre várva" [Waiting for Commissions], *Világosság* (June 1986).

13 *Budapesti Mérnöki Kamara Közleményei* [Reports of the Budapest Chamber of Engineers], 1942.

reproduces our old problems, this wealth should be directly appropriated by the government to initiate a fundamental reform.[14]

Old-right circles had a similarly disillusioned evaluation of anti-Jewish legislation and wartime developments, as expressed by the influential architect Guidó Hoepfner in 1942:

> We Hungarian engineers fail to comprehend why the power of capital may continue to exercise a tyranny over industrial production. We fail to comprehend why we are told, over and again, by our own government that the utilization of our available capacities is curtailed by an alleged shortage of capital. Our economy still resembles a village in which a peasant is sitting on a pyramid of grain, suffering from the cold because he has no boots. Opposite him, a cobbler is sitting on a pyramid of boots, suffering from hunger because he has no food. But they may not come to each other's rescue, because neither of them will ever get hold of those magic pieces of paper.[15]

At this point we might conclude that these long years of discrimination against Jewish engineers and, later, against Jewish capitalists had left the Gentile majority of the profession with virtually no sense of fulfillment. It is not hard to see how the frustration of their corporate aspirations could induce the most fundamentalist faction of the profession to lend their hands to the shameful acts of persecution during the final denouement of 1944.

To this I would like to add one final remark. For two or three years after 1945 no one would have predicted the enormous rise in status of the profession that was to come under Stalinism. Nevertheless, during the denazification screenings engineers could not fail to notice the efforts of the Communist-dominated government to win over not only the rank and file of the profession, but also its interwar corporate leaders, including some who were compromised by undeniable acts of persecution.[16] This may help us see, if not understand, how the first engineer awarded the highest distinction of the newly established State Prize in 1948 was the wartime president of the Chamber of Engineers. The next year, the country embarked on a *fully orchestrated national policy of industrialization*, which though it may have done very little to bring peasants and cobblers together, yet elicited quite a lot of sympathy from the engineering profession.

14 *Ibid.*, 1941, p. 133.

15 *Ibid.*, p. 15.

16 Documents on the screenings are to be found in the Archives of the Hungarian Trade Unions *[Szakszervezetek Központi Levéltára]*, File "Mérnök/1."

VII

Propensities or Circumstances? A Debate

Patterns of Jewish Economic Behavior in Central Europe in the Twentieth Century*

Yehuda Don

This paper constitutes an attempt to find some characteristic and common patterns in the economic behavior of Jews in Central Europe between the two World Wars. The geographical concept of "Central Europe" is open to various definitions. In the widest sense it included the area east of the Rhein to west of the Vistula (to the Baltic Sea in the north, northern Italy and the northern provinces of Yugoslavia in the south), encompassing Switzerland, Germany, together with Austria, Hungary, Czechoslovakia and present-day Poland.[1] I have used, in this paper, a much narrower definition which includes Austria, Hungary and Czechoslovakia, the three major heirs of the Austro-Hungarian Empire. Admittedly, the definition is not thoroughly consistent as it omits the eastern and southern provinces of the Habsburg Empire, namely Galicia, Bukovina and Transylvania, incorporated in eastern European states (Poland and Romania) as well as the provinces of the Voyvodina, Croatia, Dalmatia and Slovenia which became parts of Yugoslavia. My definition contains also a measure of thematic inconsistency, as it includes the Jewish communities of Subcarpathian Rus, which by all socioeconomic criteria, belong to the eastern European model,[2] while it excludes the Jewish population of southern Transylvania and the Banat, both of them very similar, structurally as well as economically, to Hungarian Jewry.[3] The reason for such transgression in consistency was practical, stemming from the prosaic fact that statistical information is published on a national basis and very little regional statistics were available for this study.

* This is a slightly different version of my paper in Yehuda Don and Victor Karady, eds., *A Social and Economic History of Central European Jewry* (New Brunswick, 1990).

1 See *The New York Times Atlas of the World*, new edition (London, 1983), pp. 30-31.

2 "The Jewish community of Subcarpathian Rus...possessed its own very special character. This was the most backward region in all Hungary inhabited by peasant Rusyns...and a Jewish community of the classic East European type." See Ezra Mendelsohn, *The Jews of East Central Europe between the World Wars* (Bloomington, 1983), p. 141.

3 "....in Transylvania proper and in the Banat there lived a Hungarian-type Jewry which in certain cities was as germanized as it was magyarized." See *ibid*., p. 173.

The overwhelming unifying influence on Central European Jews was their common legacy within the Habsburg Empire. This legacy granted about fifty years of peaceful, undisturbed development under a liberal constitution which opened a wide range of socio-economic opportunities to the Jewish population, and led to a rapid process of structural transformation.

The Habsburg Empire with its relatively liberal economic and social policy created a vast internal market of about 50 million consumers. Factors of production, namely capital and labor, moved freely within the boundaries of the Empire, and the existence of free trade within those boundaries led to processes of regional specialization, for each region according to its comparative advantages. Thus, Bohemia and Moravia developed into major industrial suppliers of the Empire, mainly of consumers' goods, such as textiles, footware and metal goods. Hungary became the granary of the Empire with highly developed flour milling and food processing industries. Vienna and Budapest became the central financial and commercial centers, and so on.

Within this rather liberal framework migration of labor from the poor to the developed regions, and from the provinces to the big cities was an expected socio-economic phenomenon. Jews took an active part in this internal migration, wandering from the underdeveloped regions such as Galicia, Bukovina, Subcarpathian Rus to rapidly growing industrial and financial centers in Austria and Hungary and particularly to their rapidly growing capitals, Vienna and Budapest.

This tendency is clearly demonstrated in the composition of Austrian Jewry including, apart from Austria, two of its most underdeveloped provinces, Galicia and Bukovina.

Table 1: Distribution of Jewish Population in Three Austrian Regions, 1847 and 1900[4]

Years	1847		1900		Average Annual Growth
Austria	15,000	3.0%	193,000	17.5%	4.94%
Bukovina	29,000	5.9%	96,000	8.7%	2.28%
Galicia	449,000	91.1%	811,000	73.7%	1.12%
Total	493,000	100%	1,100,000	100%	1.53%

4 Sources: for 1847, Arthur Ruppin, *The Sociology of the Jews* [Hebrew] (Tel Aviv, 1934), vol. I, p. 57; for 1900 in Galicia and Bukovina, U.Z. Engelman, "Sources of Jewish Statistics," in Louis Finkelstein, ed., *The Jews*, 3rd ed. (New York, 1960), vol. II, p. 1523; for 1900 in Austria, see "Austria," *Encyclopaedia Judaica*.

These results seem particularly interesting in view of the very big differences in the net demographic growth rates, which were by the end of the nineteenth century as follows:[5]

Austria	(1900)	9.3	per thousand per year
Bukovina	(1896-1900)	18.7	per thousand per year
Galicia	(1895-1900)	19.6	per thousand per year

The reason for such rapid growth of this Austrian Jewry was obviously the constant stream of Jewish immigrants from Galicia and Bukovina to Vienna. In due course the majority of the Viennese Jews were in fact immigrants from Hungary and the Austrian Eastern provinces. This stream of migrants continued throughout the first two decades of the twentieth century and in the first years after the dissolution of the Empire. One of the major excuses for the antisemitic riots in Austria was the presence of Galician and Bukovinian Jews who had once been Austrian citizens and then ceased to be after 1918. The expulsion of these Jews was a permanent issue on the Austrian agenda in the early 1920s.[6]

Similar developments took place in the second senior partner of the Empire, Hungary, and particularly in Budapest, which also absorbed tens of thousands of immigrants from the impoverished Hungarian region of Subcarpathian Rus as well as from Galicia.[7]

II

The dissolution of the Habsburg Empire terminated all these economic developments and population movements.

The dissolution of the Habsburg Empire also terminated the vast and open market of goods and inputs and created five small states hostile to each other and eager to develop easy and rapid substitutes for the advantages they had enjoyed before World War I. Hungary embarked on extreme autarkic economic policies and pushed for rapid industrialization. Austria, which found itself with a huge

5 "Sources of Jewish Statistics," pp. 1524-1525. The figures for Vienna stand for "Austria." Since close to 90 per cent of all Austrian Jews resided in Vienna, it can be considered an appropriate surrogate for Austria. The figures for Romania stand for Bukovina. Apparently little demographic differences existed between Bukovina and Romania as a whole. This contention is supported by Mendelsohn, *Jews of East Central Europe,* p. 148.

6 See the reports in the *American Jewish Yearbooks*. See for instance the yearbook for 1920/1, pp. 169-171.

7 On immigration to Hungary, see Yehuda Don and George Magos, "The Demographic Development of Hungarian Jewry," *Jewish Social Studies* 45 (1983), 189-216.

and mostly redundant network of financial and administrative infrastructure, experimented with various policies to divest itself of its imperial economic legacies and adjust to the fact of being a small landlocked country in Central Europe. Czechoslovakia, which lost most of her traditional markets for her industrial products as a result of the protectionist policies of her neighbors from the south and the east, developed relentless export-oriented economic policies which made her the seventh largest exporter in Europe.[8] These new gravitations in economic policies brought about unique problems to particular segments, regional or sectorial, of the respective countries, which became the victims of the new economic policies. Thus, in Hungary, rapid industrialization worsened the relative position of the countryside and of the agrarian sector.[9] In Czechoslovakia the pursuit of exportation through large and cost-efficient plants in the industrial centers in Bohemia, Moravia and Silesia ruined beginnings of industrial experiments and also the traditional handicrafts in the poor southern and eastern provinces of Slovakia and Subcarpathian Rus.[10] Finally, both in Austria and in Hungary, the vast bureaucracy of the past, now redundant, created critical problems of employment for a formerly privileged class which lost its economic raison d'etre and was not qualified to do anything else but administration. The impoverished position of this class stood in sharp contrast to its aspirations and it became a potential reservoir for extreme right wing opposition.[11]

All these developments had visible impact upon the economic readjustment of the Jews to the post-Habsburg era in Central Europe. The disintegration of the Empire terminated the overall liberal policy towards the Jews. Following World War I every country developed its own Jewish policy. Czechoslovakia was established as a liberal democracy and remained so "...until the very end of

8 J.C. Pick in his study on the economy of the Jews in Czechoslovakia suggested mistakenly that Czechoslovakia was the sixth largest exporter in the world. See J.C. Pick, "The Economy," in *The Jews of Czechoslovakia* (New York-Philadelphia, 1968), vol. I, pp. 359-438. According to the authoritative figures of Svennilson, the position of Czechoslovakia was that of the seventh largest exporter in Europe. See I. Svennilson, "Growth and Stagnation in the European Economy," *The U.N. Economic Commission for Europe* (Geneva, 1954), pp. 312-313. As of the early 1930s the relative position of Czechoslovakia was relegated below the seventh place in Europe, as the Great Depression plagued Czechoslovakia's exports more than those of other countries.

9 T. Iván Berend and György Ránki, *A Magyar gazdaság száz éve* [A Century of the Hungarian Economy] (Budapest, 1972).

10 Aryeh Soleh, "Subcarpathian Ruthenia, 1918-1938," in *The Jews of Czechoslovakia*.

11 The role of the redundant civil servants in the political right from the point of view of Hungary, is analyzed in detail by Ottó Szabolcs, *Köztisztviselők az ellenforadalmi rendszer bázisában 1920-1926* [The Civil Servants in the Social Basis of the Counterrevolutionary Regime 1920-1926], (Budapest, 1965).

the 1930s."[12] The Jewish policy of Czechoslovakia was decisively affected by the political convictions of Thomas Masaryk, and remained liberal and reasonably tolerant throughout the independent existence of the state. In this respect the Jewish policy in Czechoslovakia was in fact a continuation of the Habsburg Empire's attitude to the Jews.

In Hungary, on the other hand, the transition in Jewish policy was immediate and drastic. Following the collapse of the brief Communist episode, the white terror revived for a while in Hungary the most brutal and violent antisemitic outbursts, condoned by the authorities.[13] Eventually power was taken over by Regent Miklós Horthy, himself a self-declared lifelong antisemite[14] and by the "sane" constitutional right headed by Count Stephen Bethlen. The official approach was that existing discriminatory laws, such as the *Numerus Clausus* were not to be formally suspended, but nor were they to be vigorously enforced. This type of modus vivendi enabled the Jewish population to function economically more or less in a normal fashion until the late 1930s.

In Austria, though the old liberal attitude to Jews was, after 1918, a matter of the past, the Christian Socialists with explicitly conservative to reactionary policies, were successful in containing the extreme right's violently antisemitic propaganda. The Jews, most of whom were associated with the Social Democratic Party, carried on with their normal business activities until German occupation in 1938, though as of 1934 the official policy was to squeeze Jews out of important economic positions. The Austrian public displayed a much higher degree of popular antisemitism than was actually instigated by the authorities.[15]

Another important change that evolved in Central European Jewry from the early 1920s was the phenomenon of a steady to slightly declining population as indicated in Table 2. The stability of the population was the combined result of an almost stagnant, slightly negative, natural growth rate and the heavy decline in emigration, particularly to the United States, after the enactment of the 1922

12 Mendelsohn, *Jews of East Central Europe*, p. 131.

13 The *American Jewish Yearbook* of 1920-21 reports in detail of the widespread atrocities committed by the Hungarian military and paramilitary units and condoned by the authorities. These atrocities led, according to the *American Jewish Yearbook*, to a petition of the Jews in Budapest, with 100,000 signatures, "...to be forwarded to the Peace Conference, asking that Romanian troops should return to Budapest to reestablish order and to put an end to persecution...of Jews." See *ibid.*, p. 225.

14 There is a now a well-known declaration to this effect in a letter of Miklós Horthy to his friend and political ally Count Pál Teleky in 1940. See *Horthy Miklós Titkos Iratai* [The Secret Documents of Miklós Horthy], 2nd ed. (Budapest, 1963), document no. 51.

15 On Austrian antisemitism see the brief review in *The Jewish Communities of Nazi-Occupied Europe*. Originally prepared in 1944 and published in 1982 by the American Jewish Committee. See the report on Austria, p. 6.

and 1924 immigration laws.[16] Thus, until the late 1930s, when the territorial changes, designed by Nazi Germany, redrew the population map of Central European Jewry, the economic processes that we try to portray took place within a steady population.

Table 2: Jewish Population in 1920 and 1930 in Central Europe[17]

	1920	1930	Annual rate of change
Austria	201,513*	191,485*	- 0.51%
Hungary	473,310	444,567	- 0.62%
Czechoslovakia	368,970	356,830	- 0.33%

* Figures for Austria are for 1923 and 1933 respectively.

III

The basic model for investigating the economic behavior of Jews in the diaspora or indeed of any ethnic or religious minority, is that of Professor Simon Kuznets. In a long and seminal study Kuznets laid down the analytical framework for the recently developed subject of Jewish economic history.[18] The analysis of Kuznets refers to what he calls a "small minority," constituting less than 10 per cent of the overall population in a country. In this respect the Jewish minorities of Central Europe, with the unique regional exception of Carpathian Rus,[19] qualify as "small minorities." The share of Jews in the respective populations of the Central European states was as follows:

Austria	2.85%	1934-5
Hungary	5.12%	1930
Czechoslovakia	2.42%	1930

16 A detailed description of these laws can be found in Arthur Ruppin, *Jews in the Modern World* (London, 1934), pp. 48-52. Total Jewish immigration was down from 141,411 in 1921 to an average of 42,300 for 1926-30. See *ibid.*, p. 47. The share of Central Europe in the Jewish immigration to the U.S. in the early 1920s was about 6.5 per cent. For figures see the various volumes of the *American Jewish Yearbook.*

17 Figures are census figures. See *Encyclopaedia Judaica* entries "Austria," "Hungary," and "Czechoslovakia."

18 Simon Kuznets, "Economic Structure and Life of the Jews," in Finkelstein, ed., *The Jews*, vol. II, pp. 1597-1666.

19 In Subcarpathian Rus the share of Jews in the total population in 1930 was 16.12%.

Following the basic premises of the Kuznets model we hypothesize that the economic behavior of the Jews was unique in the following aspects:

1) The occupational composition of the Jews was different from that of the population at large. Its basis was narrower. Jews concentrated in a smaller number of occupations than the population. Such a narrow basis may appear in the selection of industries as well as in the composition of economic status.[20]

2) Jews tended to gravitate to economic branches which were either relatively new or expanding at a faster rate than others. The reason for such orientation is twofold. On the one hand new industries were not yet occupied by the majority, as they had not acquired the necessary skill to conquer the best posts created in those new industries. Thus the resistance of the majority to the penetration of Jews to such industries was expected to be milder. Secondly, new and fast growing industries were, by nature, more profitable and offered better economic opportunities than old and stagnant ones.

3) Jews were endowed with certain skills as a heritage from their countries of emigration. This is what Kuznets called "the economic heritage" which had been brought over at the time of their immigration from their old countries. Pre-migration skill structure was thus an important factor in the initial process of selection of new occupations in their new countries.

In view of these three Kuznetsian hypotheses it seems that the pace and the extent of the economic adjustment of Jews to their host countries depended on the following:

1) The numerical weight of the Jewish minority, whereby the smaller it was the easier it adjusted, economically, to the conditions and opportunities of their host country.

2) The "Jewish policy," or indeed the general attitude to immigrants and minorities of the host country's government and people.

3) Various exogenous factors such as economic heritage, language differences between the old and new country, etc.

Consequently, after some initial processes of economic adjustment it is expected that in certain industries Jews will occupy a significant and even dominating share, due to their tendency to converge in a narrow range of industries. Furthermore, within any given industry the employment status structure of the Jews is likely to be different from that of the Gentiles, whereby the share of independent entrepreneurs and of white collar salaried employees will be relatively high and that of blue collar workers relatively low.

20 Kuznets, with a penetrative insight, remarked that if the economic composition of the minority is similar to that of the majority, then the independent identity of the minority will be short-lived.

Considering the fact that the share of immigrants among the Jews in Western Europe and other immigration countries[21] was large, and that recent immigrants start, as a rule, their economic careers at the bottom, and in view of the hypothesis that Jews will be found in rapidly growing and new industries, it is expected that the pace of economic advancement of the Jews will be faster than that of the majority. Generally speaking one may contend that distinct economic behavior of the Jews correlates negatively with the tolerance and liberalism of the host country. The more liberal the Jewish policy of the host country becomes, the easier and the faster processes of assimilation will set in, and the smaller the difference between the economic structure of the majority and the Jewish minority will eventually become.

Let us now examine more closely some of our hypotheses. With respect to the narrow occupational base, the most visible fact was the extremely low representation of Jews in agriculture. The almost complete absence of Jews from farming, richly documented by all students of Jewish social and economic history,[22] has been attributed mainly to historical developments. Before emancipation Jews had been, in most countries, prevented from owning land. This was true in Central Europe until the second half of the nineteenth century. After the abolition of most formal restrictions upon entering agriculture, the proportion of Jews did not increase. The reasons given were a combination of arguments of socio-political nature. Land, even after emancipation, symbolized,

21 For a detailed description of immigration countries for the Jews see Jacob Lestchinsky "Jewish Migrations 1840-1956," in Finkelstein, ed., *The Jews*, vol. II, pp. 1536-1596. See in particular, pp. 1554-1555.

22 Arthur Ruppin collected rich statistical information, all of which indicates very low percentages of Jews in agriculture in the first quarter of the twentieth century in most Central European countries. Ruppin's figures for the percentage of Jews in agriculture of total Jewish labor force in the early 1920s were:

Percentage of Jews in Agriculture

Bohemia & Moravia	Bavaria	Hungary	Lithuania	Poland	Slovakia	Carpathian Rus
(1921)	(1925)	(1920)	(1923)	(1921)	(1921)	(1921)
2.8	3.6	4.2	6.0	9.6	10.7	26.9

Ruppin, *The Sociology of the Jews*, vol. II, ch. 19. See also the comparative statistics of Kuznets, "Economic Structure and Life of the Jews," p. 1605 corroborating the same point.

more than any other form of capital, long term power base, and the historical owners of land were often disinclined to transfer such symbols of power into the possession of people with strange and basically alien background. Also, Jews well understood that agriculture was physically very heavily demanding and thus stayed away from it. Without attempting to corroborate or refute these arguments, it is claimed that the absence of Jews from agriculture even after the removal of all legal barriers, was a perfectly rational reaction to given economic conditions. When emancipation became a legal and social reality, agriculture was a declining sector. As of the second half of the nineteenth century, the number of workers in agriculture rapidly diminished due to higher productivity in agriculture, industrialization and its concomitant urbanization. Jews, therefore, obviously refrained from entering agriculture when millions of non-Jews were all attempting to leave it.[23] Such was the reaction to traditional agriculture. Modernized agrarian capitalism was a different issue. Rationally managed large scale agro-business was profitable, and Jewish entrepreneurs did play an active role in such enterprises, particularly in Hungary. In that country as late as in 1942, three years after the enactment of the Second Jewish Law[24] which ordered the total expropriation of Jews from all landholding, 1.5 million acres of agricultural land was still in the hands of Jewish entrepreneurs.[25]

There was also a sociological angle to the evasion of agriculture. Jews urbanized ahead of the general population in every country.[26] Urbanization meant to the Jews more than a chance for improved economic opportunities and better educational social and cultural services.[27] The city, and particularly the big

23 An interesting observation of Lestchinsky in his study on Jewish migration shows that migrating Jews to the U.S. during 1900-1925 also stayed away from agriculture, though none of the institutionally constraining factors existed in the U.S. According to Lestchinsky only 2.4 per cent of all Jewish immigrants turned to agriculture, compared to 26.6 per cent of non-Jewish immigrants. (See Lestchinsky, "Jewish Migrations 1840-1956," in *The Jews*, pp. 1568-9). The economic reason for such an occupation selection of the Jews was, of course, that they completely lacked any comparative advantage due to previously acquired skills in agriculture, in sharp contrast to the Irish, the Italians and the Poles who had been overwhelmingly farmers prior to immigration to the U.S.

24 For the Second Jewish Law, see Randolph L. Braham, *The Politics of Genocide: The Holocaust in Hungary*, 2 vols. (New York, 1981), vol. I, pp. 123-125.

25 See Yehuda Don, "The Economic Dimension of Antisemitism," *East European Quarterly* 20 (1986), 447-465.

26 U. Z. Engelman makes this point very explicit by stating "Jews massed into cities earlier than other population groups and at a faster tempo." See his "Sources of Jewish Statistics," *The Jews*, p. 1530.

27 M. Todaro in his numerous studies on urbanization in developing countries emphasized that the central expectations of migrating populations from rural to metropolitan areas were a better chance for occupational improvement, better schooling and better municipal services. See for instance M. Todaro, "Internal Migration in Developing Countries," in R.

city, provided a framework to live among their peer group. Furthermore, the big city provided much desired anonymity and a shelter of personal security vis-a-vis antisemitic outbursts. Thus a tendency of convergence of Jews in the largest cities has been apparent since the early days of urbanization.[28] It should, therefore, be quite obvious that Jews, wherever possible, evaded rural communities. The exceptions to this pattern of accelerated urbanization were found in the poorest Jewish regions of Central Europe, in Subcarpathian Rus, where two-thirds of all Jews lived in rural communities, and one third of them found their livelihood in agriculture.[29] A second example, which belonged to the Habsburg Empire before World War I was Galicia, where according to Arthur Ruppin 13.6 per cent of all Jews worked in agriculture.[30] Not accidentally, Subcarpathian Rus and Galicia were the most eagerly deserted provinces in Central Europe.

The three sectors most frequently patronized by Jews were 1) Industry and Handicraft, 2) Trade and Finance and 3) the Liberal Professions. Table 3 presents the distribution of Jewish labor force among these sectors in Central Europe in the 1930s. Occupational distribution in other European countries, such as Germany or Latvia, was quite similar.

A. Esaterlin, ed., *Population and Economic Change in Developing Countries* (Chicago, 1980), N.B.E.R. No. 30.

28 This tendency of European Jews to concentrate in the capital cities of their host countries was observed by Ruppin. See *Jews in the Modern World*, pp. 36-38. The following table demonstrates this tendency of Jewish concentration in the capital cities in four capitals with very large Jewish population in the 1920s, namely Warsaw, Budapest, Vienna and Berlin.

	% of Population in Capital			% of Jews in the		% Capital / % Country
	Jews	Non-Jews	Jews/Non-Jews	Capital	Country	
	1	2	3 = 1 / 2	4	5	6 = 4/5
Poland	10.16	8.66	1.17	10.95	9.49	1.15
Hungary	44.82	9.24	4.85	32.19	5.50	5.85
Austria	91.20	26.36	3.46	10.80	3.38	3.20
Germany	30.65	6.23	4.92	4.30	0.90	4.78

With the exception of Poland, where, as a late result of the Pale of Settlement limitations of the nineteenth century, the Jewish population was still basically rural, the heavily urban character of the Jews is very visible (see columns 3 through 6).

29 See Soleh's study in the *The Jews of Czechoslovakia*.

30 See Ruppin, *The Sociology of the Jews*, vol. II, ch. 19 and above, note 22.

Table 3: Proportion of Non-agricultural Labor among Jews by Major Occupational Sectors in the 1930s[31]

	Non-agricultural	Of all Non-agricultural labor employed in				
	Labor	Industry	Trade	Professions	Others	Total
Austria	99.9	23.8	36.9	23.1	16.2*	100
Hungary	97.0	35.4	44.9	9.1	5.6**	100
Czechoslovakia	91.0	27.0	56.8	10.1	6.1**	100

* Including unemployed
** Including transportation, personal services, etc.

The first impression from Table 3 is the very significant role of industry in the employment structure of the Jews. Measuring the share of industry in the occupational composition of non-agricultural Jewish and non-Jewish labor force, leads to some rather unexpected results. As shown in Table 4, in five of the eight countries covered by the Kuznets statistics, industry occupied a more important place in the employment structure of non-agricultural labor among Jews than non-Jews.

Table 4: The Share of Industry in the Employment Structure of Jews and Non-Jews in Eight Countries in the 1930s (in percents)[32]

	Germany	Czecho-slovakia	USA	Hungary	Latvia	Canada	Poland	Romania
Jews	23.3	24.6	28.0	34.4	28.8	33.0	44.8	33.4
Non-Jews	47.3	45.3	32.0	28.2	19.3	19.2	25.4	17.4
Jews/Non-Jews	0.49	0.54	0.88	1.22	1.49	1.72	1.76	1.92

The high proportion of Jews in commerce and finance was expected. Indeed, the conventional wisdom on Jewish occupational structure has been that Jews acquired dominating positions in commerce and banking, and held thus in their grips the economies of their host countries. Statistics are clearly indicative,

31 Sources for Hungary and Czechoslovakia, Kuznets, "Economic Structure and Life of the Jews," p. 1608, for Austria, *The Jewish Communities of Nazi Occupied Europe*, p. 8.
32 Kuznets, "Economic Structure and Life of the Jews," *passim*.

however, that the value judgements attached to them are simplistic. Growth patterns of Central and Eastern Europe in the nineteenth and twentieth centuries were such that with higher productivity in agriculture and manufacture, the share of the tertiary sectors (services and commerce) in the labor force was increasing. The expansion of trade became thus concurrent with economic growth, and since commerce was a rapidly growing sector, Jews gravitated to it. But so did non-Jewish labor, and probably with even greater thrust. Consequently, a negative correlation seems to be seen between the share of trade in the occupational composition of the Jews in different countries, and the share of Jews in the overall employment in trade in the same countries. In other words, in those countries in Central Europe, where the percentage of trade in the employment structure of the Jews was high, the percentage of Jews employed in trade out of total labor force in trade was low. Table 5 demonstrates this development for two Central European countries (Hungary and Czechoslovakia), one Central-Western (Germany) and one Central-Eastern (Poland).

Table 5: Indicators of Jewish Share in Commerce in the 1930s in Four Countries[33]

	I[34]	II	III	IV	V	VI
Poland (1931)	53.4	36.7	39.2	51.3	9.7	5.3
Hungary (1930)	48.2	29.7	49.9	35.4	5.1	6.9
Czechoslovakia (1930)	27.3	22.0	56.8	12.9	2.4	5.3
Germany (1933)	16.9	11.1	62.8	3.4	0.8	4.1

The first column in Table 5 shows the share of agriculture in total labor force. This ratio is frequently used as an indicator for the level of economic development. By this indicator Poland was the least and Germany the most developed economy, with Hungary close to Poland and Czechoslovakia close to Germany.[35] The second column measures the effect of economic development

33 *Ibid.*

34 A United Nations' sponsored study on the European economies between the two world wars indicated different figures for the share of agriculture in total labor force (Poland: 60.4 per cent; Germany: 21.4 per cent). Though the figures were different, apparently due to definitional and computational differences, the order remained unchanged. See Svennilson, "Growth and Stagnation in the European Economy," p. 241.

35 Other indicators of economic development, such as industrial production value per capita or steel and cement consumption per capita are perfectly consistent with our indicator of the share of agriculture in total labor force. See *ibid.*, pp. 306, 311.

on the standard of commercial services. It shows the number of people in each country served by one worker in the commercial-financial sector. The results are perfectly consistent with the message of column I. The more advanced the economy the larger its commercial sector becomes, absorbing large numbers of new employees in commerce, capable of improving the standard of commercial services to the population. Column III measures the share of commerce in the total Jewish labor force. Figures are quite clear, indicating that the more advanced the economy, i.e. the larger the country's commercial sector, the relatively greater the share of commerce in the occupational structure of the Jews.[36] Column IV measures the weight of Jews in commerce in total commerce, i.e., the percentage of Jewish employees in trade and commerce in the overall labor force in that sector. Figures of this column support our basic proposition, that the larger the commercial sector in the economy, the smaller the share of Jews and their significance in it. The weight of Jews in any segment of the economy is of course the function of the relative size of the Jews in the population of the host country. This percentage is presented in column V. Finally, column VI is an attempt to compute a "Relative Domination Index" trying to measure the effective power of Jews in commerce taking into consideration their weight in the population.

The index is obtained through dividing column IV by column V.[37] Whenever the value of the index is larger than unity, the share of Jews in

36 This observation was already made by Ruppin in his *The Sociology of the Jews*, vol. II, ch. 19. Ruppin did not, however, elaborate on his observation further than tabulating statistics. It is however interesting that Ruppin's figures, from the early 1920s, are invariably lower than those of Kuznets, from the 1930s, indicating that the trend of entering commerce by Jews continued.

37 Let L, M, J_L and J_M be respectively total labor force (standing for total population), total labor force in commerce, Jewish labor force (standing for Jewish population) and Jewish labor force in commerce. Then, columns II to V of Table 5 will be as follows:

Columns: $II = 1/\ M/L$; $III = J_M/J_L$; $IV = J_M/M$; $V = J_L/L$

Let $M/L = m$; $J_M/J_L = j_m$; $J_M/M = m_j$ and $J_L/L = l_j$

"Relative Domination Index" (i) (Column VI) will thus be $m_j / l_j = j_m / m$

If we assume the existence of a Jewish problem, i.e. $L > J_L > 0$ we shall find that the range of the parameters will be as follows:

$1 > m > 0$ $\quad 1 \geq j_m \geq 0$ $\quad 1 \geq m_j \geq 0$ $\quad 1 > l_j > 0$

Consequently the range of (i) is as follows:

if (m_j) or (j_m) equal zero, $(i) = 0$; if $(m_j) = 1 \Rightarrow (i) = L/J_L$; if $(j_m) = 1 \Rightarrow (i) = L/M$.

Consequently, the "Relative Domination Index" (i) correlates positively with the share of commerce in Jewish occupational structure (j_m) and with the share of Jews in commerce

commerce surpasses their share in the population (labor force). As indicated in column VI of Table 5, index numbers in Central Europe ranged from 4.1 (Germany) to 6.9 (Hungary). Consequently, commerce was and remained a typical Jewish occupation, and with the growth of new employment openings, Jews entered commerce together with non-Jews. Another interesting conclusion emerging from Table 5 is that the "Relative Domination Index" did not seem to be effected by the level of development of the countries examined.

As indicated above, commerce was a sector which grew with economic development. Where did the additional labor force come from to feed the growing demand of commerce for labor? Non-Jewish labor force to commerce accrued from the ongoing process of urbanization. Migrants from agriculture fed the cities with a new labor force to be absorbed by all urban economic sectors. Jewish labor to commerce originated partially also from rural-urban migrations, and, at least partially, it came from a shift of urban workers from manufacture and handicraft to commerce. This contention of ours is demonstrated in Table 6.

Table 6: Ratios of Labor in Commerce, Industry and Agriculture among Jews and Non-Jews in Four European Countries[38]

	Non-Jews in Commerce/ Non-Jews in Industry I	Non-Jews in Commerce/ Non-Jews in Agriculture II	Jews in Commerce/ Jews in Industry III
Poland	0.21	0.09	0.84
Hungary	0.20	0.12	1.41
Czechoslovakia	0.20	0.33	2.10
Germany	0.33	0.92	2.67

Column I indicates very little. No trend seems to emerge in the ratio in view of the ascending order in terms of economic development. The same ratio of "Labor in Commerce"/"Labor in Industry" applied to the Jewish labor force displays a very clear ascending tendency, pointing to the fact that the higher the level of economic development of the country the more labor is employed in commerce per unit of labor in industry (Column III). These results support the

(m_j), while it correlates negatively with the share of Jews in the labor force (population) (l_j) as well as with the share of commerce in total labor force (population) (m).
Thus $\partial i/\partial j_m = 1/m > 0$; $\partial i/\partial m_j = 1/l_j > 0$ and $\partial i/\partial l_j = -mj/lj^2 < 0$; $\partial i/\partial m = -j_m/m^2 < 0$.

38 Kuznets, "Economic Structure and Life of the Jews."

proposition, that with the expansion of commerce, as a concomitant of economic development, Jewish labor shifted from industry into commerce. The clearly ascending order in Column II, showing the number of non-Jewish workers employed in commerce for every unit of labor in agriculture, makes analogy between columns II and III unavoidable. The proposition that additional labor to commerce among Jews originated in occupational migration from industry and among non-Jews in occupational and spatial migration from agriculture stands to reason. Obviously, the ratio of non-Jewish "Labor in Industry"/"Labor in Agriculture" also resulted in ascending coefficients,[39] indicating that the higher the level of development the more workers were found in industry for every unit of labor in agriculture. Indeed, contracting agriculture fed demand for additional labor both in industry and in commerce. However, labor force from industry feeding increasing employment in commerce was a unique, typically Jewish phenomenon.

The reason for such evolvement of the coefficients for non-Jewish labor was evident. The rapidly declining agrarian sector provided labor force to the growing industrial and commercial sectors. The reasons for Jews to shift from industry to commerce seemed more complex. Industry was by no means a declining sector in Central Europe in the 1930s. Why then did Jewish labor desert industry in response to economic development?

Some reasons can directly be learned from the Kuznets theses. The propensity to trade and exchange was a part of the historical occupational heritage of the Jews for many generations. In most immigration countries there existed an initial critical mass of Jewish merchants, who assisted new immigrants, or at least set examples for them for a model of remunerative occupational integration through commerce. Secondly, with economic development the composition of industrial labor force went through some conspicuous metamorphosis. Average firm size increased, in terms of labor force. The share of the small to medium, independent workshops declined, as increasingly more artisans were pushed out of business by the mass production

39 The ratio Labor in Industry/Labor in Agriculture can easily be obtained through the Column II/Column I ratio from Table 6. The results are the following:

Poland	Hungary	Czechoslovakia	Germany
0.43	0.60	1.65	3.79

of highly mechanized, capital intensive, large factories.[40] Jewish artisans, losing the battle against the modern factory, faced the option to chose between the career of a factory worker and that of an independent vendor or pedlar, or an employee in a merchant's establishment. In view of the above mentioned "propensity to trade" and considering the special characteristic of the Jewish employee, mentioned later in this study, we contend that relatively more Jewish than non-Jewish artisans preferred the commercial option over that of a factory worker.[41] Thus technical progress which converted the gentile small artisan into a factory worker, pushed the Jewish artisan out of industry and into commerce.

At this juncture let us examine some profiles of the manufacturing branches in which Jews were, and to a great extent still are, particularly active. Kuznets established that the typical industries most frequently patronized by Jews were clothing, food, leather, furs, printing, paper and jewelry. Obviously there are some common denominators for these industries.

1) All these industries manufacture final consumers' goods sold directly, on competitive markets, to the final consumers. The typical buyer of the output of these industries was the individual consumer and not institutional buyers or other manufacturing establishments.

2) The typical manufacturing unit of such products tends to be relatively small, its technology relatively simple and its capital requirement relatively modest.

Generally speaking, Jewish industrialists refrained from entering the metal industry, heavy engineering, textiles (in contrast to clothing), mining and the production of building material. These industries manufactured mainly capital goods, raw material and other inputs for industry; they operated, as a rule, as large plants and were capital intensive. There were, obviously, conspicuous exceptions. Prominent were the huge metal and engineering works, the mines and the foundries as well as the great electrical plants in Jewish hands in Hungary. Likewise, about 16.3 per cent of all mining works, 15.9 per cent of the chemical industry and 10 per cent of all foundries in Bohemia and Moravia were under Jewish control.[42] The role of Emil Rathenau in the establishment of

40 This is basically the Marxian analysis, originally applied by Marx to early nineteenth century England. Analogous conditions emerged fifty to a hundred years later in Central and East Central Europe.

41 Obviously, the commercial option was not always accessible. An example when such options were limited and the Jewish worker in the big textile city of Lodz willy-nilly accepted the path of a factory worker, is beautifully described by I. J. Singer in his novel *Brothers Ashkenazi* (New York, 1967).

42 These figures were reported to the American Jewish Committee immediately after World War II and published in 1982 in "Czechoslovakia," *Jewish Communities in Nazi Occupied Europe*, p. 6. The reliability of the Czechoslovakian figures do not seem to be very high as, apparently, the anonymous authors relied on data about Nazi procedures of de-

the giant electrical firm in Germany, the A.E.G. is also well known. There were numerous metal works in Germany controlled by orthodox Jews,[43] and the list is far from complete.

Although these plants and great names are of special interest, and have drawn much attention of social and economic historians, the vast majority of Jewish labor, whether independent workshop operators or hired employees, worked in industries which served directly the final consumers, sold their merchandise on the competitive markets and produced in relatively small plants with relatively little capital.

The profile of Jewish commerce was quite similar to that of Jewish industry. The typical Jewish commercial establishment operated in the retail business. The Jewish tradesman preferred, as a rule, to sell consumers' goods, particularly in the clothing and footware and in the food and drinks business. Though exceptions were not particularly rare, Jewish merchants tended to stay away from trading in raw materials and in industrial inputs. The extension of our examination to the post-World War II era seems to corroborate these observations. The size of the store may have changed, yet its basic features remained the same. The heirs of the small Jewish shopkeepers are Marks and Spencer, the Great Universal Stores, Macy's, Abraham & Strauss' and their parallels in France, Austria, Brazil and Holland.[44]

The target group has remained the individual consumer and the arena of operation has remained the fiercely competitive consumers' market, mainly in clothing and food.

The obvious question is why did these characteristics crystallize and why have they been sustained? Kuznets's answer was that Jewish tradesmen and artisans sought objects of trade and patterns of organization which enabled rapid turnover of the working capital, which required much ingenuity but little capital, sharp instincts but little training. One may add the propensity of the Jew to operate on such markets where individual dexterity and inventiveness matter more than business connections to other major sectors in the economy or to the authorities.

Discrimination, open or subtle, can be better countervailed in a business sector in which all participants have an equal access to the market and an equal chance to gain the patronage of the individual, anonymous customer, who is more likely, than any institutional buyer, to maximize his benefit by buying from

Judafication of the economy which also included enterprises with partial Jewish ownership.

43 These plants are mentioned by Mordechai Breuer in *Jüdische Orthodoxie im Deutschen Reich 1871-1918* (Frankfurt, 1986), p. 14.

44 On the profile of Jewish retail trade in the Netherlands see a new major work by B. DeVries, *From Pedlars to Textile Barons* (North Holland, Amsterdam, 1989).

the most price efficient sources. Then, once Jews succeeded in a specific branch, intra-communal connections eased the extension of their activities in the same branch. This seems to explain the statistical observation that Jewish merchants or artisans occupied dominant shares of the business in certain specific sub-sectors in the garment industry or in other industries with similar features. Gravitation to some narrow niches, both in production and in trade, in which the comparative advantage of the Jewish merchant and artisan came to fruition, was a comfortable occupational solution for the new immigrants or for people who were on the market seeking new occupations. On the other hand, however, the general profile of such branches, as indicated above, was a reasonable safeguard against turning industries dominated by Jews into cartel type havens. Examples of such industrial niches were hat-making in France, Austria and Germany, furriery in Hungary, Austria and Czech lands, furniture trade in Hungary and Austria and leather in Germany and Hungary.[45]

Let us sum up this topic by presenting a set of comparative tables, based on the Kuznets statistics, which summarize the issue of relative concentration of Jewish industrial activity in different branches.

The picture that emerges in Table 7 is quite clear. In all four countries, food, leather, paper and printing, and above all clothing were patronized by Jews much more intensively than their share in industrial employment. For clothing this overrepresentation in Germany and Czechoslovakia was three times as high as their proportional representation in industry. On the other hand, in the metal and textile industries Jewish labor force was underrepresented.

Table 8 examines the comparative distribution by branches of the industrial labor force among Jews and among non-Jews, with branches aggregated into three groups:

a) the "Jewish branches," i.e. food, clothing, leather, paper and printing
b) textiles, metals, wood
c) all other branches

45 See for instance *Encyclopaedia Judaica*, entry "Austria." See also H. Silbergleit, *Die Bevölkerungs und Berufsverhältnisse der Juden im Deutschen Reich* (Berlin, 1930), as well as the reports on Czechoslovakia and Hungary in *The Jewish Communities of Nazi Occupied Europe*.

Table 7: Concentration Index of Industrial Activity of Jews in Four Countries, by Branches[46]

	Food	Clothing	Leather	Printing	Textile	Wood	Metals
Germany	2.4	3.0	2.0	1.4	0.6	0.6	0.6
Austria	2.2	2.0	1.4	1.4	0.5	0.9	0.6
Czechoslovakia	2.3	3.1	2.1	2.0	0.3	1.1	0.9
Poland	1.3	1.8	1.9	1.2	0.6	0.7	0.6

Table 8: Distribution by Industrial Aggregates of Jewish and Non-Jewish Labor in Four Countries (in per cent)[47]

	Group (a)		Group (b)		Group (c)	
	Jews	non-Jews	Jews	non-Jews	Jews	non-Jews
Germany	70.3	30.3	19.0	35.0	10.7	34.7
Austria	63.2	30.4	23.5	36.7	13.3	32.9
Czechoslovakia	60.5	22.1	27.6	42.8	11.9	35.1
Poland	68.4	35.6	21.3	36.3	10.3	28.1

The "Jewish branches" employed on the average about two-thirds of all Jewish labor in industry, as compared to less than one-third of the non-Jewish labor. This one observation supports statistically the contention of Kuznets with

46 Sources: Kuznets, "Economic Structure and Life of the Jews," pp. 1612-1613. The data pertains to different dates in different countries (Austria, 1910; Germany, 1907; Czechoslovakia, 1921; Poland, 1921), nevertheless, in view of the internal consistency of each country data, indices are comparable. Concentration Index for industry j be (I_j) was calculated as follows: Let Jews in industry and in industry J be (J_i) and (J_{ij}) respectively. Gentiles in industry and industry J will thus be (G_i) and (G_{ij}) respectively.

$$I_j = \frac{J_{ij}/J_i}{G_{ij}/G_i} = \frac{J_{ij}/G_{ij}}{J_i/G_i}$$

or, in other words

$$I_j = \frac{\text{Percentage of Jews in industry (j) and of all Jews in industry}}{\text{Percentage of Gentiles in industry (j) and of all Gentiles in industry}}$$

The figures for Austria pertain to "total attached" Jews and Gentiles; for Germany and Poland to "gainfully occupied" Jews and Gentiles and for Czechoslovakia to "wage earners" Jews and Gentiles.

47 Source: Kuznets *ibid.*

respect of the relatively narrow branch base of Jews in industry. The share of Jewish labor in the third group of branches (group C) further corroborates the thesis of "narrow base." Employment in all industry, besides the seven aforementioned branches, employed about one-third of the non-Jewish labor force as compared to about one-ninth of the Jewish employed persons in industry. Indeed, the relative difference between non-Jewish and Jewish labor's share in the three branch aggregates was consistently the highest for group (C) as indicated in Table 9.

Table 9: Branch Aggregate Percentage Ratios Among Non-Jewish and Jewish Labor in Industry in Four Countries[48]

	Group (a)		Group (b)	Group (c)
Germany	0.43	(2.33)[x]	1.84	3.24
Austria	0.48	(2.08)[x]	1.56	2.47
Czechoslovakia	0.37	(2.70)[x]	1.55	2.95
Poland	0.52	(1.92)[x]	1.70	2.73

x The figures in brackets are the reciprocal of the ratio, brought for more meaningful intergroup comparison.

Further examination of the ratio from Table 8 leaves little doubt as to the existence of a uniquely different Jewish branch structure in contrast to the branch structure of the non-Jewish industrial employment. For the corroboration of this statement we calculated a rather simplistic variation of distribution index for each country examined in Tables 7 to 9, comparing the branch distribution among Jews and non-Jews. Then we calculated the same index coefficient for each country's non-Jewish industrial distribution in comparison to the non-weighted average distribution of the other three countries examined. Finally, the same index coefficient was calculated for each country's Jewish branch distribution compared to the non-weighted average distribution of the Jewish sector in the other three countries. The results are summed up in Tables 10a, b and c.[49]

48 Source: Table 8. The figures for each group of industries in each country are the ratios of the Jewish/Gentile percentages.

49 Source: Table 8. The Variation of Distribution Index between Population a and Population b (I_{ab}) was calculated as follows:

Table 10: Variation of Distribution Indexes

a. Among Jewish and Non-Jewish Aggregated Branch: Distribution in Four Countries

	Non-Jews in				Non-weighted
Distribution of Jews in	Germany	Austria	Czechoslovakia	Poland	Average
Germany	16.44				
Austria		13.48			
Czechoslovakia			15.79		
Poland				13.41	
Jews non-weighted average					14.79

b. Among Non-Jewish Branch: Distribution in Four Countries

	All Countries non-weighted average except			
Distribution of non-Jews	Germany	Austria	Czechoslovakia	Poland
Germany	1.53			
Austria		0.57		
Czechoslovakia			4.17	
Poland				3.39

c. Among Jewish Branch: Distribution in Four Countries

	All Countries non-weighted average except			
Distribution of Jews in	Germany	Austria	Czechoslovakia	Poland
Germany	2.73			
Austria		1.35		
Czechoslovakia			3.09	
Poland				1.53

$$I_{ab} = \frac{\sum_{i=1}^{n} (X_{ia} - X_{ib})^2}{n}$$

when X_{ia} and X_{ib} are the percentage of employed persons in industry i of populations a and b respectively, and n is the number of industries examined. In our case (see Table 8) industry was divided into three groups, thus n = 3. In Table 10a, a = Gentiles in country j; b = Jews in country j. In Table 10b, a = Gentiles in all countries, but country j, averages, b = Gentiles in country j. In Table 10c, same as above, but substitute Jews for Gentiles.

In summary, our conclusion from the branch composition differences in the four countries between Jews and non-Jews in industry is that Jews developed a pattern of strong preference to converge in a relatively small number of branches, the common denominators of which were a) the typical plant was relatively small; b) the output was aimed mainly for final consumption and sold on the open marketplace.[50]

Another well-known feature of Jewish economic behavior is the drive for economic independence, i.e. the drive for a status of self-employed. Kuznets emphasized this preference of the Jewish participants in labor force, and brought rich statistical support for his thesis.[51] Furthermore, and as an obvious inference from the very explicit preference for economically independent status of self-employment, Jews tended to be more likely employed in relatively small establishments. There are illuminating figures on Polish Jewry in industry. There were close to 225,000 dwarf workshops in Poland operated by the artisan-owner without any employee.[52] The same applied to the Jews in commerce. Of the close to 450,000 persons gainfully occupied in commerce and finance some 350,000 were self-employed pedlars or dwarf shopkeepers without any employee on the premises.[53] A similar picture emerges from the analysis of Bennathan about the sector of self-employed among German Jewry. Of the close to 130,000 self-employed Jewish persons in Germany, well over 50,000 (42 per cent) lived, using the term of Bennathan, in a "proletarian environment".[54] The situation in Hungary was very similar during the 1930s,[55] and in Czechoslovakia and Austria the picture was basically the same.

50 The only country in which Jewish industry carried a measure of structural similarity to non-Jewish industry was Palestine. Using branch composition figures of Ruppin for Palestine in 1931 (*The Jews in the Modern World*, p. 187) and aggregating branches into the three groups of Table 8 we obtain the following results for Jewish industries:

group a 37.7% group b 17.0% group c 45.3%

When (a) = non-Jewish industry in Palestine, (b) = Jewish industry in Palestine, the Variation of Distribution Index (I_{ab}): I_{ab} = 8.52.

When (a) = Jewish industry in Germany, Austria, Czechoslovakia and Poland calculated as unweighted averages, and (b) = Jewish industry in Palestine: I_{ab} = 14.74.

Comparing this result with the figures in Table 10c is interesting.

51 Kuznets, "Economic Structure and Life of the Jews," pp. 1617, 1618. Others who mention this are Ruppin, *The Sociology of the Jews*, vol. II, ch. 19; E. Bennathan, "Die demographische und wirtschaftliche Struktur der Juden," in W.K. Mosse, ed., *Entscheidungsjahr 1932* (Tübingen, 1932); Mendelsohn, *The Jews of East Central Europe*, pp. 27-28; Raphael Mahler, *Jews in Poland Between The Two World Wars* [Hebrew] (Tel Aviv, 1968), pp. 78-79.

52 *Ibid.*

53 Bennathan, "Die demographische und wirtschaftliche Struktur der Juden," p. 113.

54 Yehuda Don, "Economic Effects of Antisemitic Discrimination: The Case of the Hungarian Anti-Jewish Legislation, 1938-1944," *Jewish Social Studies* 48 (1986), 63-82.

Table 11: Jewish and Non-Jewish Persons Employed in Industry by Size of Establishment in Poland in 1931[56]

Establishment	Percentage of Non-Jews	Percentage of Jews	Share of Jews
Large	27.3	2.0	1.8
Medium	16.6	10.0	13.0
Small	56.1	88.0	28.1
Total	100.0	100.0	20.0

Thus the profile of the economic behavior of the Jews in Central Europe and bordering countries can be summed up as follows:

1) Jews rarely sought their living in agriculture.

2) In industry and commerce, which together employed the vast majority of the economically active Jewish population, the following characteristics could be observed and attributed to the unique behavioral model of the Jews:

a) the commodities produced were, generally, designed for the final consumption of the individual consumer;

b) the commodities produced were designed to be marketed on the open competitive market place through retail marketing channels;

c) the establishments tended to be relatively small and not particularly capital intensive.

d) the preferred status of employment was that of an independent, self-employed owner of a producing or marketing business establishment.

The reasons for such economic idiosyncrasies, typical of Jews throughout Central Europe, must primarily be related to their status as a minority, in accordance with the Kuznetsian thesis. However, other minorities behaved differently and developed different patterns of economic interaction with the majority, still in line with the theoretical framework of Kuznets. For the Jews' pattern of economic interaction with their host countries, factors additional to their minority status should be sought, such as:

1) the status of landlessness;

2) the awareness of the existence of a dormant or active situation of antisemitic prejudices.

55 See the reports on Jews in Austria and Czechoslovakia in *The Jewish Communities of Nazi Occupied Europe.*

56 *Ibid.*

Landlessness, or the absence of a specific territorial base, where the minority may assume the role of the regional establishment, creates a situation which, in certain aspects, is similar to that of an immigrating minority. The minority, in both cases, is devoid of any unofficial contact or association with the authorities as well as with the socio-political and economic elite of the country. The member of the landless or immigrating minority, an outsider for the "establishment," may accept reality, resign himself to the status of an outsider alien, and seek to reduce contacts with the authorities to the bureaucratically unavoidable minimum. He will pursue channels for economic existence which are independent of the public sector as well as of semi-public organizations which are linked, formally or through a web of informal personal contacts among the members of the "establishment," to the public sector. In avoiding the public or semi-public sector, the obvious stage of operation becomes the atomistically structured, competitive market place. There the rules of survival are rational and instrumental, and elements such as personal contacts, pedigree, nepotism and class allegiance are of minor significance. Consumer goods are more easily exchanged on such a competitive and anonymous market place than factors of production or capital goods. Operating an independent, small establishment, whether in production or in commerce, is a better agent for the safeguard of freedom of action and anonymity than association with a large organization as a manager, an official or a worker. The status of employee in a large organization many expose the individual to institutional constraints, such as trade unions, which could be conceived undesirable by the member of the minority. Besides, self-employment is often more lucrative than income from salary and wages.

Thus, the desire to minimize contact with the public sector and its business satellites, motivated either by a sense of alienation and perhaps fear, or by the suspicion that as an outsider he would suffer from discrimination were he try to integrate into that sector, drove the Jew to the open market place, which became the central stage for his economic endeavor. Preferring self-employment and independence, he selected the optimum plant size and product mix within the existing constraints of institutional reality, market situation and available technology. Consequently, the economic behavior of the Jew reflected a high degree of rationality in view of the socio-economic circumstances and the realistically feasible set of options. The shadow of latent or overt antisemitism contributed to his tendency to keep wealth in relatively liquid assets, to establish businesses with a relatively quick turnover and to acquire foot-loose, universally utilizable skills.

However, these patterns and preferences stood in sharp contrast to the dynamics of economic development. Some of the more conspicuous trends of economic change as of the beginning of the twentieth century were:

a) Technological progress and improved financial organization enhanced the importance of economies of scale.

b) New marketing techniques granted great advantages to the large scale commercial enterprises.

c) Advanced technology has been positively correlated with high capital intensity.

d) There has been a dramatic increase in the role and functions of the public sector.

All these changes affected adversely the above suggested socio-economic optimum of the Jew in Central Europe, or indeed anywhere else, where similar behavioral patterns were adopted by the Jewish minority. The trend went towards a continuous increase in the "employees"/"employed persons" ratio, leaving fewer fields in which small establishments were competitive with the large organizations. Supermarkets cut into the business of the small groceries, and department stores eliminated many tiny shopkeepers. Mass production put out of business most small producers in the garment, footware, leather and food industries and the sharp rise of government intervention in the economy vastly increased the absolute and relative numbers of employees working for the Government or other agencies of the public and semi-public sector.

The reaction of the Jewish minority to these, prima facie, adverse developments reconfirmed its great art of flexibility and the capacity to adjust to new situations. The principal expression of such an occupational readjustment was the thrust into new professions, particularly by the second generation of the immigrants and of the emancipated. The intensive Jewish penetration into the liberal professions, as of the beginning of the twentieth century, is a well-known and well documented fact.[57] Jewish lawyers, Jewish engineers, and above all Jewish dentists and physicians assumed dominating positions in post-World War I Central and Eastern Europe. Penetration into the liberal professions was facilitated by the utmost utilization of new learning opportunities, which obviously coincided with the proliferation of academic studies at a time when universities ceased to be the exclusive haven of the privileged classes and

57 For Jews in the liberal professions see Jacob Lestchinsky, "The Liberal Professions," in B. Dinur, A. Tartakover and J. Lestchinsky, eds., *Klal Yisrael, Chapters in the Sociology of the Jewish People* [Hebrew] (Jerusalem, 1954), pp. 292-299. Recently two fascinating studies were completed on Hungarian physicians and lawyers, Jewish and non-Jewish, and the organizational differences between the two. See Mária M. Kovács, "Luttes professionelles et antisemitisme: Chronique de la montée du fascisme dans les corps medical hongrois 1920-1940," *Actes de la Recherche en Science Social* 56 (1985), 31-44 and Mária M. Kovács, "Lawyers Against the Current: Antisemitism and Liberal Response in Interwar Hungary," in Yehuda Don and Victor Karady, eds., *A Social and Economic History of Central European Jewry* (New Brunswick, 1990), pp. 249-256.

became the major vehicle for professional education and diffusion of technology and science. Before Jews entered the liberal professions, they made their appearance in increasing numbers in universities. The process was that of a transformation of the ancient Jewish tradition of learning from the holy to the secular and from learning for its own sake to learning for the pragmatic objectives of skill acquisition.

However, the fundamental features of the occupational priorities of the Jewish professionals were not different from those of their fathers. The liberal professions most frequently chosen by Jews display similar characteristics to those observed in Jewish industry and commerce. Physicians, dentists, lawyers, chartered accountants and architects are very often independent operators of small to medium sized offices, who provide services to customers from the non-public sectors. The stage of operation for these private professionals is the highly competitive market where the stakes are high and income differentials, between the successful and the unsuccessful, vast. Most of these skills are footloose, and their practitioners can transplant their establishments from one location to the other at relatively low transfer costs. Such a competitive existence of professionals is in sharp contrast to the safe and tenured working conditions of professionals in the public and semi-public sectors, where income is the function of rank, and ranks depend on seniority.

Another indication to the same tendencies is the relatively low popularity of the teaching profession among Jews. In those countries where education was public, and thus the teachers were employees of the authorities, the share of Jews in the teaching profession—elementary and high-schools—was well below their share among physicians, lawyers, chartered accountants, journalists or artists.[58] Likewise, professions which promised employment mainly in the public sector, such as agronomy and veterinary medicine were hardly ever chosen by Jews. Obviously, the army, the police and other military professions were, in peace-times, virtually free of Jews.

In summary, the patterns of occupational composition of the Jewish minority went during the first four decades of the twentieth century, through a radical metamorphosis. The most prominent changes were the ascendance of the liberal professions, a disproportionate rise in the share of white collar employees and a decline in the share of industrial employees. However, in spite of these profound changes, the basic profile of the Jewish occupational preference remained by and large unchanged. Jews preferred to minimize, as far as possible, business association with the public and semi-public sectors, preferred

58 On the scanty representation of Jews in a number of liberal professions in Hungary, see Don, "Economic Effects of Antisemitic Discrimination."

to operate on the competitive market place, and tended to give priority to risk-taking independence over the status of salaried employees.

It is possible that our findings about Jewish economic behavior are not uniquely Jewish but reflect patterns of behavior of minorities with certain cultural attributes at large. The Chinese in the Western Hemisphere are an immediate subject for comparison. Further comparative research is needed to examine this question in depth.

The Occupational Structure of Hungarian Jews in the Interwar Period*

György Ránki

Over the decades and centuries, their propensity to trade shaped the historical legacy of European Jewry and deeply influenced their occupational structure in both Eastern and Central Europe. However, if we attempt to explain the dominant role of the Jews in trade or commerce as primarily the result of their propensity to trade and their historical legacy, and much less the result of historical circumstances, then one might assume that the proportion of tradesmen and merchants would decrease among those Jews who were more assimilated into the gentile milieu, and whose social structure and cultural attitudes had thereby been profoundly modified. In theory, those countries at the forefront of Jewish emancipation offered better opportunities for the Jews to abandon the occupational structure that had been partly formed in the ghettos and adapt themselves to the demands of the modern world. The leaders of the Jewish community who had a secular education should have strongly influenced this process. Put in another way, if the Jews' heavy participation in trade was rooted in the traditional development processes, we could expect to find the strongest survival of the traditional Jewish occupation structure in those countries less advanced in their economic, social and political transformation.

This thesis is not borne out, however, by a comparison of the occupational structure of German and Hungarian Jews. In the case of Germany, whose territorial losses consequent on World War I were not extreme, we can use the censuses of both 1907 and 1925; for Hungary, pre- and post-war censuses are not comparable, because the truncation of Hungary imposed by the Trianon Treaty caused a profound change in the size and structure of the Hungarian Jewish community.

* This lecture was presented at the last public appearance of the late Prof. Ránki. A slightly different version has appeared in Hungarian as György Ránki, "A magyarországi zsidóság foglalkozási szerkezete a két világháború között," *Történelmi Szemle* XXX (1987-88), 256-266.

Table 1: Occupational Structure of German Jews, 1907-1933[1]

	1907	1925	1933
Agriculture	1.6	1.8	1.7
Industry	27.1	24.5	23.1
Trade and transport	62.6	61.3	61.3
Liberal professions and civil service	8.1	9.3	12.5

We can ignore the changes in the occupational structure of German Jewry, since that is not our major interest. What is important is that even in early-twentieth-century Germany nearly two-thirds of the Jews were engaged in trade. We can compare these data with the occupational structure of Hungarian Jews at roughly the same time. We see that only 44% of the Jews in Hungary were engaged in trade, while their role in industry (35%) was much more significant than in Germany.

Table 2: Occupational Structure of Hungarian Jews, 1920-1935[2]

	1920	1930	1935 (Budapest)
Agriculture	4.3	2.0	0.4
Industry	34.7	35.0	36.0
Trade	42.5	44.0	42.8
Professions	18.5	19.0	21.8

The obvious conclusion is that trade was far less important in the occupational structure of the Hungarian Jews than it was for their German co-religionists. It follows that we must relate cautiously to any explanation of Jewish occupational structure based mainly upon a Jewish propensity to trade. The issue involves another important point as well, raised long ago by Simon Kuznets.[3] Kuznets stressed that the social structure of the Jews was determined only in part by internal factors. At least as much attention must be devoted to the economic and social structure of the particular country, since that is what provided the general condition for the social development of the Jews, created

1 *Entscheidungsjahr 1932. Zur Judenfrage in der Endphase der Weimarer Republik*, edited by Werner E. Mosse (Tübingen, 1966), pp. 104-105.

2 Based on the censuses of 1920 and 1930.

3 Simon Kuznets, "Economic Structure and Life of the Jews," in Louis Finkelstein, *The Jews: Their History, Culture, and Religion* (New York, 1960[3]), vol. II, pp. 1597-1666.

the opportunities, and determined the borders and obstacles to Jewish social mobility. According to Kuznets, Jews—like most minorities—tried to turn to "new" activities in which the majority of the country's population had not yet acquired the proper skills. Consequently the Jews displayed strong interest in those industrial branches where rapid development was translated into higher profits or better opportunities for success.

The argument cannot be limited to the profit motive, though, since it is clear that there was higher Jewish participation in those sectors of the economy in which the Hungarians were less interested and the balance of supply and demand favored the former. Taking into consideration the level and dynamism of German industry during the period of Jewish emancipation, it is clear that it was much easier for Jews to get involved in industry in Hungary, where industrial development was in its infancy, than in Germany, where most of the seats were already taken.

Yehuda Don has called our attention to the fact that the ratio of Jews in trade, to Jews in industry, was much lower in Germany than anywhere else in Central Europe. While this ratio was 1:2.7 in Germany, it was 1:2.1 in Czechoslovakia, 1:1.4 in Hungary, and was even inverted in Poland, where more Jews were engaged in industry than in trade (1:0.8).[4]

Since Germany had proportionally the highest industrial population of all these countries, Kuznets' theory—that where the policy towards the Jews was more liberal, the process of assimilation was faster and easier and the difference between the occupational structure of the population at large and the Jews was lower—does not hold.[5]

Based upon the data for these four countries, we can suggest that in proportion as a country was more industrialized and the deeper the roots of industrialization (proto-industrialization), Jewish participation in industry was smaller. It is premature, however, to express this as a firm conclusion based only on the data for these four countries.

Nevertheless, it cannot be denied that a larger proportion of the Jews of Germany and Czechoslovakia engaged in trade than in Hungary and Poland, with their more agrarian character. Yehuda Don explains this as follows: In a more developed country, the role of the third sector of the economy is usually stronger. Obviously one can refer to the well-known economic processes whereby there is a constant flow of labor from agriculture to industry during the earlier stage of development and a flow from industry to the service sector in a later stage. Due to these processes, in those countries where trade dominated the

4 Yehuda Don, "Patterns of Jewish Economic Behavior in Central Europe in the Twentieth Century," in this volume.

5 *Ibid.*

Jewish occupational structure, the proportion of Jews among all people working in trade was usually smaller.[6]

Although we accept Don's interpretation, we wish to go one step further and extend the size and scope of the research. For this, a deeper analysis of the industrial structure seems to be indispensable. Kuznets was able to locate a strong Jewish presence in four industrial sectors—food, clothing, printing, and jewelry. Since the size of the labor force in the last two was insignificant, we may concentrate our study on the food and clothing sectors.

In Germany, at least two-thirds of all Jews employed in industry were employed by these two branches—and two-thirds of these in the garment industry. Both branches were traditional consumer-good industries producing directly for human needs. According to the typology of Hoffman,[7] they were both among the dominant branches in the process of industrialization in the nineteenth century. Their share was constantly declining, however, due to the second industrial revolution in which Germany was the pioneer. Heavy industry, with its substantial demand for labor, became the most dynamic sector of the economy. The process of concentration ran in parallel with this change, and the importance of small enterprises was declining even in the older sectors, like the garment industry. It is true that, in spite of all expectations, small enterprises did not entirely disappear from the scene. Moreover, technological development gave birth to a number of new branches in the service sector. Still, the role of the Jews in these branches cannot compare with their share in the traditional industries.

The thesis must accordingly be reformulated, as an addendum to Yehuda Don's interpretation, as follows: The increased Jewish participation in trade is a function of a particular country's industrial development and cannot be separated from the place of industry in the economy as a whole and from the structure of industry (ratio of heavy to light industry and of large to small enterprises). In this respect it does not matter how many Jews can be found among the owners and managers, since the Jewish role in heavy industry was usually low; it was in those branches that favored the survival of small enterprise that most of the Jewish small businesses and Jewish labor force were to be found. In the iron and textile industries, despite their divergent technologies, the Jewish role was

6 In Warsaw more Jews were involved in industry (artisans and factories) than in trade. See Arcadius Kahan, *Essays in Jewish Social and Economic History* (Chicago, 1986). In Zurich in 1936, two-thirds of the Jewish work-force was engaged in trade, while in Cisleithania before World War I, 27.5 percent of the Jewish population worked in industry and 39.6 percent in trade. See Uri Robert Kaufman, "Swiss Jewry from the Jewish Village to the City," *Leo Baeck Yearbook* XXX (1985), 294 and Ivor Oxaal and Walter Weitzmann, "The Jews in pre-1914 Vienna," *Leo Baeck Yearbook* XXX (1985), 421-422.

7 W. Hoffman, *Stadien und Typen der Industrialisierung* (Jena, 1931).

insignificant, since in those branches economies of scale prevail and most of the enterprises were relatively large factories.

According to Kuznets, in addition to the Jewish propensity to trade, Jews tended to gravitate to those branches where goods were produced or sold directly to the individual consumer. One may wonder what the attraction of these branches was. I think we must supplement Kuznets' view by noting that these were the branches favoring small enterprises over large, where independence was more likely to be maintained, and where manufacture and sales were conducted by the same person, namely, the workshop owner. Those industries in Germany in which Jews were concentrated, were precisely those with a relatively high percentage of self-employed persons. In the food industry, 15.1 percent of the labor force at large, but 37.3 percent of the Jews, were self-employed. The difference was less extreme in the case of the garment industry, where 32 percent of the labor force at large, and 37.5 percent of the Jewish labor force, were self-employed. These sectors stood in strong contrast to the textile and iron industries, where only 2.6 and 13.9 percent were self-employed, respectively. In these branches Jewish participation was quite limited; but among the Jews involved in them, 32.6 percent were self-employed in the textile industry and 31 percent were self-employed in the iron industry. Whereas the ratio of self-employed to blue-collar workers in the food industry was 1:2, and 1:6 in the garment industry—which certainly proves the strong survival of the small enterprise—those industries with minor Jewish participation were dominated by large enterprises and the ratio of self-employed to blue-collar workers was quite different.

In this respect the Hungarian data are basically identical with those for Germany. In 1920 the share of the self-employed in industry was slightly higher than in Germany and hovered around 42 percent. There were more important differences in the industrial structures of the two countries. According to the 1930 census, there were 23,866 Jewish artisans with workshops in Hungary. Of these, 1894 were shoemakers or cobblers, 1925 butchers, 6092 tailors or dressmakers, and 2845 innkeepers. Since the 2845 innkeepers can be regarded more as merchants than as artisans, the Hungarian statistics, which include them under industry, need to be modified. If we deduct the persons working in bars, restaurants, and the like from the industrial sector and add them to the trade sector, the total number of Jews in trade would increase from 94,200 to 100,000, while Jews in industry would decrease from 73,800 to 68,000. We should also note that the other three branches mentioned above are affiliated with the food and clothing industries.

If we extend our investigation from the self-employed to the total labor force the dominant role of these two branches becomes even clearer. The garment industry—tailors and dressmakers—employed 8485 blue collar workers, of whom two-thirds were women. Butchers and bakers dominated in the food industry. The number of Jewish printers and locksmiths did not fall far behind either.

A clear profile of the Jewish labor force emerges from a division of the blue-collar workers into those working in small workshops and those working in large enterprises. In 1930, of the 35,410 Jewish blue-collar workers in Hungary, only 7371 were working in factories employing more than 20 workers. In addition to the textile and garment industry, the printing and—interestingly enough—the machine and electrotechnical industries employed most of the Jewish blue-collar workers. Among the Jewish blue-collar laborers working in large enterprises, 15 to 20 percent were employed in printing, 10 to 15 percent in the machine and electrotechnical industry, another 10 percent in the garment industry, and approximately the same percentage in the textile industry. The proportions of self-employed, white-collar, and blue-collar workers presented in the following table clearly demonstrate the peculiar social structure of the Jewish labor force in Hungary.

Table 3: The Occupational Structure of the Active Population in Hungary According to Religion, 1930

	Jews	Catholics	Lutherans	Calvinists
		Industry		
Self-employed	32.2	22.2	24.6	29.6
White collar	19.6	3.7	5.2	2.7
Blue collar	48.1	74.1	70.2	67.7
		Trade		
Self-employed	45.5	37.8	33.7	38.5
White collar	25.5	16.0	19.7	14.5
Blue collar	29.0	46.2	46.6	47.0

The proportion of self-employed is substantially higher among the Jews than among the non-Jews in both industry and trade.

Even the Calvinists, who have the largest proportion of self-employed after the Jews, lag behind them by 3 percent in industry and by 7 percent in trade. Yet I do not believe that the large proportion of self-employed can be regarded as the most important peculiarity of the Jewish occupational structure in Hungary. It is clear from the data that the differences are more significant when it comes to white-collar workers. While every fifth Jew employed in industry was a white-collar worker, the corresponding figure for the second-ranking Lutherans was only one in twenty. The disparity is less striking in trade; but even here, whereas 25 percent of the Jewish population were white-collar workers, the corresponding figure for the Lutherans (who had a strongly German background) was 19 percent. If we include banking and finance in the service sector, along with trade, then the proportion of Jewish white-collar workers is even higher. This is partly due to the nature of the sector, since in banking and finance the number of self-employed was insignificant—the age of Jewish private bankers had passed—nor was there a large number of blue-collar laborers. On the other hand, whereas 50 percent of the white-collar workers in trade were Jewish, in banking and finance their share was slightly more than one third.

Compared with the situation in other countries, however, the high proportion of white-collar workers does not seem to be a peculiar feature of the Hungarian Jewish occupational structure. In Germany in 1933, 34.5 percent of the Jewish population were recorded as *Angestellte und Beamte*, compared to 29.8 percent in the same category in Hungary, according to our calculation[8]—an insignificant difference for our purposes. Similarly, 46 percent of the Jewish workforce in Germany were self-employed, compared to only 38 percent in Hungary.

But the most striking difference can be found in the proportion of blue-collar workers in the two populations. In Germany only 10 percent of the working Jewish population fell into this category (even including domestics), whereas in Hungary 30 percent of the Jewish workforce were blue-collar workers. Even if we accept the assumption that in Germany another 10 percent or so of those listed as "helping family members" can be regarded as close to this category, whereas in Hungary those distinctions were never made, we must still explain why the number of blue-collar workers was so much higher among Hungarian than among German Jews.

Here I think we can perceive the most important difference between the two social structures, deriving from the greater *Verbürgerlichung* of the German Jews on the one hand, and their smaller participation in industry, on the other. To approach the same issue from another angle, the Hungarian Jews, or at least some of them, were more strongly rooted in the proletariat. If we consider that

8 Our calculation differs here from the official statistics which present the share of white-collar workers among the Hungarian Jews as 26 percent. The discrepancy stems from the different interpretation of a category that the Hungarian statistics describe as "pensioners and rentiers." The official statistics regarded everyone in this category (15,440 bread-winners) as self-employed, whereas we have divided them up equally among white-collar workers and self-employed. Hence there is a discrepancy for the share of self-employed as well: the official statistics gave this as 44.7 percent of the active Jewish population, our estimates reduce this to only 40.3 percent.

industrial workers accounted for 47 percent of the German population, but only 23 percent of the German Jews, whereas in Hungary 24 percent of the population, but 39 percent of the Jews were employed in industry, it is obvious that greater weight of industry in the occupational structure of Hungarian Jews contributed significantly to the formation of a Jewish working class. In Poland, where the weight of industry in the Jewish occupational structure was even larger than in Hungary, the proportion of blue-collar workers among the Jews was even larger.

Table 4: Occupational Structure of Hungarian Jews, 1930

	Budapest	Provinces	Total
Self-employed	38.0	40.7	38.9
White collar	32.1	24.7	28.7
Blue collar	29.8	35.0	32.3

It may seem surprising that there is almost no difference in the proportion of self-employed between the Jews of the capital and the provinces. We must assume, however, that in Budapest the large number of independent professionals swelled the number of independent self-employed persons. If we narrow our research to industry and trade, we obtain quite different results. Among the industrialized population of the countryside, 42.9 percent were self-employed, 23.3 percent white-collar workers, and 43.8 blue-collar workers; in Budapest the proportions were 24.9 percent self-employed, 24.6 white collar, and 50.5 blue collar. In trade, Budapest had 35.7 self-employed, 39 percent white collar, and 25.4 percent blue collar, while in the provinces 57.5 percent of the Jews in trade were self-employed, 33 percent blue collar, and only 10 percent white collar. It is obvious from these figures that most of the Jewish merchants in the countryside worked alone or had no more than one employee. While in Budapest there were 1.7 employees for each self-employed, in the countryside there were only 0.57 employees for each independent shopkeeper. In the capital, all employees (blue- and white-collar workers taken together) exceeded the number of self-employed by 60 percent, whereas in the countryside the number of employees was less than 70 percent the number of self-employed.

In any discussion of the occupational structure of the Jews of the capital, however, another correction is required. The "self-employed" category aggregates people with very different social status; by lumping together self-employed market women with wholesale merchants, and rural artisans with wealthy entrepreneurs, it camouflages true class distinctions instead of contributing to proper quantitative analysis. Moreover, it also includes the liberal-professional intellectuals, who by their education and training are sometimes closer to a large segment of the white-collar workers than to the rural artisans. If we modify the occupational categorization of the Jews accordingly, white-collar workers and liberal professionals would account for the largest fraction of Budapest Jews (40 percent).

Yehuda Don, in his excellent study, emphasizes that the Jewish population demonstrated a most explicit preference for economic independence, which is why so many of them were self-employed or employed in small workshops. He refers to Poland, where, among 450,000 persons gainfully occupied in commerce and finance, some 350,000 were self-employed peddlers or shopkeepers[9] (a dubious figure, by the way); one can add the figures from Warsaw, where alongside 14,450 independent shopkeepers and 9550 self-employed peddlers there were only 13,100 employees in trade i.e., no more than 30 percent of the Jewish commercial workforce.[10] Generally speaking, self-employed small shopkeepers and artisans represented the majority in the occupational structure of Polish Jewry.

These figures support Don's view. When we turn our attention to industry, however, the situation is not so clear. While there were 21,830 Jewish industrial entrepreneurs and independent artisans in Poland, there were 60,470 Jews among the white- and blue-collar workers. In industry, the proportions are reversed: 27 percent self-employed versus 73 percent employees.

Table 5: Distribution of Gainfully Employed Jews in Poland (excluding agriculture)[11]

Self-employed small shopkeepers and artisans	58.5
Entrepreneurs	3.4
White-collar workers	8.8
Blue-collar workers	36.3
Others	3.0
Total	100.0

Although the figures for Warsaw and Eastern Europe should not be excessively generalized, an economic explanation of this disproportion is wanted. Don emphasizes that the independent small workshop made good economic sense in the nineteenth century, but was bucking the trend in the

9 Don, "Patterns of Jewish Economic Behavior," table 11 ff..

10 Kahan, *Essays,* p. 172.

11 Joseph Marcus, *Social and Political History of the Jews in Poland* (Berlin-Amsterdam, 1985), p. 31.

twentieth, when, due to technological progress, the importance of economies of scale gained ground. The new demand for large capital-intensive enterprises was hardly reconcilable with the traditional Jewish pattern of doing business—relatively large liquid assets and quick turnover. Modern economy required large fixed capital and increased the scale of commercial and financial enterprises. According to Don, in the twentieth century the Jewish occupational pattern underwent a major readjustment to fit the new circumstances; the propensity to trade was replaced or partly replaced by the propensity to learn. The second or third generation aimed at the intellectual professions—not just the liberal professions, but also highly qualified white-collar positions in large industrial corporations and financial institutions, where the demand for experts and managers was constantly growing.

The flexible readjustment to the new need started as early as the turn of the century. Let us examine this for the Hungarian case. The census of 1930 reveals that the Jewish population spent more years in school than the population at large. While 5.8 percent of the male population of Hungary were high-school graduates and 2.1 had university degrees, among Jewish males in Budapest 31.7 percent were high-school graduates and 8.1 percent were university graduates. The proportion was lower in the countryside, where 17 percent of Jewish males had completed high school and 5 percent were university graduates, but even this figure was two or three times higher than the average.[12]

Nevertheless, one should not simplify the matter of the propensity to learn. The strong social mobility, the different social structure, the stronger urbanization and the better economic conditions have quite as much to do with the higher educational level of the Jews in Hungary. In this respect I differ with Don. According to him, although the occupational composition of the Jewish minority went through a radical metamorphosis during the first decades of the century, nevertheless the basic profile of the Jewish occupational preference remained by and large unchanged. In this special interplay of change and continuity, the occupational readjustment led to Jewish penetration into the liberal professions; yet, says Don, the fundamental features of the occupational priorities of the Jewish professionals were not different from those of their fathers. Don argues that the explanation of this seeming contradiction is to be found in the fact that even Jewish professionals, seeking independence, maintained and operated small or medium-sized offices providing services in a highly competitive market. Their preference for this niche is explained by the high income differentials and the fact that potential Jewish professionals were looking for branches where skills are easily transportable.

12 Victor Karády, "Jewish Enrollment Patterns in Classical Secondary Education in Old Regime and Inter-war Hungary," *Studies in Contemporary Jewry* I (1984), 225-252.

Marsha Rozenblit, in her work on the Jews in Vienna,[13] sums up the decisive changes in their occupational structure in a chapter entitled "From Trader to Clerk." She concludes that the assumption of the liberal emancipation that assimilated Jews would leave trade for industry proved to be erroneous. "Far more typically Jews joined the ranks of salaried white-collar employees as clerks, salesmen, and managers in commercial and industrial enterprises." In my opinion, Rozenblit's study neglects the economic background of these changes; but she makes the valid point that "by choosing new occupations as clerks, salesmen, and managers Viennese Jews improved their social status and announced their successful acculturation."

Rozenblit published representative data according to which 25 percent of the Jews in Vienna in the early twentieth century were white-collar workers, and another 11 percent professionals. We can extend her argument concerning the economic background of those changes. The children of well-to-do merchants probably did not increase their income by leaving trade to become clerks; on the other hand, the great majority of independent Jewish shopkeepers and artisans had a very modest income, usually less than the average salary of a white-collar employee of an insurance company, bank, or industrial enterprise. Furthermore, the salary provided a fixed income.

This movement from trader to clerk can be observed in Budapest as well. Between 1920 and 1930 the number of Jewish white-collar employees in industry rose from 10,107 to 14,466 and the number of clerks in trade or finance rose from 22,097 to 27,579; this translates into 40 percent growth in the first case and 25 percent growth in the second case. Whereas in 1920 15.6 of the Jewish workforce held white-collar positions, the corresponding figure for 1930 was 19.8 percent.

Thus in explaining Jewish occupational patterns we must be more cautious about talk of innate propensities or the urge for independence as a Jewish trait. We may, however, restate the thesis, and say that in their quest for independence they gravitated to self-employment where it meant higher income and social prestige, but where those targets could be achieved as an employee that status exercised an equal or even greater attraction on them. Hence I take issue with statements that overemphasize innate propensities, since they largely disregard those political and social circumstances that pushed Jewish university graduates to certain professions and blocked them from others. To what extent can one say that the Jews, due to their longing for independence, disliked the public and semi-public sectors, where income is a function of rank and rank depends on seniority?[14] Would it not be better to point out that, as a matter of

13 Marsha L. Rozenblit, *The Jews in Vienna 1867-1914* (Albany, NY., 1983), chapter 3.
14 Don, "Patterns of Jewish Economic Behavior," pp. 33-34.

fact, even in the most liberal state the public or semi-public sector was much less accessible to Jews than was the private sector? This statement is even more valid with regard to interwar Hungary, where very few doctors,[15] lawyers, judges, and even teachers of Jewish origins were employed in the public sector, because they were regarded as politically unreliable. We can hardly say that the Jews preferred to minimize their involvement in the public and semi-public sectors. On the contrary, it is well-known how strongly Jewish business was involved—if permitted—in public contracts; the king of Jewish industry in Hungary, Manfréd Weiss, built up his factory mainly on public contracts. Rather, we should point out that the occupational structure of the Jews was partly shaped by political and social discrimination, which largely closed off the public sector to them. Here, then, I would explain the Jewish occupational structure by external circumstances rather than by inner propensity. One should not make a virtue out of compulsion. The occupational structure was shaped under constraint and pressure.[16]

We are led to the conclusion that, in the analysis of the Jewish occupational structure, less importance should be attributed to Jewish propensities or preferences and more to the interplay of market forces—never forgetting that, in the case of the Jews, market forces were strongly influenced by state and political intervention and the existence of discrepancies between social prestige and economic power (income level). In this respect the occupational structure of the Jews in interwar Hungary was the combined result of the following factors:

- The traditional occupational structure of the Jews and its continuity;
- The traditional occupational structure of the gentiles, and its modification;
- The level and dynamism of the country's economic development;
- The structural changes of the modern economy and its needs (e.g., the bureaucratization of the economy and the increase of professionals);
- Government policy, which sought to change the composition of the Hungarian intellectuals and to preserve and strengthen the Christian middle class.

15 Maria M. Kovács, "Professionelles et antisémitisme," *Actes de la recherche* 56 (1985) emphasized that in Hungary medicine was long regarded as not quite a proper calling for a nobleman, and a physician's social prestige was far behind that of an army officer, lawyer, or civil servant. The major push for medical posts began only after World War I. This is why Jews and non-Jews were equally represented on the faculty of medicine before the war, but after the twenties the number of gentiles was several times that of the number of the Jews. The new non-Jewish doctors benefited from the expansion of the health services, which, due to the expansion of insurance, became more and more a public sector from which Jewish competitors were excluded.

16 Don refers to the small number of teachers among the Jews. However, a study of the Jewish occupational structure after World War II makes it clear that when the social obstacles disappeared Jews began teaching in universities.

In conclusion, let me say that when Jews are different from other social groups it does not follow that we can regard them as a corporate estate within a particular society. For one, we must not ignore their internal stratification. We cannot explain their difference merely by the manifold qualities of Jewishness or by some long-standing Jewish preferences; we must look to more complex interactions of Jewish propensities and the forces of supply and demand on the market.[17] In our economic model, Jewishness must be regarded as a dependent and not as an independent variable.

17 See Lawrence Schofer, "The History of European Jews—Search for a Method," *Leo Baeck Yearbook* XXIV (1979), 19.

Contributors

Vera Bácskai	Professor, Dept. of History, Karl Marx University of Economic Sciences, Budapest
George Deak	Dr. Deak works for a Boston bank
Yehuda Don	Professor, Dept. of Economics, Bar-Ilan University
Zvi Erényi	Librarian, Yeshiva University
Péter Hanák	Member of the Hungarian Academy of Sciences and Head of Section at the Institute of History of the Hungarian Academy of Sciences
Avraham Harman	Chancellor, Hebrew University
Peter Hidas	Professor, Dept. of History, Dawson College, Montreal
Victor Karady	Research Director, École des Hautes Études en Sciences Sociales, Paris
László Katus	Professor, Dept. of History, University of Pécs
Jacob Katz	Professor Emeritus, Dept. of Sociology, Hebrew University
John Komlos	Professor, Dept. of History, University of Pittsburgh
Maria Kovács	Research Fellow, Institute of History, Hungarian Academy of Sciences, Budapest
György Lengyel	Research Fellow, Department of Sociology, Karl Marx University of Economic Sciences, Budapest
William McCagg	Professor, Dept. of History, Michigan State University, East Lansing, Michigan
Juliánna Puskás	Senior Research Fellow, Institute of History, Hungarian Academy of Sciences, Budapest
György Ránki	(1931-1988) was a Member of the Hungarian Academy of Sciences and Director of its Institute of History
Michael K. Silber	Lecturer, Dept. of Jewish History, Hebrew University
Lászlo Varga	Director of Budapest Municipal Archives
Károly Vörös	Senior Research Fellow, Institute of History, Hungarian Academy of Sciences, Budapest
Eliyahu Yeshurun	Dr. Yeshurun, a journalist, lives in Netanya, Israel

Index